SGT FROG

KERORO GUNSO

Volume #3

by Mine Yoshizaki

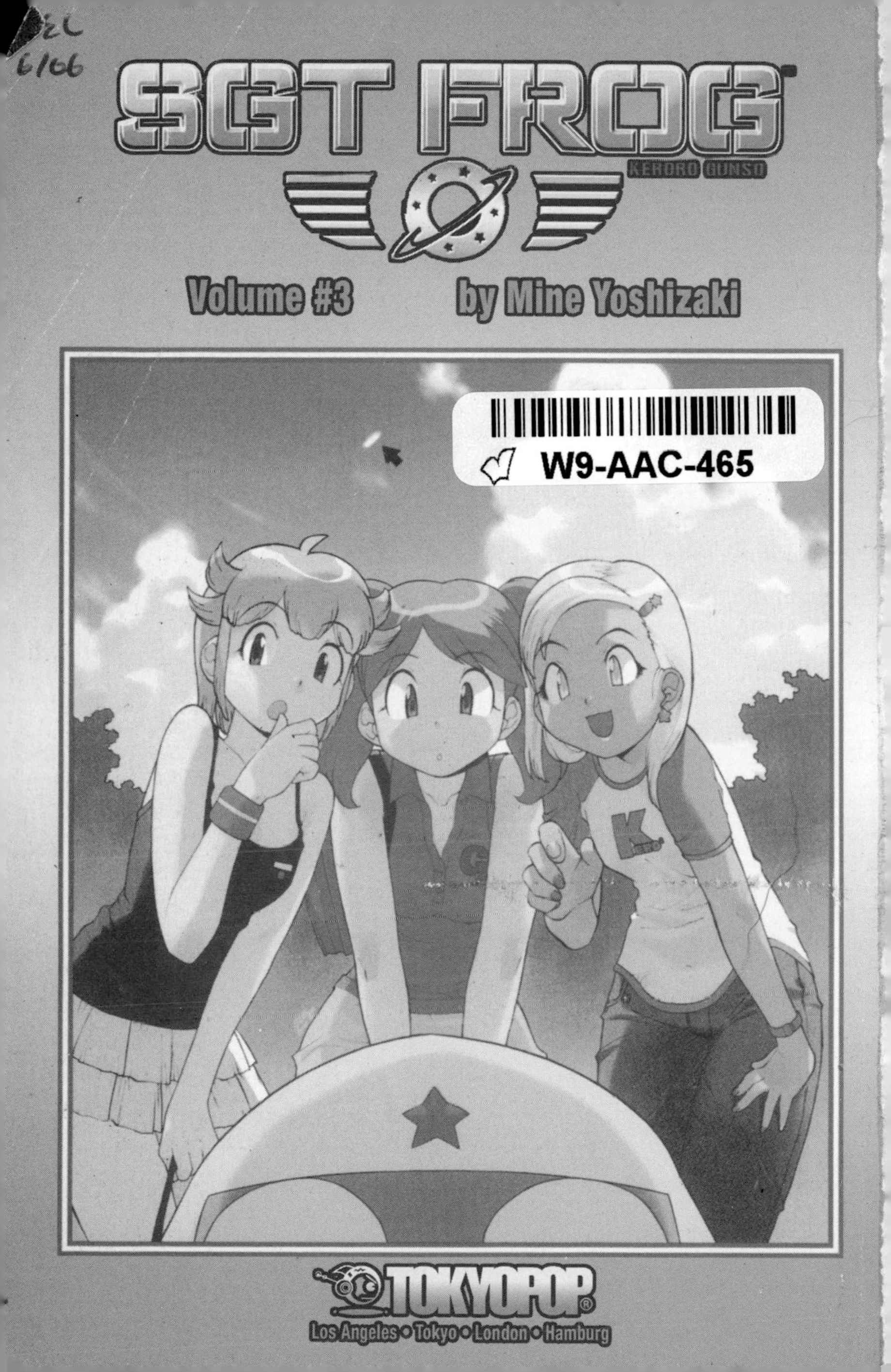

TOKYOPOP®
Los Angeles • Tokyo • London • Hamburg

SERGEANT KERORO 2001

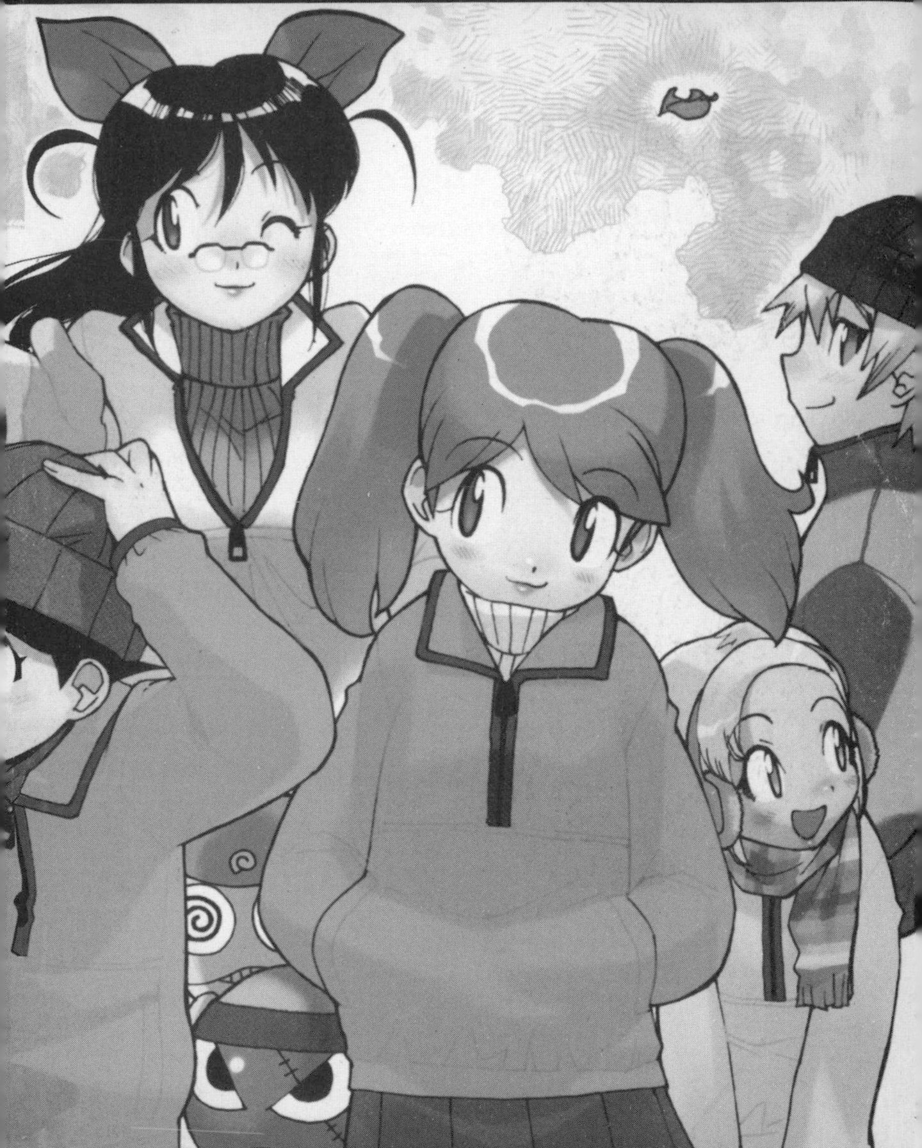

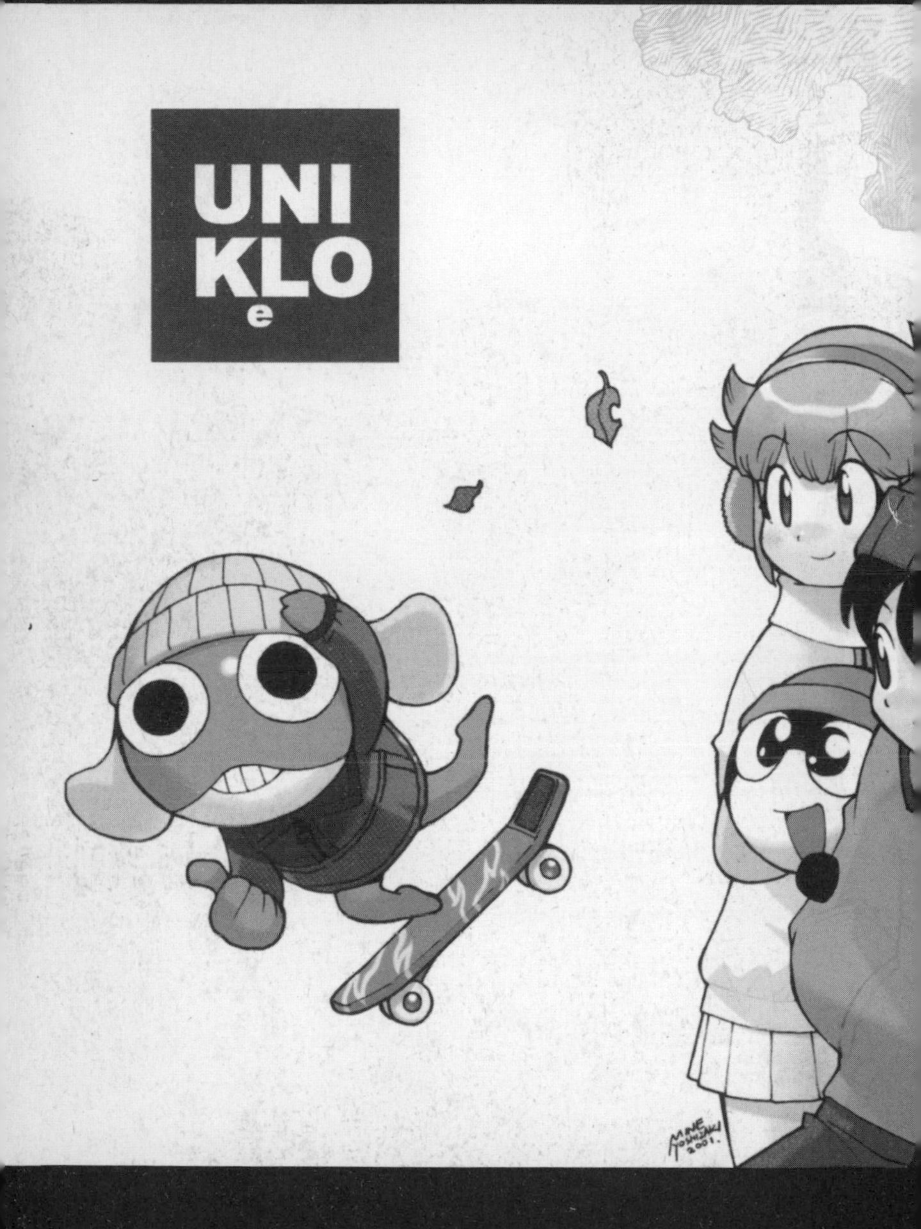
UNI
KLO
e
MINE YOSHIZAKI 2001.

KERORO PINUP

SGT. FROG 3 • TABLE OF CONTENTS

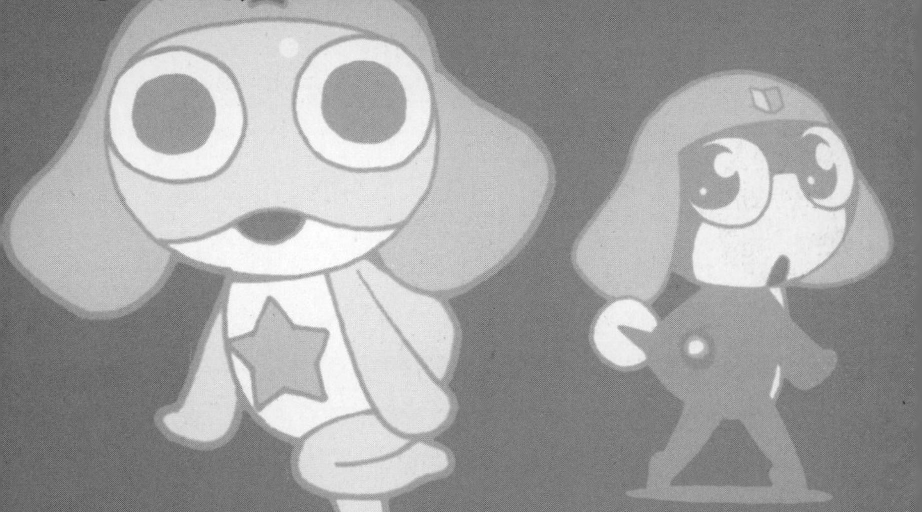

SGT FROG

KERORO GUNSOU

CHARACTER RELATIONSHIPS AND THE STORY SO FAR

(FACT-CHECKING PERFORMED BY SHONEN ACE MAGAZINE)

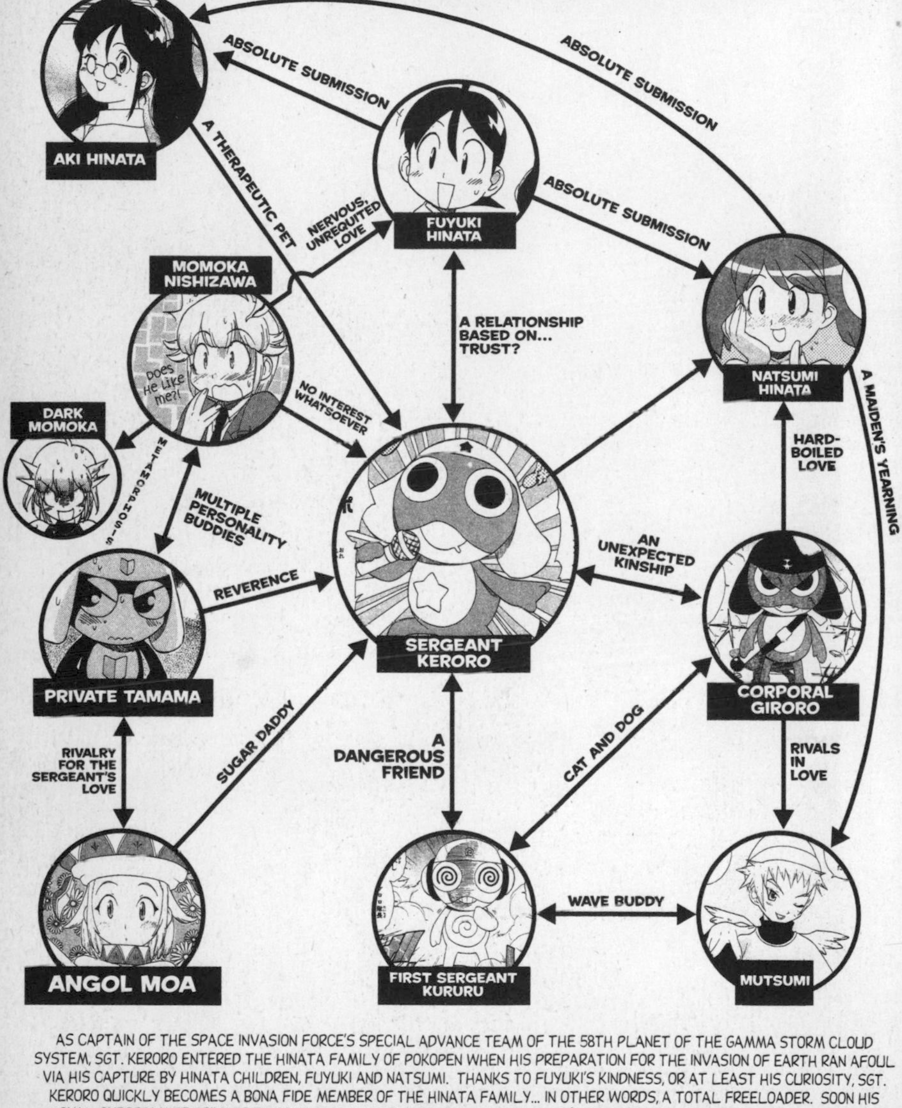

AKI HINATA
ABSOLUTE SUBMISSION
ABSOLUTE SUBMISSION
A THERAPEUTIC PET
FUYUKI HINATA
NERVOUS, UNREQUITED LOVE
ABSOLUTE SUBMISSION
MOMOKA NISHIZAWA
Does He like me?!
A RELATIONSHIP BASED ON... TRUST?
NATSUMI HINATA
DARK MOMOKA
NO INTEREST WHATSOEVER
METAMORPHOSIS
MULTIPLE PERSONALITY BUDDIES
HARD-BOILED LOVE
A MAIDEN'S YEARNING
AN UNEXPECTED KINSHIP
REVERENCE
PRIVATE TAMAMA
SERGEANT KERORO
CORPORAL GIRORO
SUGAR DADDY
A DANGEROUS FRIEND
CAT AND DOG
RIVALRY FOR THE SERGEANT'S LOVE
RIVALS IN LOVE
WAVE BUDDY
ANGOL MOA
FIRST SERGEANT KURURU
MUTSUMI

AS CAPTAIN OF THE SPACE INVASION FORCE'S SPECIAL ADVANCE TEAM OF THE 58TH PLANET OF THE GAMMA STORM CLOUD SYSTEM, SGT. KERORO ENTERED THE HINATA FAMILY OF POKOPEN WHEN HIS PREPARATION FOR THE INVASION OF EARTH RAN AFOUL VIA HIS CAPTURE BY HINATA CHILDREN, FUYUKI AND NATSUMI. THANKS TO FUYUKI'S KINDNESS, OR AT LEAST HIS CURIOSITY, SGT. KERORO QUICKLY BECOMES A BONA FIDE MEMBER OF THE HINATA FAMILY... IN OTHER WORDS, A TOTAL FREELOADER. SOON HIS LOYAL SUBORDINATE PRIVATE TAMAMA AND UNLIKELY RELATIVE ANGOL MOA (A.K.A. THE LORD OF TERROR FORETOLD BY NOSTRADAMUS) ARE FOISTING FURTHER CHAOS ONTO THE HINATA FAMILY UNIT. MEANWHILE, THE SERGEANT AND HIS GANG CONTINUE TO HATCH THEIR PLANS TO INVADE THE EARTH, RIGHT UNDER THE HINATAS' WELL-INTENTIONED NOSES...

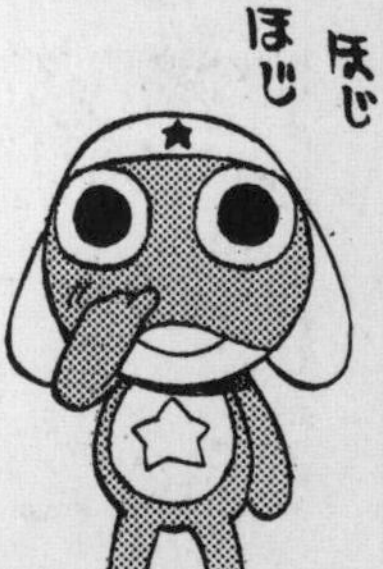
ほじ
ほじ

ENCOUNTER XXI

WELCOME TO RADIO-FREE KERORO

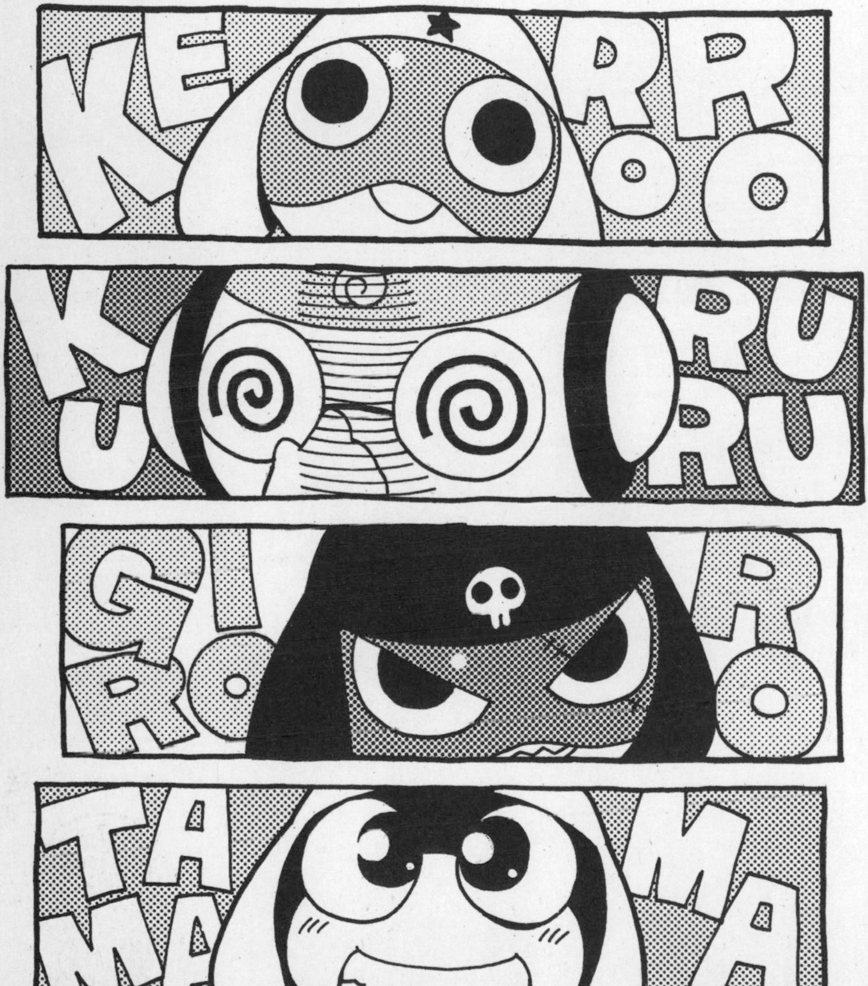
KERORO
KURURU
GIRORO
TAMAMA

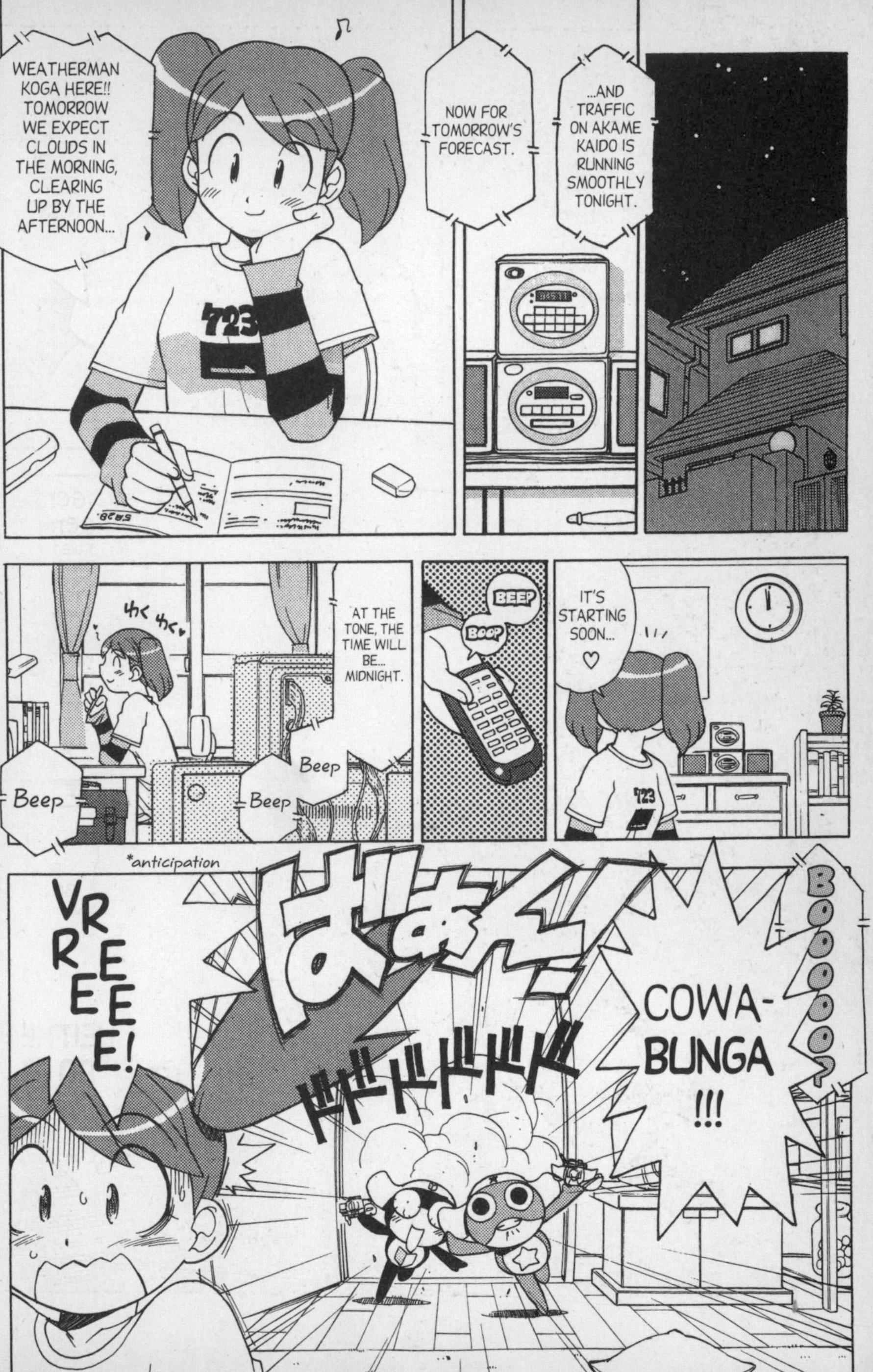

WEATHERMAN KOGA HERE!! TOMORROW WE EXPECT CLOUDS IN THE MORNING, CLEARING UP BY THE AFTERNOON...
NOW FOR TOMORROW'S FORECAST.
...AND TRAFFIC ON AKAME KAIDO IS RUNNING SMOOTHLY TONIGHT.
AT THE TONE, THE TIME WILL BE... MIDNIGHT.
Beep
Beep
Beep
わく わく
*anticipation
BEEP
BOOP
IT'S STARTING SOON...
VREEEEE!
ばあん
ドドドドド
COWA-BUNGA!!!
BOOOOOO

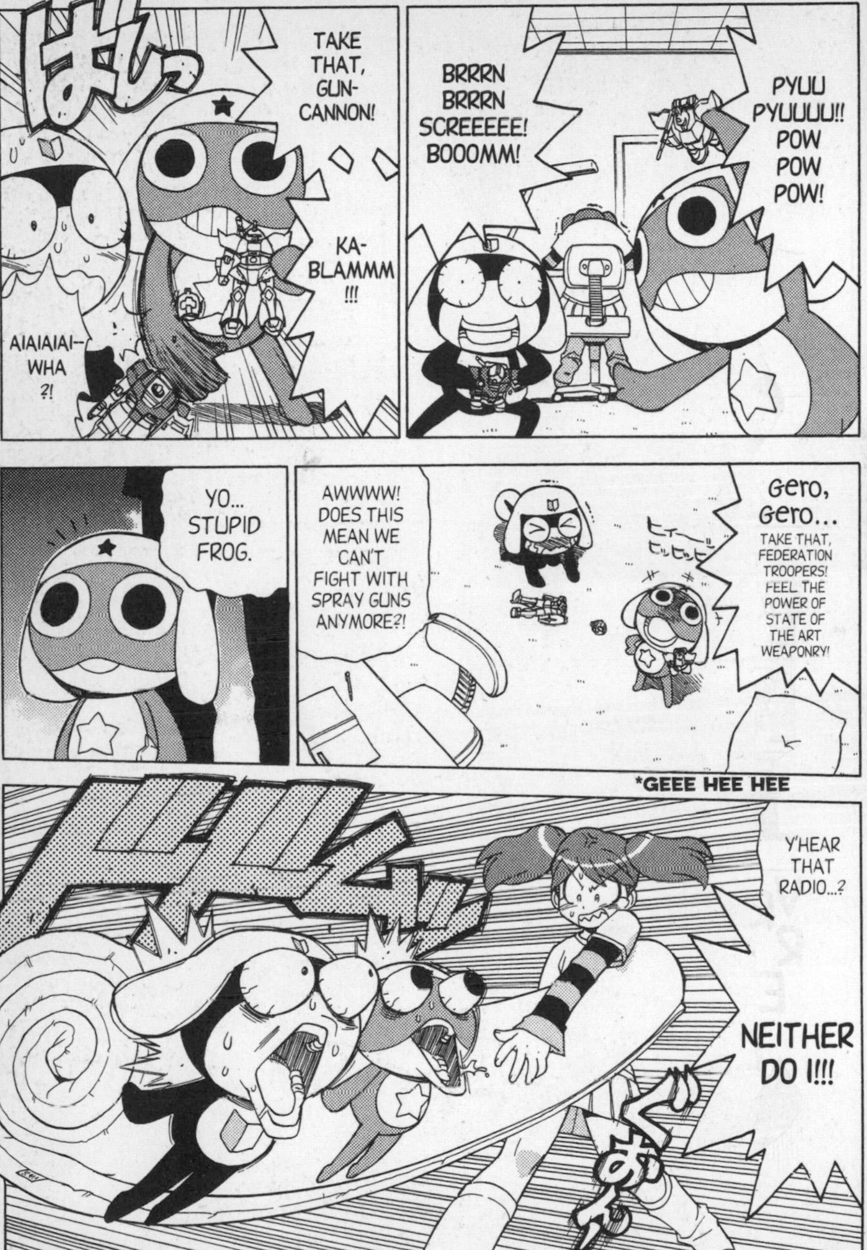
BRRRN BRRRN SCREEEEE! BOOOMM!
PYUU PYUUUU!! POW POW POW!
TAKE THAT, GUN-CANNON!
KA-BLAMMM!!!
AIAIAIAI--WHA?!
Gero, Gero... TAKE THAT, FEDERATION TROOPERS! FEEL THE POWER OF STATE OF THE ART WEAPONRY!
AWWWW! DOES THIS MEAN WE CAN'T FIGHT WITH SPRAY GUNS ANYMORE?!
YO... STUPID FROG.
*GEEE HEE HEE
Y'HEAR THAT RADIO...?
NEITHER DO I!!!

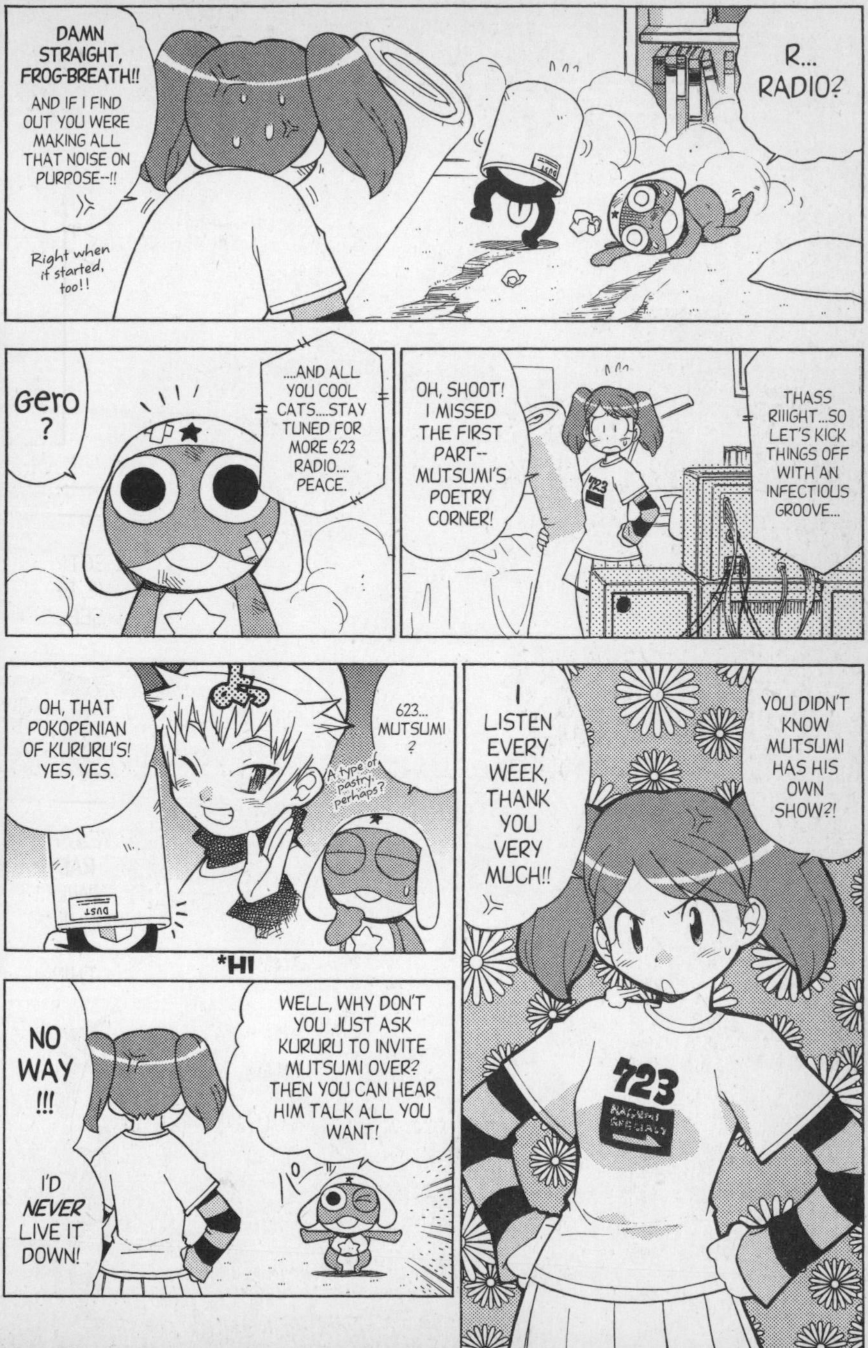
R... RADIO?
DAMN STRAIGHT, FROG-BREATH!!
AND IF I FIND OUT YOU WERE MAKING ALL THAT NOISE ON PURPOSE--!!
Right when it started, too!!
THASS RIIIGHT...SO LET'S KICK THINGS OFF WITH AN INFECTIOUS GROOVE...
OH, SHOOT! I MISSED THE FIRST PART-- MUTSUMI'S POETRY CORNER!
....AND ALL YOU COOL CATS....STAY TUNED FOR MORE 623 RADIO.... PEACE.
Gero?
YOU DIDN'T KNOW MUTSUMI HAS HIS OWN SHOW?!
I LISTEN EVERY WEEK, THANK YOU VERY MUCH!!
623... MUTSUMI?
A type of pastry, perhaps?
OH, THAT POKOPENIAN OF KURURU'S! YES, YES.
*HI
WELL, WHY DON'T YOU JUST ASK KURURU TO INVITE MUTSUMI OVER? THEN YOU CAN HEAR HIM TALK ALL YOU WANT!
NO WAY!!!
I'D *NEVER* LIVE IT DOWN!

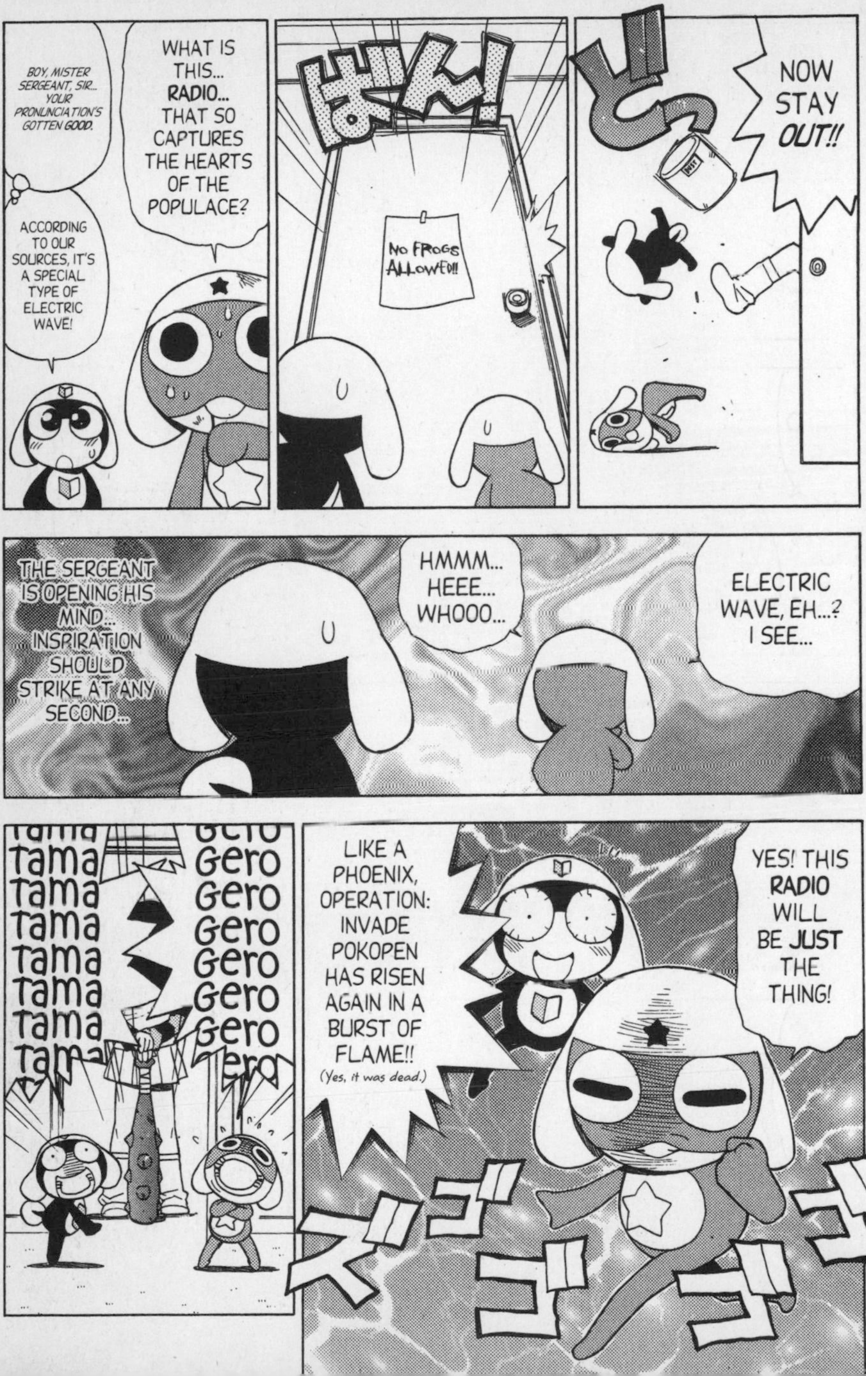
NOW STAY OUT!!
NO FROGS ALLOWED!!
WHAT IS THIS... RADIO... THAT SO CAPTURES THE HEARTS OF THE POPULACE?
BOY, MISTER SERGEANT, SIR... YOUR PRONUNCIATION'S GOTTEN GOOD.
ACCORDING TO OUR SOURCES, IT'S A SPECIAL TYPE OF ELECTRIC WAVE!
ELECTRIC WAVE, EH...? I SEE...
HMMM... HEEE... WHOOO...
THE SERGEANT IS OPENING HIS MIND... INSPIRATION SHOULD STRIKE AT ANY SECOND...
YES! THIS RADIO WILL BE JUST THE THING!
LIKE A PHOENIX, OPERATION: INVADE POKOPEN HAS RISEN AGAIN IN A BURST OF FLAME!!
(Yes, it was dead.)
Gero Gero Gero Gero Gero Gero Gero
Tama Tama Tama Tama Tama Tama Tama

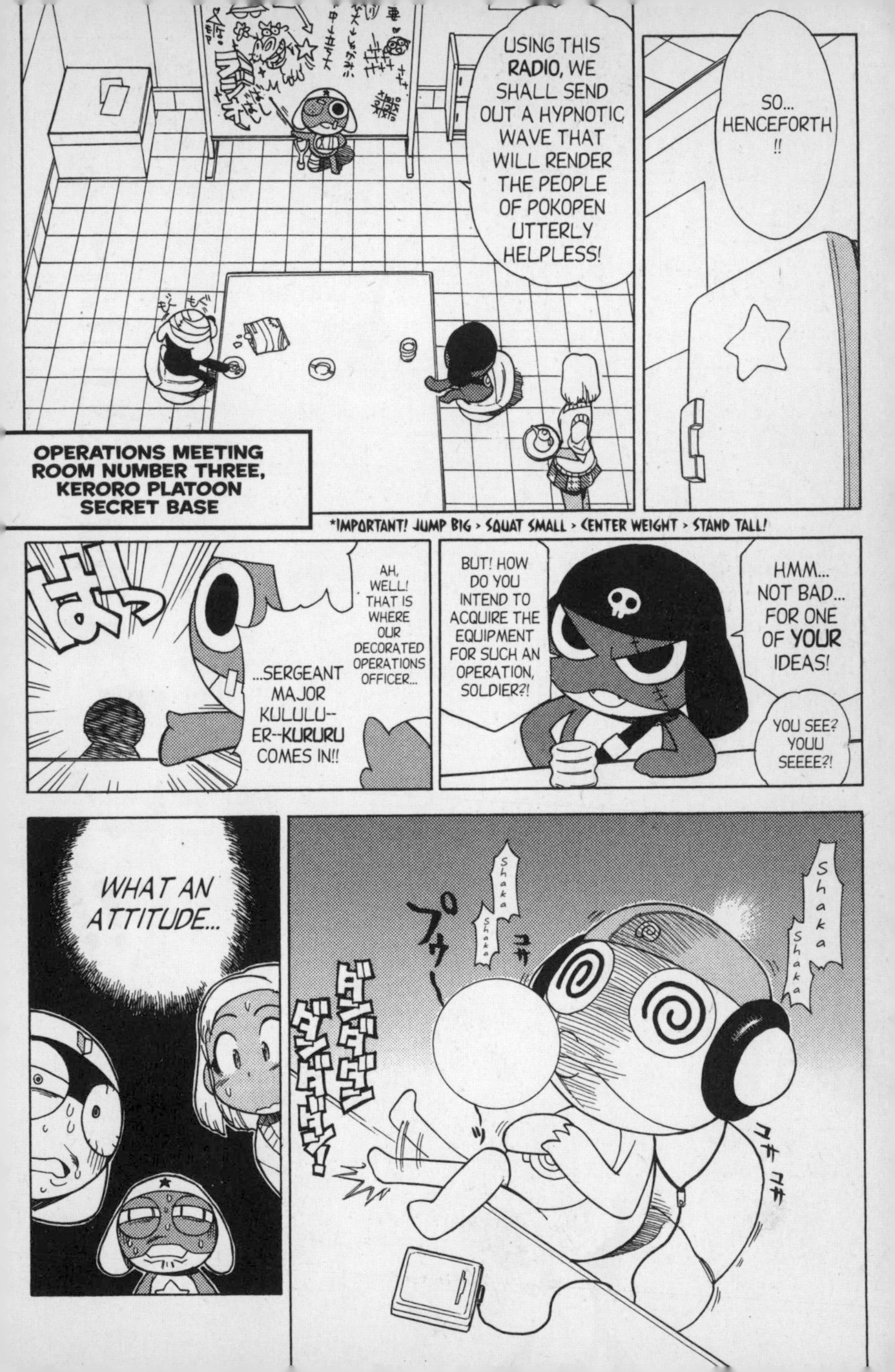

SO... HENCEFORTH !!
USING THIS RADIO, WE SHALL SEND OUT A HYPNOTIC WAVE THAT WILL RENDER THE PEOPLE OF POKOPEN UTTERLY HELPLESS!
OPERATIONS MEETING ROOM NUMBER THREE, KERORO PLATOON SECRET BASE
*IMPORTANT! JUMP BIG > SQUAT SMALL > CENTER WEIGHT > STAND TALL!
HMM... NOT BAD... FOR ONE OF YOUR IDEAS!
YOU SEE? YOUU SEEEE?!
BUT! HOW DO YOU INTEND TO ACQUIRE THE EQUIPMENT FOR SUCH AN OPERATION, SOLDIER?!
AH, WELL! THAT IS WHERE OUR DECORATED OPERATIONS OFFICER...
...SERGEANT MAJOR KULULU-- ER--KURURU COMES IN!!
はっ
Shaka Shaka
Shaka Shaka
プゥ~
WHAT AN ATTITUDE...

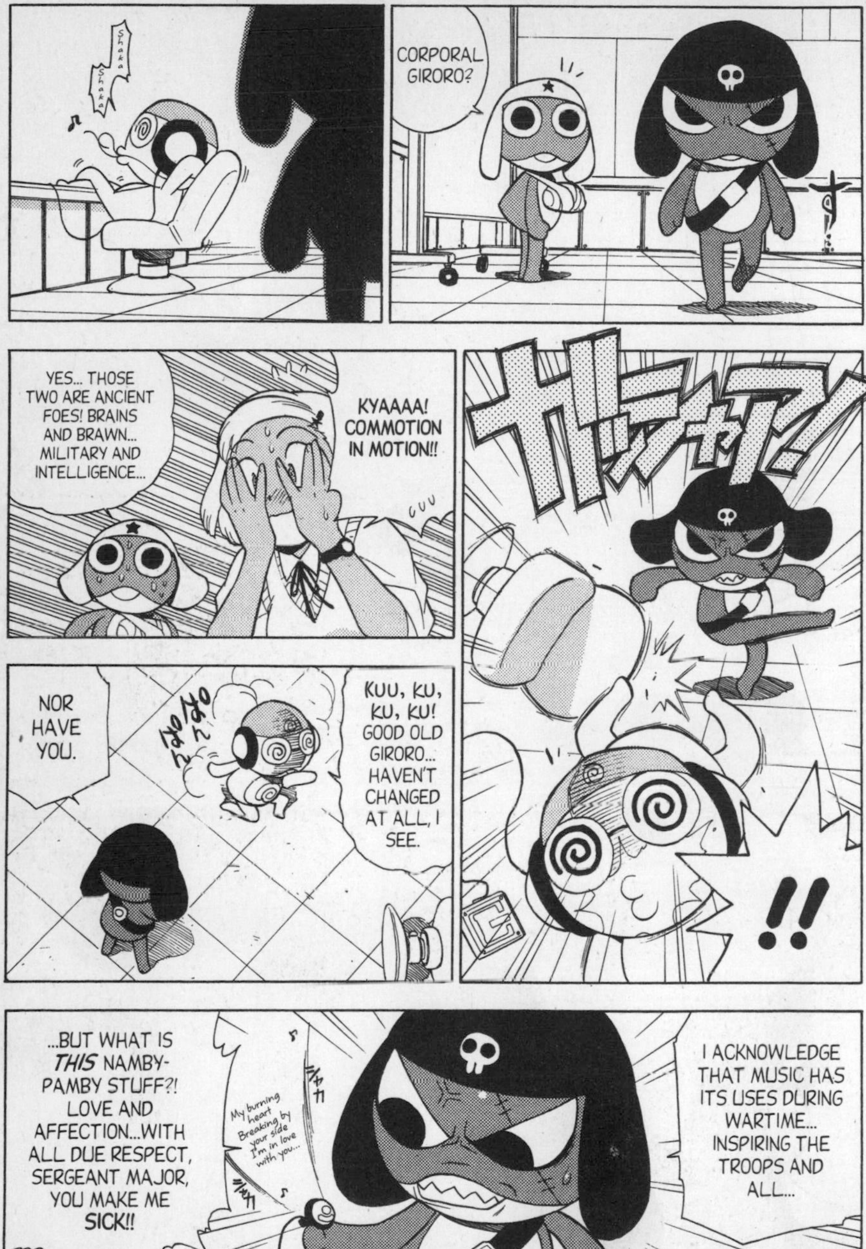
Shaka Shaka
CORPORAL GIRORO?
KYAAAA! COMMOTION IN MOTION!!
YES... THOSE TWO ARE ANCIENT FOES! BRAINS AND BRAWN... MILITARY AND INTELLIGENCE...
!!
KUU, KU, KU, KU! GOOD OLD GIRORO... HAVEN'T CHANGED AT ALL, I SEE.
NOR HAVE YOU.
I ACKNOWLEDGE THAT MUSIC HAS ITS USES DURING WARTIME... INSPIRING THE TROOPS AND ALL...
My burning heart Breaking by your side I'm in love with you...
...BUT WHAT IS THIS NAMBY-PAMBY STUFF?! LOVE AND AFFECTION...WITH ALL DUE RESPECT, SERGEANT MAJOR, YOU MAKE ME SICK!!

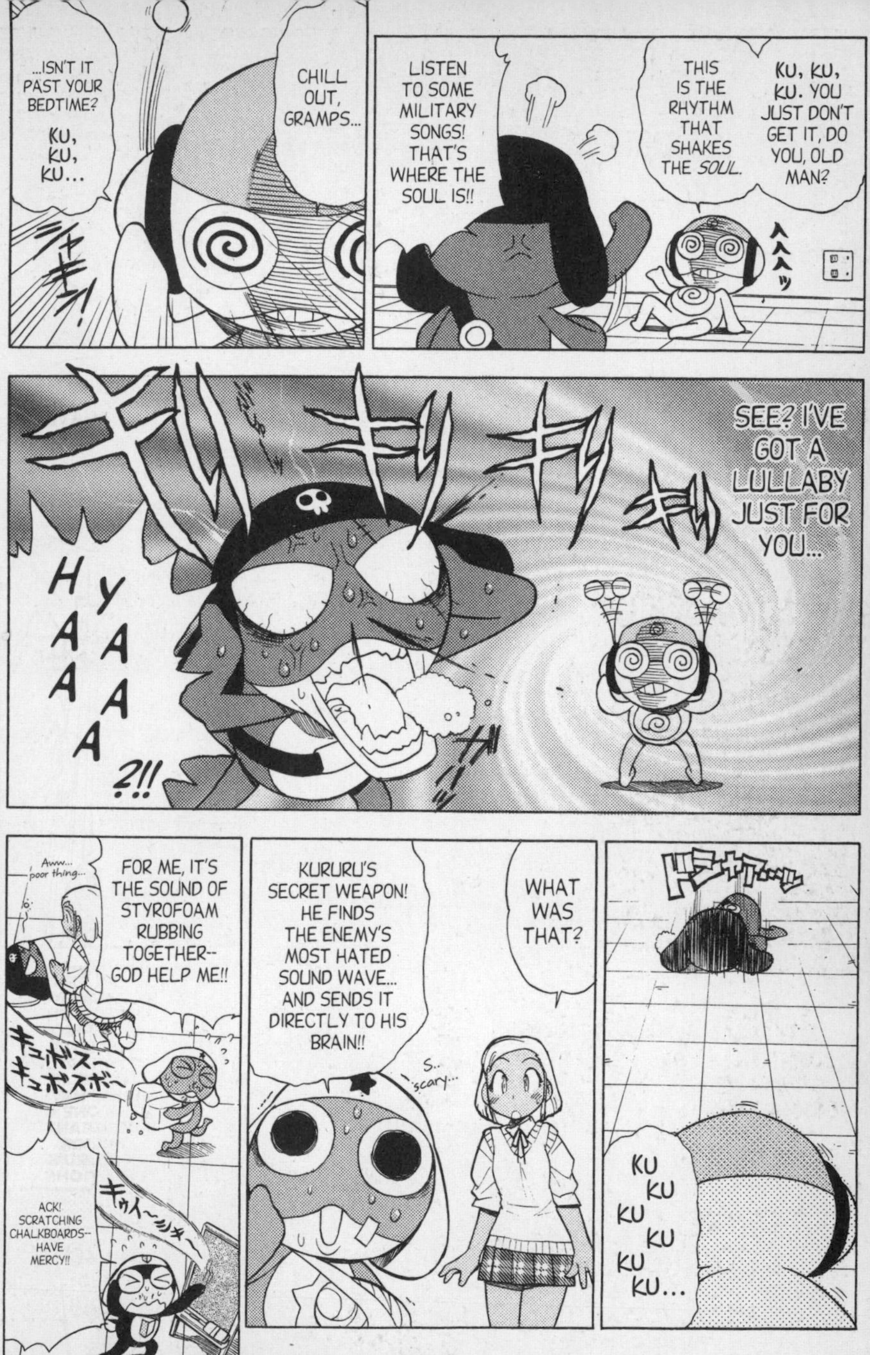
KU, KU, KU. YOU JUST DON'T GET IT, DO YOU, OLD MAN?
THIS IS THE RHYTHM THAT SHAKES THE *SOUL*.
LISTEN TO SOME MILITARY SONGS! THAT'S WHERE THE SOUL IS!!
CHILL OUT, GRAMPS...
...ISN'T IT PAST YOUR BEDTIME?
KU, KU, KU...
シャキーン!
SEE? I'VE GOT A LULLABY JUST FOR YOU...
ギリ キリ キリ キリ
HYAAAAAA ?!!
ドシャアーッ
KU KU KU KU KU KU...
WHAT WAS THAT?
KURURU'S SECRET WEAPON! HE FINDS THE ENEMY'S MOST HATED SOUND WAVE... AND SENDS IT DIRECTLY TO HIS BRAIN!!
S.. scary...
FOR ME, IT'S THE SOUND OF STYROFOAM RUBBING TOGETHER-- GOD HELP ME!!
Aww... poor thing...
キュボスー キュボスボー
ACK! SCRATCHING CHALKBOARDS-- HAVE MERCY!!

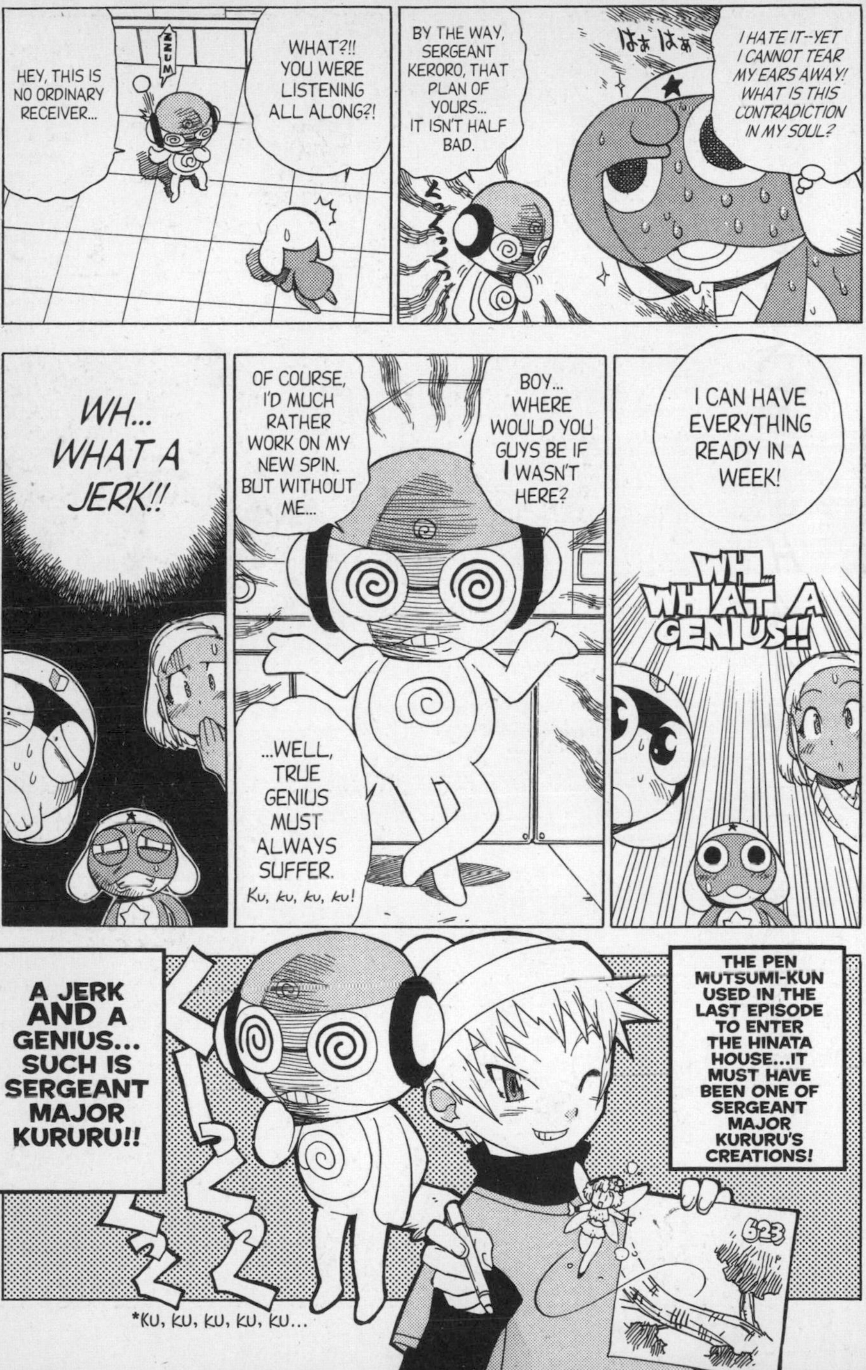

HEY, THIS IS NO ORDINARY RECEIVER...
ZZUM
WHAT?!! YOU WERE LISTENING ALL ALONG?!
BY THE WAY, SERGEANT KERORO, THAT PLAN OF YOURS... IT ISN'T HALF BAD.
はぁ はぁ
I HATE IT--YET I CANNOT TEAR MY EARS AWAY! WHAT IS THIS CONTRADICTION IN MY SOUL?
OF COURSE, I'D MUCH RATHER WORK ON MY NEW SPIN. BUT WITHOUT ME...
BOY... WHERE WOULD YOU GUYS BE IF I WASN'T HERE?
...WELL, TRUE GENIUS MUST ALWAYS SUFFER.
Ku, ku, ku, ku!
WH... WHAT A JERK!!
I CAN HAVE EVERYTHING READY IN A WEEK!
WH... WHAT A GENIUS!!
A JERK AND A GENIUS... SUCH IS SERGEANT MAJOR KURURU!!
THE PEN MUTSUMI-KUN USED IN THE LAST EPISODE TO ENTER THE HINATA HOUSE...IT MUST HAVE BEEN ONE OF SERGEANT MAJOR KURURU'S CREATIONS!
623
*KU, KU, KU, KU, KU...

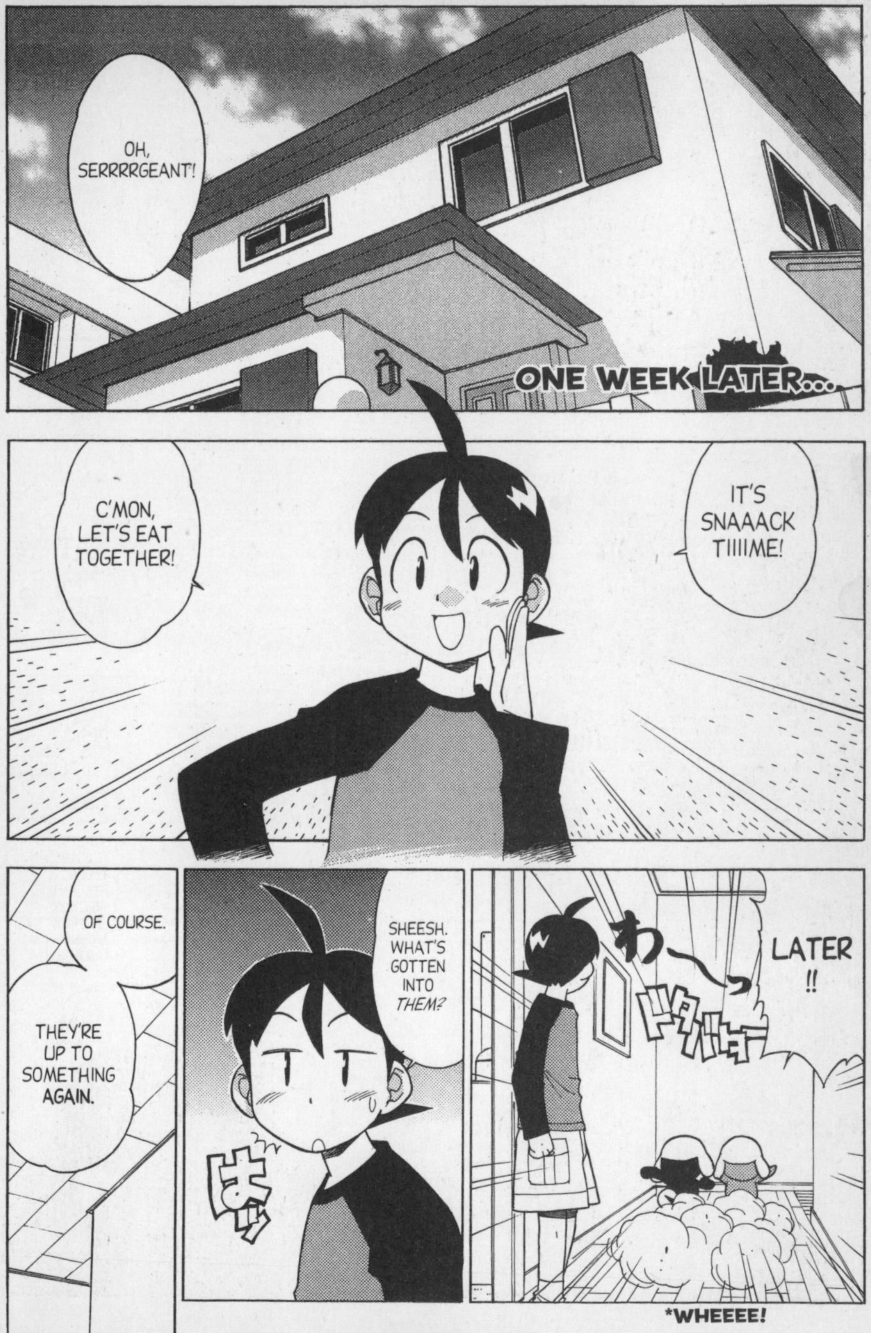
ONE WEEK LATER...
OH, SERRRRGEANT!
IT'S SNAAACK TIIIIME!
C'MON, LET'S EAT TOGETHER!
わ〜っ
LATER !!
SHEESH. WHAT'S GOTTEN INTO *THEM?*
OF COURSE.
THEY'RE UP TO SOMETHING **AGAIN.**

*WHEEEE!

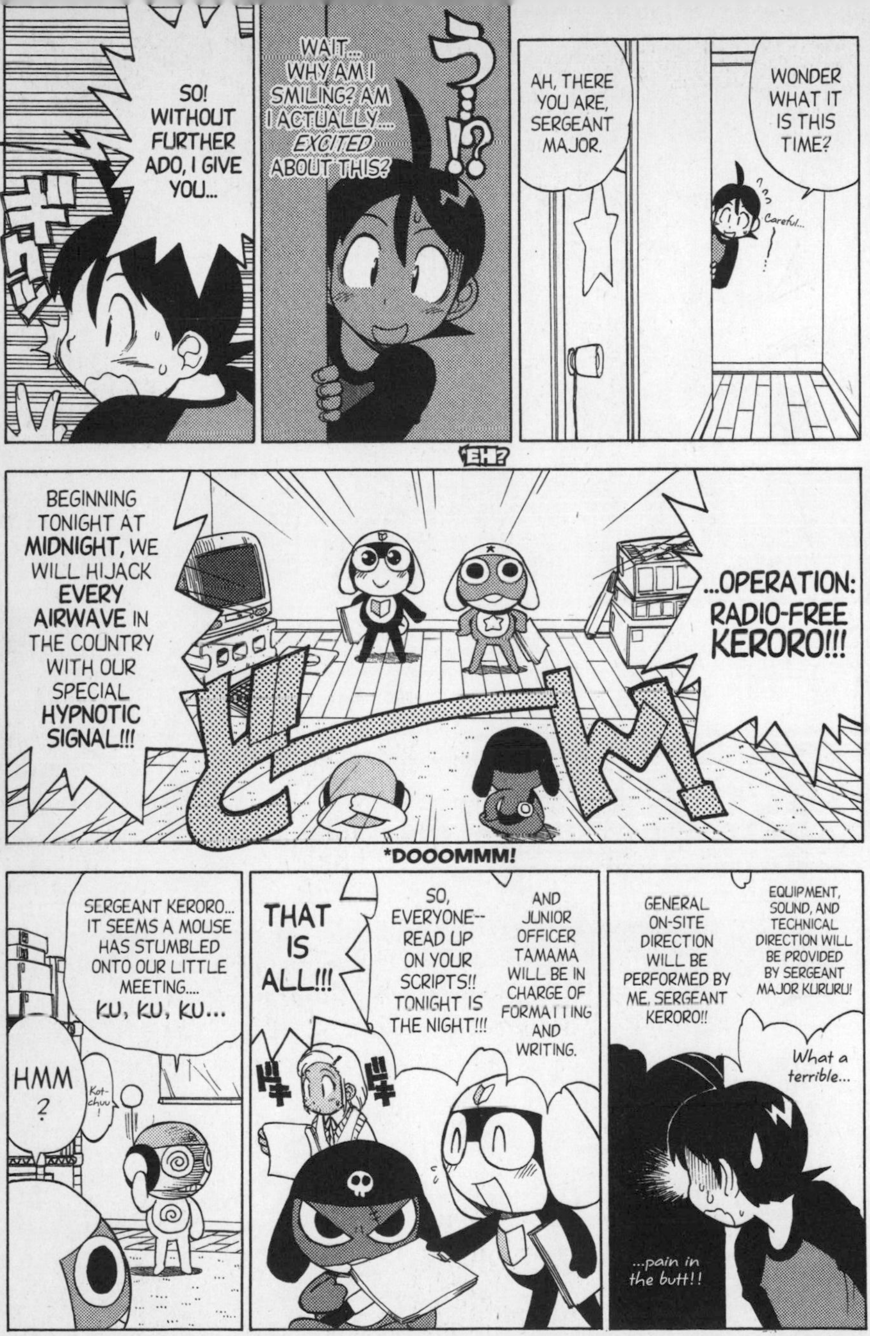
WONDER WHAT IT IS THIS TIME?
Careful...
AH, THERE YOU ARE, SERGEANT MAJOR.
WAIT... WHY AM I SMILING? AM I ACTUALLY... EXCITED ABOUT THIS?
SO! WITHOUT FURTHER ADO, I GIVE YOU...
*EH?
...OPERATION: RADIO-FREE KERORO!!!
BEGINNING TONIGHT AT MIDNIGHT, WE WILL HIJACK EVERY AIRWAVE IN THE COUNTRY WITH OUR SPECIAL HYPNOTIC SIGNAL!!!
*DOOOMMM!
EQUIPMENT, SOUND, AND TECHNICAL DIRECTION WILL BE PROVIDED BY SERGEANT MAJOR KURURU!
GENERAL ON-SITE DIRECTION WILL BE PERFORMED BY ME, SERGEANT KERORO!!
What a terrible...
...pain in the butt!!
AND JUNIOR OFFICER TAMAMA WILL BE IN CHARGE OF FORMATTING AND WRITING.
SO, EVERYONE-- READ UP ON YOUR SCRIPTS!! TONIGHT IS THE NIGHT!!!
THAT IS ALL!!!
SERGEANT KERORO... IT SEEMS A MOUSE HAS STUMBLED ONTO OUR LITTLE MEETING.... KU, KU, KU...
Kot-chuu!
HMM?

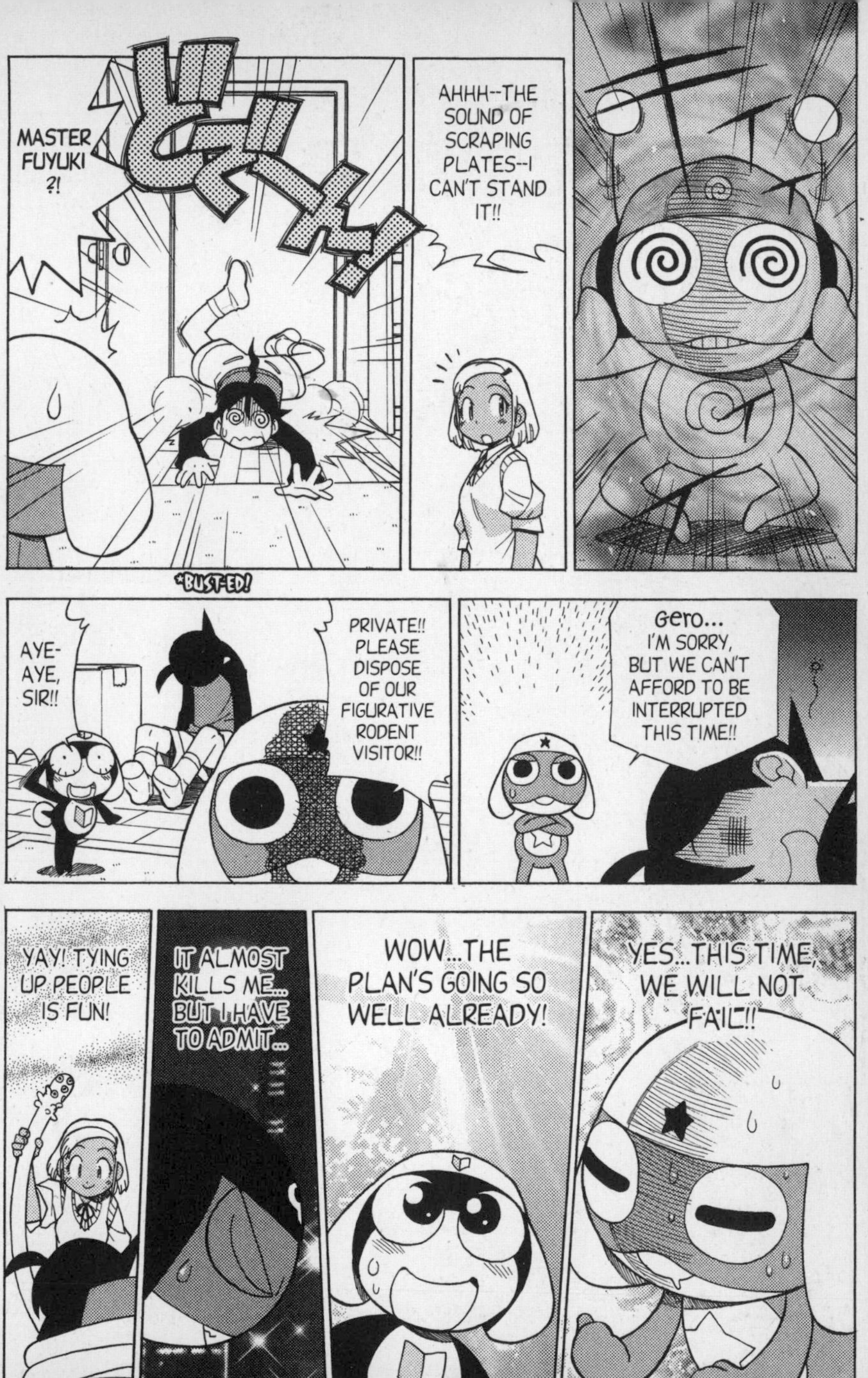
AHHH--THE SOUND OF SCRAPING PLATES--I CAN'T STAND IT!!
MASTER FUYUKI ?!
*BUST-ED!
Gero... I'M SORRY, BUT WE CAN'T AFFORD TO BE INTERRUPTED THIS TIME!!
PRIVATE!! PLEASE DISPOSE OF OUR FIGURATIVE RODENT VISITOR!!
AYE-AYE, SIR!!
YES...THIS TIME, WE WILL NOT FAIL!!
WOW...THE PLAN'S GOING SO WELL ALREADY!
IT ALMOST KILLS ME... BUT I HAVE TO ADMIT...
YAY! TYING UP PEOPLE IS FUN!

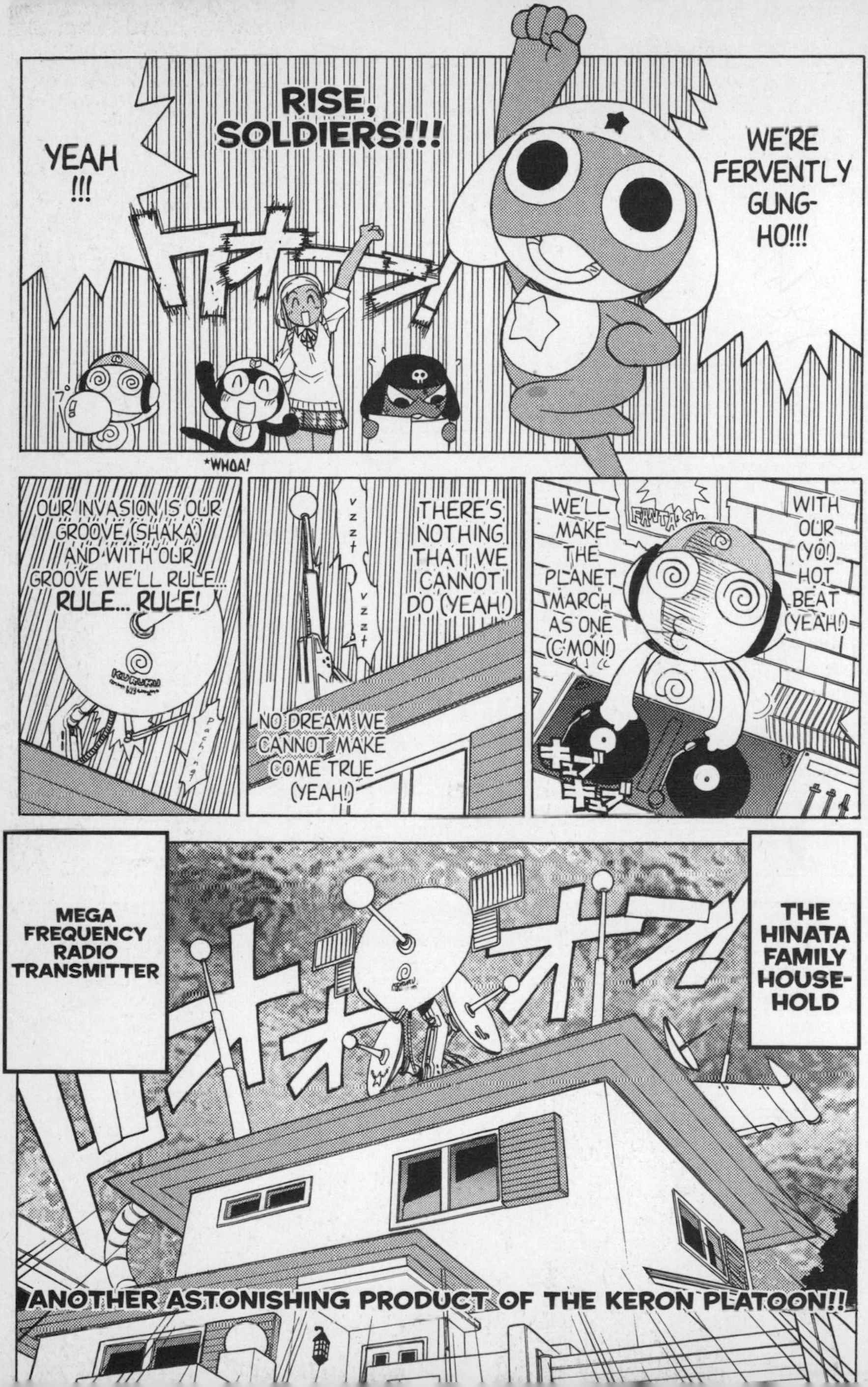
RISE, SOLDIERS!!!
WE'RE FERVENTLY GUNG-HO!!!
YEAH !!!
*WHOA!
OUR INVASION IS OUR GROOVE (SHAKA) AND WITH OUR GROOVE WE'LL RULE... RULE... RULE!
THERE'S NOTHING THAT WE CANNOT DO (YEAH!)
NO DREAM WE CANNOT MAKE COME TRUE (YEAH!)
WE'LL MAKE THE PLANET MARCH AS ONE (C'MON!)
WITH OUR (YO!) HOT BEAT (YEAH!)
MEGA FREQUENCY RADIO TRANSMITTER
THE HINATA FAMILY HOUSE-HOLD
ANOTHER ASTONISHING PRODUCT OF THE KERON PLATOON!!

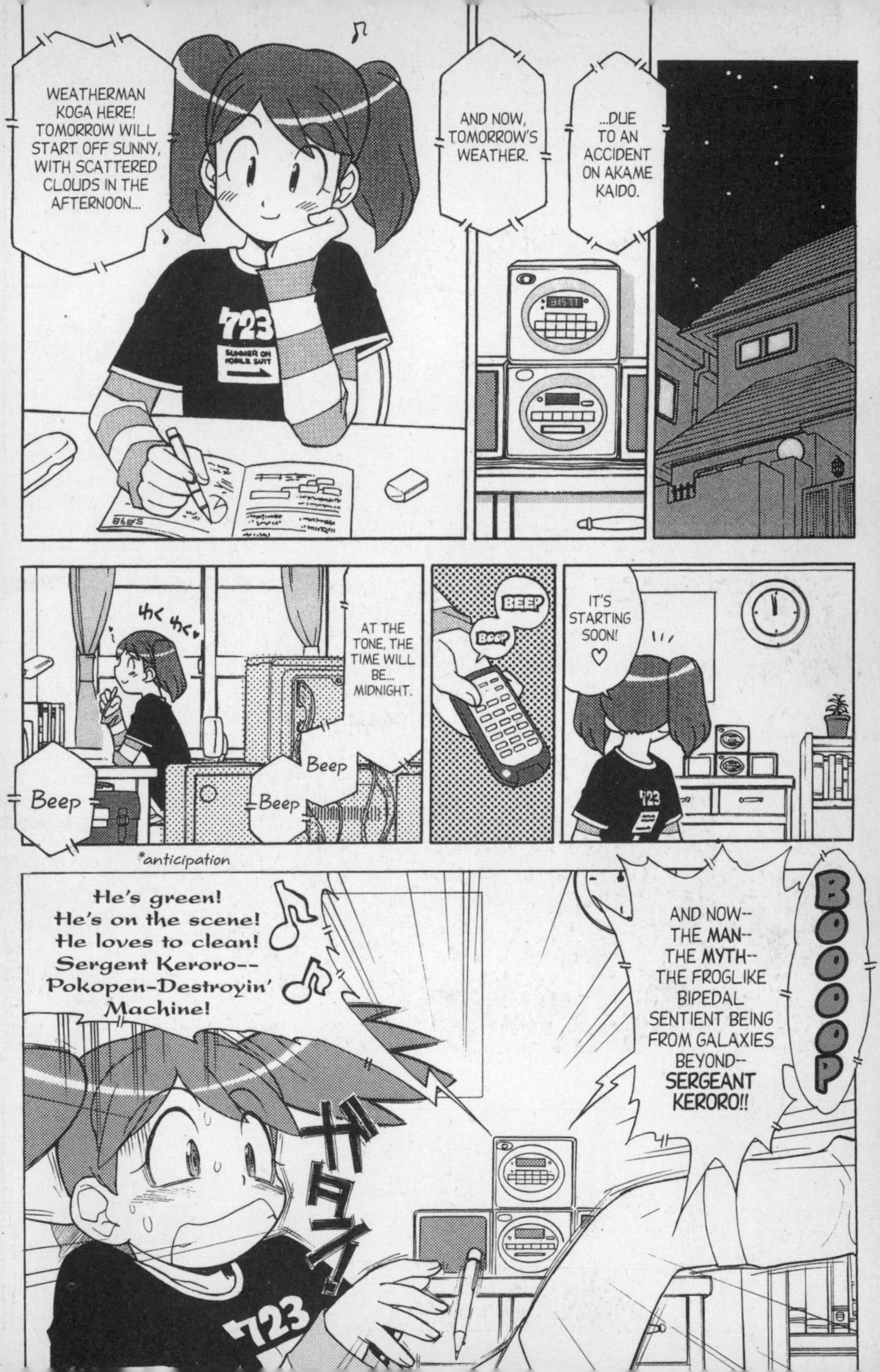
...DUE TO AN ACCIDENT ON AKAME KAIDO.
AND NOW, TOMORROW'S WEATHER.
WEATHERMAN KOGA HERE! TOMORROW WILL START OFF SUNNY, WITH SCATTERED CLOUDS IN THE AFTERNOON...
IT'S STARTING SOON! ♡
BEEP
BOOP
AT THE TONE, THE TIME WILL BE... MIDNIGHT.
Beep
Beep
Beep
*anticipation
BOOOOOP
AND NOW-- THE MAN-- THE MYTH-- THE FROGLIKE BIPEDAL SENTIENT BEING FROM GALAXIES BEYOND-- SERGEANT KERORO!!
He's green! He's on the scene! He loves to clean! Sergent Keroro-- Pokopen-Destroyin' Machine!

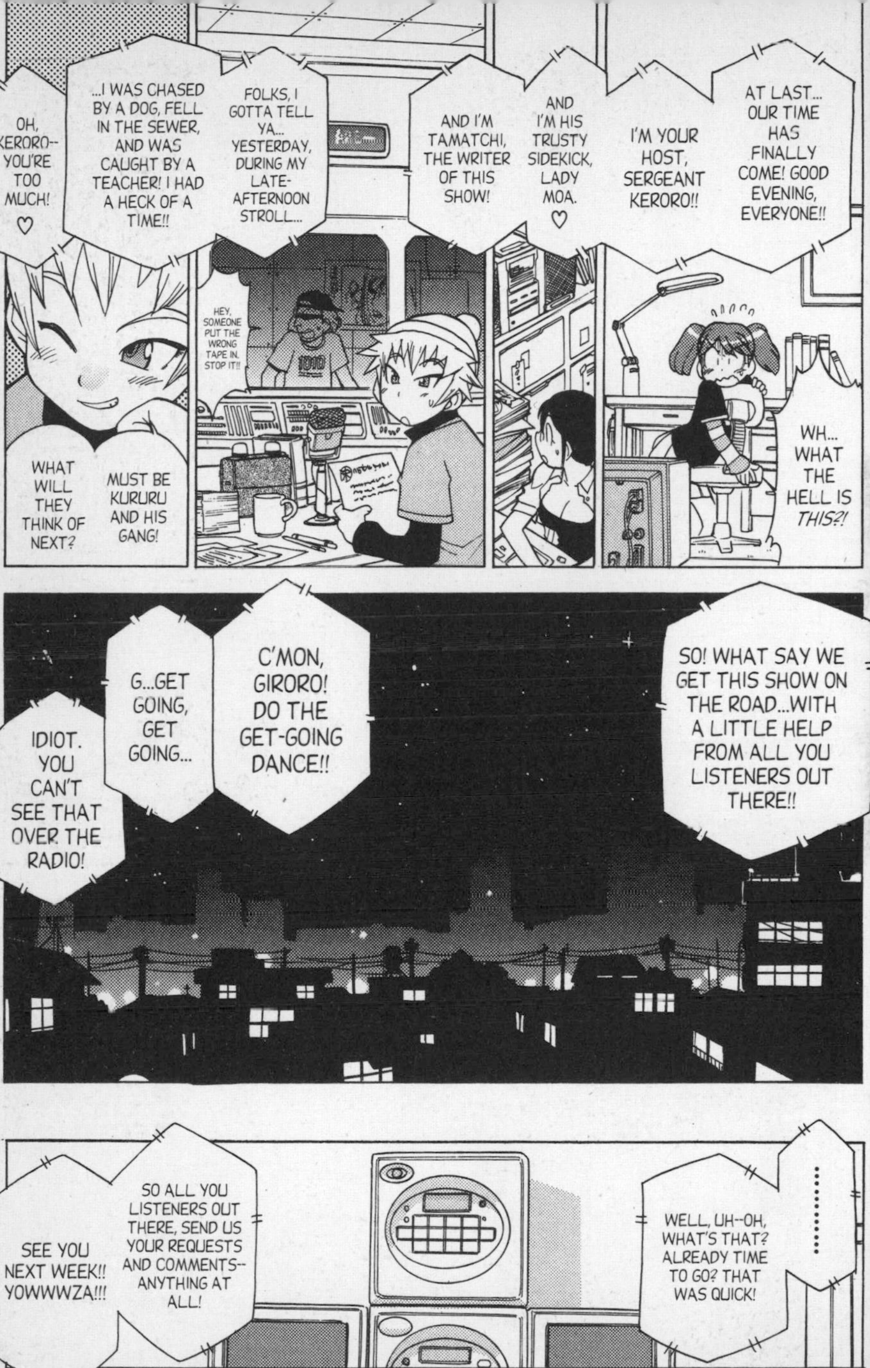
AT LAST... OUR TIME HAS FINALLY COME! GOOD EVENING, EVERYONE!!
I'M YOUR HOST, SERGEANT KERORO!!
AND I'M HIS TRUSTY SIDEKICK, LADY MOA. ♡
AND I'M TAMATCHI, THE WRITER OF THIS SHOW!
FOLKS, I GOTTA TELL YA... YESTERDAY, DURING MY LATE-AFTERNOON STROLL...
...I WAS CHASED BY A DOG, FELL IN THE SEWER, AND WAS CAUGHT BY A TEACHER! I HAD A HECK OF A TIME!!
OH, KERORO-- YOU'RE TOO MUCH! ♡
WH... WHAT THE HELL IS *THIS?!*
HEY, SOMEONE PUT THE WRONG TAPE IN. STOP IT!!
MUST BE KURURU AND HIS GANG!
WHAT WILL THEY THINK OF NEXT?
SO! WHAT SAY WE GET THIS SHOW ON THE ROAD...WITH A LITTLE HELP FROM ALL YOU LISTENERS OUT THERE!!
C'MON, GIRORO! DO THE GET-GOING DANCE!!
G...GET GOING, GET GOING...
IDIOT. YOU CAN'T SEE THAT OVER THE RADIO!
....
WELL, UH--OH, WHAT'S THAT? ALREADY TIME TO GO? THAT WAS QUICK!
SO ALL YOU LISTENERS OUT THERE, SEND US YOUR REQUESTS AND COMMENTS-- ANYTHING AT ALL!
SEE YOU NEXT WEEK!! YOWWWZA!!!

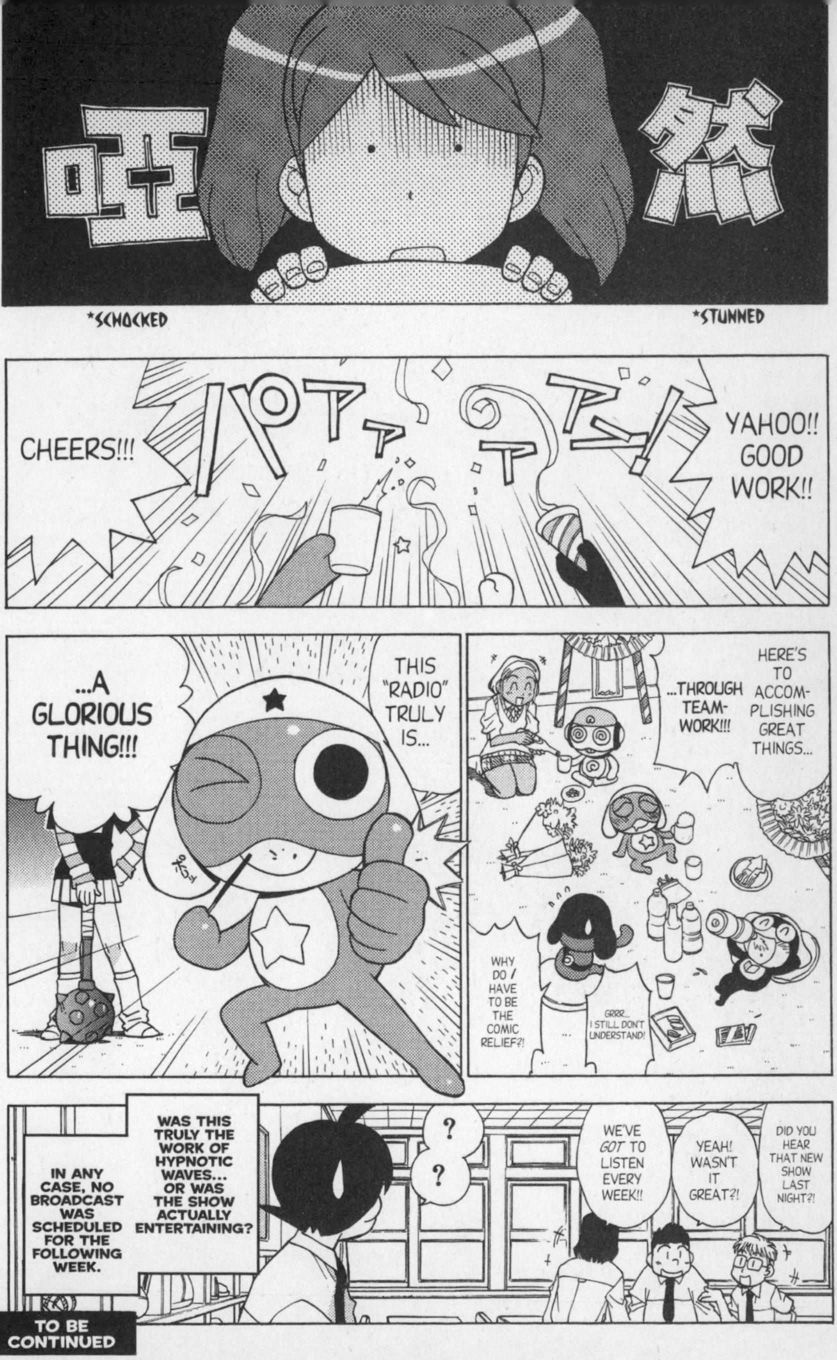
唖然
*SCHOCKED
*STUNNED
YAHOO!! GOOD WORK!!
CHEERS!!!
HERE'S TO ACCOMPLISHING GREAT THINGS...
...THROUGH TEAMWORK!!!
GRRR... I STILL DON'T UNDERSTAND!
WHY DO I HAVE TO BE THE COMIC RELIEF?!
THIS "RADIO" TRULY IS...
...A GLORIOUS THING!!!
DID YOU HEAR THAT NEW SHOW LAST NIGHT?!
YEAH! WASN'T IT GREAT?!
WE'VE *GOT* TO LISTEN EVERY WEEK!!
? ?
WAS THIS TRULY THE WORK OF HYPNOTIC WAVES... OR WAS THE SHOW ACTUALLY ENTERTAINING?
IN ANY CASE, NO BROADCAST WAS SCHEDULED FOR THE FOLLOWING WEEK.
TO BE CONTINUED

ENCOUNTER XXII

NATSUMI'S NUMBER IS UP

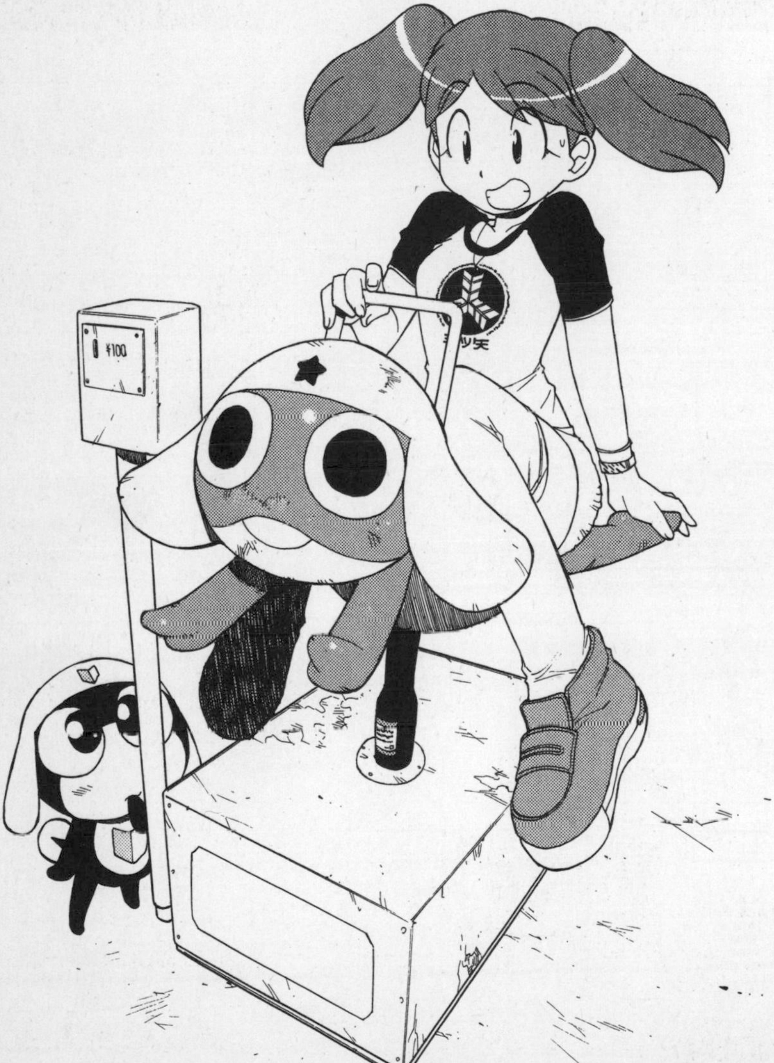
¥100

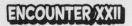

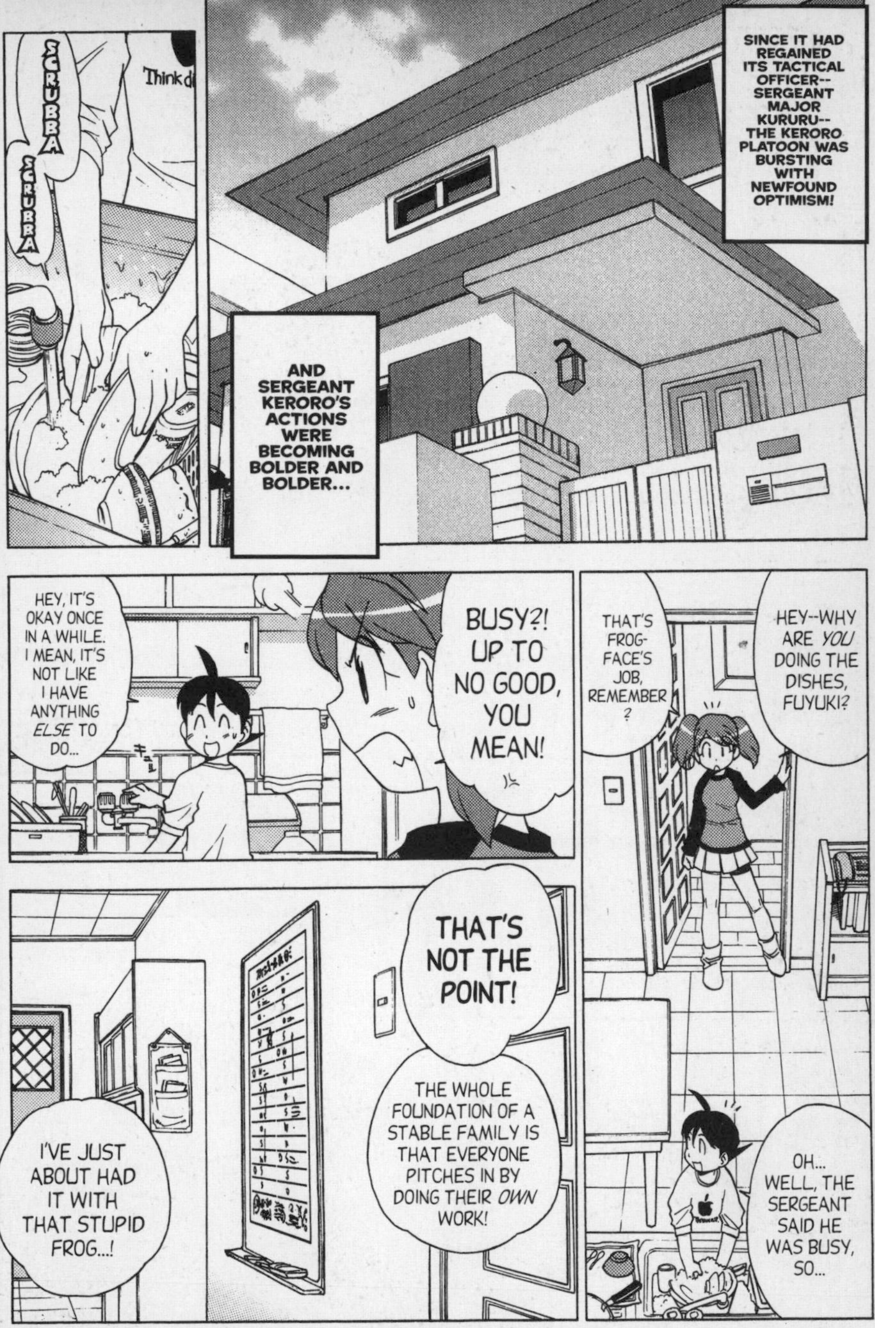
SINCE IT HAD REGAINED ITS TACTICAL OFFICER--SERGEANT MAJOR KURURU--THE KERORO PLATOON WAS BURSTING WITH NEWFOUND OPTIMISM!
AND SERGEANT KERORO'S ACTIONS WERE BECOMING BOLDER AND BOLDER...
SCRUBBA SCRUBBA
SCRUBBA
HEY--WHY ARE *YOU* DOING THE DISHES, FUYUKI?
THAT'S FROG-FACE'S JOB, REMEMBER?
OH... WELL, THE SERGEANT SAID HE WAS BUSY, SO...
BUSY?! UP TO NO GOOD, YOU MEAN!
HEY, IT'S OKAY ONCE IN A WHILE. I MEAN, IT'S NOT LIKE I HAVE ANYTHING *ELSE* TO DO...
THAT'S NOT THE POINT!
THE WHOLE FOUNDATION OF A STABLE FAMILY IS THAT EVERYONE PITCHES IN BY DOING THEIR *OWN* WORK!
I'VE JUST ABOUT HAD IT WITH THAT STUPID FROG...!

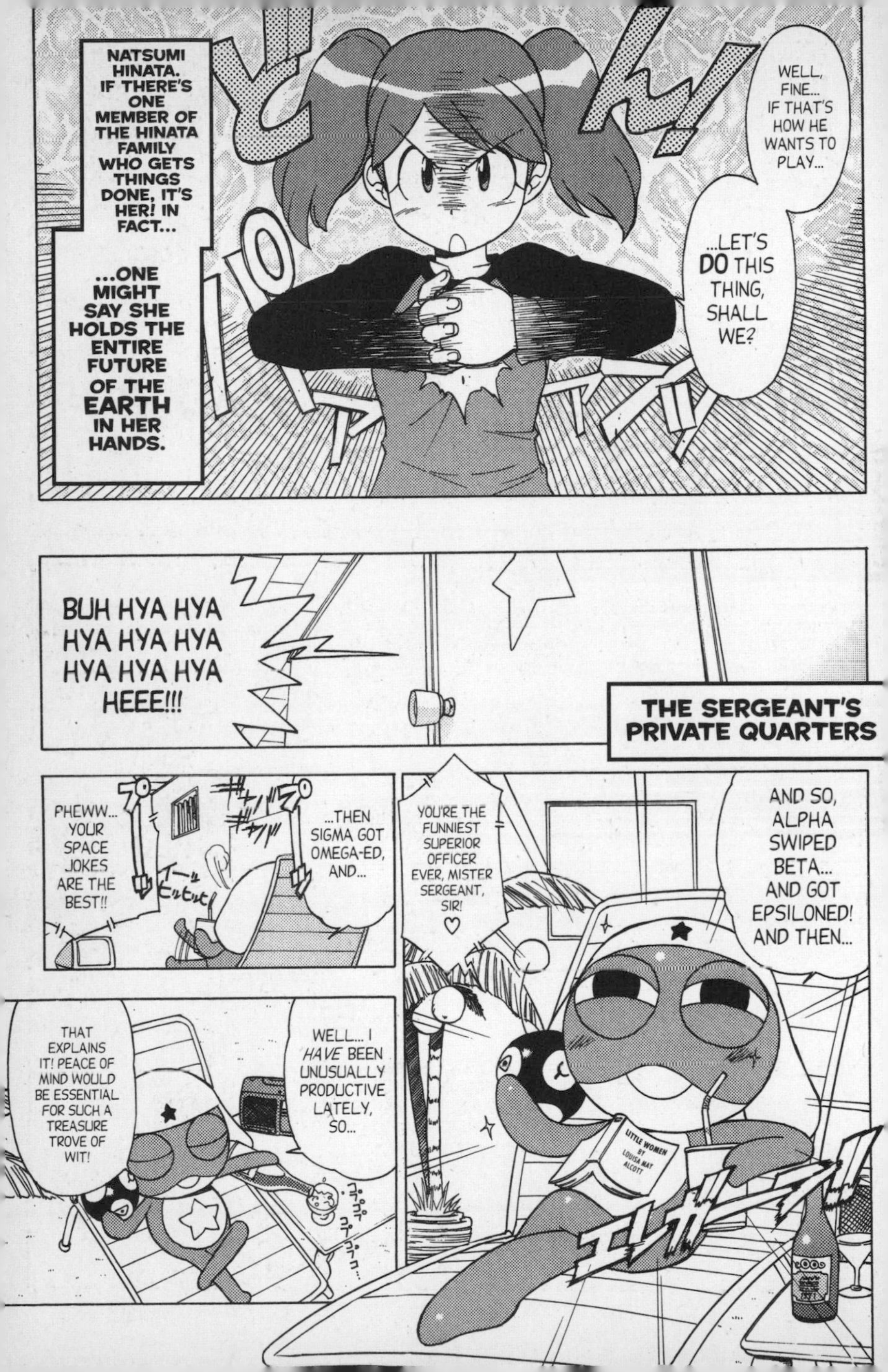
NATSUMI HINATA. IF THERE'S ONE MEMBER OF THE HINATA FAMILY WHO GETS THINGS DONE, IT'S HER! IN FACT...
...ONE MIGHT SAY SHE HOLDS THE ENTIRE FUTURE OF THE EARTH IN HER HANDS.
WELL, FINE... IF THAT'S HOW HE WANTS TO PLAY...
...LET'S DO THIS THING, SHALL WE?
BUH HYA HYA HYA HYA HYA HYA HYA HYA HEEE!!!
THE SERGEANT'S PRIVATE QUARTERS
...THEN SIGMA GOT OMEGA-ED, AND...
PHEWW... YOUR SPACE JOKES ARE THE BEST!!
AND SO, ALPHA SWIPED BETA... AND GOT EPSILONED! AND THEN...
YOU'RE THE FUNNIEST SUPERIOR OFFICER EVER, MISTER SERGEANT, SIR! ♡
WELL... I HAVE BEEN UNUSUALLY PRODUCTIVE LATELY, SO...
THAT EXPLAINS IT! PEACE OF MIND WOULD BE ESSENTIAL FOR SUCH A TREASURE TROVE OF WIT!
LITTLE WOMEN BY LOUISA MAY ALCOTT

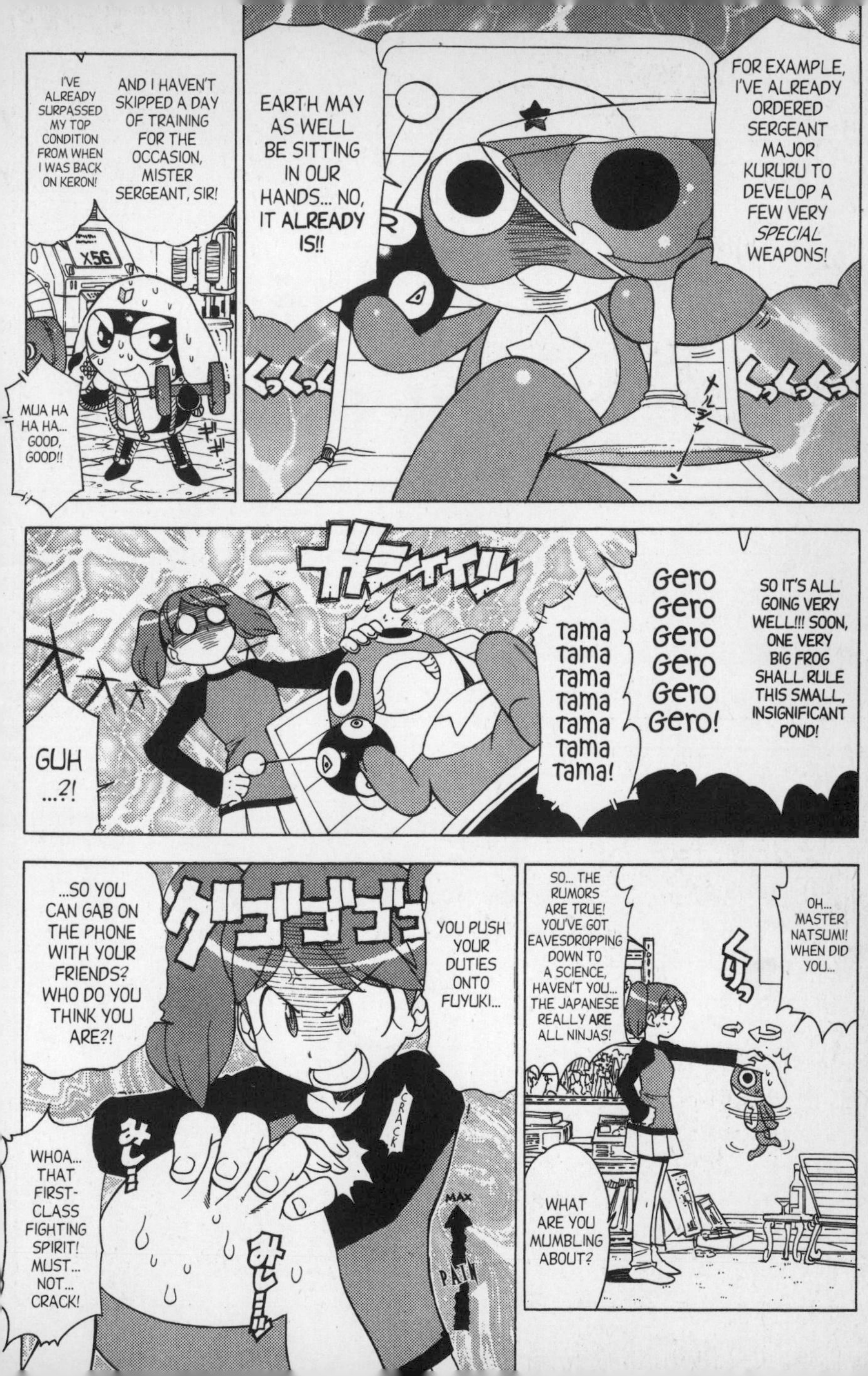
FOR EXAMPLE, I'VE ALREADY ORDERED SERGEANT MAJOR KURURU TO DEVELOP A FEW VERY SPECIAL WEAPONS!
EARTH MAY AS WELL BE SITTING IN OUR HANDS... NO, IT ALREADY IS!!
くっくっくっく
くっくっく
AND I HAVEN'T SKIPPED A DAY OF TRAINING FOR THE OCCASION, MISTER SERGEANT, SIR!
I'VE ALREADY SURPASSED MY TOP CONDITION FROM WHEN I WAS BACK ON KERON!
X56
MUA HA HA HA... GOOD, GOOD!!
SO IT'S ALL GOING VERY WELL!!! SOON, ONE VERY BIG FROG SHALL RULE THIS SMALL, INSIGNIFICANT POND!
Gero Gero Gero Gero Gero Gero!
Tama Tama Tama Tama Tama Tama Tama!
GUH ...?!
OH... MASTER NATSUMI! WHEN DID YOU...
SO... THE RUMORS ARE TRUE! YOU'VE GOT EAVESDROPPING DOWN TO A SCIENCE, HAVEN'T YOU... THE JAPANESE REALLY ARE ALL NINJAS!
WHAT ARE YOU MUMBLING ABOUT?
YOU PUSH YOUR DUTIES ONTO FUYUKI...
...SO YOU CAN GAB ON THE PHONE WITH YOUR FRIENDS? WHO DO YOU THINK YOU ARE?!
CRACK
MAX
PAIN
WHOA... THAT FIRST-CLASS FIGHTING SPIRIT! MUST... NOT... CRACK!

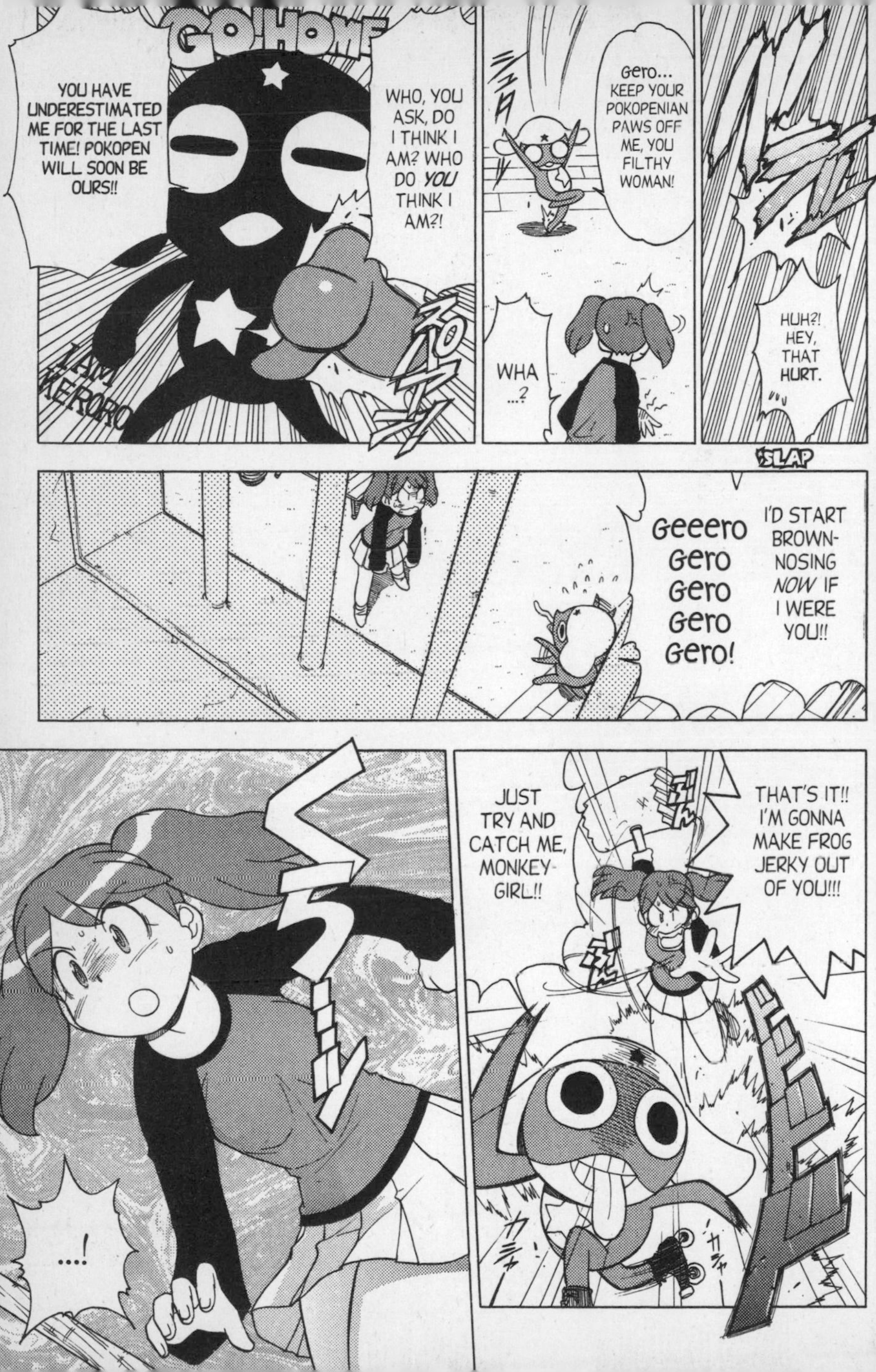
HUH?! HEY, THAT HURT.
SLAP
Gero... KEEP YOUR POKOPENIAN PAWS OFF ME, YOU FILTHY WOMAN!
WHA ...?
WHO, YOU ASK, DO I THINK I AM? WHO DO *YOU* THINK I AM?!
YOU HAVE UNDERESTIMATED ME FOR THE LAST TIME! POKOPEN WILL SOON BE OURS!!
GO!HONF
I AM KERORO
I'D START BROWN-NOSING *NOW* IF I WERE YOU!!
Geeero Gero Gero Gero Gero!
THAT'S IT!! I'M GONNA MAKE FROG JERKY OUT OF YOU!!!
JUST TRY AND CATCH ME, MONKEY-GIRL!!
...!

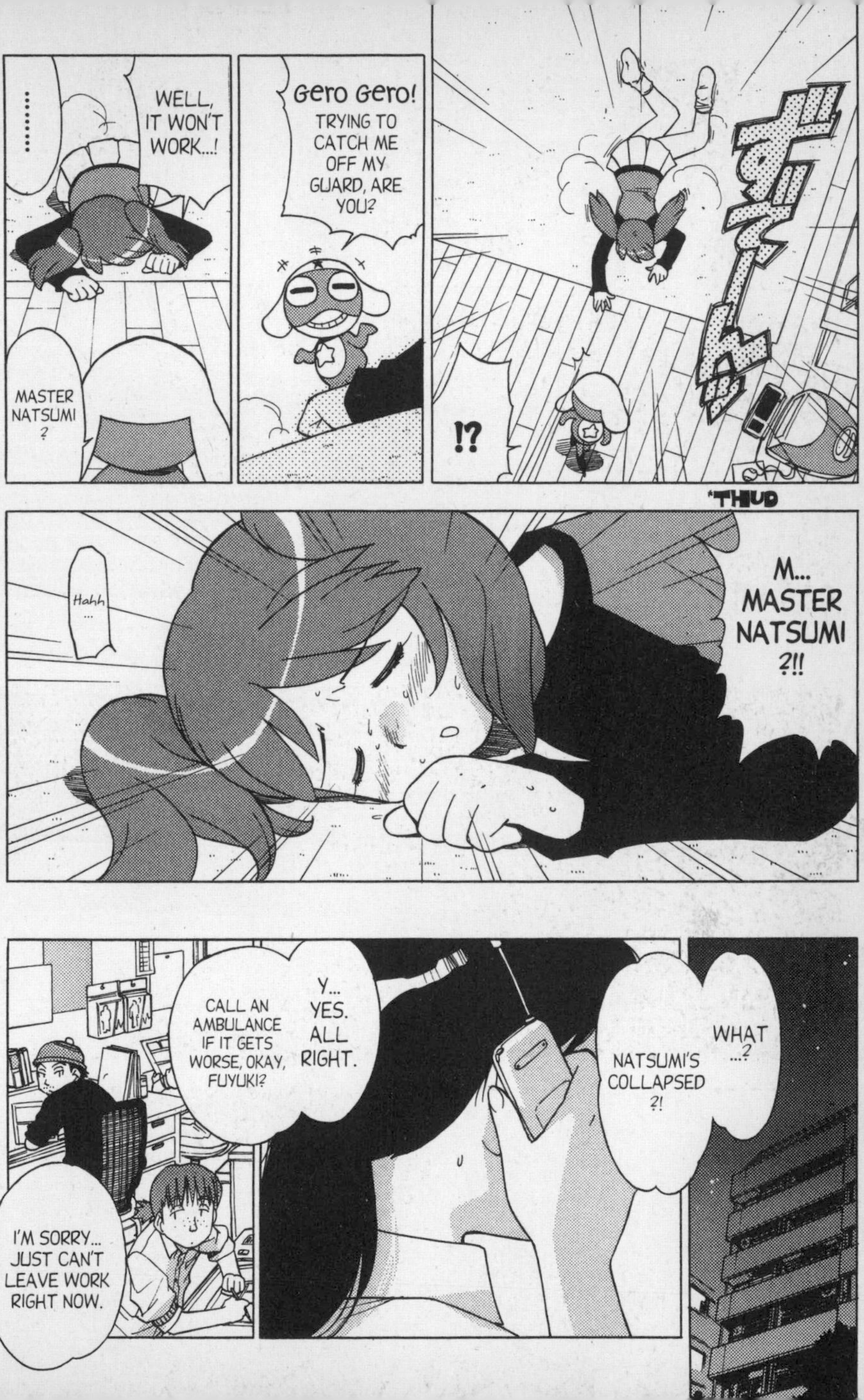
!?
*THUD
Gero Gero!
TRYING TO CATCH ME OFF MY GUARD, ARE YOU?
WELL, IT WON'T WORK...!
......
MASTER NATSUMI?
M... MASTER NATSUMI?!!
Hahh ...
WHAT ...?
NATSUMI'S COLLAPSED?!
Y... YES. ALL RIGHT.
CALL AN AMBULANCE IF IT GETS WORSE, OKAY, FUYUKI?
I'M SORRY... JUST CAN'T LEAVE WORK RIGHT NOW.

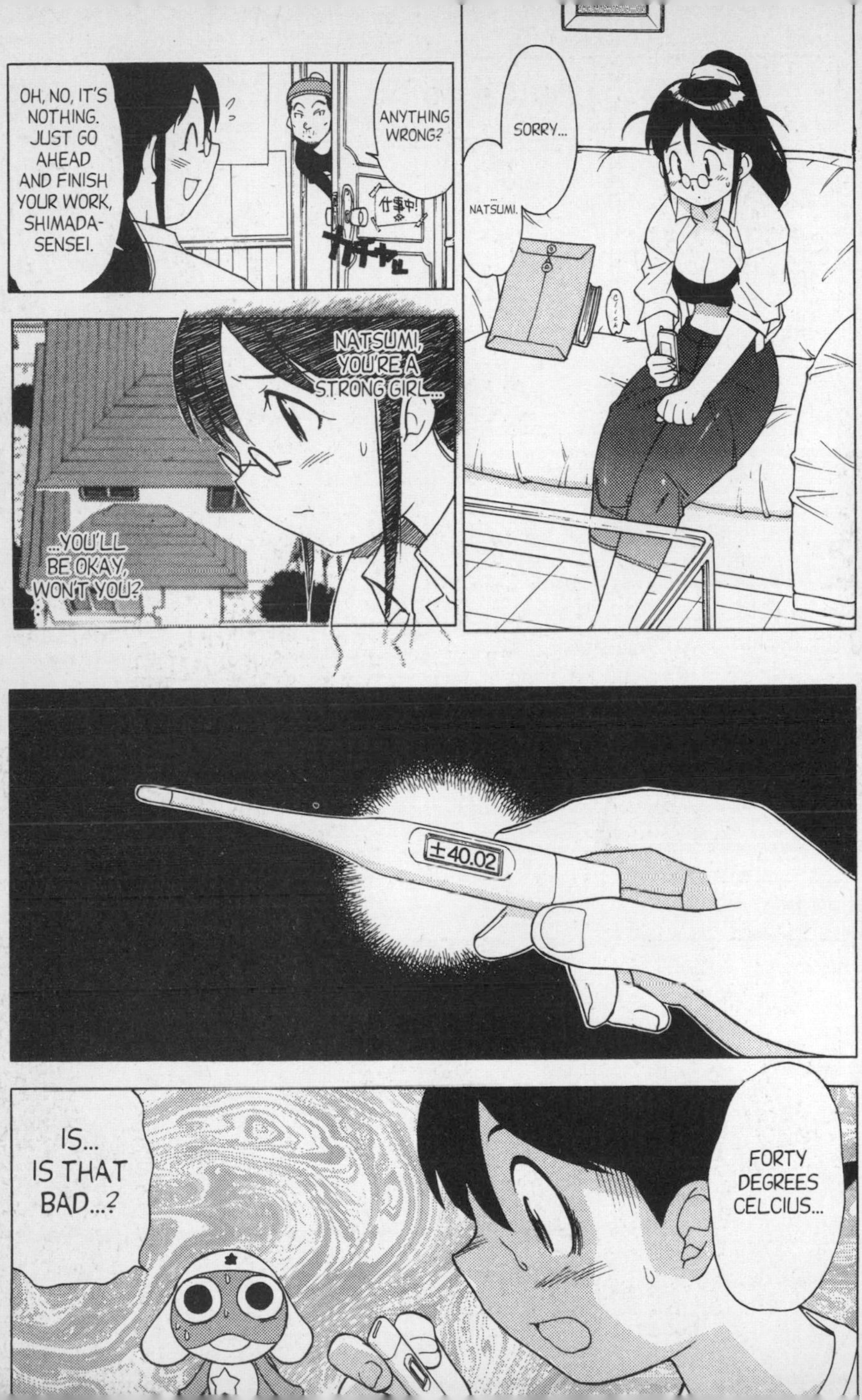

SORRY...
...NATSUMI.
ANYTHING WRONG?
OH, NO, IT'S NOTHING. JUST GO AHEAD AND FINISH YOUR WORK, SHIMADA-SENSEI.
NATSUMI, YOU'RE A STRONG GIRL...
...YOU'LL BE OKAY, WON'T YOU?
±40.02
FORTY DEGREES CELCIUS...
IS... IS THAT BAD...?

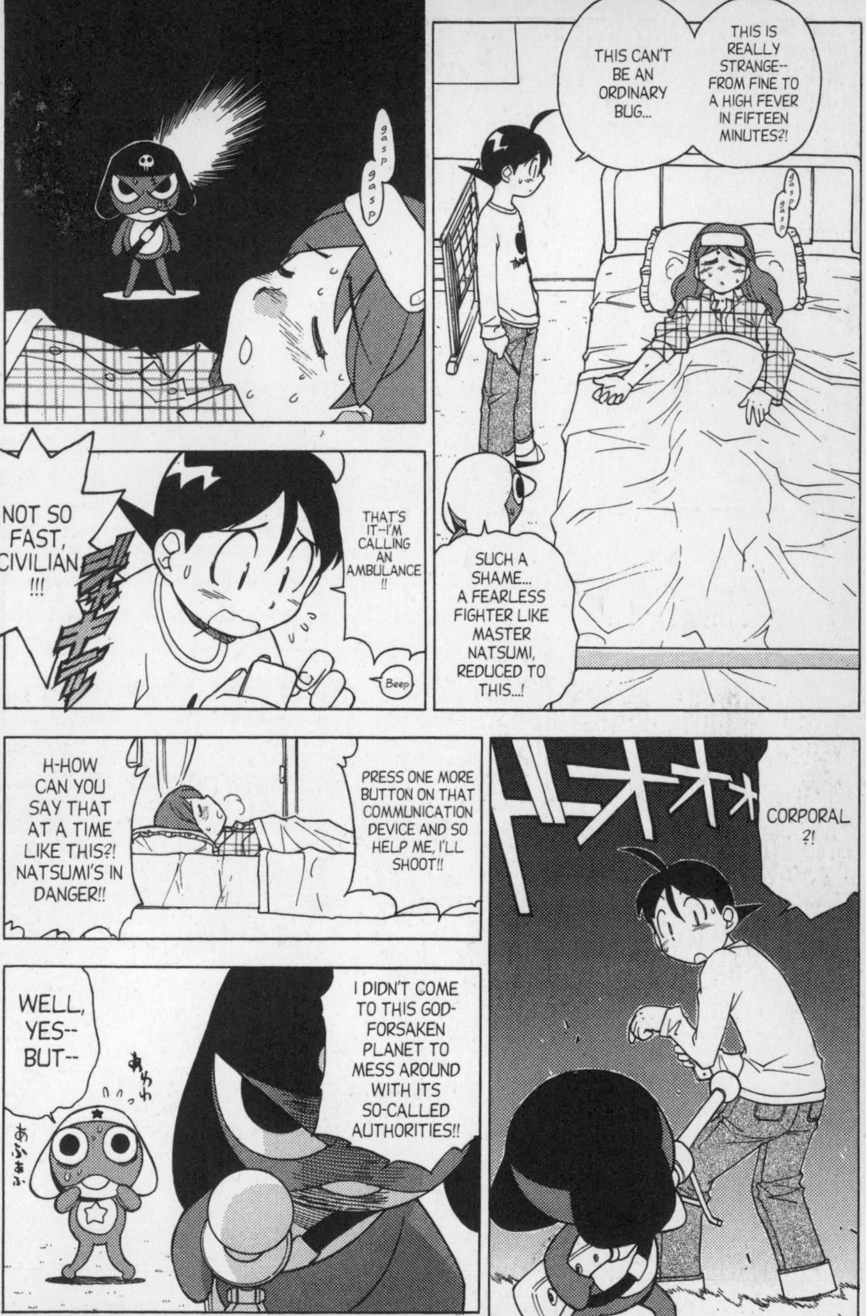
THIS IS REALLY STRANGE-- FROM FINE TO A HIGH FEVER IN FIFTEEN MINUTES?!
THIS CAN'T BE AN ORDINARY BUG...
gasp gasp
gasp gasp gasp
SUCH A SHAME... A FEARLESS FIGHTER LIKE MASTER NATSUMI, REDUCED TO THIS...!
THAT'S IT--I'M CALLING AN AMBULANCE!!
Beep
NOT SO FAST, CIVILIAN!!!
CORPORAL?!
PRESS ONE MORE BUTTON ON THAT COMMUNICATION DEVICE AND SO HELP ME, I'LL SHOOT!!
H-HOW CAN YOU SAY THAT AT A TIME LIKE THIS?! NATSUMI'S IN DANGER!!
I DIDN'T COME TO THIS GOD-FORSAKEN PLANET TO MESS AROUND WITH ITS SO-CALLED AUTHORITIES!!
WELL, YES-- BUT--

*tremble

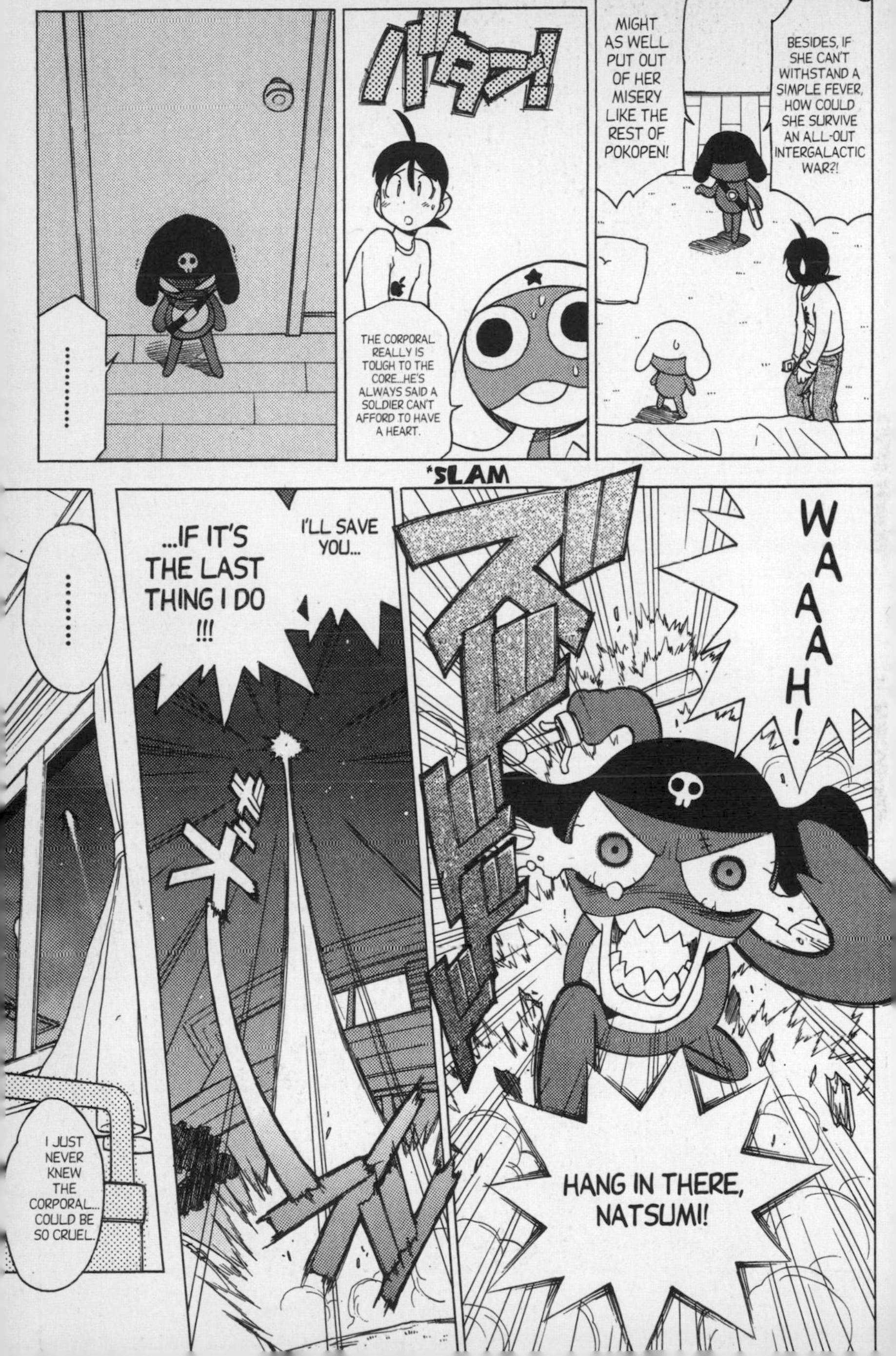
BESIDES, IF SHE CAN'T WITHSTAND A SIMPLE FEVER, HOW COULD SHE SURVIVE AN ALL-OUT INTERGALACTIC WAR?!
MIGHT AS WELL PUT OUT OF HER MISERY LIKE THE REST OF POKOPEN!
THE CORPORAL REALLY IS TOUGH TO THE CORE...HE'S ALWAYS SAID A SOLDIER CAN'T AFFORD TO HAVE A HEART.
....
*SLAM
WAAAAH!
HANG IN THERE, NATSUMI!
I'LL SAVE YOU...
...IF IT'S THE LAST THING I DO !!!
....
I JUST NEVER KNEW THE CORPORAL... COULD BE SO CRUEL.

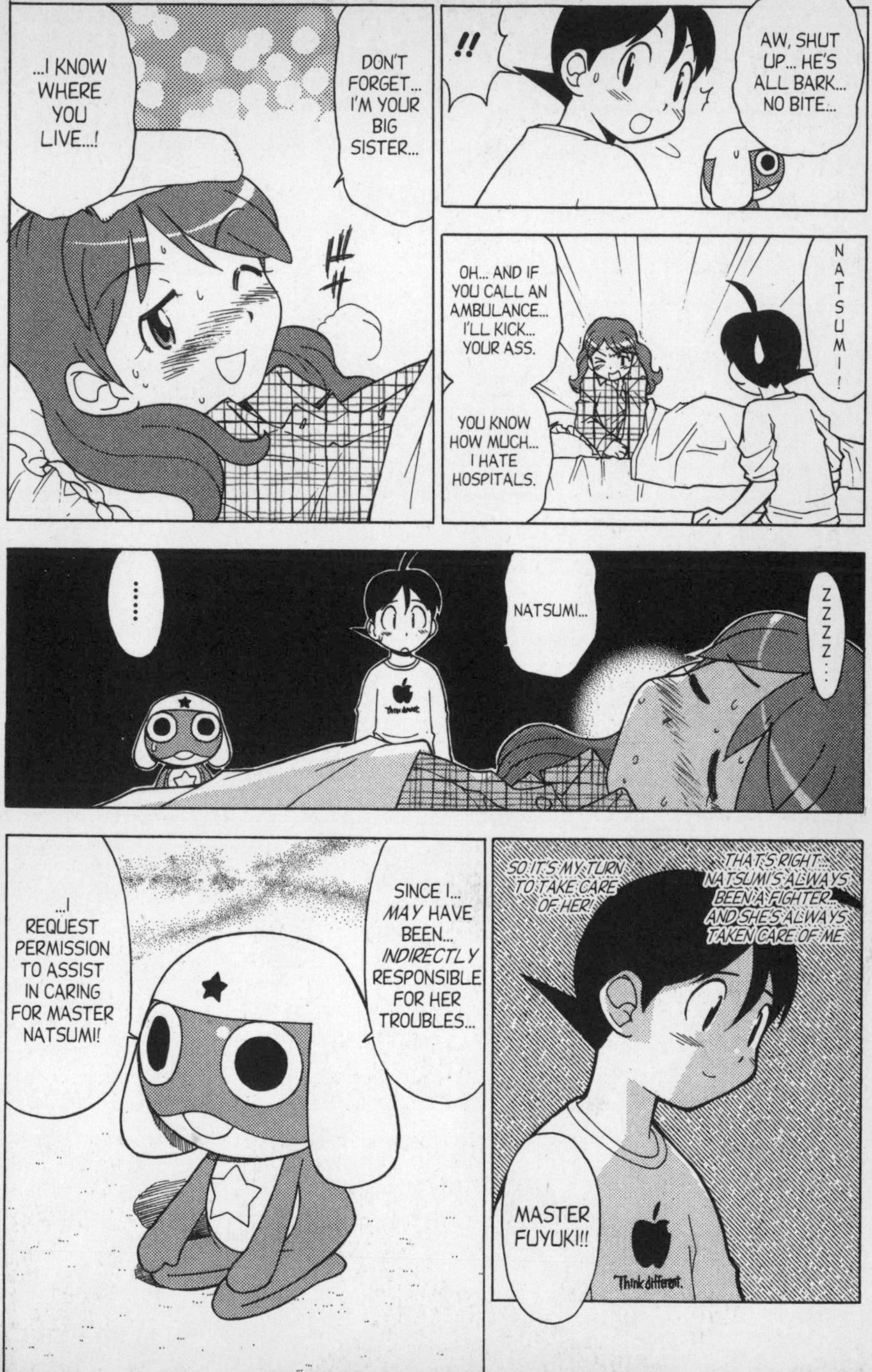
AW, SHUT UP... HE'S ALL BARK... NO BITE...
!!
DON'T FORGET... I'M YOUR BIG SISTER...
...I KNOW WHERE YOU LIVE...!
NATSUMI!
OH... AND IF YOU CALL AN AMBULANCE... I'LL KICK... YOUR ASS.
YOU KNOW HOW MUCH... I HATE HOSPITALS.
ZZZ...
NATSUMI...
......
THAT'S RIGHT... NATSUMI'S ALWAYS BEEN A FIGHTER... AND SHE'S ALWAYS TAKEN CARE OF ME.
SO IT'S MY TURN TO TAKE CARE OF HER!
MASTER FUYUKI!!
Think different.
SINCE I... *MAY* HAVE BEEN... *INDIRECTLY* RESPONSIBLE FOR HER TROUBLES...
...I REQUEST PERMISSION TO ASSIST IN CARING FOR MASTER NATSUMI!

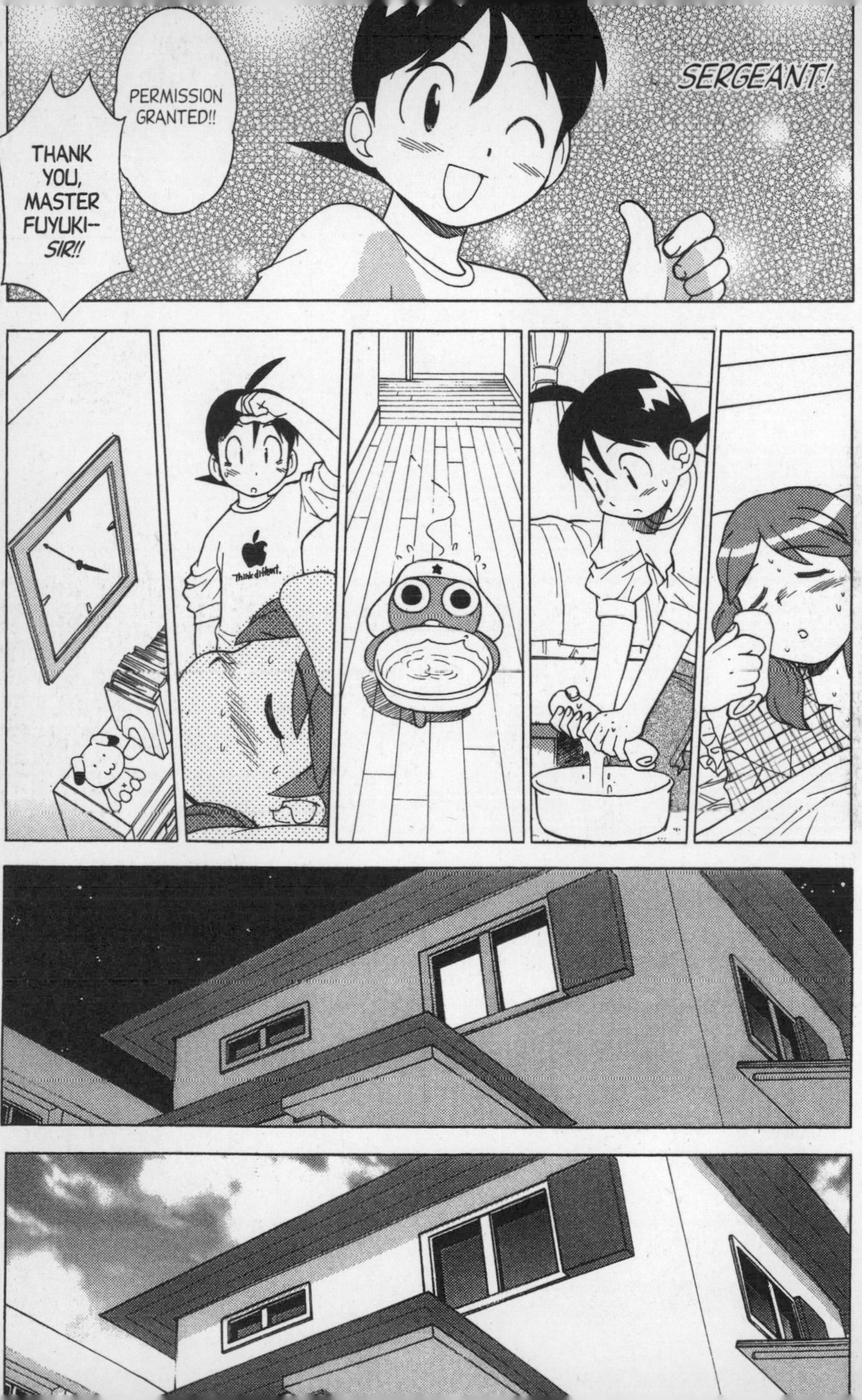
SERGEANT!
PERMISSION GRANTED!!
THANK YOU, MASTER FUYUKI--SIR!!
Think different.

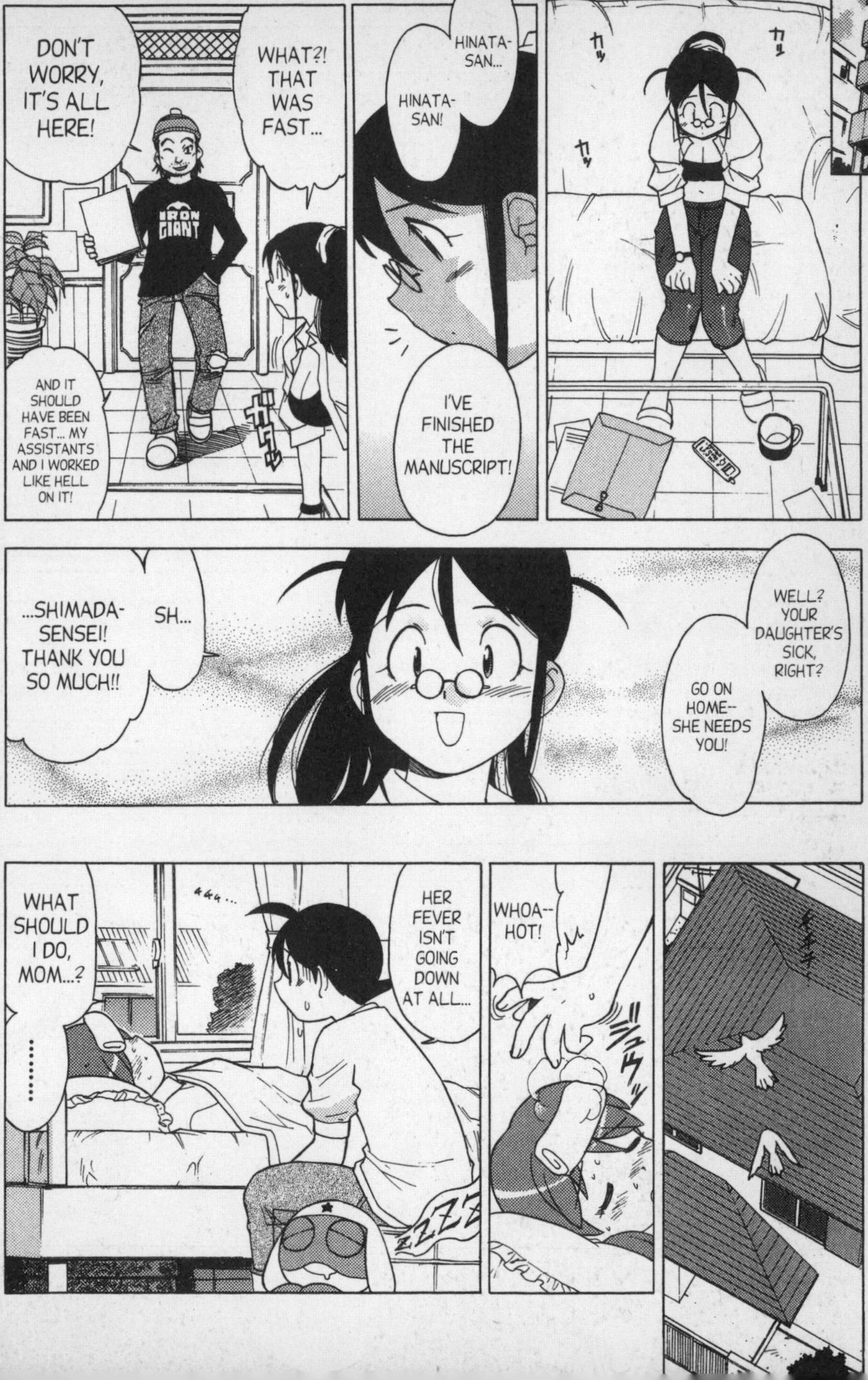
HINATA-SAN...
HINATA-SAN!
I'VE FINISHED THE MANUSCRIPT!
WHAT?! THAT WAS FAST...
DON'T WORRY, IT'S ALL HERE!
AND IT SHOULD HAVE BEEN FAST... MY ASSISTANTS AND I WORKED LIKE HELL ON IT!
WELL? YOUR DAUGHTER'S SICK, RIGHT?
GO ON HOME-- SHE NEEDS YOU!
SH...
...SHIMADA-SENSEI! THANK YOU SO MUCH!!
WHOA-- HOT!
HER FEVER ISN'T GOING DOWN AT ALL...
WHAT SHOULD I DO, MOM...?
....

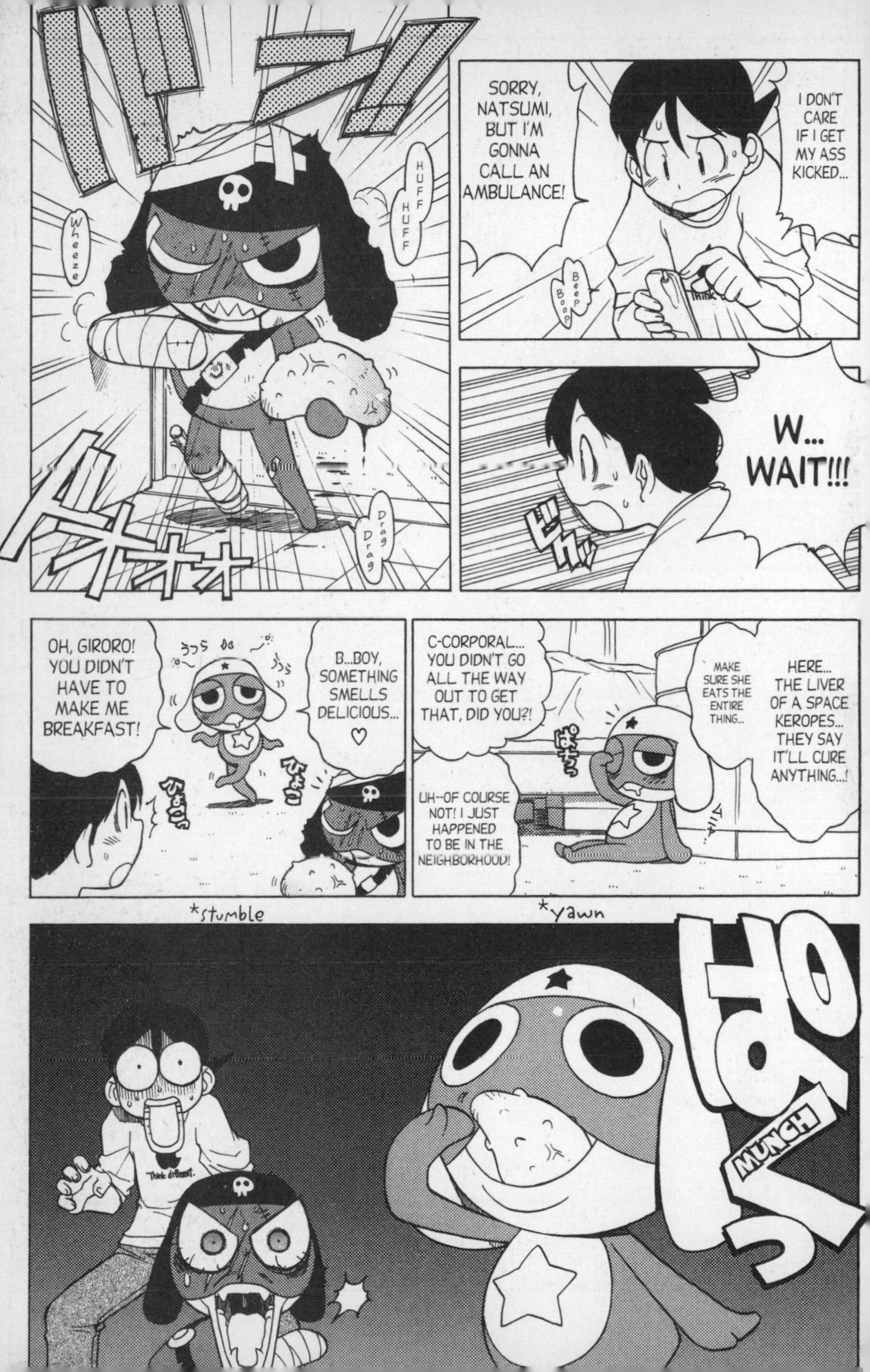
I DON'T CARE IF I GET MY ASS KICKED...
SORRY, NATSUMI, BUT I'M GONNA CALL AN AMBULANCE!
Beep Boop
W... WAIT!!!
HUFF HUFF
Wheeze
Drag Drag
HERE... THE LIVER OF A SPACE KEROPES... THEY SAY IT'LL CURE ANYTHING...!
MAKE SURE SHE EATS THE ENTIRE THING...
C-CORPORAL... YOU DIDN'T GO ALL THE WAY OUT TO GET THAT, DID YOU?!
UH--OF COURSE NOT! I JUST HAPPENED TO BE IN THE NEIGHBORHOOD!
*yawn
B...BOY, SOMETHING SMELLS DELICIOUS... ♡
OH, GIRORO! YOU DIDN'T HAVE TO MAKE ME BREAKFAST!
*stumble
MUNCH
Think different.

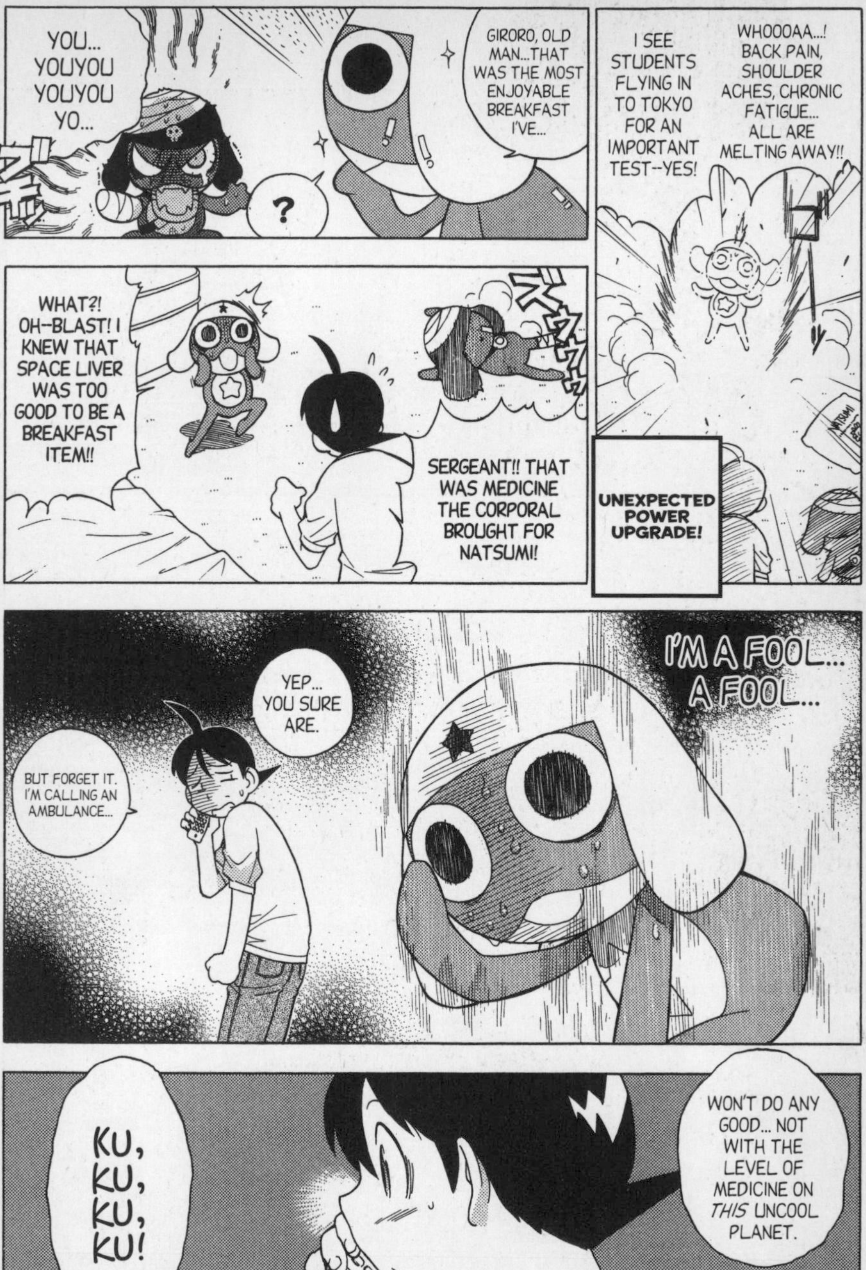
GIRORO, OLD MAN...THAT WAS THE MOST ENJOYABLE BREAKFAST I'VE...
YOU... YOUYOU YOUYOU YO...
?
WHOOOAA...! BACK PAIN, SHOULDER ACHES, CHRONIC FATIGUE... ALL ARE MELTING AWAY!!
I SEE STUDENTS FLYING IN TO TOKYO FOR AN IMPORTANT TEST--YES!
SERGEANT!! THAT WAS MEDICINE THE CORPORAL BROUGHT FOR NATSUMI!
WHAT?! OH--BLAST! I KNEW THAT SPACE LIVER WAS TOO GOOD TO BE A BREAKFAST ITEM!!
UNEXPECTED POWER UPGRADE!
I'M A FOOL... A FOOL...
YEP... YOU SURE ARE.
BUT FORGET IT. I'M CALLING AN AMBULANCE...
WON'T DO ANY GOOD... NOT WITH THE LEVEL OF MEDICINE ON THIS UNCOOL PLANET.
KU, KU, KU, KU!

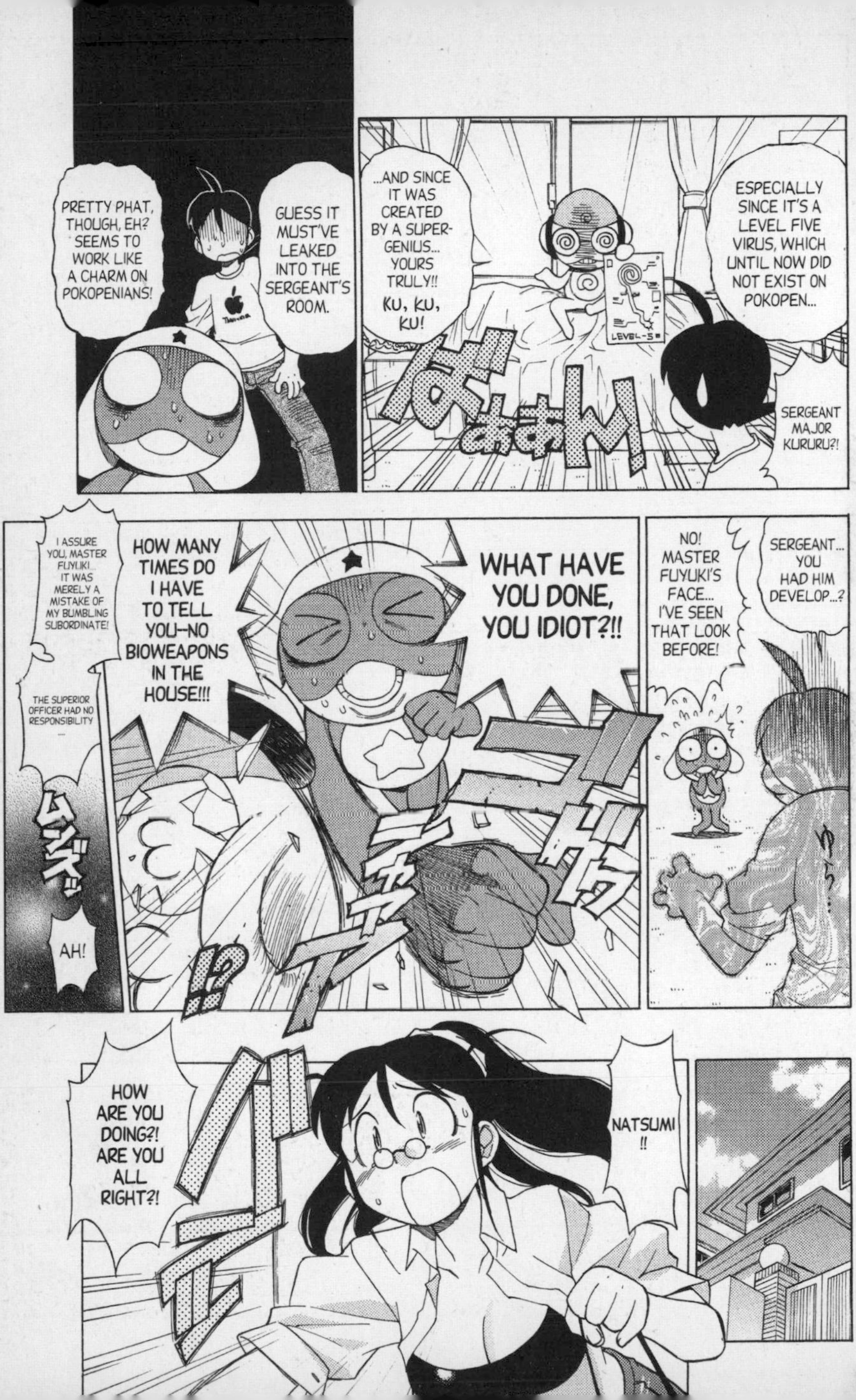
ESPECIALLY SINCE IT'S A LEVEL FIVE VIRUS, WHICH UNTIL NOW DID NOT EXIST ON POKOPEN...
...AND SINCE IT WAS CREATED BY A SUPER-GENIUS... YOURS TRULY!! KU, KU, KU!
LEVEL-5
SERGEANT MAJOR KURURU?!
GUESS IT MUST'VE LEAKED INTO THE SERGEANT'S ROOM.
PRETTY PHAT, THOUGH, EH? SEEMS TO WORK LIKE A CHARM ON POKOPENIANS!
SERGEANT... YOU HAD HIM DEVELOP...?
NO! MASTER FUYUKI'S FACE... I'VE SEEN THAT LOOK BEFORE!
WHAT HAVE YOU DONE, YOU IDIOT?!!
HOW MANY TIMES DO I HAVE TO TELL YOU--NO BIOWEAPONS IN THE HOUSE!!!
!?
I ASSURE YOU, MASTER FUYUKI... IT WAS MERELY A MISTAKE OF MY BUMBLING SUBORDINATE!
THE SUPERIOR OFFICER HAD NO RESPONSIBILITY —
AH!
NATSUMI !!
HOW ARE YOU DOING?! ARE YOU ALL RIGHT?!

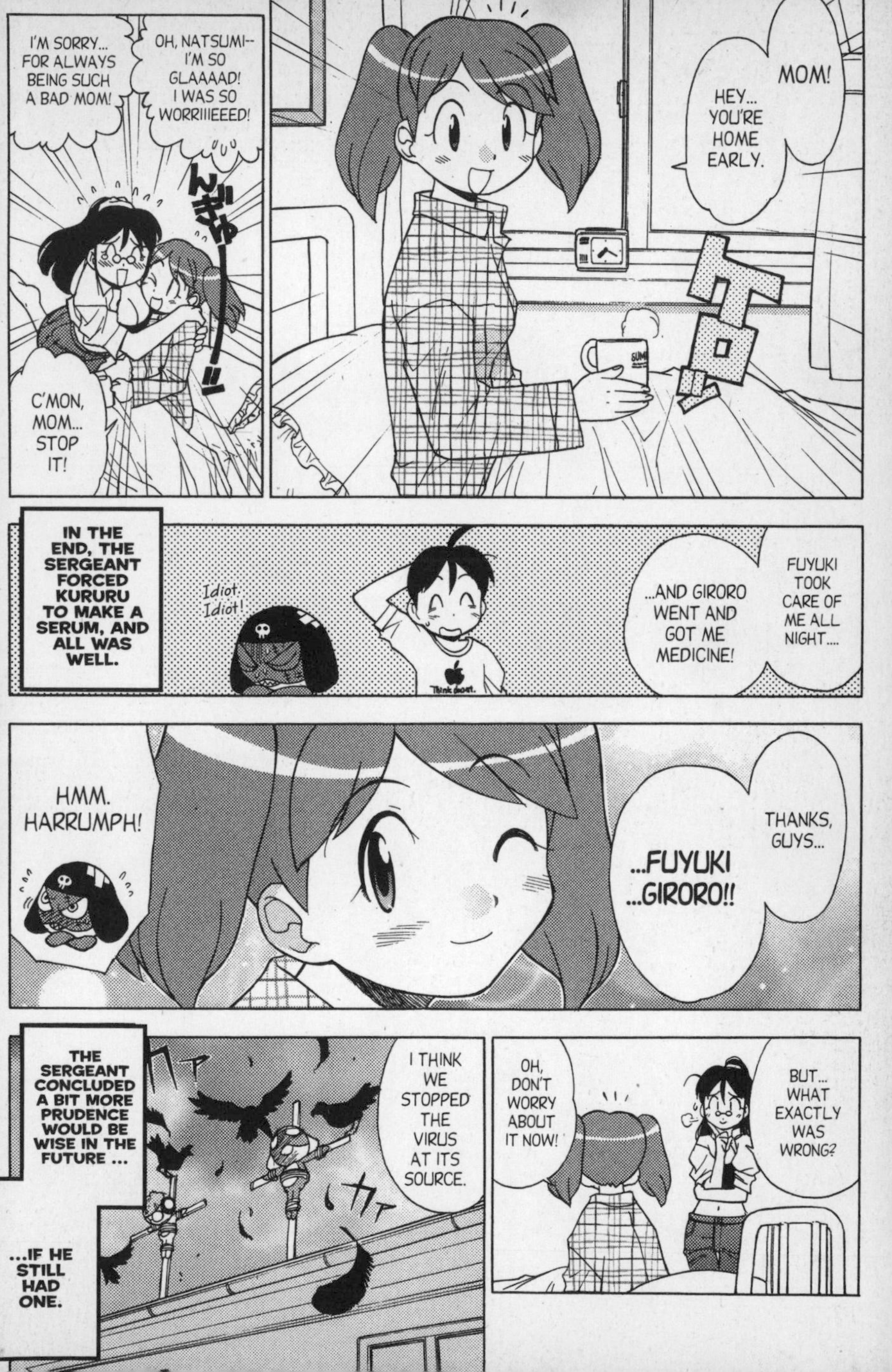
MOM!
HEY... YOU'RE HOME EARLY.
ケロッ
OH, NATSUMI-- I'M SO GLAAAAD! I WAS SO WORRIIIEEED!
I'M SORRY... FOR ALWAYS BEING SUCH A BAD MOM!
んぎゅ〜〜っ!!
C'MON, MOM... STOP IT!
FUYUKI TOOK CARE OF ME ALL NIGHT....
...AND GIRORO WENT AND GOT ME MEDICINE!
Idiot. Idiot!
IN THE END, THE SERGEANT FORCED KURURU TO MAKE A SERUM, AND ALL WAS WELL.
THANKS, GUYS...
...FUYUKI ...GIRORO!!
HMM. HARRUMPH!
BUT... WHAT EXACTLY WAS WRONG?
OH, DON'T WORRY ABOUT IT NOW!
I THINK WE STOPPED THE VIRUS AT ITS SOURCE.
THE SERGEANT CONCLUDED A BIT MORE PRUDENCE WOULD BE WISE IN THE FUTURE ...
...IF HE STILL HAD ONE.

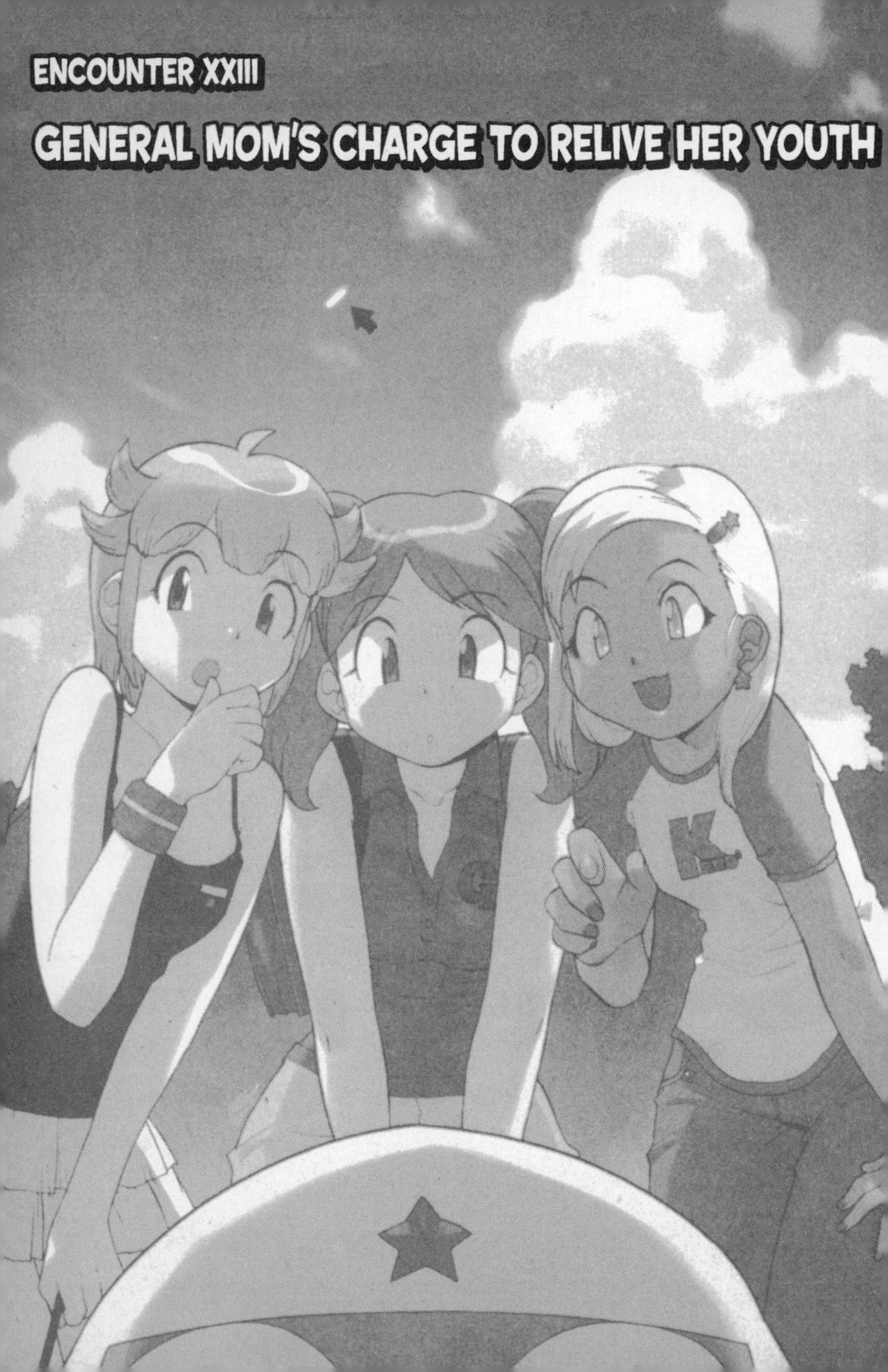
ENCOUNTER XXIII
GENERAL MOM'S CHARGE TO RELIVE HER YOUTH

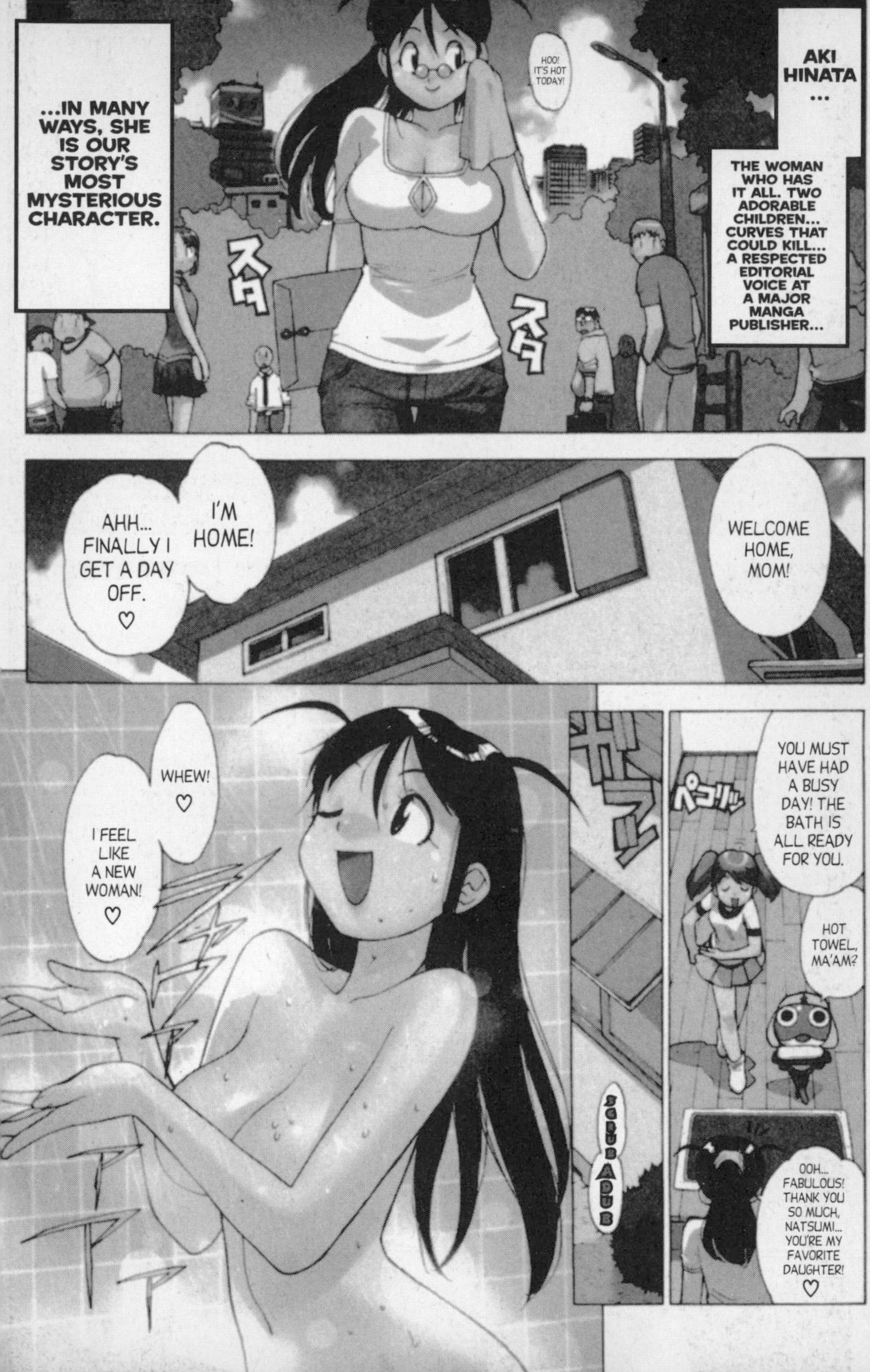
AKI HINATA ...
THE WOMAN WHO HAS IT ALL. TWO ADORABLE CHILDREN... CURVES THAT COULD KILL... A RESPECTED EDITORIAL VOICE AT A MAJOR MANGA PUBLISHER...
HOO! IT'S HOT TODAY!
...IN MANY WAYS, SHE IS OUR STORY'S MOST MYSTERIOUS CHARACTER.
スタ
スタ
WELCOME HOME, MOM!
I'M HOME!
AHH... FINALLY I GET A DAY OFF. ♡
YOU MUST HAVE HAD A BUSY DAY! THE BATH IS ALL READY FOR YOU.
HOT TOWEL, MA'AM?
OOH... FABULOUS! THANK YOU SO MUCH, NATSUMI... YOU'RE MY FAVORITE DAUGHTER! ♡
SCRUB A DUB
WHEW! ♡
I FEEL LIKE A NEW WOMAN! ♡

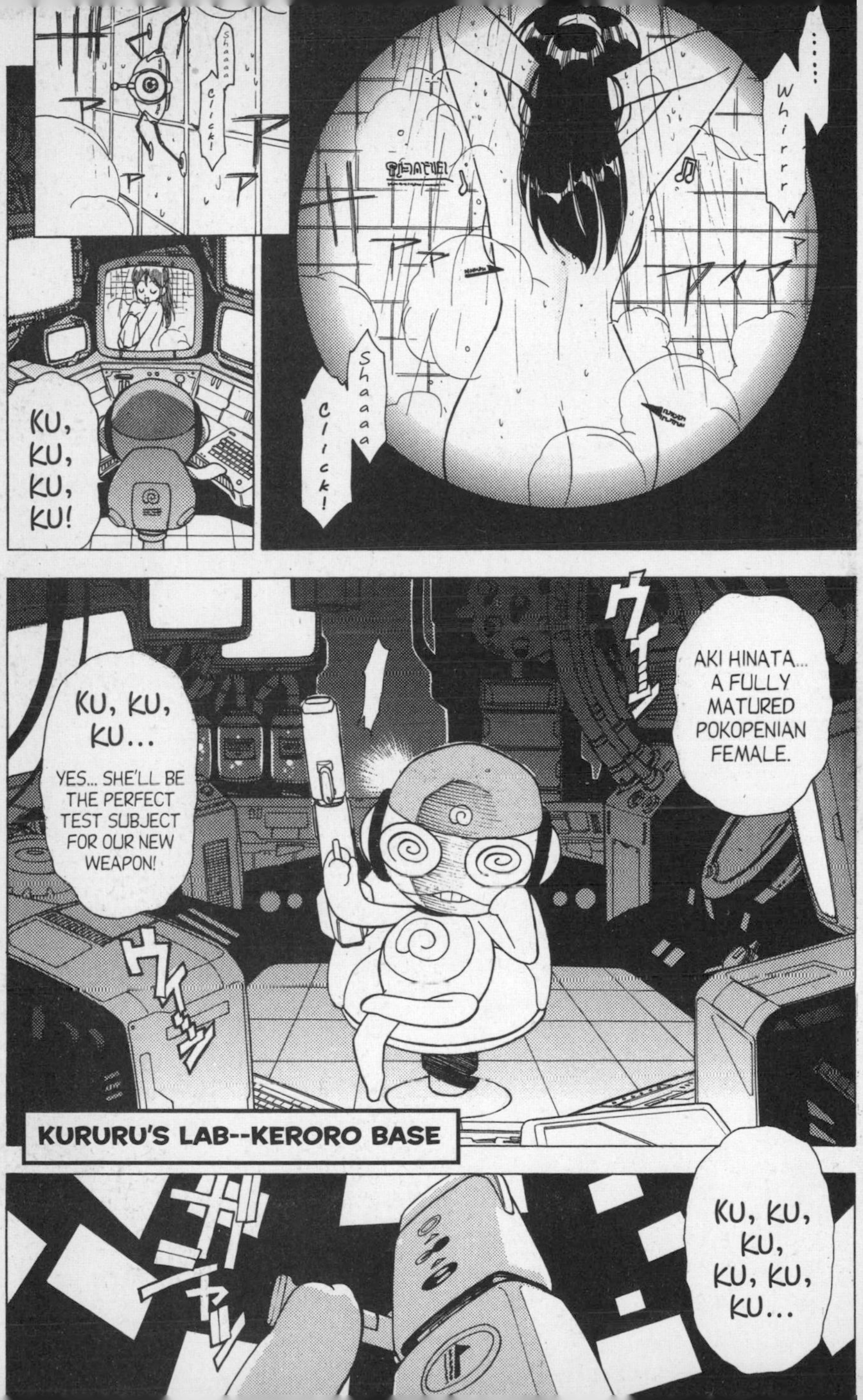
......
Whirrr
Shaaaa
Click!
Shaaaa
Click!
KU, KU, KU, KU!
AKI HINATA... A FULLY MATURED POKOPENIAN FEMALE.
KU, KU, KU...
YES... SHE'LL BE THE PERFECT TEST SUBJECT FOR OUR NEW WEAPON!
KURURU'S LAB--KERORO BASE
KU, KU, KU, KU, KU, KU...

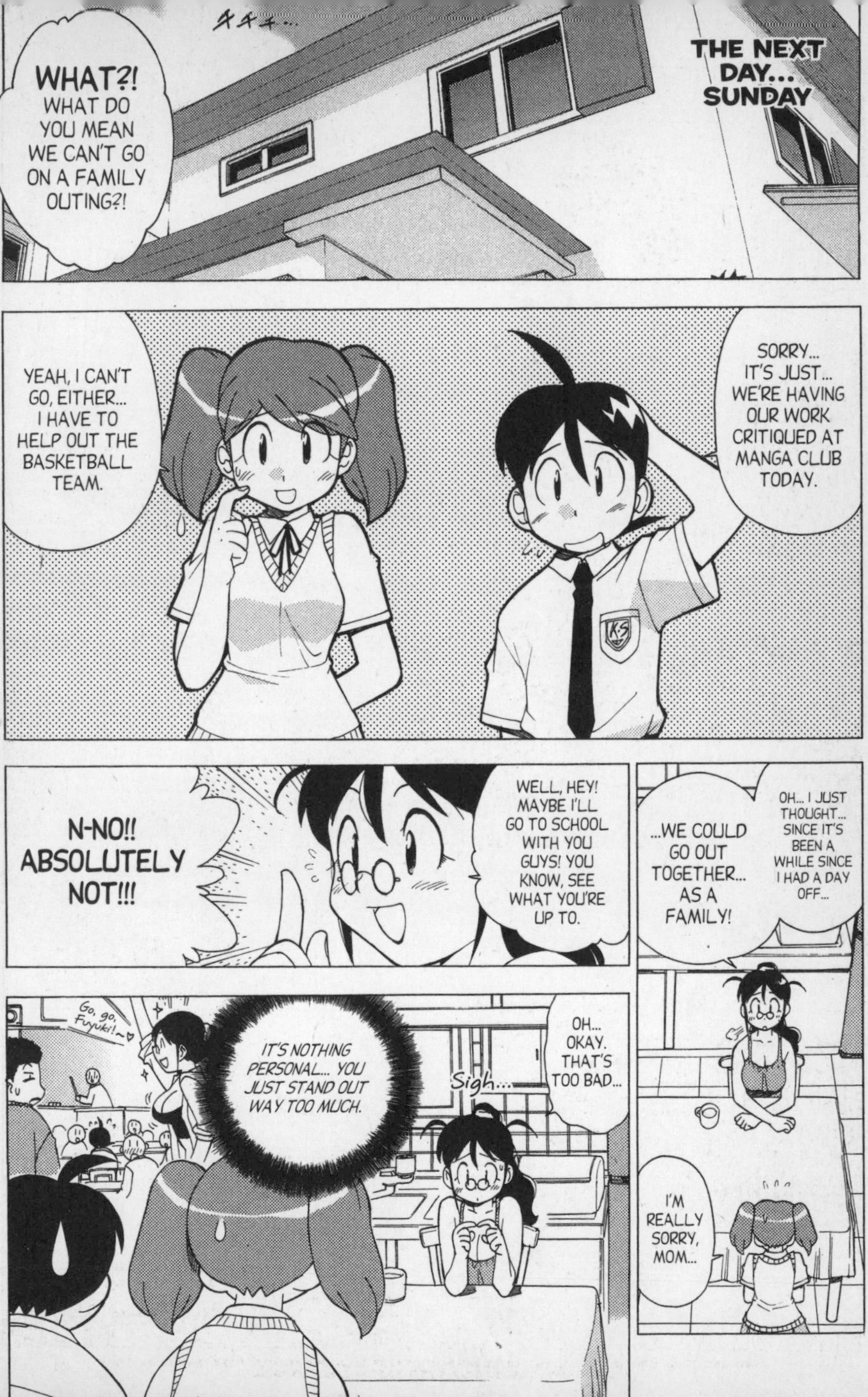
THE NEXT DAY... SUNDAY
WHAT?! WHAT DO YOU MEAN WE CAN'T GO ON A FAMILY OUTING?!
SORRY... IT'S JUST... WE'RE HAVING OUR WORK CRITIQUED AT MANGA CLUB TODAY.
YEAH, I CAN'T GO, EITHER... I HAVE TO HELP OUT THE BASKETBALL TEAM.
OH... I JUST THOUGHT... SINCE IT'S BEEN A WHILE SINCE I HAD A DAY OFF...
...WE COULD GO OUT TOGETHER... AS A FAMILY!
WELL, HEY! MAYBE I'LL GO TO SCHOOL WITH YOU GUYS! YOU KNOW, SEE WHAT YOU'RE UP TO.
N-NO!! ABSOLUTELY NOT!!!
I'M REALLY SORRY, MOM...
OH... OKAY. THAT'S TOO BAD...
Sigh...
IT'S NOTHING PERSONAL... YOU JUST STAND OUT WAY TOO MUCH.
Go, go, Fuyuki!~♥

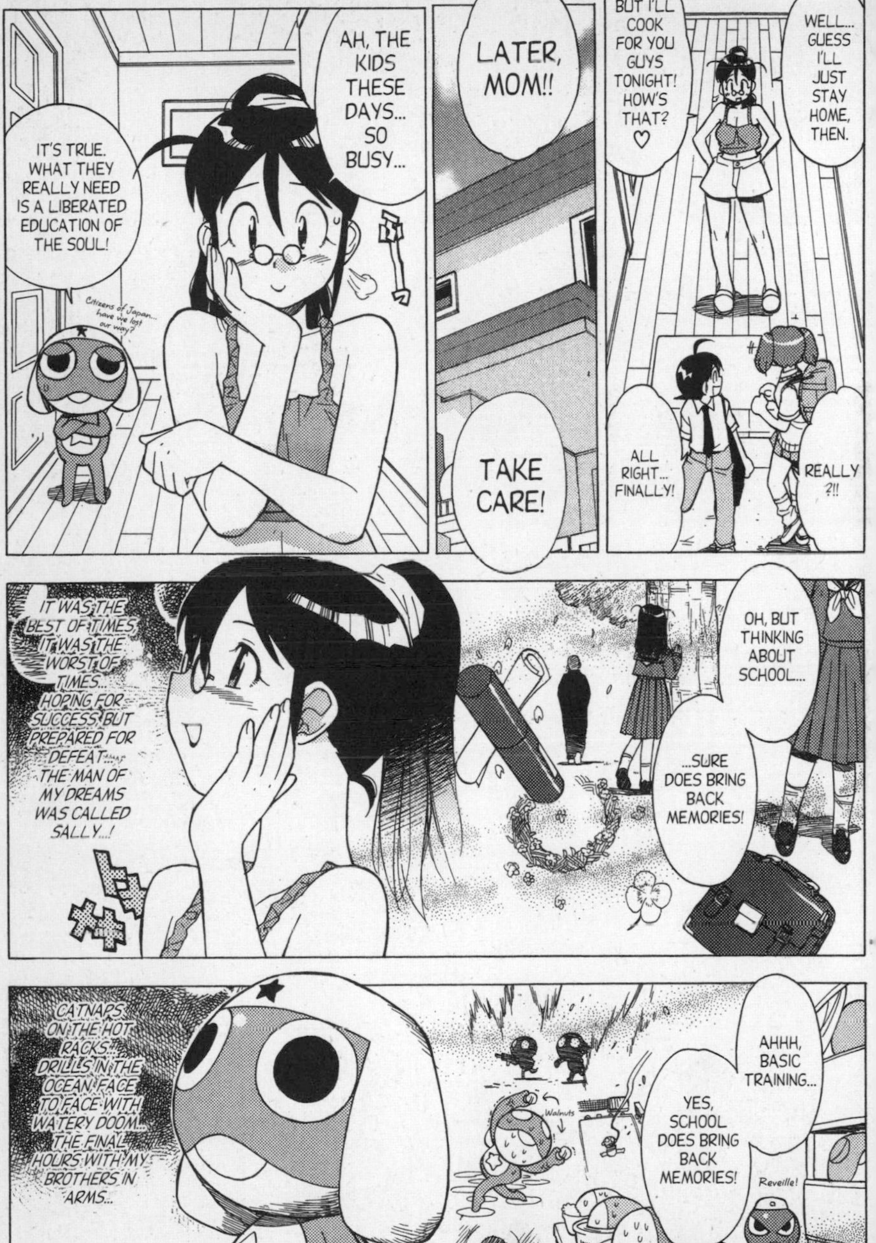
WELL... GUESS I'LL JUST STAY HOME, THEN.
BUT I'LL COOK FOR YOU GUYS TONIGHT! HOW'S THAT? ♡
REALLY?!!
ALL RIGHT... FINALLY!
LATER, MOM!!
TAKE CARE!
AH, THE KIDS THESE DAYS... SO BUSY...
IT'S TRUE. WHAT THEY REALLY NEED IS A LIBERATED EDUCATION OF THE SOUL!
Citizens of Japan... have we lost our way?
OH, BUT THINKING ABOUT SCHOOL...
...SURE DOES BRING BACK MEMORIES!
IT WAS THE BEST OF TIMES, IT WAS THE WORST OF TIMES... HOPING FOR SUCCESS, BUT PREPARED FOR DEFEAT... THE MAN OF MY DREAMS WAS CALLED SALLY...!
AHHH, BASIC TRAINING...
YES, SCHOOL DOES BRING BACK MEMORIES!
Reveille!
Walnuts
CATNAPS ON THE HOT RACKS... DRILLS IN THE OCEAN FACE TO FACE WITH WATERY DOOM... THE FINAL HOURS WITH MY BROTHERS IN ARMS...

* HOT RACKS--SO CALLED BECAUSE THE TURNOVER WAS SO FAST THAT THE WARMTH FROM THE LAST PERSON DIDN'T HAVE TIME TO DISSIPATE BEFORE THE NEXT PERSON.

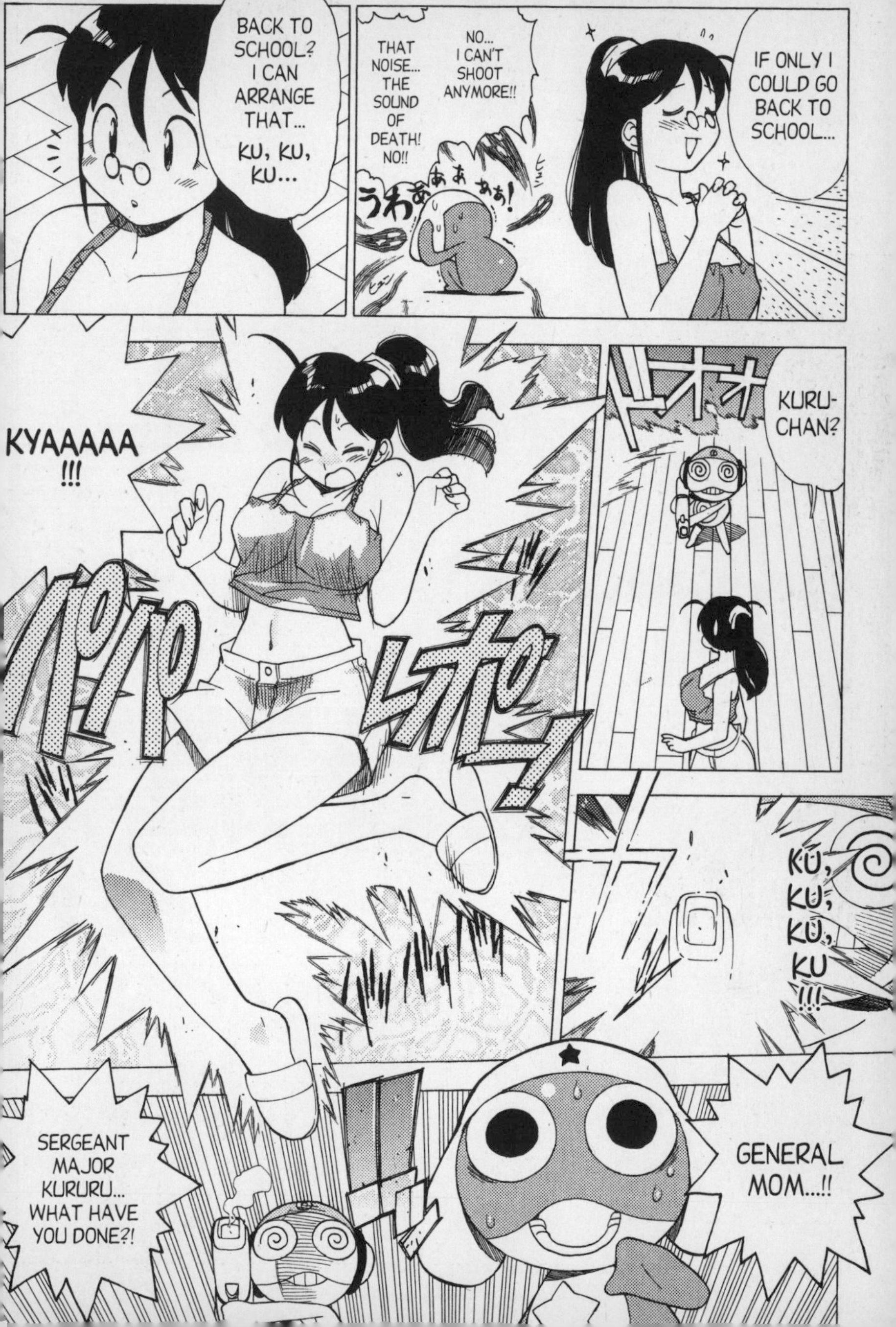
IF ONLY I COULD GO BACK TO SCHOOL...
NO... I CAN'T SHOOT ANYMORE!!
THAT NOISE... THE SOUND OF DEATH! NO!!
BACK TO SCHOOL? I CAN ARRANGE THAT... KU, KU, KU...
KURU-CHAN?
KYAAAAA!!!
KU, KU, KU, KU!!!
GENERAL MOM...!!
SERGEANT MAJOR KURURU... WHAT HAVE YOU DONE?!

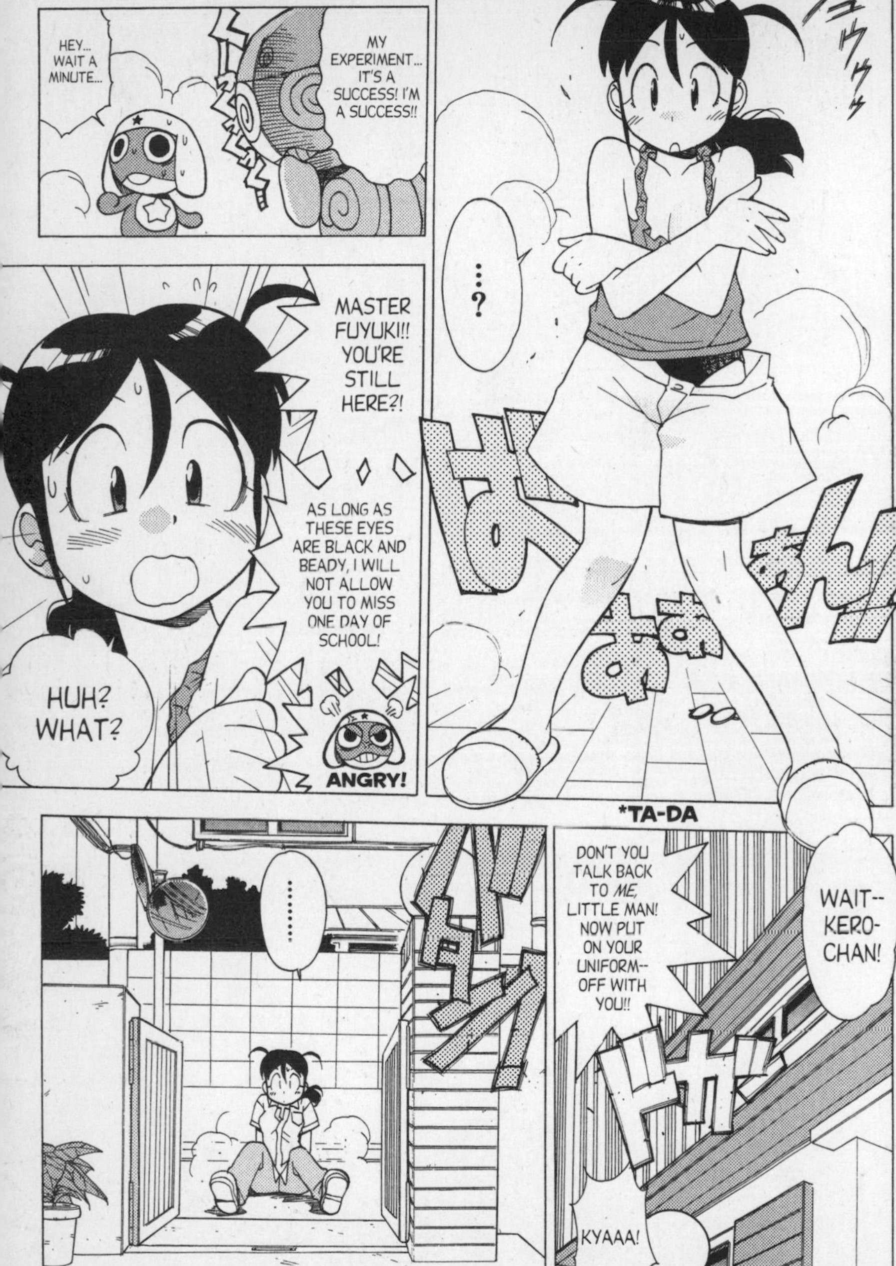
...?
*TA-DA
MY EXPERIMENT... IT'S A SUCCESS! I'M A SUCCESS!!
HEY... WAIT A MINUTE...
MASTER FUYUKI!! YOU'RE STILL HERE?!
AS LONG AS THESE EYES ARE BLACK AND BEADY, I WILL NOT ALLOW YOU TO MISS ONE DAY OF SCHOOL!
ANGRY!
HUH? WHAT?
WAIT-- KERO-CHAN!
DON'T YOU TALK BACK TO *ME*, LITTLE MAN! NOW PUT ON YOUR UNIFORM-- OFF WITH YOU!!
KYAAA!
......

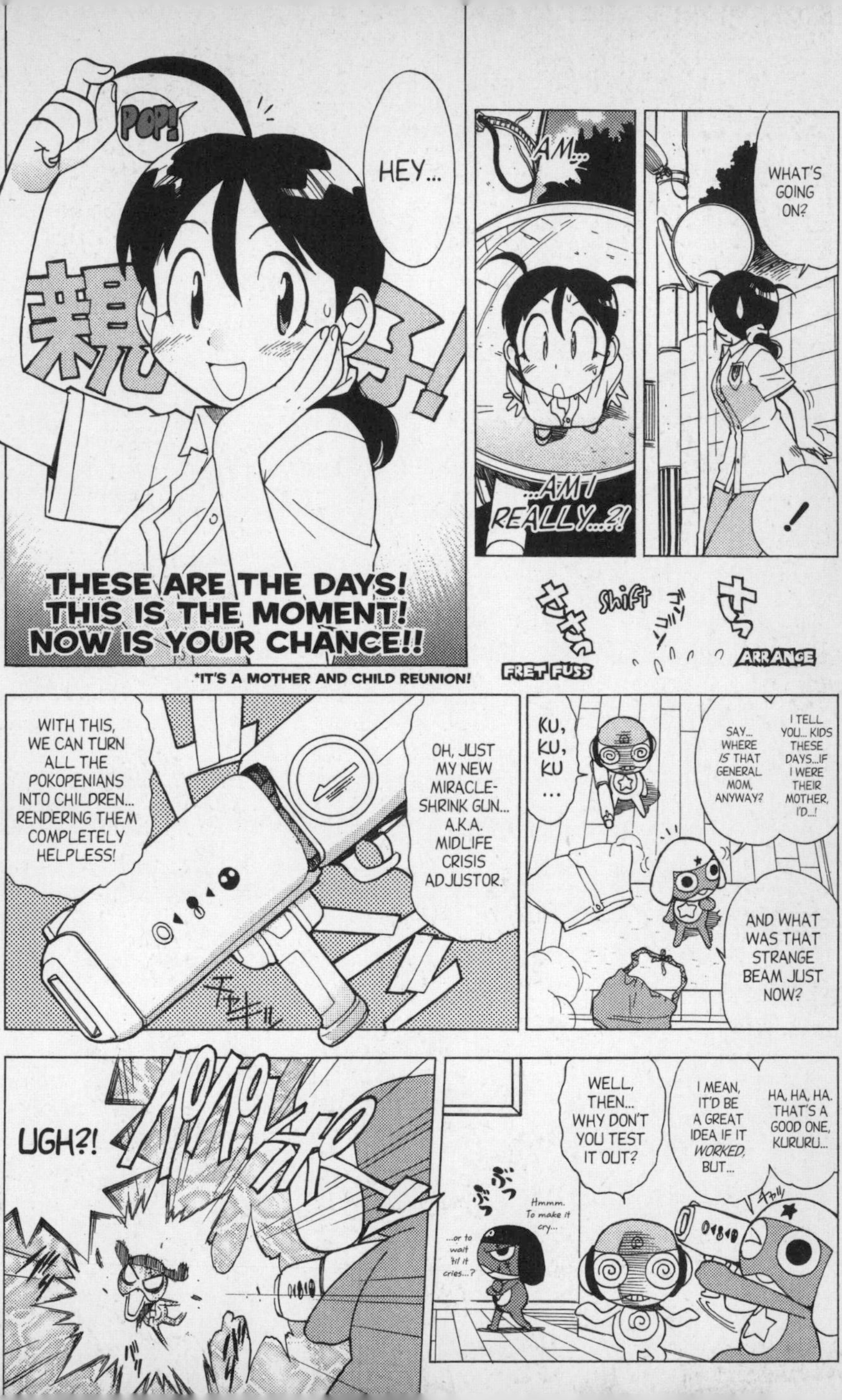

WHAT'S GOING ON?
!
AM I...
...AM I REALLY...?!
POP!
HEY...
親子!
THESE ARE THE DAYS! THIS IS THE MOMENT! NOW IS YOUR CHANCE!!
*IT'S A MOTHER AND CHILD REUNION!
ARRANGE
Shift
FRET FUSS
I TELL YOU... KIDS THESE DAYS...IF I WERE THEIR MOTHER, I'D...!
SAY... WHERE *IS* THAT GENERAL MOM, ANYWAY?
KU, KU, KU...
AND WHAT WAS THAT STRANGE BEAM JUST NOW?
OH, JUST MY NEW MIRACLE-SHRINK GUN... A.K.A. MIDLIFE CRISIS ADJUSTOR.
WITH THIS, WE CAN TURN ALL THE POKOPENIANS INTO CHILDREN... RENDERING THEM COMPLETELY HELPLESS!
HA, HA, HA. THAT'S A GOOD ONE, KURURU...
I MEAN, IT'D BE A GREAT IDEA IF IT *WORKED,* BUT...
WELL, THEN... WHY DON'T YOU TEST IT OUT?
Hmmm. To make it cry...
...or to wait 'til it cries...?
UGH?!

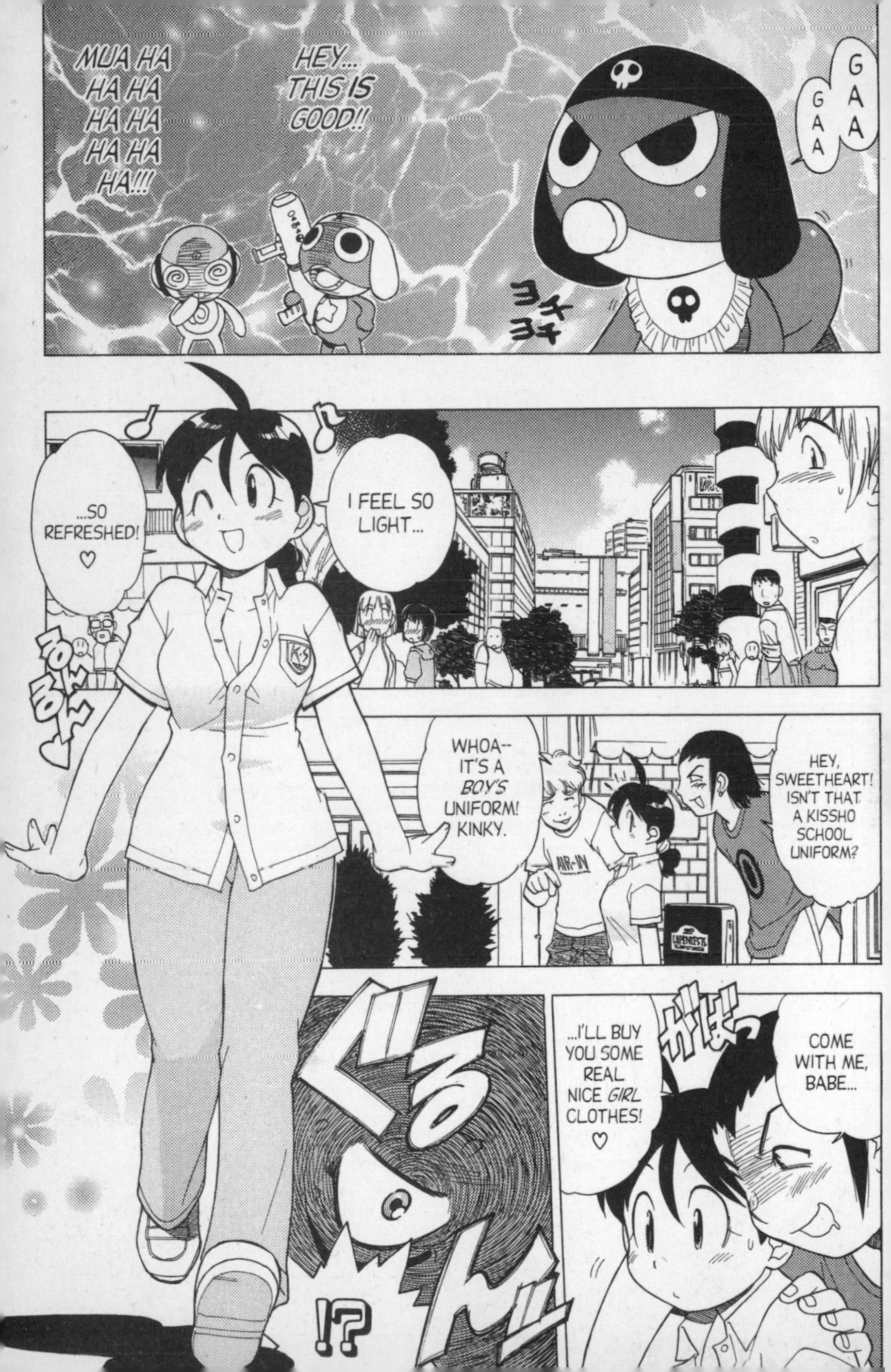
GAA GAA GAA
HEY... THIS IS GOOD!!
MUA HA HA HA HA HA HA HA HA!!!
I FEEL SO LIGHT...
...SO REFRESHED! ♡
HEY, SWEETHEART! ISN'T THAT A KISSHO SCHOOL UNIFORM?
WHOA-- IT'S A *BOY'S* UNIFORM! KINKY.
AIR-IN
COME WITH ME, BABE...
...I'LL BUY YOU SOME REAL NICE *GIRL* CLOTHES! ♡
!?

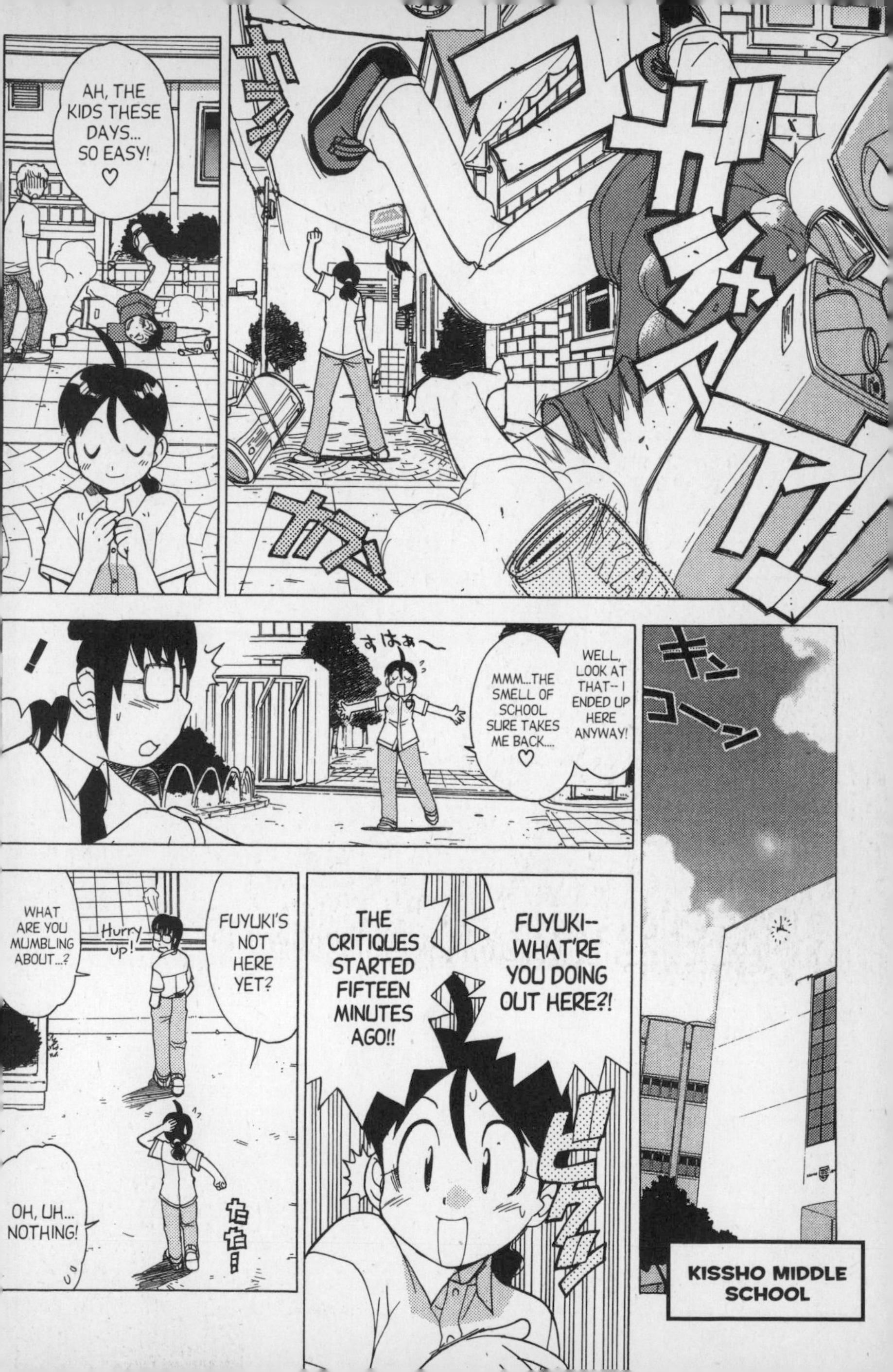

AH, THE KIDS THESE DAYS... SO EASY! ♡
KISSHO MIDDLE SCHOOL
WELL, LOOK AT THAT-- I ENDED UP HERE ANYWAY!
MMM...THE SMELL OF SCHOOL SURE TAKES ME BACK.... ♡
すはぁ～
!
FUYUKI-- WHAT'RE YOU DOING OUT HERE?!
THE CRITIQUES STARTED FIFTEEN MINUTES AGO!!
FUYUKI'S NOT HERE YET?
Hurry up!
WHAT ARE YOU MUMBLING ABOUT...?
OH, UH... NOTHING!

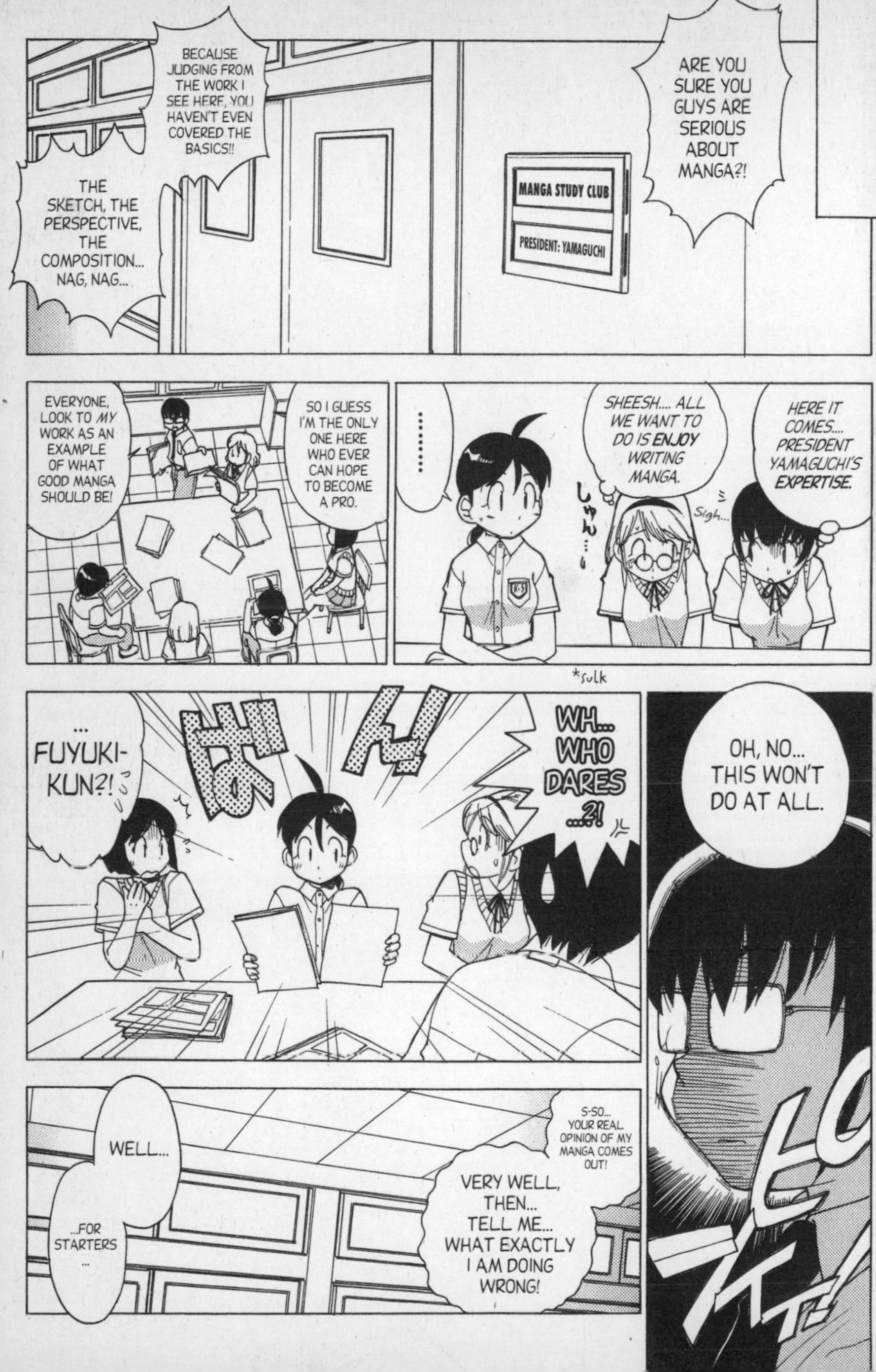
ARE YOU SURE YOU GUYS ARE SERIOUS ABOUT MANGA?!
MANGA STUDY CLUB
PRESIDENT: YAMAGUCHI
BECAUSE JUDGING FROM THE WORK I SEE HERF, YOU HAVEN'T EVEN COVERED THE BASICS!!
THE SKETCH, THE PERSPECTIVE, THE COMPOSITION... NAG, NAG...
HERE IT COMES.... PRESIDENT YAMAGUCHI'S EXPERTISE.
Sigh...
SHEESH.... ALL WE WANT TO DO IS ENJOY WRITING MANGA.
しゅん…
*sulk
....
SO I GUESS I'M THE ONLY ONE HERE WHO EVER CAN HOPE TO BECOME A PRO.
EVERYONE, LOOK TO MY WORK AS AN EXAMPLE OF WHAT GOOD MANGA SHOULD BE!
OH, NO... THIS WON'T DO AT ALL.
WH... WHO DARES ...?!
ばん!
... FUYUKI-KUN?!
S-SO... YOUR REAL OPINION OF MY MANGA COMES OUT!
VERY WELL, THEN... TELL ME... WHAT EXACTLY I AM DOING WRONG!
WELL...
...FOR STARTERS ...

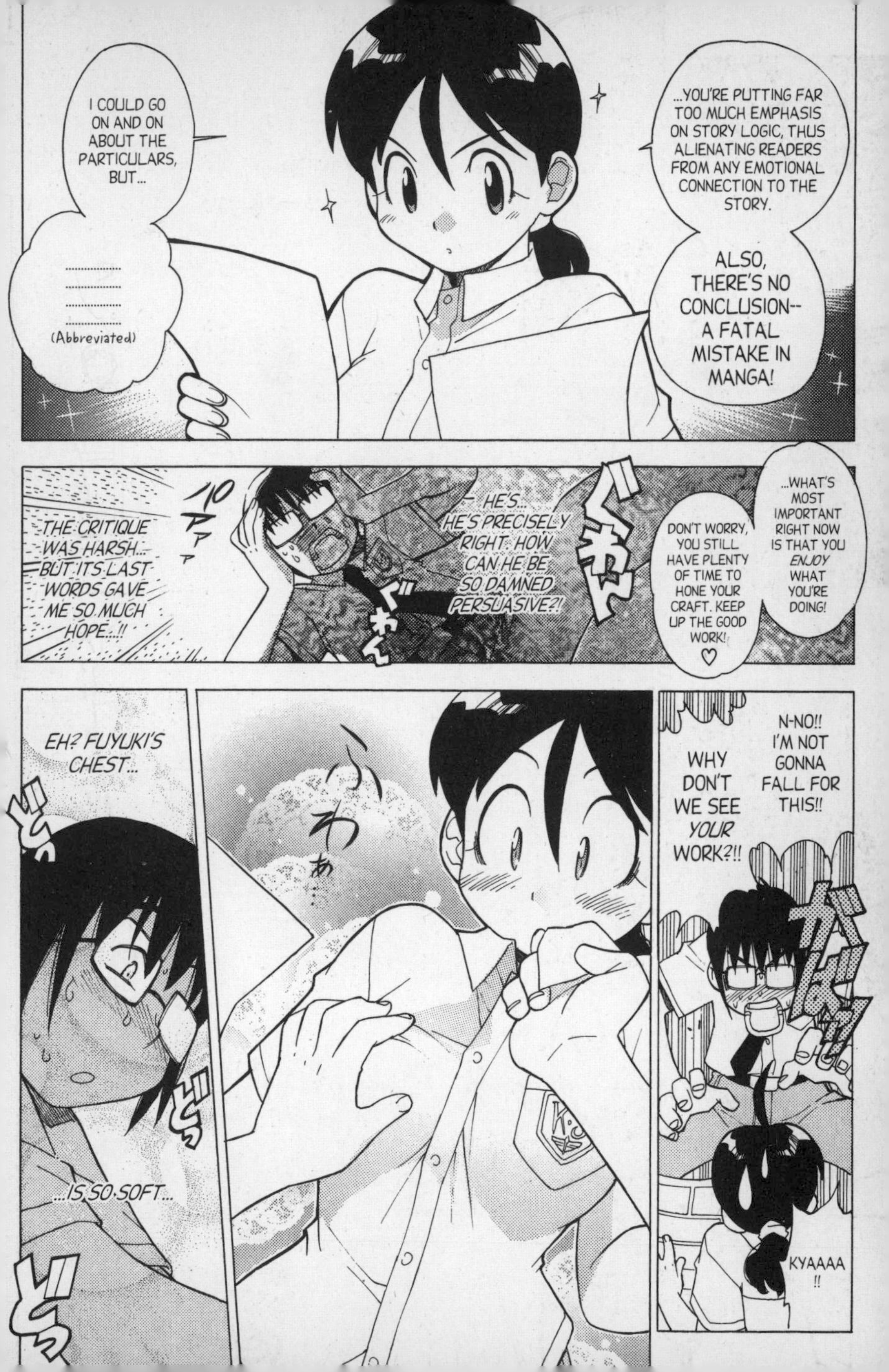
...YOU'RE PUTTING FAR TOO MUCH EMPHASIS ON STORY LOGIC, THUS ALIENATING READERS FROM ANY EMOTIONAL CONNECTION TO THE STORY.
ALSO, THERE'S NO CONCLUSION-- A FATAL MISTAKE IN MANGA!
I COULD GO ON AND ON ABOUT THE PARTICULARS, BUT...
....
(Abbreviated)
...WHAT'S MOST IMPORTANT RIGHT NOW IS THAT YOU ENJOY WHAT YOU'RE DOING!
DON'T WORRY, YOU STILL HAVE PLENTY OF TIME TO HONE YOUR CRAFT. KEEP UP THE GOOD WORK! ♡
HE'S... HE'S PRECISELY RIGHT. HOW CAN HE BE SO DAMNED PERSUASIVE?!
THE CRITIQUE WAS HARSH... BUT ITS LAST WORDS GAVE ME SO MUCH HOPE...!!
N-NO!! I'M NOT GONNA FALL FOR THIS!!
WHY DON'T WE SEE YOUR WORK?!!
KYAAAA!!
EH? FUYUKI'S CHEST...
...IS SO SOFT...

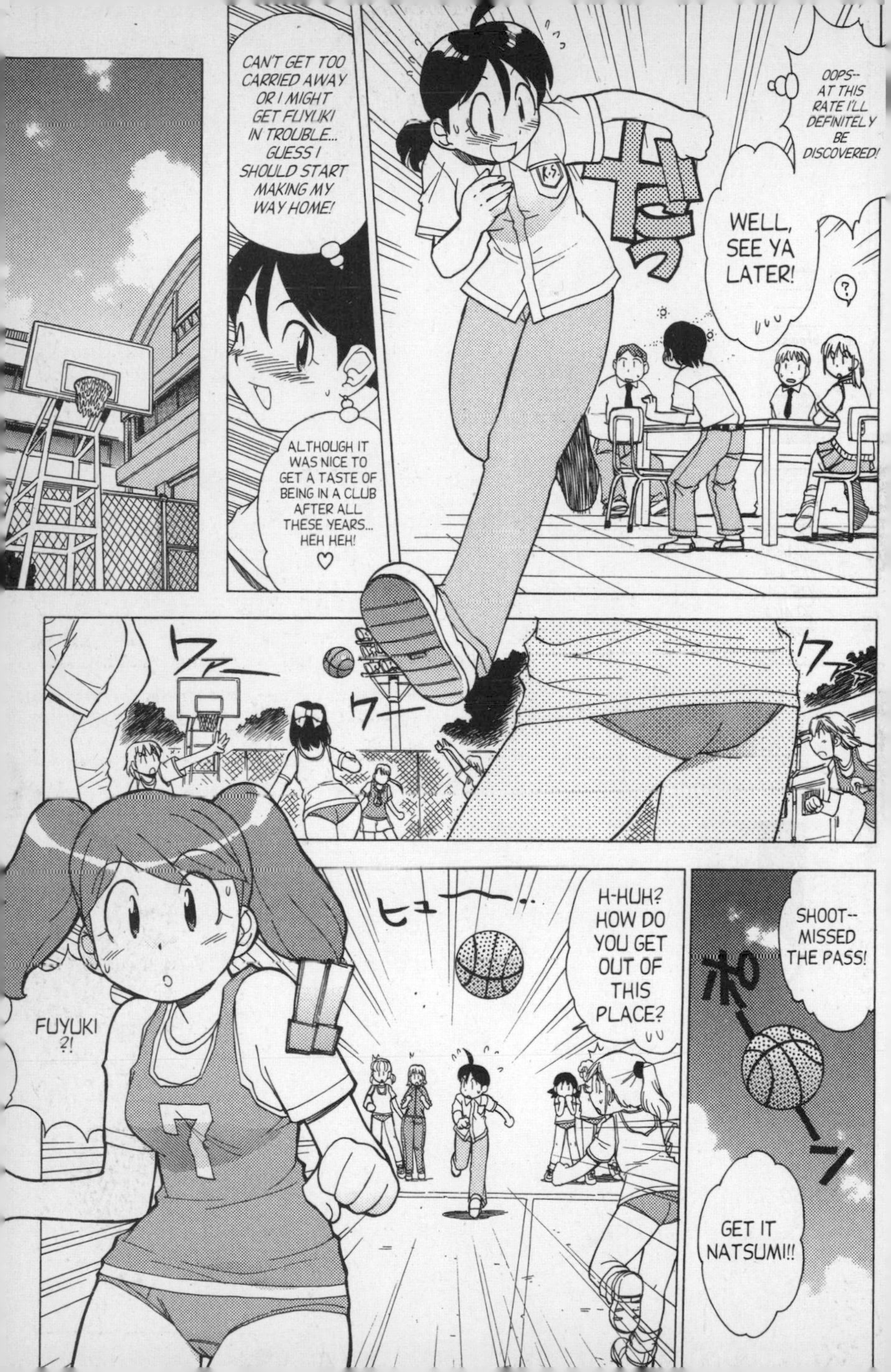
OOPS-- AT THIS RATE I'LL DEFINITELY BE DISCOVERED!
WELL, SEE YA LATER!
?
CAN'T GET TOO CARRIED AWAY OR I MIGHT GET FUYUKI IN TROUBLE... GUESS I SHOULD START MAKING MY WAY HOME!
ALTHOUGH IT WAS NICE TO GET A TASTE OF BEING IN A CLUB AFTER ALL THESE YEARS... HEH HEH! ♡
SHOOT-- MISSED THE PASS!
GET IT NATSUMI!!
H-HUH? HOW DO YOU GET OUT OF THIS PLACE?
FUYUKI ?!

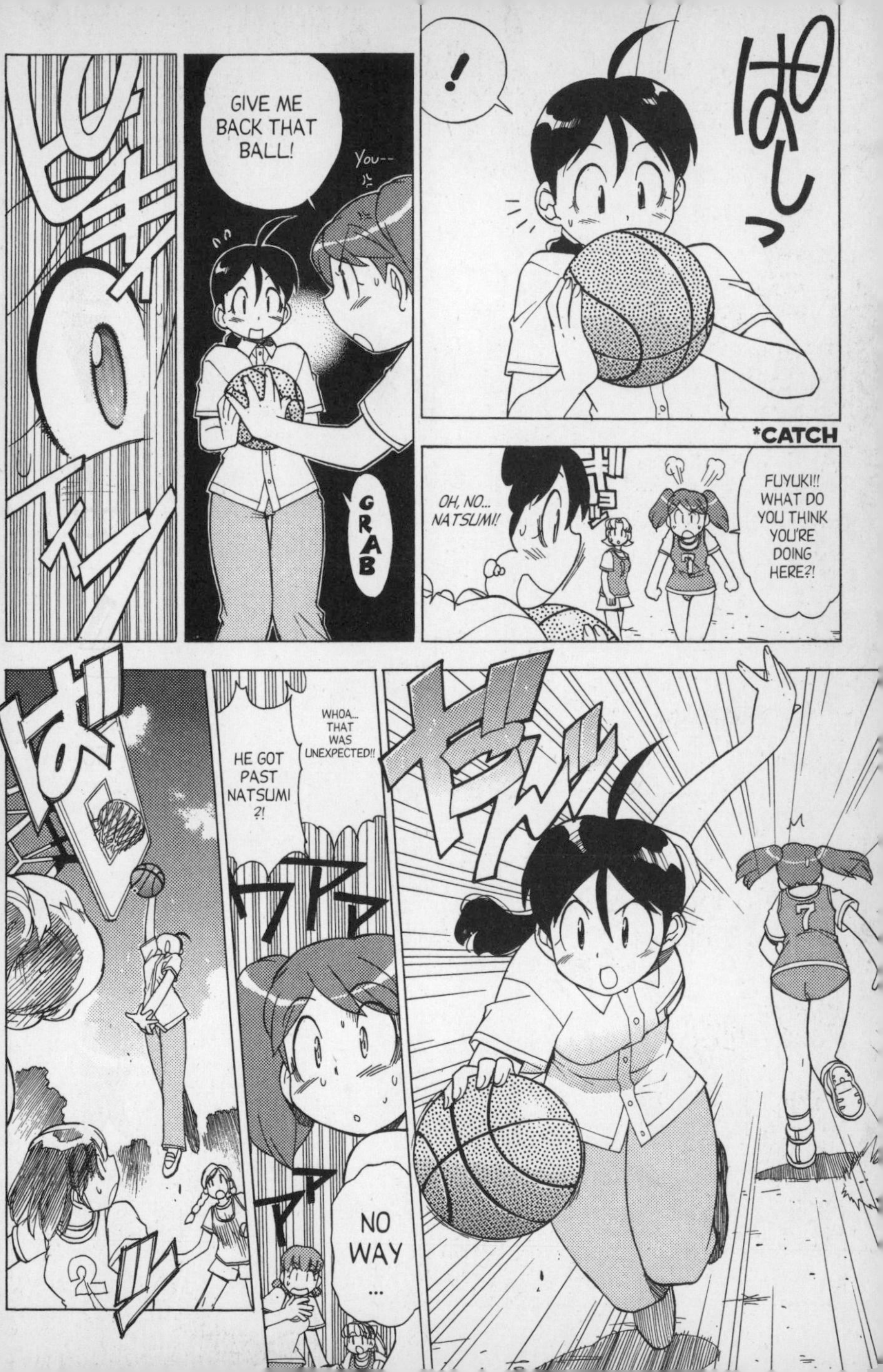
!
ぱしっ
*CATCH
FUYUKI!! WHAT DO YOU THINK YOU'RE DOING HERE?!
OH, NO... NATSUMI!
GIVE ME BACK THAT BALL!
You--
GRAB
WHOA... THAT WAS UNEXPECTED!!
HE GOT PAST NATSUMI ?!
NO WAY ...

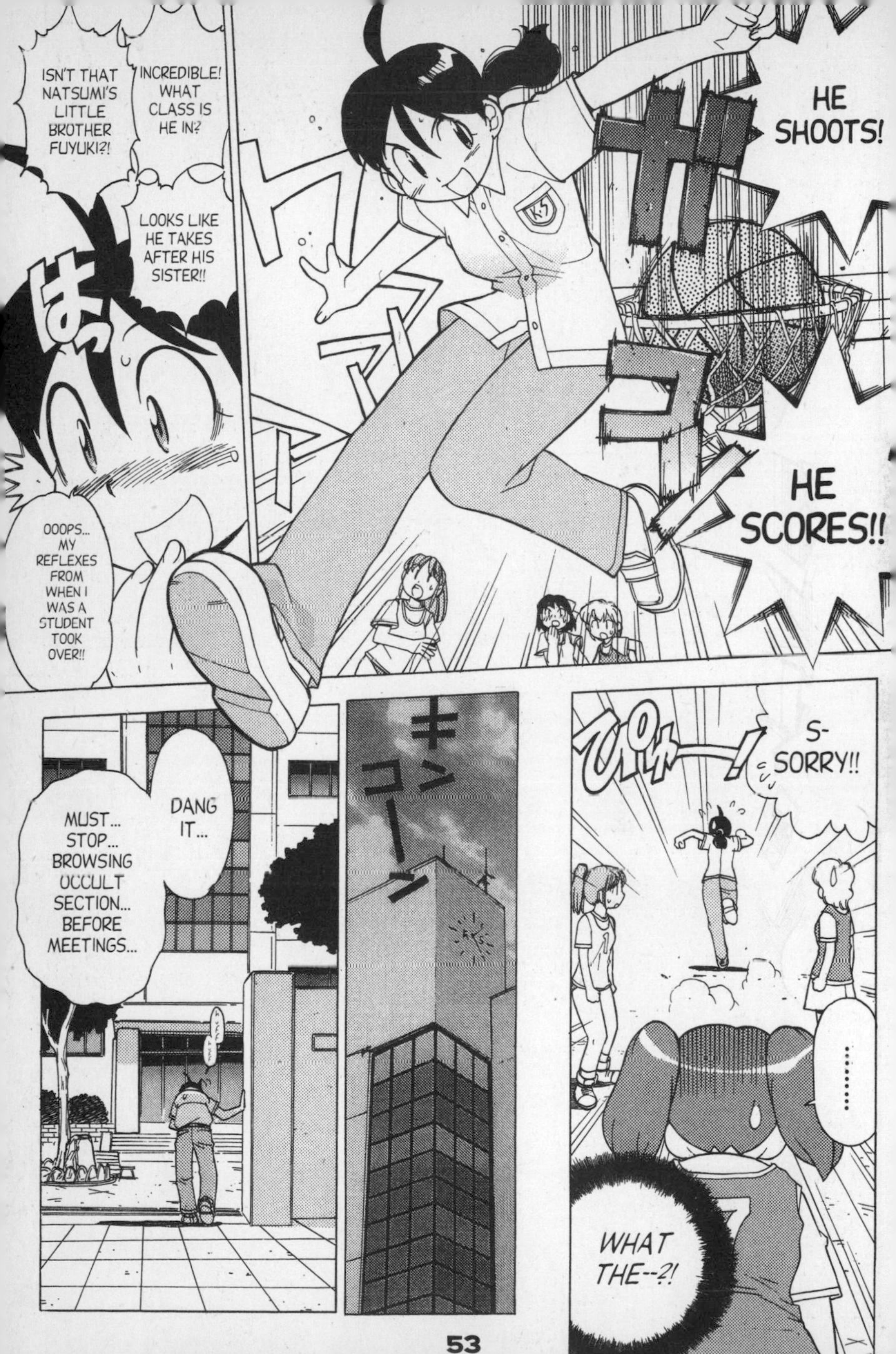
HE SHOOTS!
HE SCORES!!
INCREDIBLE! WHAT CLASS IS HE IN?
ISN'T THAT NATSUMI'S LITTLE BROTHER FUYUKI?!
LOOKS LIKE HE TAKES AFTER HIS SISTER!!
OOOPS... MY REFLEXES FROM WHEN I WAS A STUDENT TOOK OVER!!
S-SORRY!!
....
WHAT THE--?!
DANG IT...
MUST... STOP... BROWSING OCCULT SECTION... BEFORE MEETINGS...

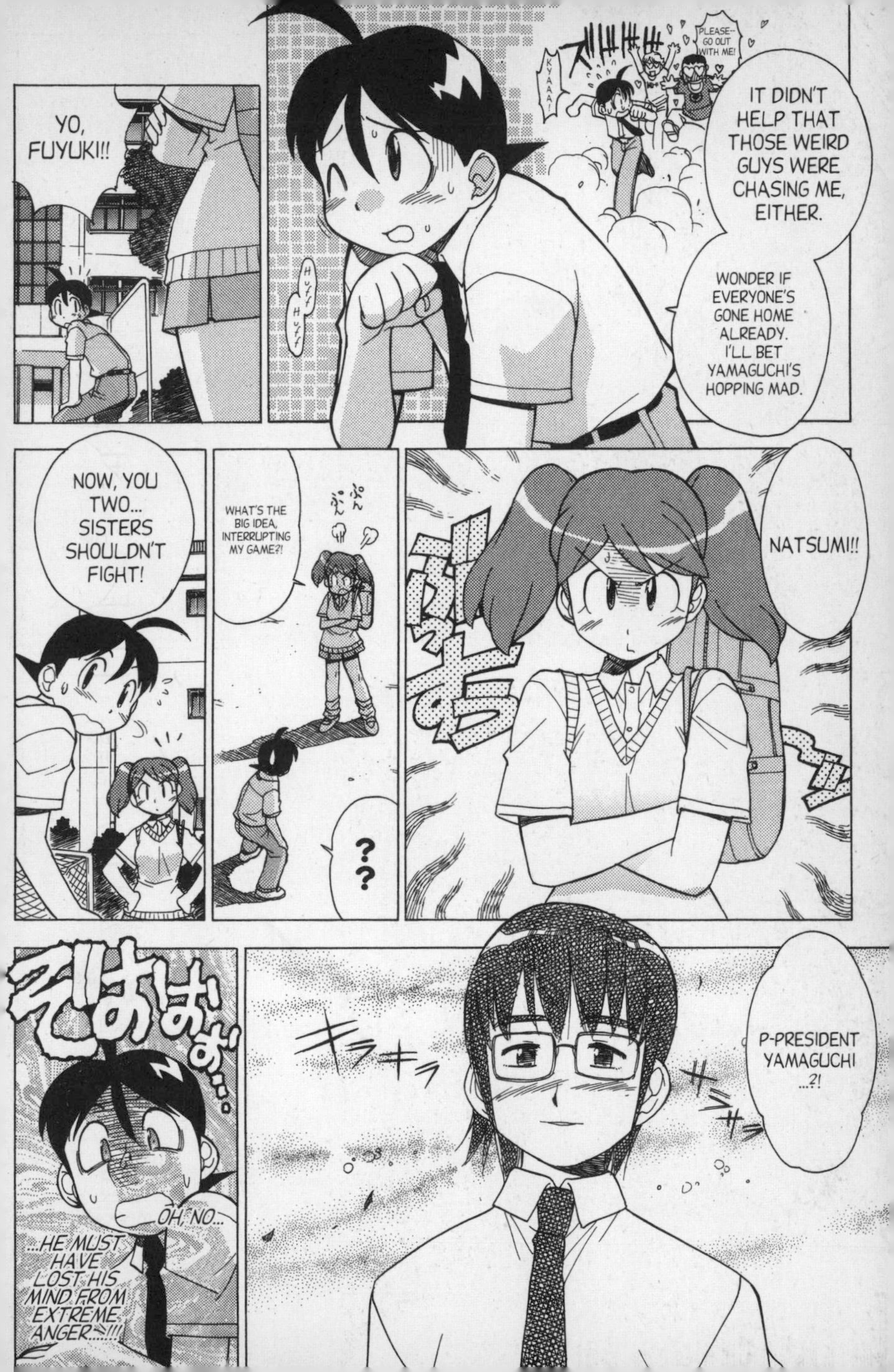
KYAAA!
PLEASE-- GO OUT WITH ME!
IT DIDN'T HELP THAT THOSE WEIRD GUYS WERE CHASING ME, EITHER.
HUFF HUFF
WONDER IF EVERYONE'S GONE HOME ALREADY. I'LL BET YAMAGUCHI'S HOPPING MAD.
YO, FUYUKI!!
NATSUMI!!
WHAT'S THE BIG IDEA, INTERRUPTING MY GAME?!
??
NOW, YOU TWO... SISTERS SHOULDN'T FIGHT!
P-PRESIDENT YAMAGUCHI ...?!
OH, NO...
...HE MUST HAVE LOST HIS MIND FROM EXTREME ANGER...!!!

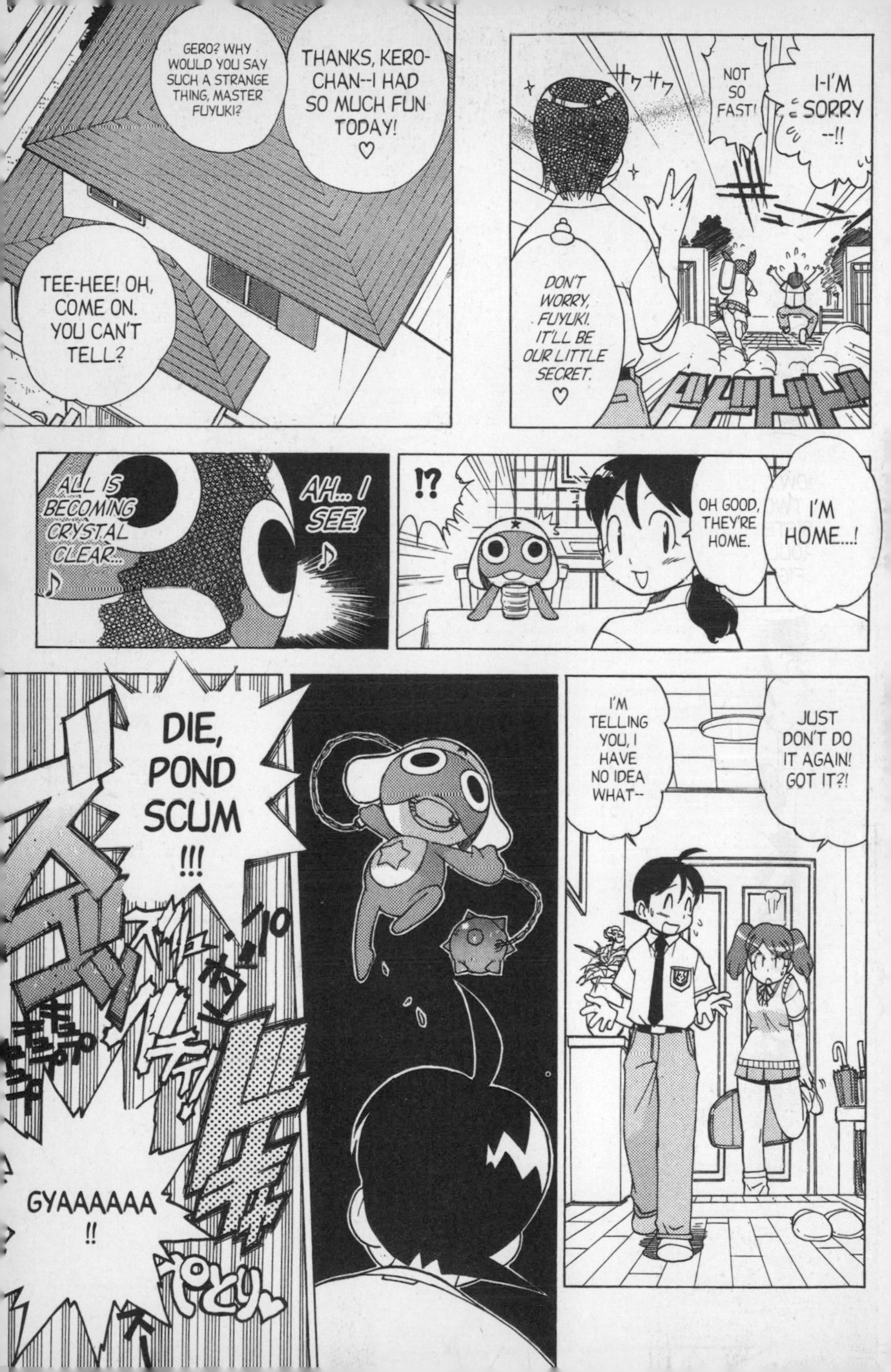
I-I'M SORRY--!!
NOT SO FAST!
DON'T WORRY, FUYUKI. IT'LL BE OUR LITTLE SECRET. ♡
THANKS, KERO-CHAN--I HAD SO MUCH FUN TODAY! ♡
GERO? WHY WOULD YOU SAY SUCH A STRANGE THING, MASTER FUYUKI?
TEE-HEE! OH, COME ON. YOU CAN'T TELL?
I'M HOME...!
OH GOOD, THEY'RE HOME.
!?
AH... I SEE! ♪
ALL IS BECOMING CRYSTAL CLEAR... ♪
JUST DON'T DO IT AGAIN! GOT IT?!
I'M TELLING YOU, I HAVE NO IDEA WHAT--
DIE, POND SCUM!!!
GYAAAAAA!!

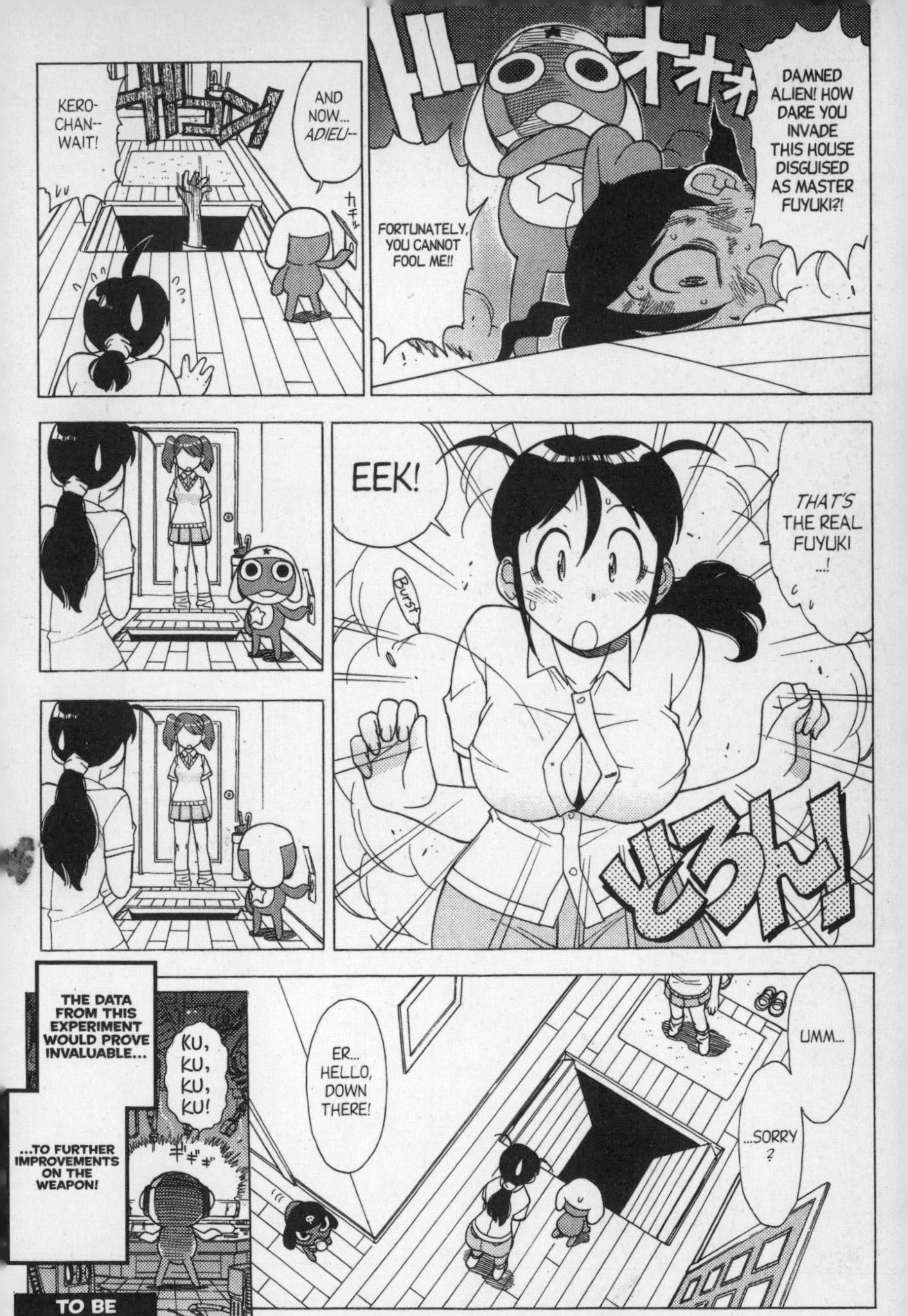
DAMNED ALIEN! HOW DARE YOU INVADE THIS HOUSE DISGUISED AS MASTER FUYUKI?!
FORTUNATELY, YOU CANNOT FOOL ME!!
AND NOW... ADIEU--
KERO-CHAN-- WAIT!
THAT'S THE REAL FUYUKI ...!
EEK!
Burst
UMM...
...SORRY ?
ER... HELLO, DOWN THERE!
THE DATA FROM THIS EXPERIMENT WOULD PROVE INVALUABLE...
KU, KU, KU, KU!
...TO FURTHER IMPROVEMENTS ON THE WEAPON!
TO BE CONTINUED

ENCOUNTER XXIV
OPERATION: SWIMSUIT ISSUE

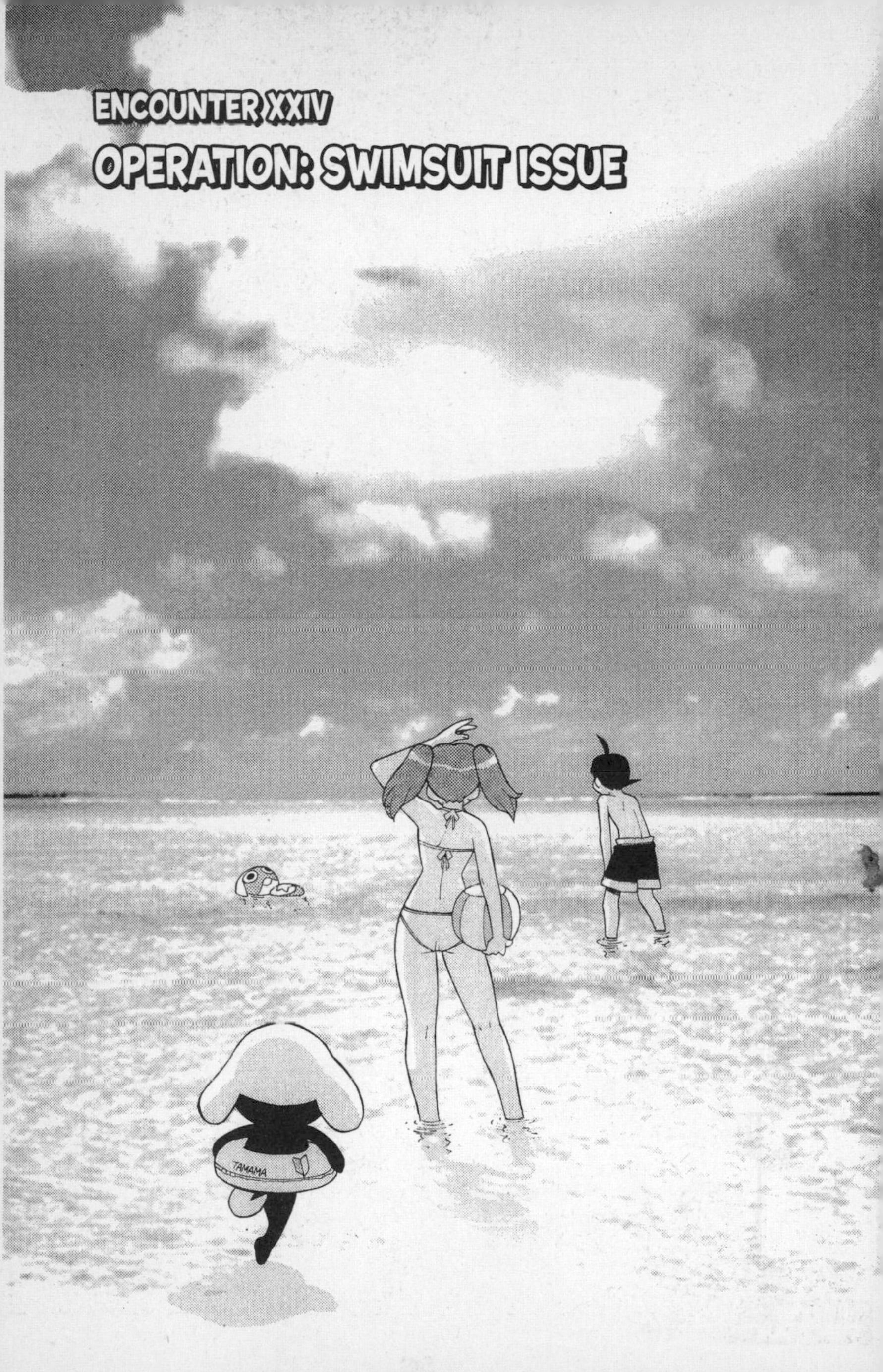
TAMAMA

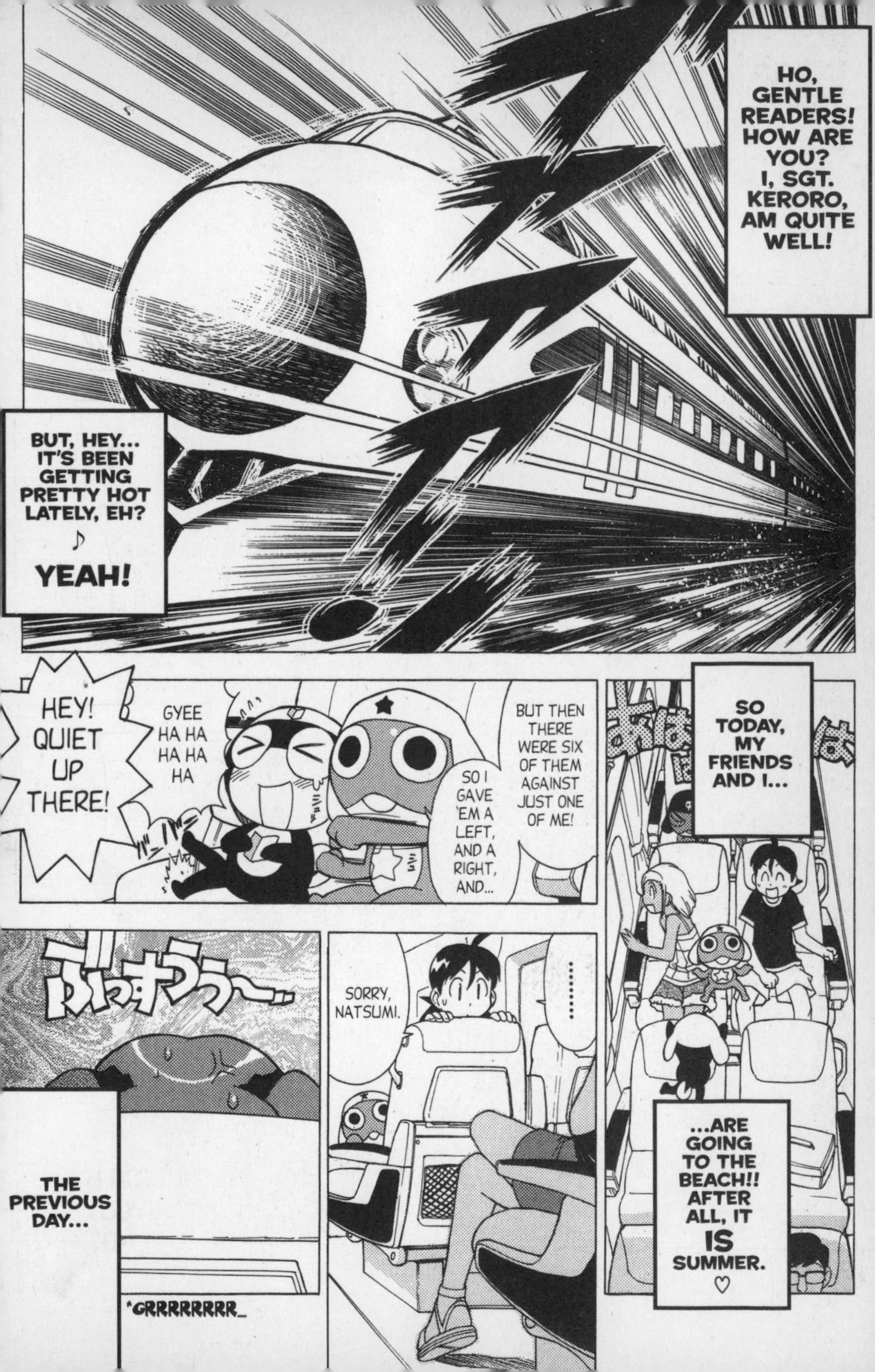
HO, GENTLE READERS! HOW ARE YOU? I, SGT. KERORO, AM QUITE WELL!
BUT, HEY... IT'S BEEN GETTING PRETTY HOT LATELY, EH? ♪ YEAH!
SO TODAY, MY FRIENDS AND I...
...ARE GOING TO THE BEACH!! AFTER ALL, IT IS SUMMER. ♡
BUT THEN THERE WERE SIX OF THEM AGAINST JUST ONE OF ME!
SO I GAVE 'EM A LEFT, AND A RIGHT, AND...
GYEE HA HA HA HA HA
HEY! QUIET UP THERE!
......
SORRY, NATSUMI.
THE PREVIOUS DAY...
*GRRRRRRRR...

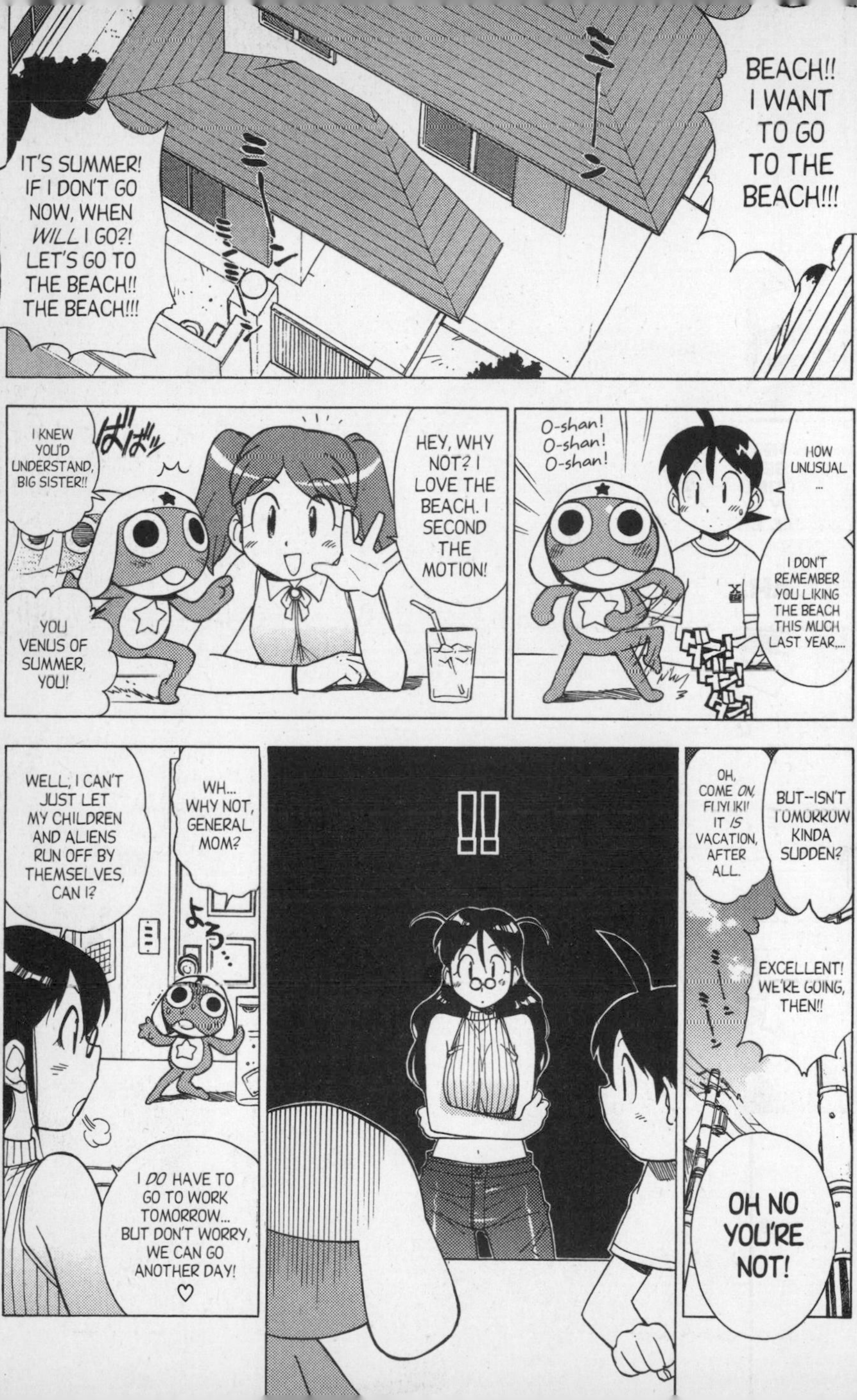

BEACH!! I WANT TO GO TO THE BEACH!!!
IT'S SUMMER! IF I DON'T GO NOW, WHEN *WILL* I GO?! LET'S GO TO THE BEACH!! THE BEACH!!!
O-shan! O-shan! O-shan!
HOW UNUSUAL ...
I DON'T REMEMBER YOU LIKING THE BEACH THIS MUCH LAST YEAR....
HEY, WHY NOT? I LOVE THE BEACH. I SECOND THE MOTION!
ばばッ
I KNEW YOU'D UNDERSTAND, BIG SISTER!!
YOU VENUS OF SUMMER, YOU!
BUT--ISN'T TOMORROW KINDA SUDDEN?
OH, COME *ON*, FUYUKI! IT *IS* VACATION, AFTER ALL.
EXCELLENT! WE'RE GOING, THEN!!
OH NO YOU'RE NOT!
!!
WH... WHY NOT, GENERAL MOM?
WELL, I CAN'T JUST LET MY CHILDREN AND ALIENS RUN OFF BY THEMSELVES, CAN I?
よろ...
I *DO* HAVE TO GO TO WORK TOMORROW... BUT DON'T WORRY, WE CAN GO ANOTHER DAY! ♡

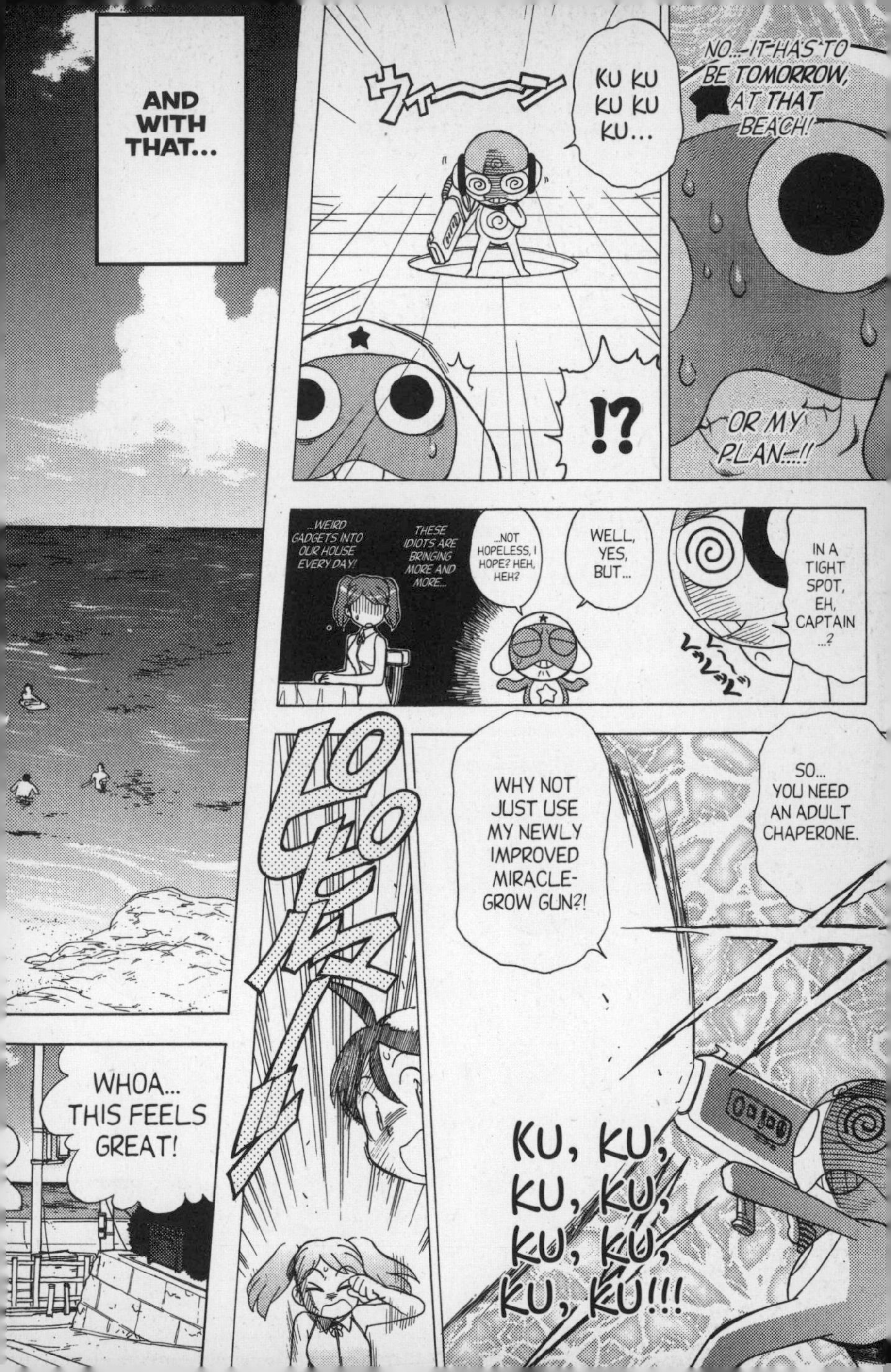

NO... IT HAS TO BE TOMORROW, AT THAT BEACH!
...OR MY PLAN...!!
ウィーーン
KU KU KU KU KU...
!?
IN A TIGHT SPOT, EH, CAPTAIN...?
WELL, YES, BUT...
...NOT HOPELESS, I HOPE? HEH, HEH?
THESE IDIOTS ARE BRINGING MORE AND MORE...
...WEIRD GADGETS INTO OUR HOUSE EVERY DAY!
SO... YOU NEED AN ADULT CHAPERONE.
WHY NOT JUST USE MY NEWLY IMPROVED MIRACLE-GROW GUN?!
KU, KU, KU, KU, KU, KU, KU, KU!!!
AND WITH THAT...
WHOA... THIS FEELS GREAT!

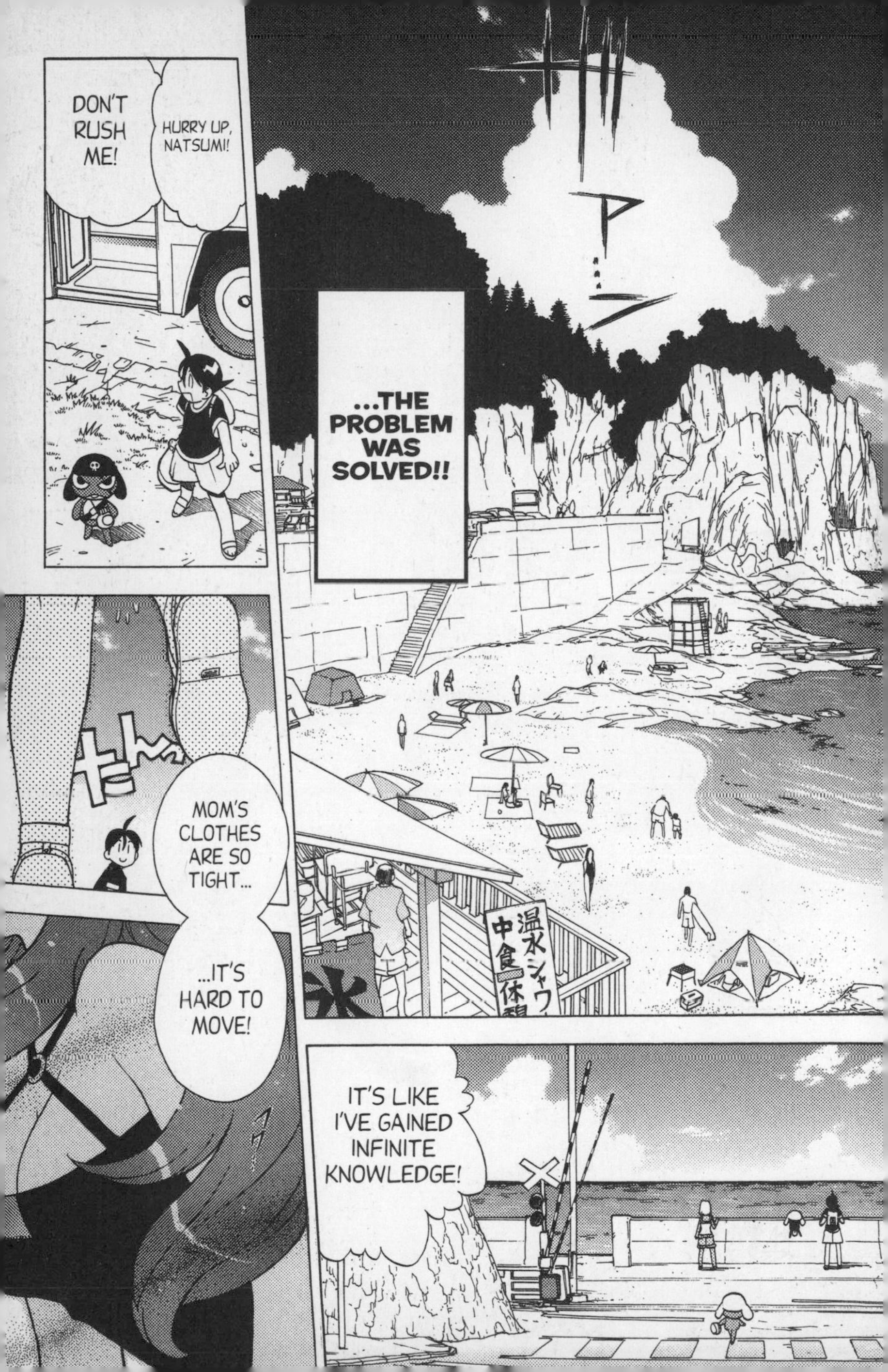
...THE PROBLEM WAS SOLVED!!
温水シャワ
中食
HURRY UP, NATSUMI!
DON'T RUSH ME!
MOM'S CLOTHES ARE SO TIGHT...
...IT'S HARD TO MOVE!
IT'S LIKE I'VE GAINED INFINITE KNOWLEDGE!

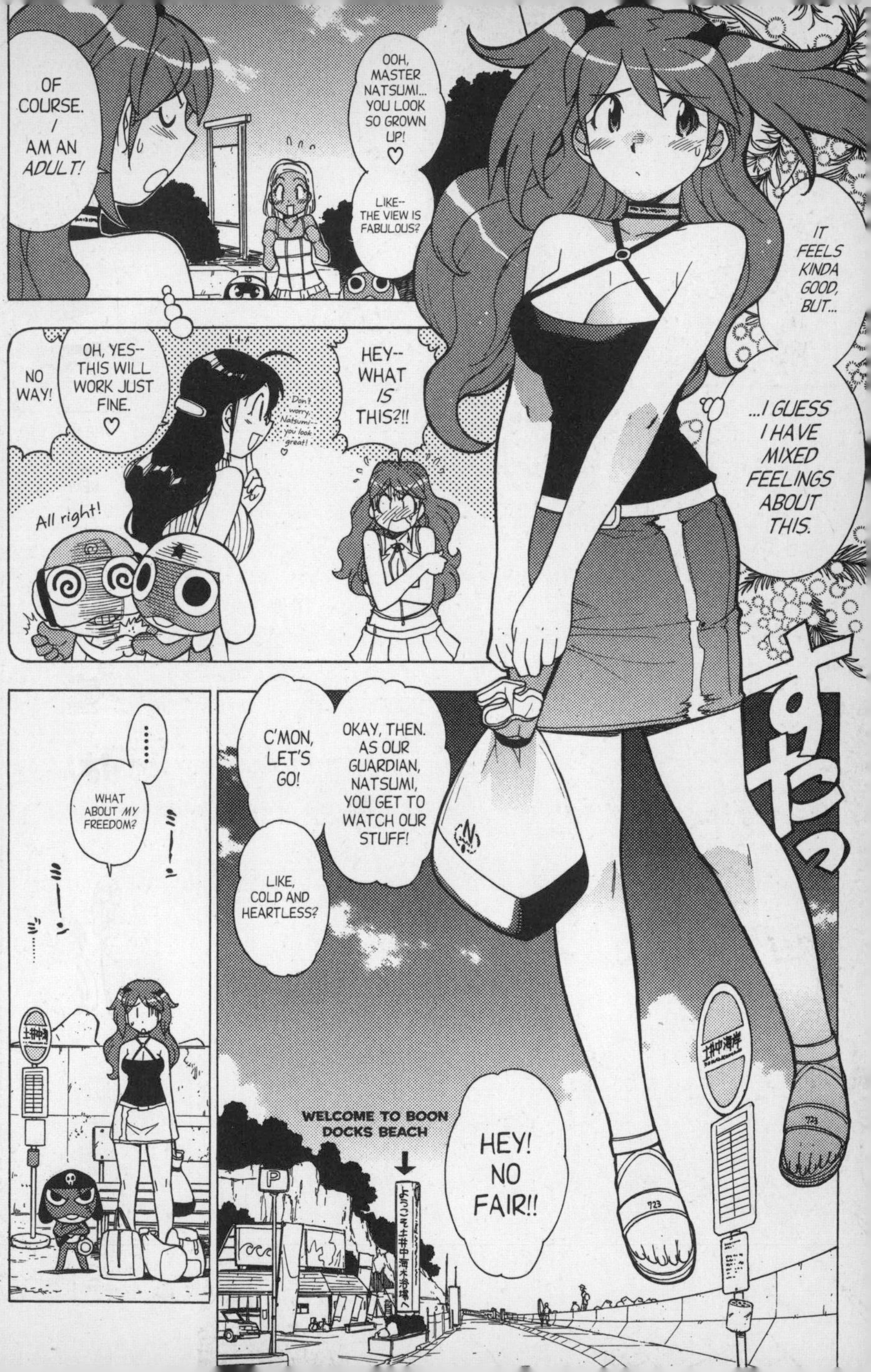
IT FEELS KINDA GOOD, BUT...
...I GUESS I HAVE MIXED FEELINGS ABOUT THIS.
OOH, MASTER NATSUMI... YOU LOOK SO GROWN UP! ♡
LIKE-- THE VIEW IS FABULOUS?
OF COURSE. I AM AN ADULT!
HEY-- WHAT IS THIS?!!
Don't worry, Natsumi-- you look great! ♡
OH, YES-- THIS WILL WORK JUST FINE. ♡
NO WAY!
All right!
すたっ
OKAY, THEN. AS OUR GUARDIAN, NATSUMI, YOU GET TO WATCH OUR STUFF!
C'MON, LET'S GO!
LIKE, COLD AND HEARTLESS?
HEY! NO FAIR!!
WELCOME TO BOON DOCKS BEACH
ようこそ土井中海水浴場へ
......
WHAT ABOUT MY FREEDOM?

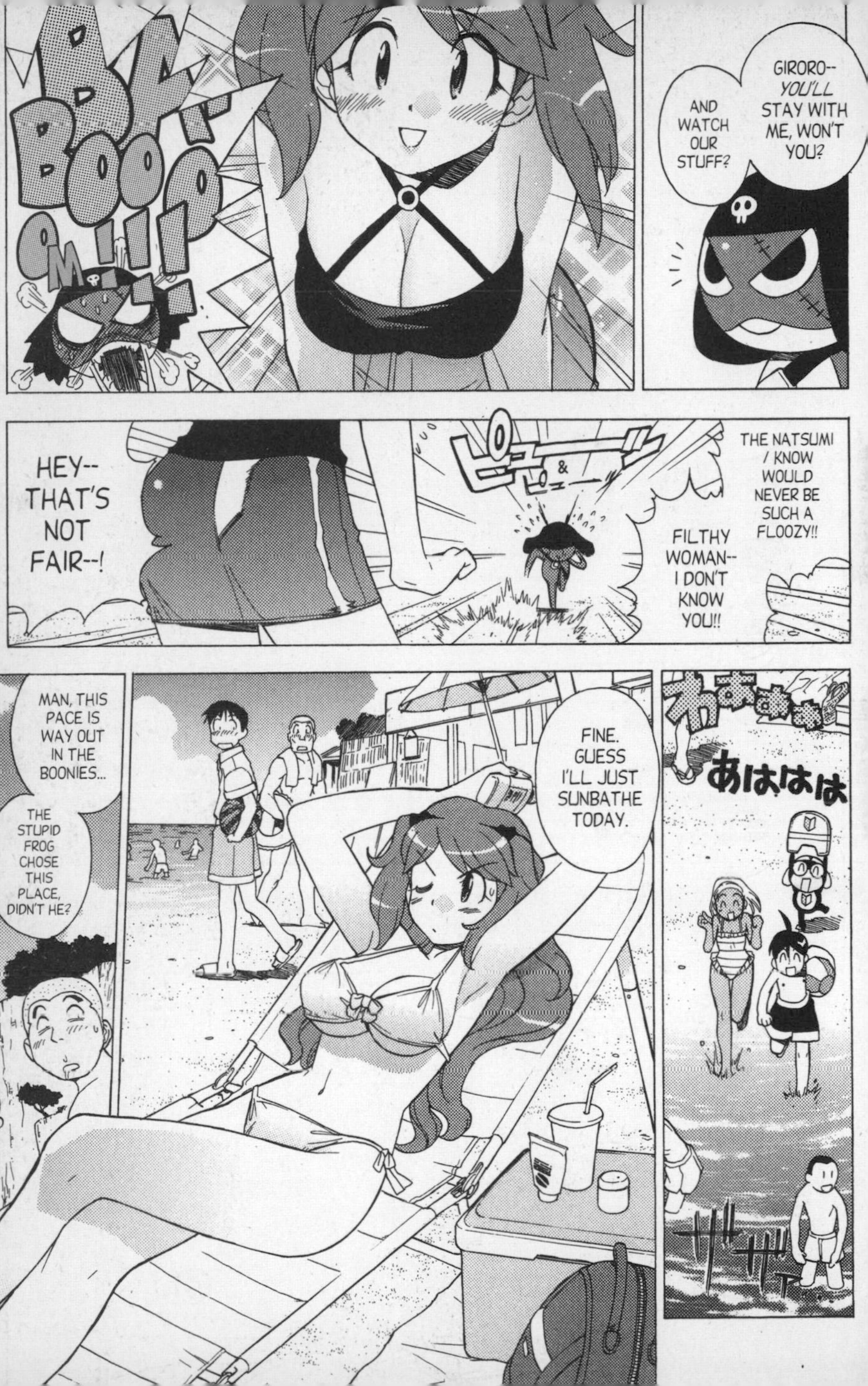
GIRORO-- YOU'LL STAY WITH ME, WON'T YOU?
AND WATCH OUR STUFF?
THE NATSUMI I KNOW WOULD NEVER BE SUCH A FLOOZY!!
FILTHY WOMAN-- I DON'T KNOW YOU!!
ピュー & ピュー
HEY-- THAT'S NOT FAIR--!
わあああ
あははは
FINE. GUESS I'LL JUST SUNBATHE TODAY.
MAN, THIS PACE IS WAY OUT IN THE BOONIES...
THE STUPID FROG CHOSE THIS PLACE, DIDN'T HE?

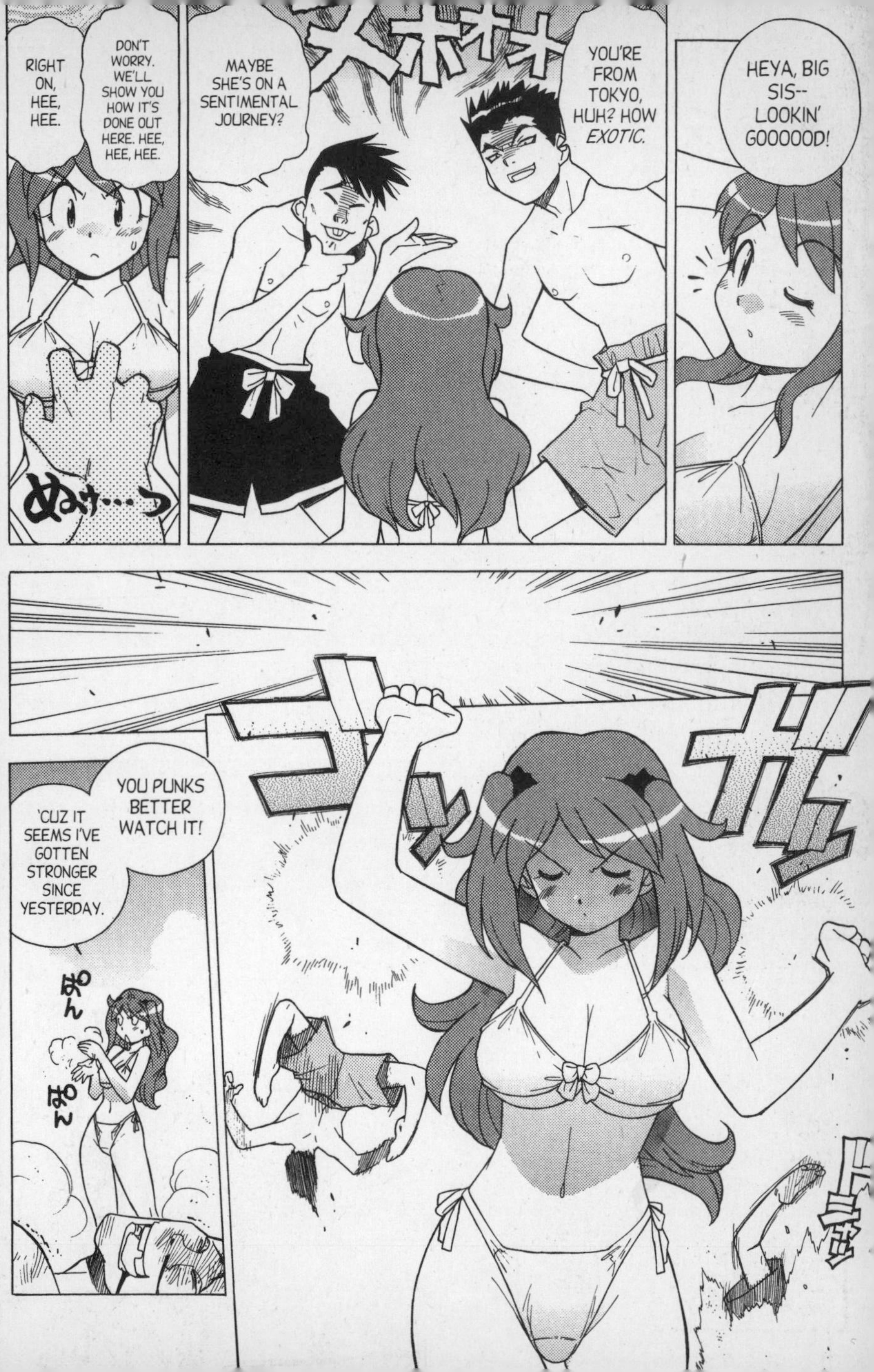
HEYA, BIG SIS-- LOOKIN' GOOOOOD!
YOU'RE FROM TOKYO, HUH? HOW *EXOTIC.*
MAYBE SHE'S ON A SENTIMENTAL JOURNEY?
DON'T WORRY. WE'LL SHOW YOU HOW IT'S DONE OUT HERE. HEE, HEE, HEE.
RIGHT ON, HEE, HEE.
YOU PUNKS BETTER WATCH IT!
'CUZ IT SEEMS I'VE GOTTEN STRONGER SINCE YESTERDAY.

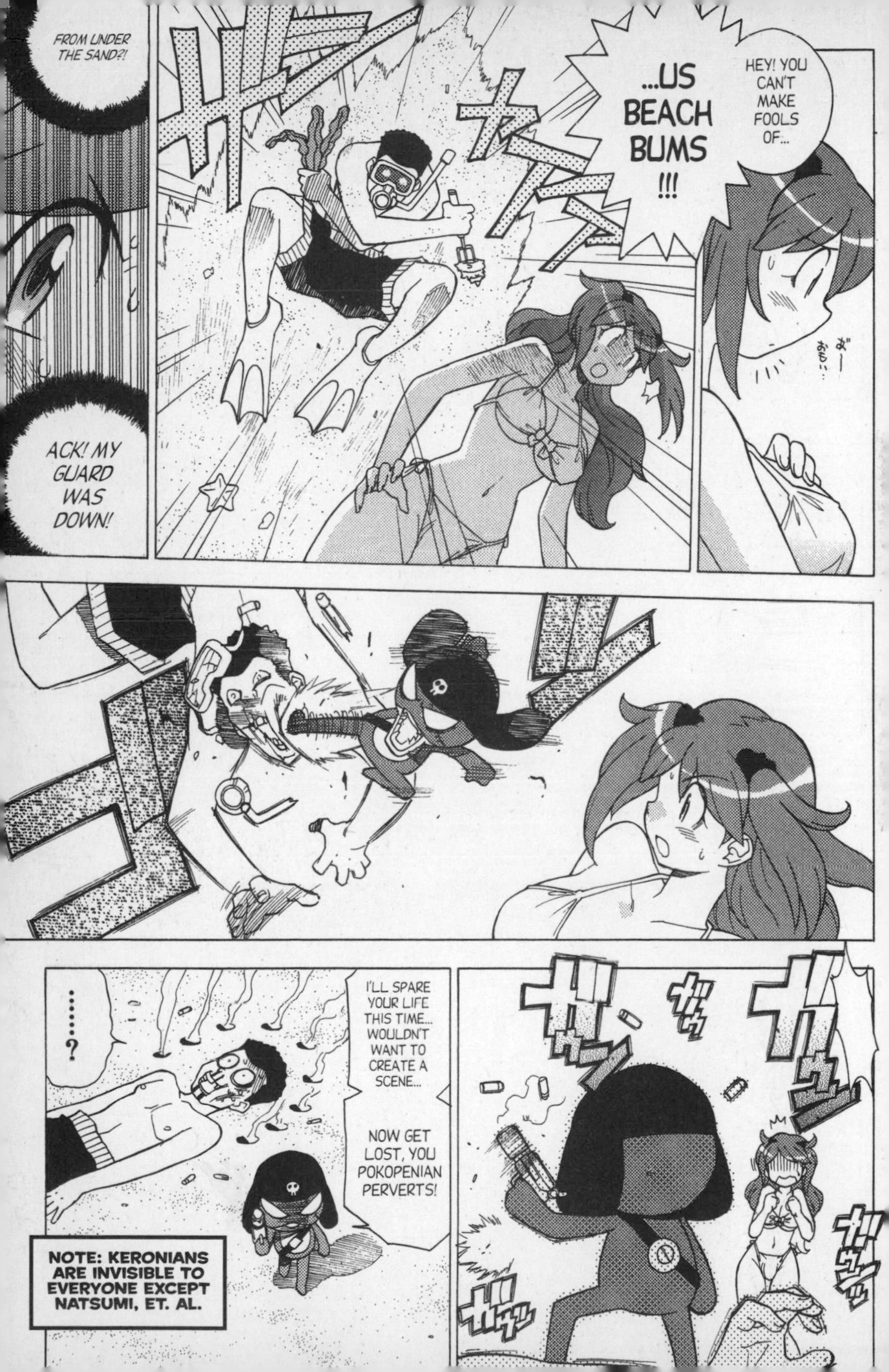
HEY! YOU CAN'T MAKE FOOLS OF...
...US BEACH BUMS !!!
FROM UNDER THE SAND?!
ACK! MY GUARD WAS DOWN!
I'LL SPARE YOUR LIFE THIS TIME... WOULDN'T WANT TO CREATE A SCENE...
NOW GET LOST, YOU POKOPENIAN PERVERTS!
......?
NOTE: KERONIANS ARE INVISIBLE TO EVERYONE EXCEPT NATSUMI, ET. AL.

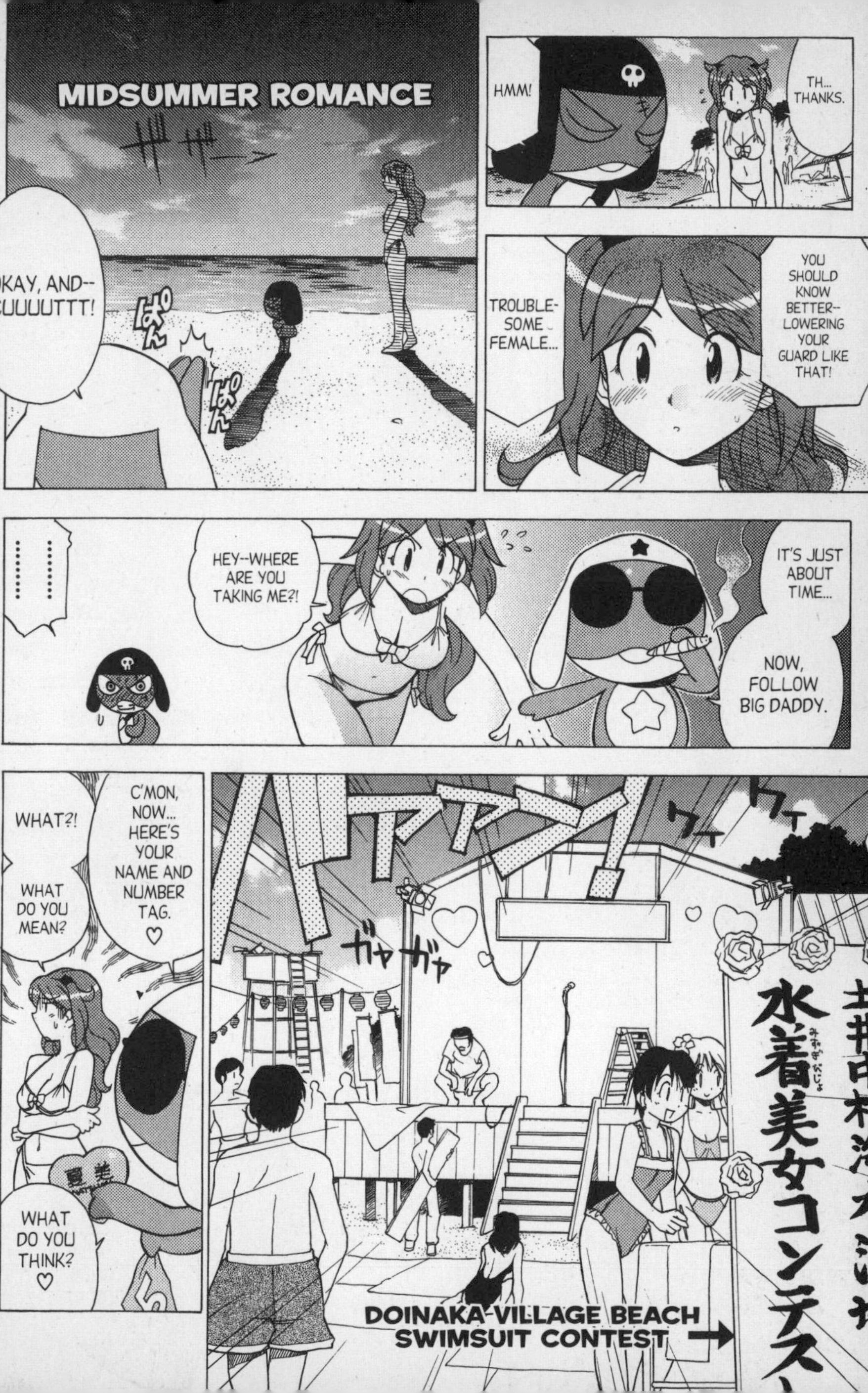
TH... THANKS.
HMM!
YOU SHOULD KNOW BETTER--LOWERING YOUR GUARD LIKE THAT!
TROUBLE-SOME FEMALE...
MIDSUMMER ROMANCE
ぱん
ぱん
OKAY, AND-- CUUUUTTT!
IT'S JUST ABOUT TIME...
NOW, FOLLOW BIG DADDY.
HEY--WHERE ARE YOU TAKING ME?!
......
土井中村海水浴場
水着美女コンテスト
DOINAKA-VILLAGE BEACH SWIMSUIT CONTEST
ガヤガヤ
C'MON, NOW... HERE'S YOUR NAME AND NUMBER TAG. ♡
WHAT?!
WHAT DO YOU MEAN?
WHAT DO YOU THINK? ♡

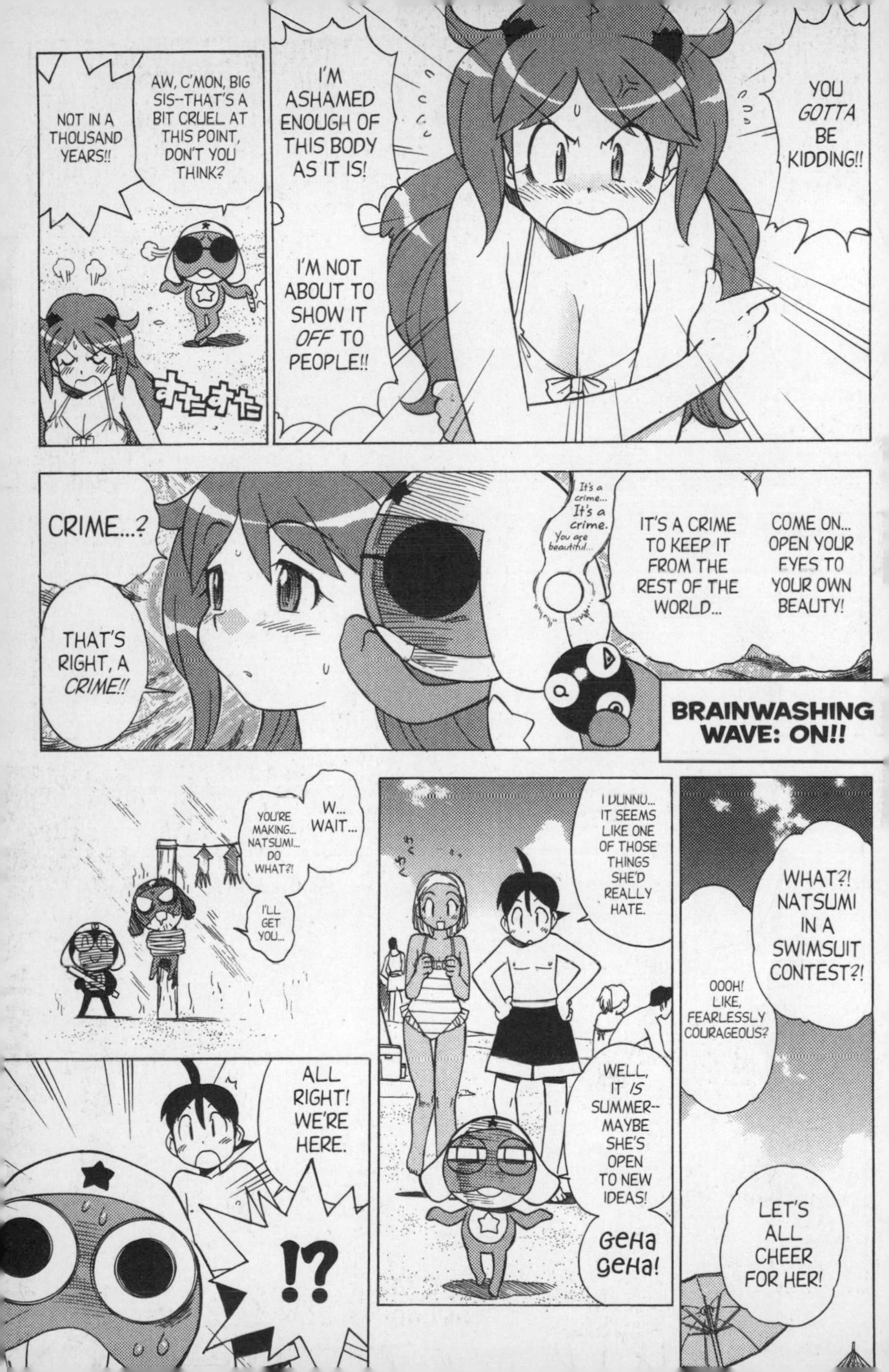
YOU *GOTTA* BE KIDDING!!
I'M ASHAMED ENOUGH OF THIS BODY AS IT IS!
I'M NOT ABOUT TO SHOW IT *OFF* TO PEOPLE!!
AW, C'MON, BIG SIS--THAT'S A BIT CRUEL AT THIS POINT, DON'T YOU THINK?
NOT IN A THOUSAND YEARS!!
すたすた
COME ON... OPEN YOUR EYES TO YOUR OWN BEAUTY!
IT'S A CRIME TO KEEP IT FROM THE REST OF THE WORLD...
It's a crime... It's a crime. You are beautiful...
BRAINWASHING WAVE: ON!!
CRIME...?
THAT'S RIGHT, A *CRIME*!!
WHAT?! NATSUMI IN A SWIMSUIT CONTEST?!
OOOH! LIKE, FEARLESSLY COURAGEOUS?
LET'S ALL CHEER FOR HER!
I DUNNO... IT SEEMS LIKE ONE OF THOSE THINGS SHE'D REALLY HATE.
WELL, IT *IS* SUMMER--MAYBE SHE'S OPEN TO NEW IDEAS!
GEHA GEHA!
W... WAIT...
YOU'RE MAKING... NATSUMI... DO WHAT?!
I'LL GET YOU...
ALL RIGHT! WE'RE HERE.
!?

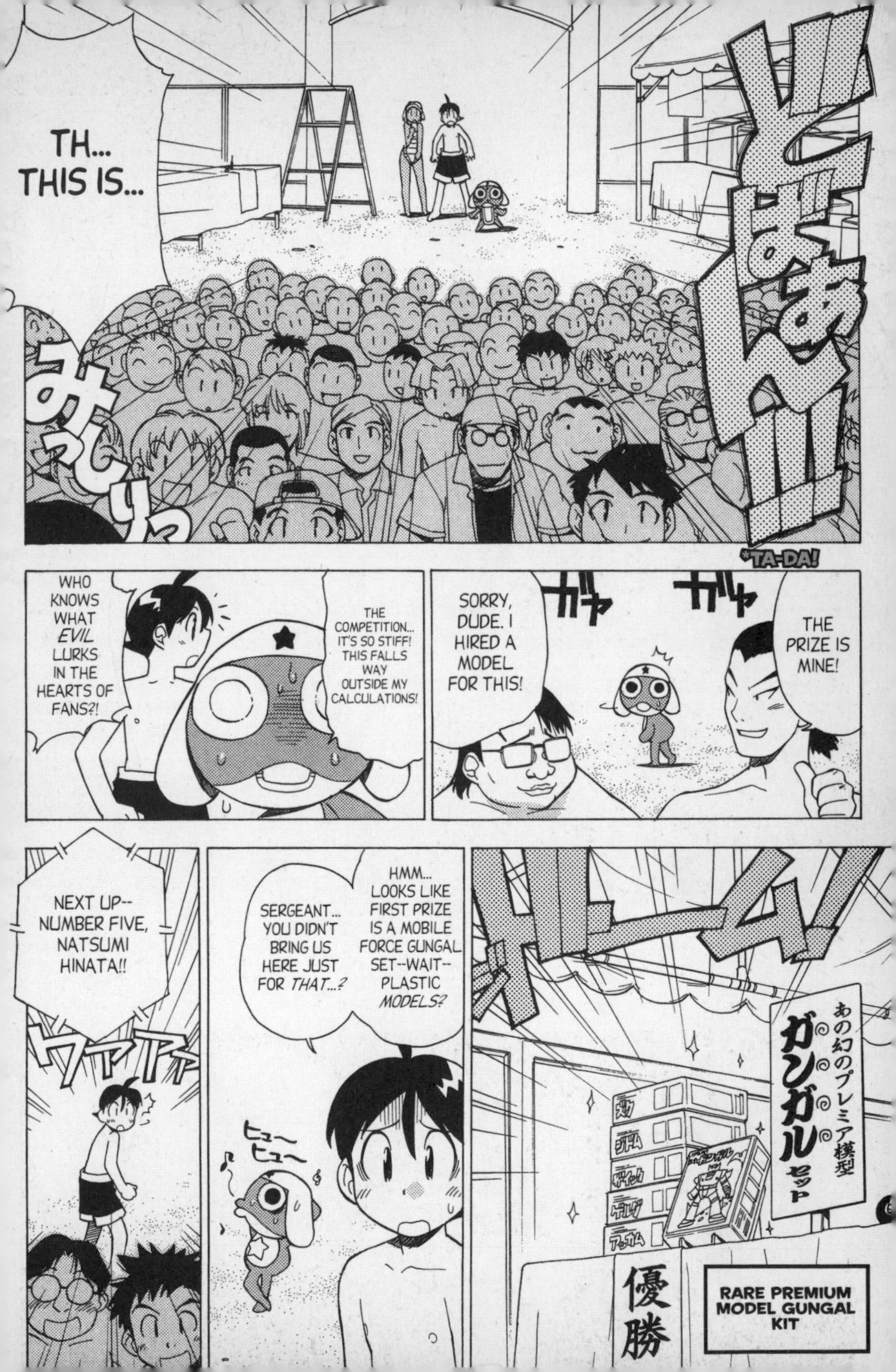
TH... THIS IS...
*TA-DA!
みっしりっ
ガヤ ガヤ
THE PRIZE IS MINE!
SORRY, DUDE. I HIRED A MODEL FOR THIS!
THE COMPETITION... IT'S SO STIFF! THIS FALLS WAY OUTSIDE MY CALCULATIONS!
WHO KNOWS WHAT *EVIL* LURKS IN THE HEARTS OF FANS?!
あの幻のプレミア模型
ガンガルセット
優勝
RARE PREMIUM MODEL GUNGAL KIT
HMM... LOOKS LIKE FIRST PRIZE IS A MOBILE FORCE GUNGAL SET--WAIT--PLASTIC *MODELS?*
SERGEANT... YOU DIDN'T BRING US HERE JUST FOR *THAT...?*
ヒュ～ ヒュ～
NEXT UP-- NUMBER FIVE, NATSUMI HINATA!!
ワァアァ

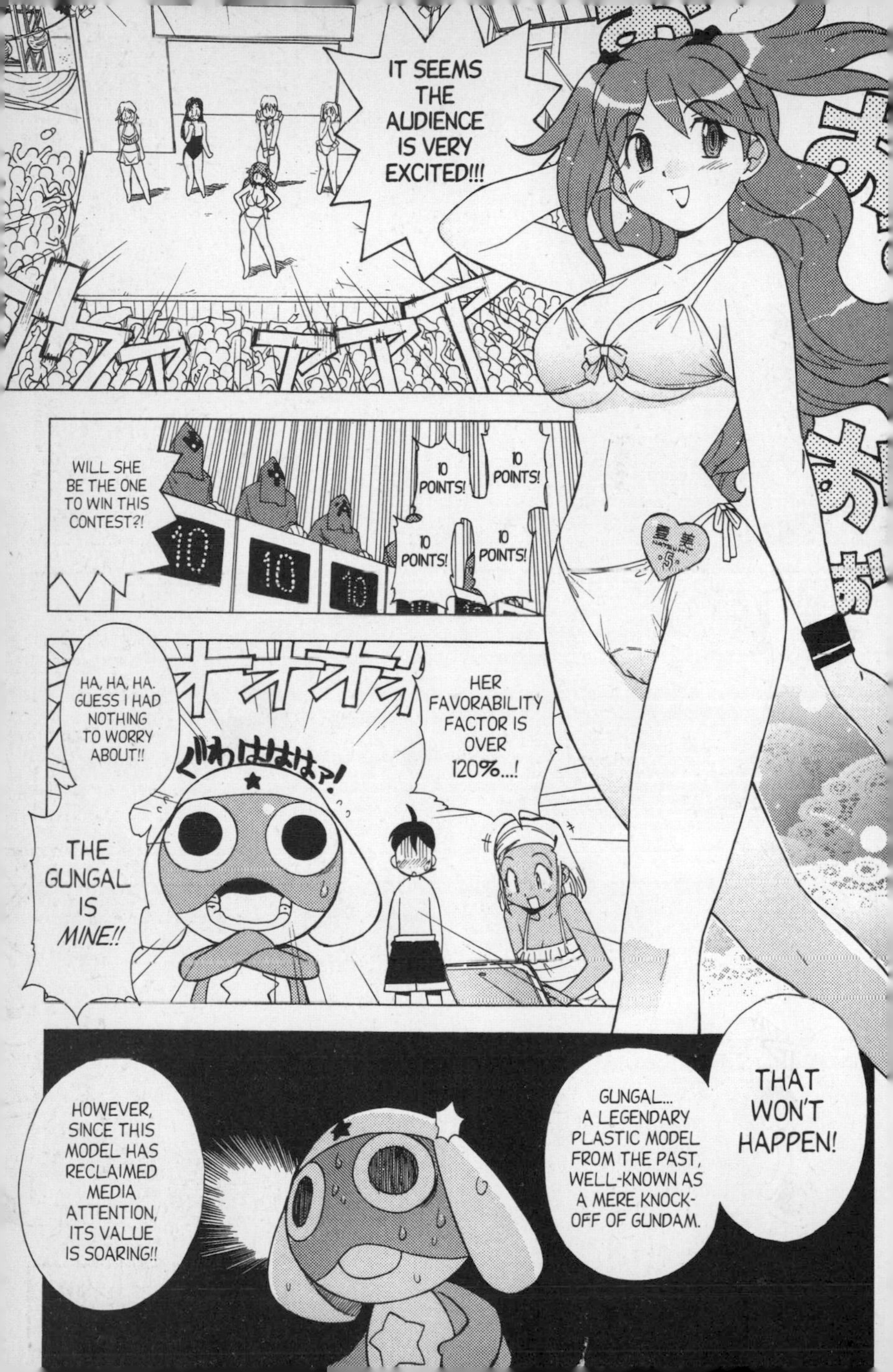
IT SEEMS THE AUDIENCE IS VERY EXCITED!!!
10 POINTS!
10 POINTS!
10 POINTS!
10 POINTS!
WILL SHE BE THE ONE TO WIN THIS CONTEST?!
HER FAVORABILITY FACTOR IS OVER 120%...!
HA, HA, HA. GUESS I HAD NOTHING TO WORRY ABOUT!!
THE GUNGAL IS *MINE!!*
THAT WON'T HAPPEN!
GUNGAL... A LEGENDARY PLASTIC MODEL FROM THE PAST, WELL-KNOWN AS A MERE KNOCK-OFF OF GUNDAM.
HOWEVER, SINCE THIS MODEL HAS RECLAIMED MEDIA ATTENTION, ITS VALUE IS SOARING!!

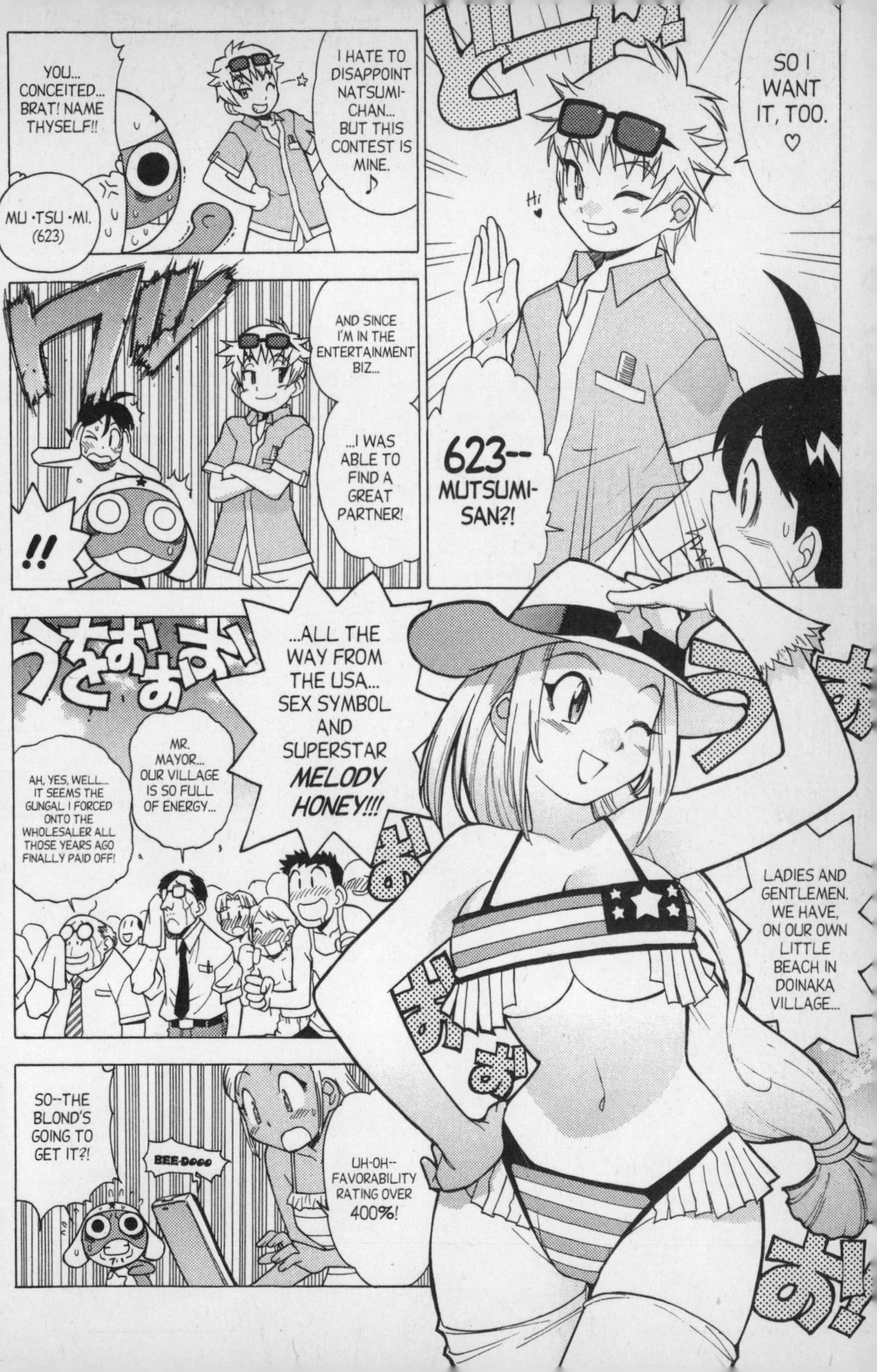

I HATE TO DISAPPOINT NATSUMI-CHAN... BUT THIS CONTEST IS MINE. ♪
YOU... CONCEITED... BRAT! NAME THYSELF!!
MU·TSU·MI. (623)
SO I WANT IT, TOO. ♡
Hi ♥
623-- MUTSUMI-SAN?!
AND SINCE I'M IN THE ENTERTAINMENT BIZ...
...I WAS ABLE TO FIND A GREAT PARTNER!
!!
LADIES AND GENTLEMEN. WE HAVE, ON OUR OWN LITTLE BEACH IN DOINAKA VILLAGE...
...ALL THE WAY FROM THE USA... SEX SYMBOL AND SUPERSTAR *MELODY HONEY!!!*
MR. MAYOR... OUR VILLAGE IS SO FULL OF ENERGY...
AH, YES, WELL... IT SEEMS THE GUNGAL I FORCED ONTO THE WHOLESALER ALL THOSE YEARS AGO FINALLY PAID OFF!
UH-OH-- FAVORABILITY RATING OVER 400%!
BEE-DOOO
SO--THE BLOND'S GOING TO GET IT?!

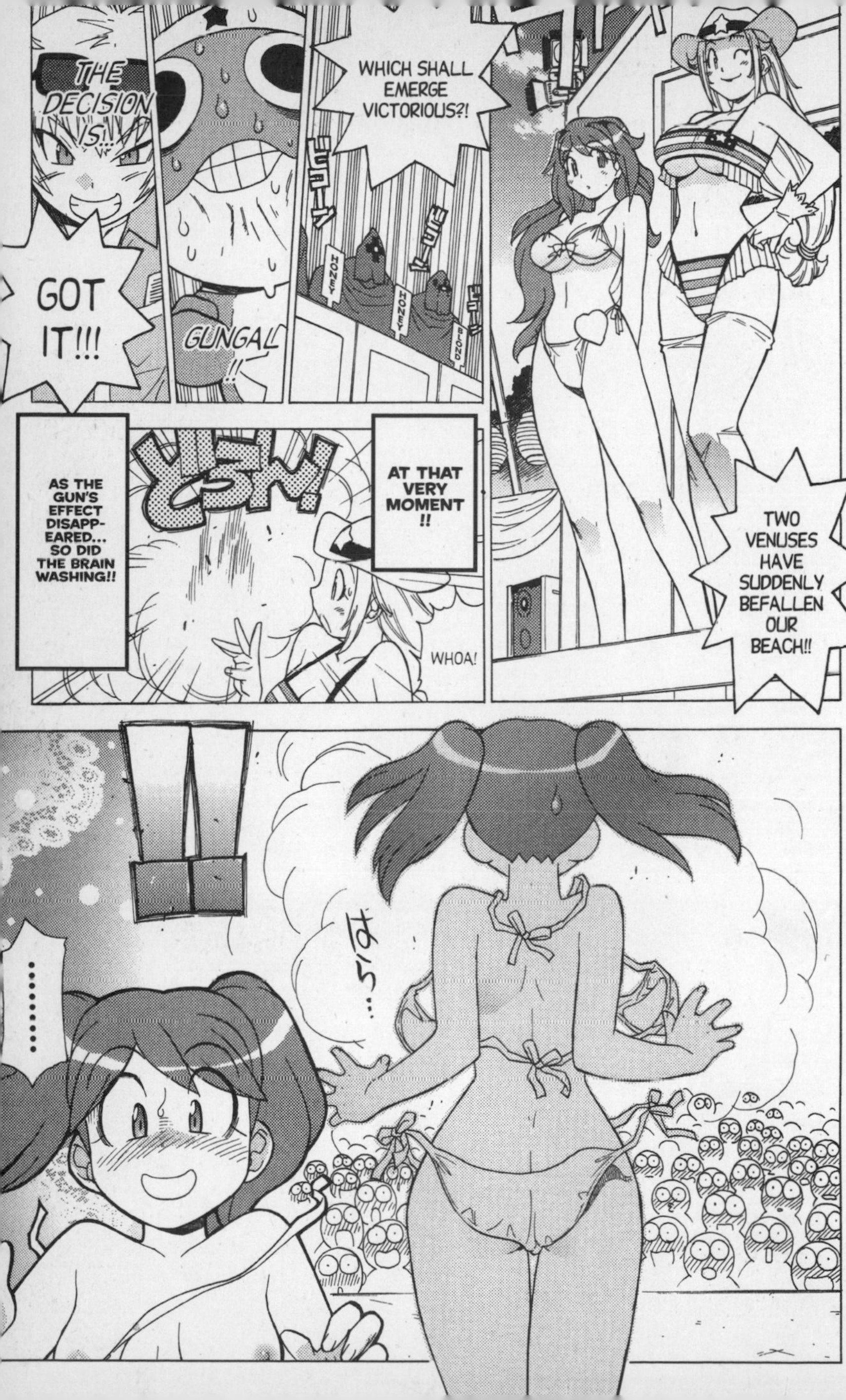
THE DECISION IS!...
GOT IT!!!
GUNGAL!!
WHICH SHALL EMERGE VICTORIOUS?!
HONEY
HONEY
BLOND
AS THE GUN'S EFFECT DISAPPEARED... SO DID THE BRAIN WASHING!!
AT THAT VERY MOMENT!!
WHOA!
TWO VENUSES HAVE SUDDENLY BEFALLEN OUR BEACH!!
!
....

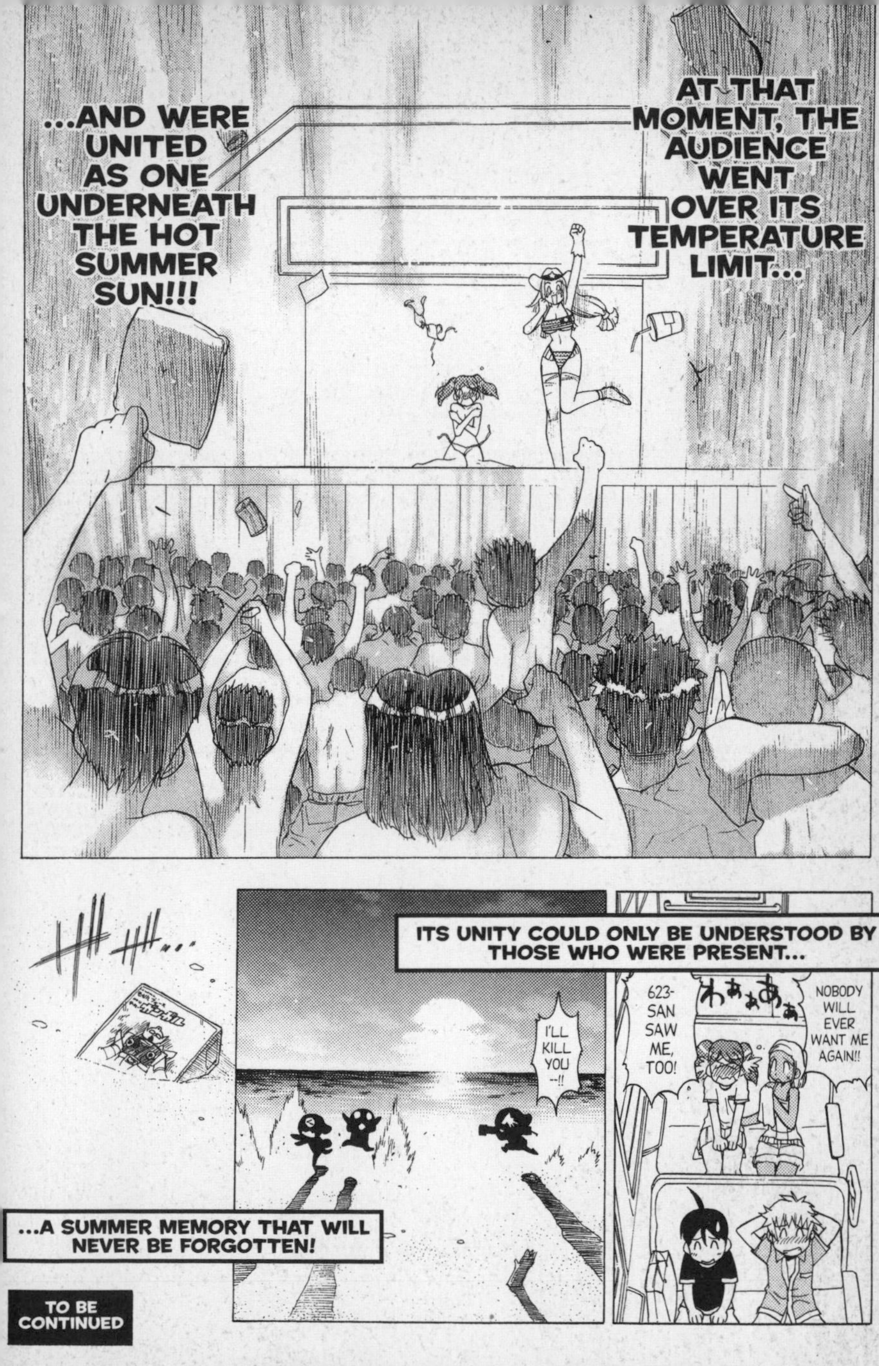
AT THAT MOMENT, THE AUDIENCE WENT OVER ITS TEMPERATURE LIMIT...
...AND WERE UNITED AS ONE UNDERNEATH THE HOT SUMMER SUN!!!
ITS UNITY COULD ONLY BE UNDERSTOOD BY THOSE WHO WERE PRESENT...
NOBODY WILL EVER WANT ME AGAIN!!
わぁぁあぁ
623-SAN SAW ME, TOO!
I'LL KILL YOU--!!
...A SUMMER MEMORY THAT WILL NEVER BE FORGOTTEN!
TO BE CONTINUED

ENCOUNTER XXV

A HORROR SHOWDOWN!

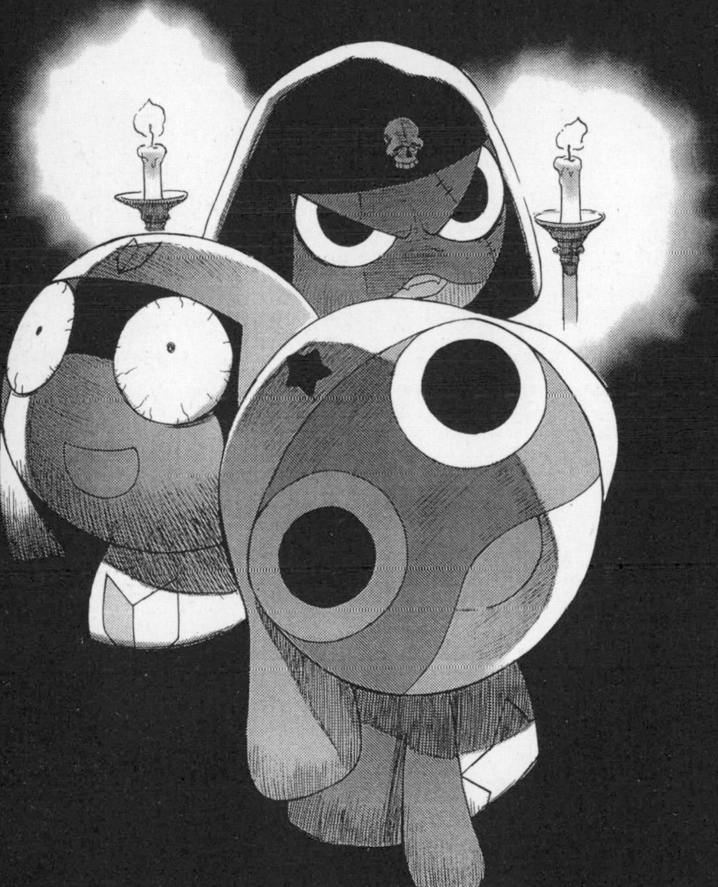

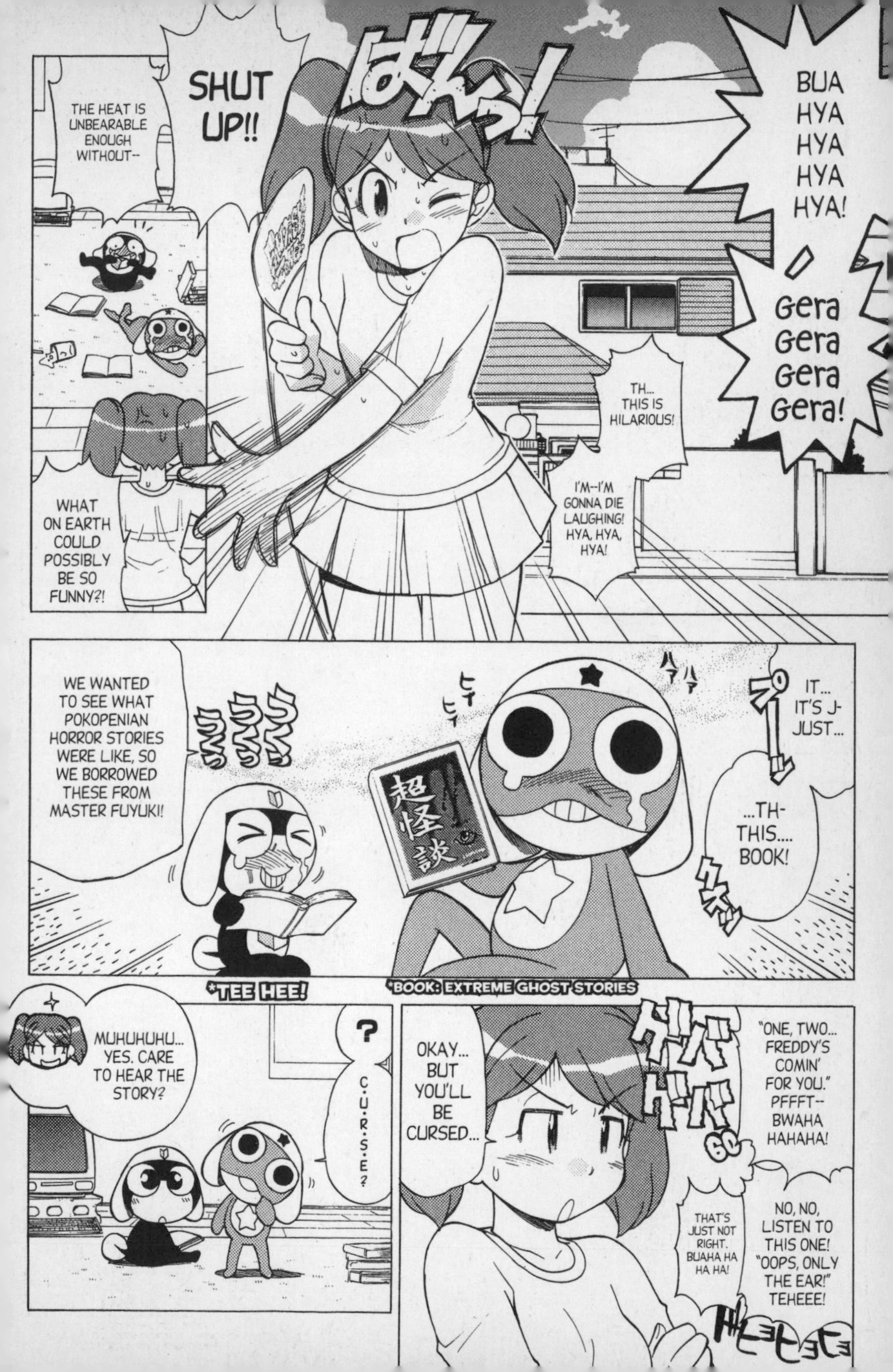

BUA HYA HYA HYA HYA!
Gera Gera Gera Gera!
TH... THIS IS HILARIOUS!
I'M--I'M GONNA DIE LAUGHING! HYA, HYA, HYA!
THE HEAT IS UNBEARABLE ENOUGH WITHOUT--
WHAT ON EARTH COULD POSSIBLY BE SO FUNNY?!
SHUT UP!!
ばんっ!
IT... IT'S J-JUST...
...TH-THIS.... BOOK!
超怪談
WE WANTED TO SEE WHAT POKOPENIAN HORROR STORIES WERE LIKE, SO WE BORROWED THESE FROM MASTER FUYUKI!
*TEE HEE!
*BOOK: EXTREME GHOST STORIES
"ONE, TWO... FREDDY'S COMIN' FOR YOU." PFFFT-- BWAHA HAHAHA!
NO, NO, LISTEN TO THIS ONE! "OOPS, ONLY THE EAR!" TEHEEE!
THAT'S JUST NOT RIGHT. BUAHA HA HA HA!
OKAY... BUT YOU'LL BE CURSED...
?
C·U·R·S·E?
MUHUHUHU... YES. CARE TO HEAR THE STORY?

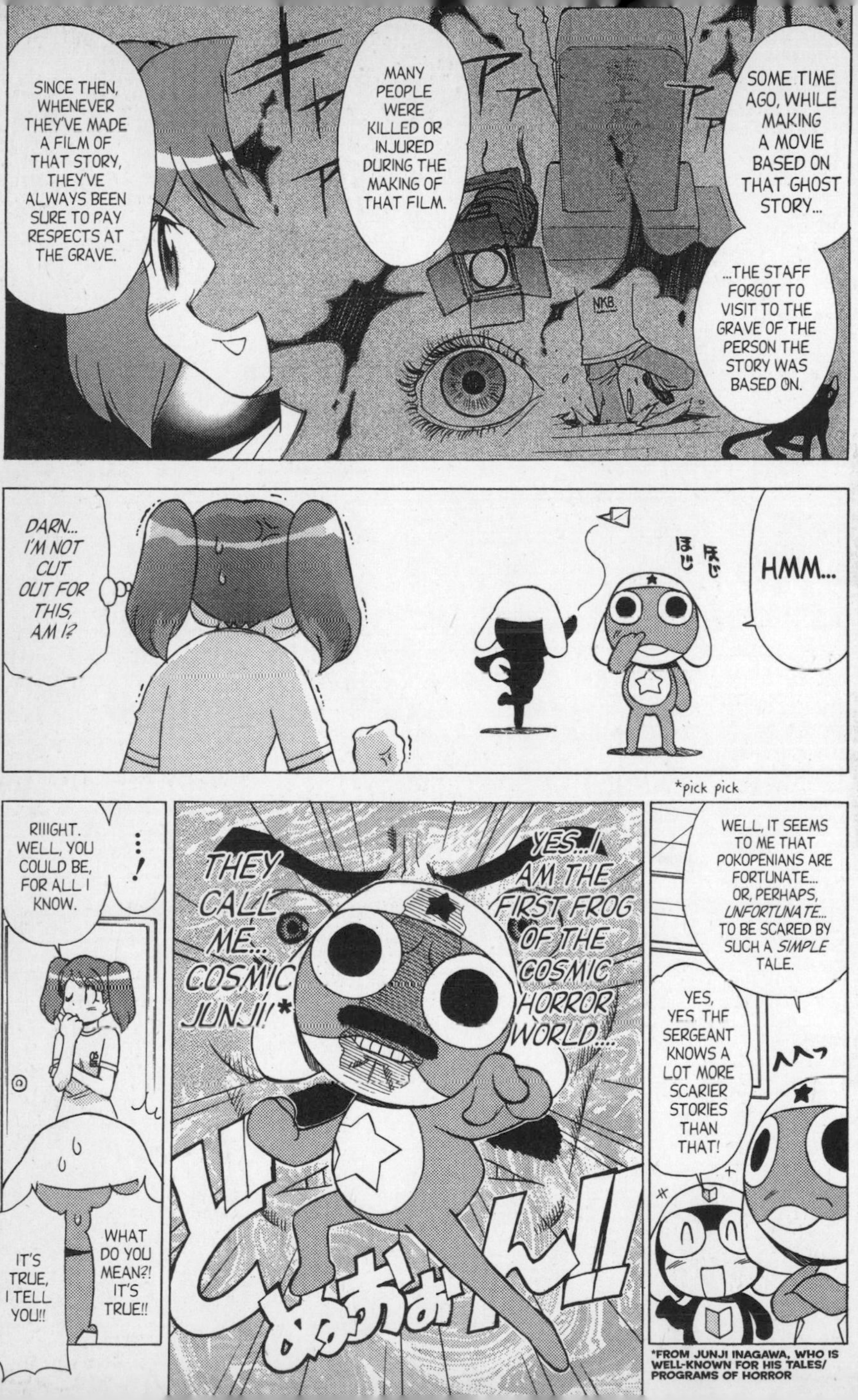
SOME TIME AGO, WHILE MAKING A MOVIE BASED ON THAT GHOST STORY...
...THE STAFF FORGOT TO VISIT TO THE GRAVE OF THE PERSON THE STORY WAS BASED ON.
MANY PEOPLE WERE KILLED OR INJURED DURING THE MAKING OF THAT FILM.
SINCE THEN, WHENEVER THEY'VE MADE A FILM OF THAT STORY, THEY'VE ALWAYS BEEN SURE TO PAY RESPECTS AT THE GRAVE.
NKB
HMM...
ほじ ほじ
*pick pick
DARN... I'M NOT CUT OUT FOR THIS, AM I!?
WELL, IT SEEMS TO ME THAT POKOPENIANS ARE FORTUNATE... OR, PERHAPS, *UNFORTUNATE*... TO BE SCARED BY SUCH A *SIMPLE* TALE.
YES, YES THE SERGEANT KNOWS A LOT MORE SCARIER STORIES THAN THAT!
へへっ
YES...I AM THE FIRST FROG OF THE COSMIC HORROR WORLD....
THEY CALL ME... COSMIC JUNJI!*
RIIIGHT. WELL, YOU COULD BE, FOR ALL I KNOW.
...!
WHAT DO YOU MEAN?! IT'S TRUE!!
IT'S TRUE, I TELL YOU!!

*FROM JUNJI INAGAWA, WHO IS WELL-KNOWN FOR HIS TALES/ PROGRAMS OF HORROR

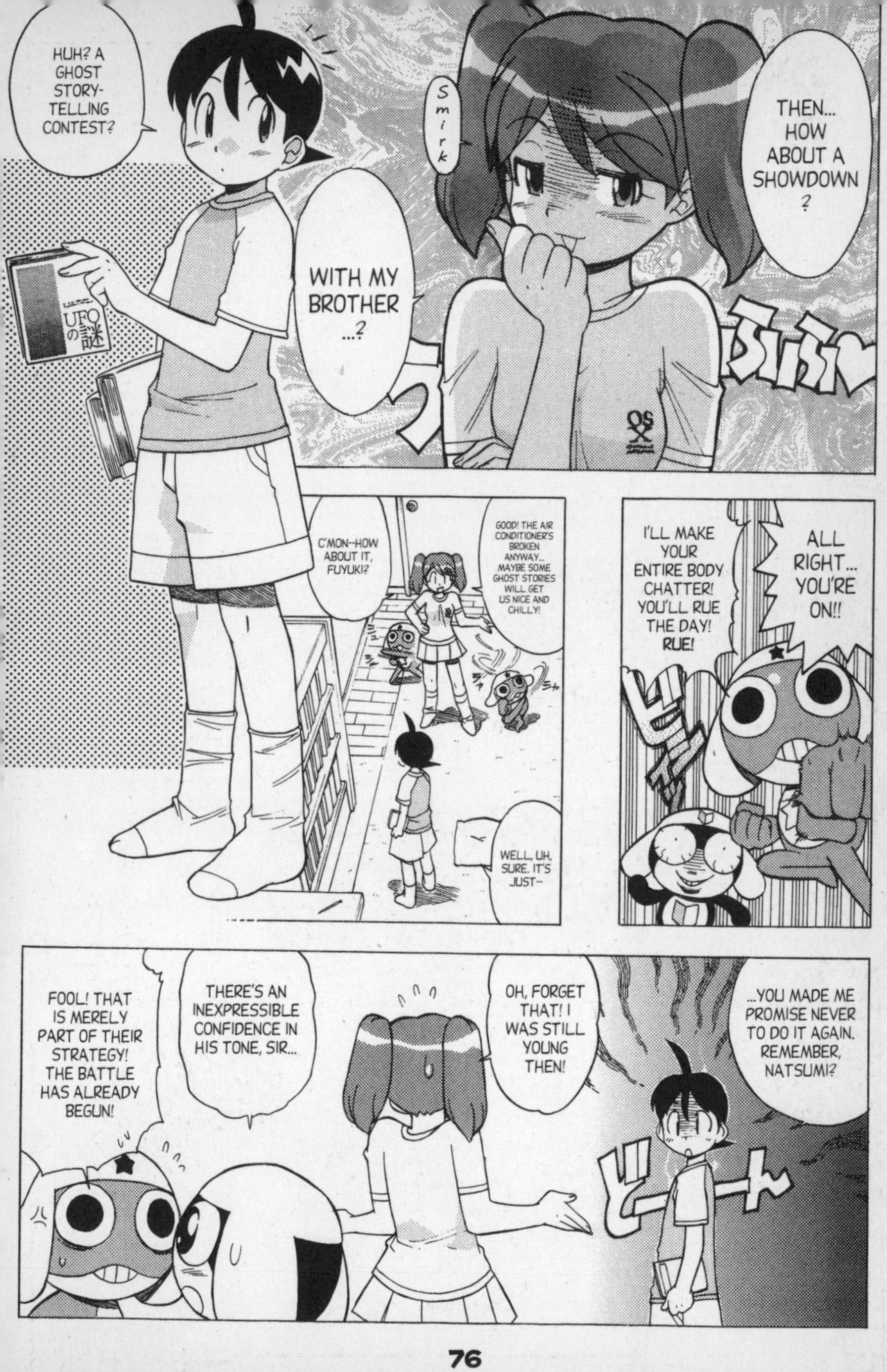
THEN... HOW ABOUT A SHOWDOWN?
Smirk
WITH MY BROTHER ...?
HUH? A GHOST STORY-TELLING CONTEST?
UFOの謎
ALL RIGHT... YOU'RE ON!!
I'LL MAKE YOUR ENTIRE BODY CHATTER! YOU'LL RUE THE DAY! RUE!
GOOD! THE AIR CONDITIONER'S BROKEN ANYWAY... MAYBE SOME GHOST STORIES WILL GET US NICE AND CHILLY!
C'MON--HOW ABOUT IT, FUYUKI?
WELL, UH, SURE. IT'S JUST--
...YOU MADE ME PROMISE NEVER TO DO IT AGAIN. REMEMBER, NATSUMI?
OH, FORGET THAT! I WAS STILL YOUNG THEN!
THERE'S AN INEXPRESSIBLE CONFIDENCE IN HIS TONE, SIR...
FOOL! THAT IS MERELY PART OF THEIR STRATEGY! THE BATTLE HAS ALREADY BEGUN!

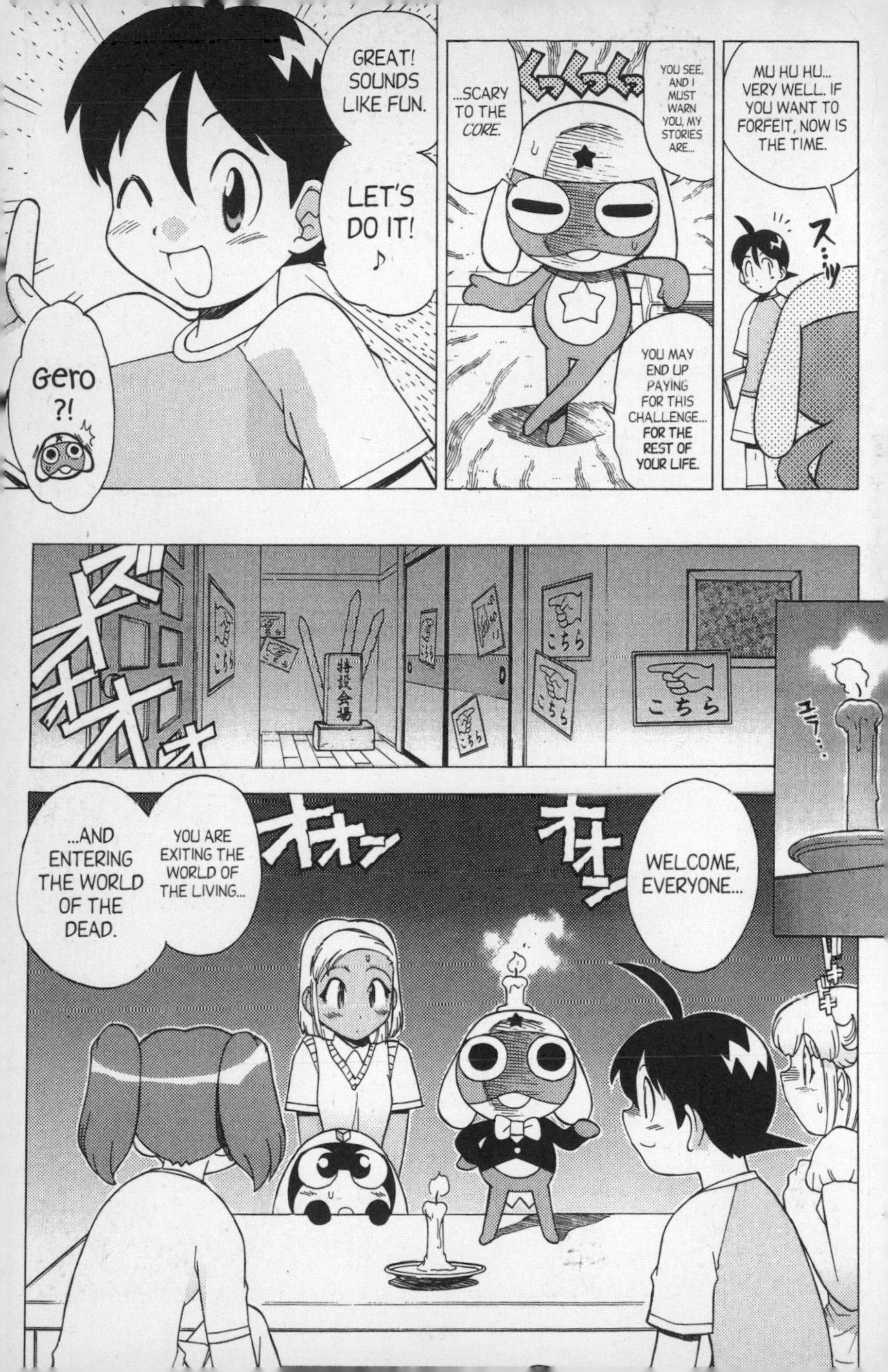
MU HU HU... VERY WELL. IF YOU WANT TO FORFEIT, NOW IS THE TIME.
YOU SEE, AND I MUST WARN YOU, MY STORIES ARE...
...SCARY TO THE CORE.
YOU MAY END UP PAYING FOR THIS CHALLENGE... FOR THE REST OF YOUR LIFE.
GREAT! SOUNDS LIKE FUN.
LET'S DO IT! ♪
Gero ?!
特設会場
こちら
こちら
こちら
WELCOME, EVERYONE...
YOU ARE EXITING THE WORLD OF THE LIVING...
...AND ENTERING THE WORLD OF THE DEAD.

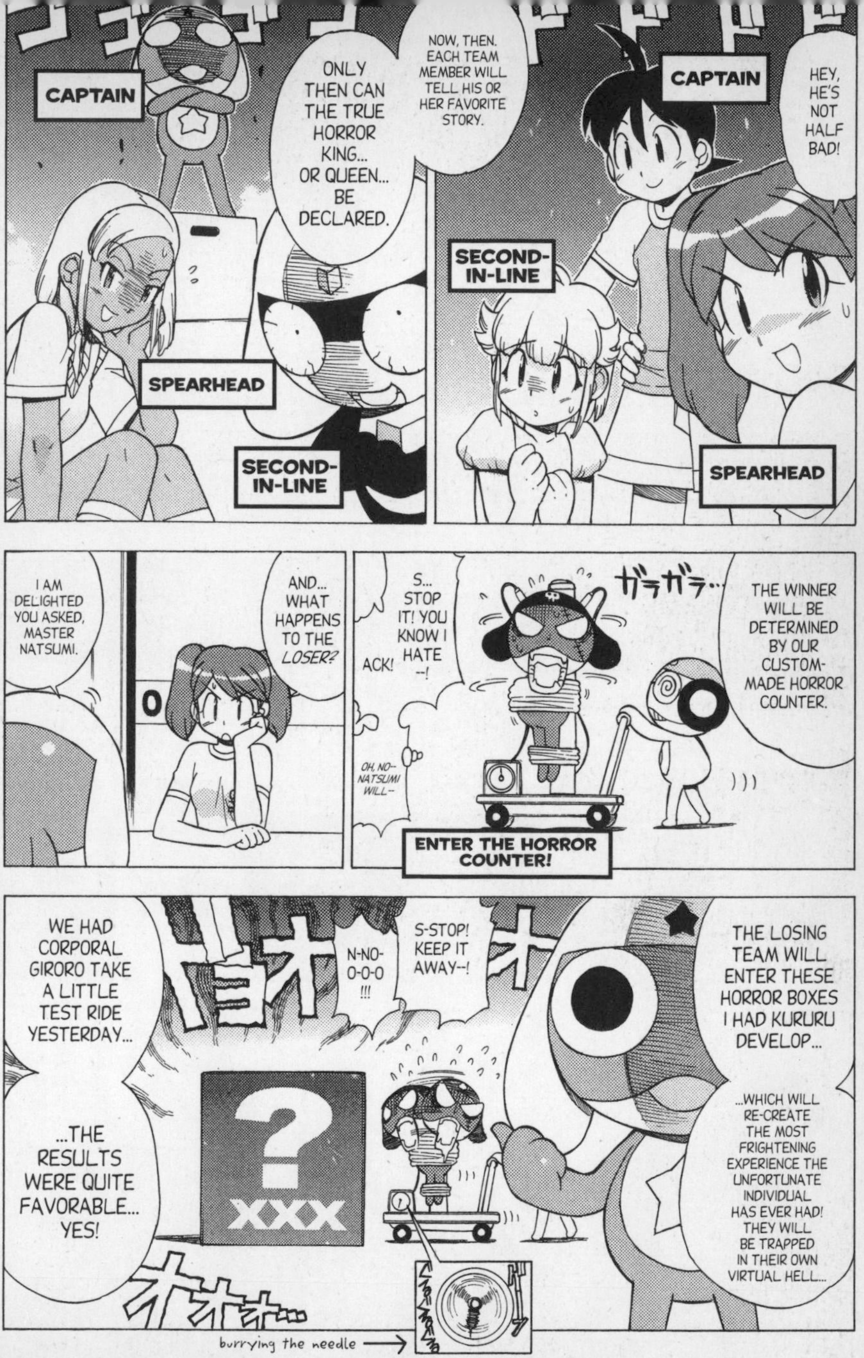

HEY, HE'S NOT HALF BAD!
CAPTAIN
SECOND-IN-LINE
SPEARHEAD
NOW, THEN. EACH TEAM MEMBER WILL TELL HIS OR HER FAVORITE STORY.
ONLY THEN CAN THE TRUE HORROR KING... OR QUEEN... BE DECLARED.
CAPTAIN
SPEARHEAD
SECOND-IN-LINE
THE WINNER WILL BE DETERMINED BY OUR CUSTOM-MADE HORROR COUNTER.
S... STOP IT! YOU KNOW I HATE --!
ACK!
OH, NO-NATSUMI WILL--
ENTER THE HORROR COUNTER!
AND... WHAT HAPPENS TO THE LOSER?
I AM DELIGHTED YOU ASKED, MASTER NATSUMI.
THE LOSING TEAM WILL ENTER THESE HORROR BOXES I HAD KURURU DEVELOP...
...WHICH WILL RE-CREATE THE MOST FRIGHTENING EXPERIENCE THE UNFORTUNATE INDIVIDUAL HAS EVER HAD! THEY WILL BE TRAPPED IN THEIR OWN VIRTUAL HELL...
S-STOP! KEEP IT AWAY--!
N-NO-O-O-O !!!
WE HAD CORPORAL GIRORO TAKE A LITTLE TEST RIDE YESTERDAY...
...THE RESULTS WERE QUITE FAVORABLE... YES!
XXX
burrying the needle

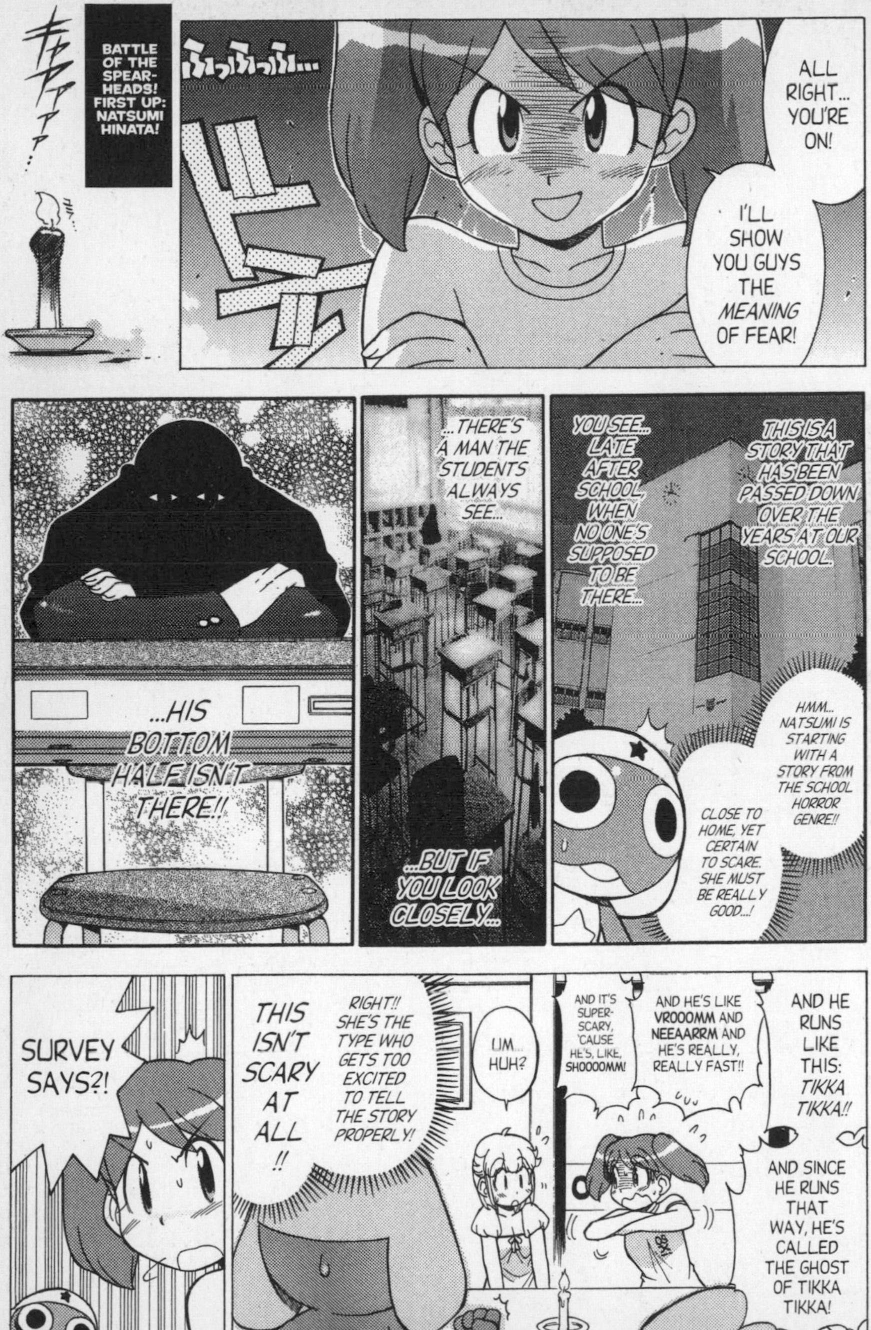
BATTLE OF THE SPEAR-HEADS! FIRST UP: NATSUMI HINATA!
ふっふっふ...
ALL RIGHT... YOU'RE ON!
I'LL SHOW YOU GUYS THE *MEANING* OF FEAR!
THIS IS A STORY THAT HAS BEEN PASSED DOWN OVER THE YEARS AT OUR SCHOOL.
YOU SEE... LATE AFTER SCHOOL, WHEN NO ONE'S SUPPOSED TO BE THERE...
HMM... NATSUMI IS STARTING WITH A STORY FROM THE SCHOOL HORROR GENRE!!
CLOSE TO HOME, YET CERTAIN TO SCARE. SHE MUST BE REALLY GOOD...!
...THERE'S A MAN THE STUDENTS ALWAYS SEE...
...BUT IF YOU LOOK CLOSELY...
...HIS BOTTOM HALF ISN'T THERE!!
AND HE RUNS LIKE THIS: *TIKKA TIKKA!!*
AND HE'S LIKE **VROOOMM** AND **NEEAARRM** AND HE'S REALLY, REALLY FAST!!
AND IT'S SUPER-SCARY, 'CAUSE HE'S, LIKE, **SHOOOOMM!**
AND SINCE HE RUNS THAT WAY, HE'S CALLED THE GHOST OF TIKKA TIKKA!
UM... HUH?
RIGHT!! SHE'S THE TYPE WHO GETS TOO EXCITED TO TELL THE STORY PROPERLY!
THIS ISN'T SCARY AT ALL !!
SURVEY SAYS?!

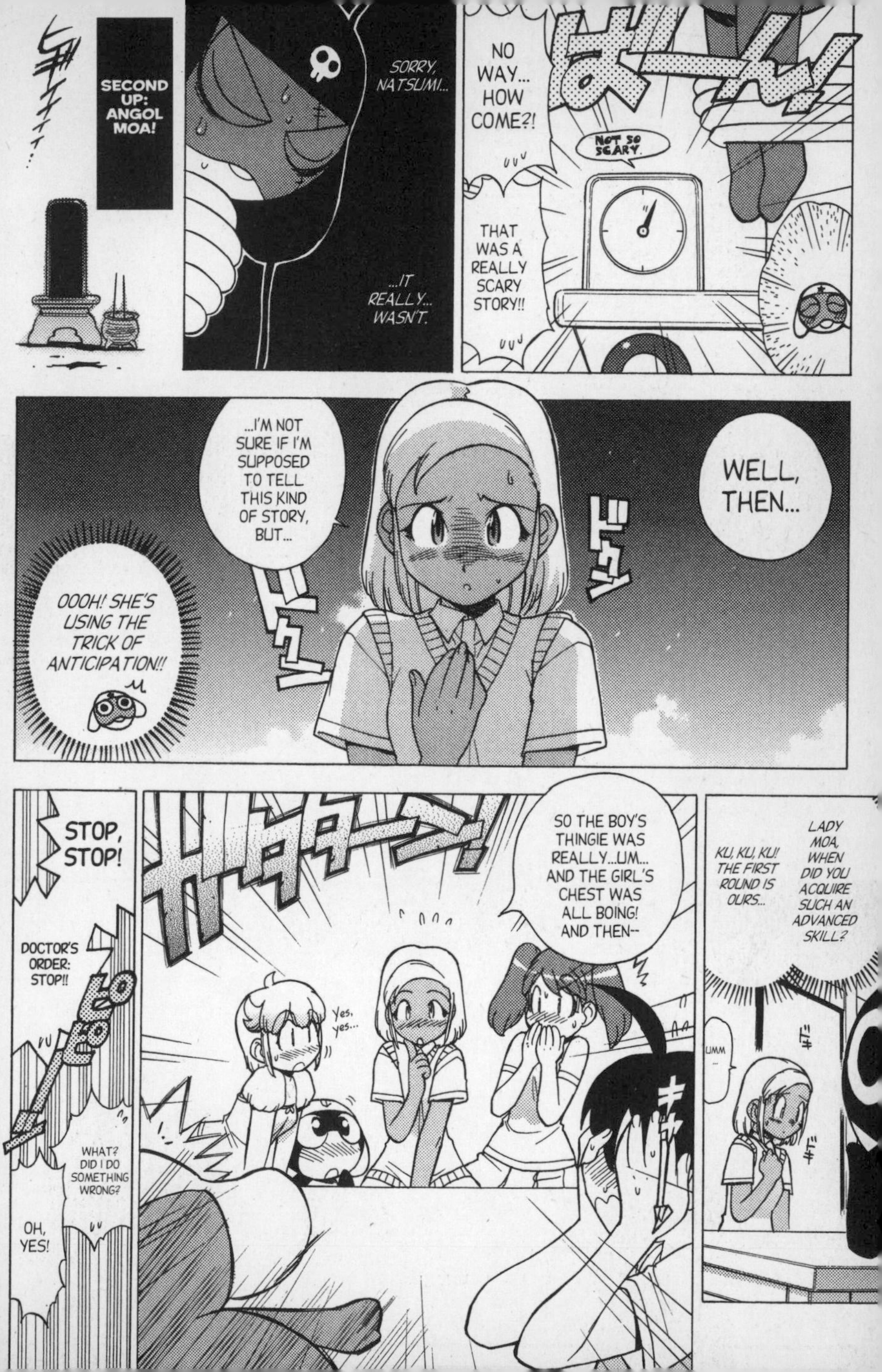

NO WAY... HOW COME?!
NOT SO SCARY.
THAT WAS A REALLY SCARY STORY!!
SORRY, NATSUMI...
...IT REALLY... WASN'T.
SECOND UP: ANGOL MOA!
WELL, THEN...
...I'M NOT SURE IF I'M SUPPOSED TO TELL THIS KIND OF STORY, BUT...
OOOH! SHE'S USING THE TRICK OF ANTICIPATION!!
LADY MOA, WHEN DID YOU ACQUIRE SUCH AN ADVANCED SKILL?
KU, KU, KU! THE FIRST ROUND IS OURS...
UMM ...
SO THE BOY'S THINGIE WAS REALLY...UM... AND THE GIRL'S CHEST WAS ALL BOING! AND THEN--
Yes, yes...
STOP, STOP!
DOCTOR'S ORDER: STOP!!
WHAT? DID I DO SOMETHING WRONG?
OH, YES!

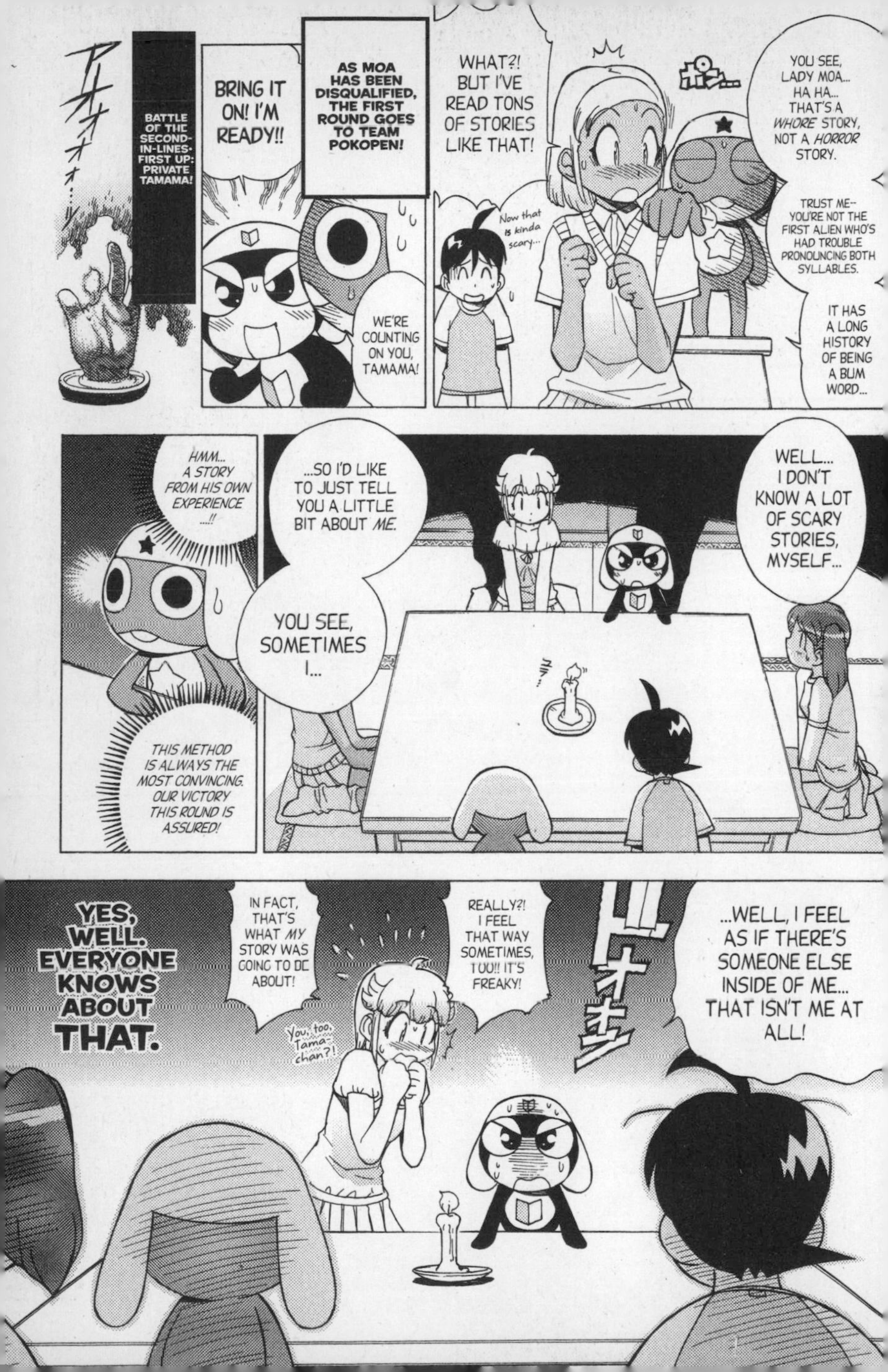

YOU SEE, LADY MOA... HA HA... THAT'S A *WHORE* STORY, NOT A *HORROR* STORY.
TRUST ME-- YOU'RE NOT THE FIRST ALIEN WHO'S HAD TROUBLE PRONOUNCING BOTH SYLLABLES.
IT HAS A LONG HISTORY OF BEING A BUM WORD...
WHAT?! BUT I'VE READ TONS OF STORIES LIKE THAT!
Now that is kinda scary...
AS MOA HAS BEEN DISQUALIFIED, THE FIRST ROUND GOES TO TEAM POKOPEN!
BRING IT ON! I'M READY!!
WE'RE COUNTING ON YOU, TAMAMA!
BATTLE OF THE SECOND-IN-LINES• FIRST UP: PRIVATE TAMAMA!
WELL... I DON'T KNOW A LOT OF SCARY STORIES, MYSELF...
...SO I'D LIKE TO JUST TELL YOU A LITTLE BIT ABOUT *ME*.
YOU SEE, SOMETIMES I...
HMM... A STORY FROM HIS OWN EXPERIENCE ...!!
THIS METHOD IS ALWAYS THE MOST CONVINCING. OUR VICTORY THIS ROUND IS ASSURED!
...WELL, I FEEL AS IF THERE'S SOMEONE ELSE INSIDE OF ME... THAT ISN'T ME AT ALL!
REALLY?! I FEEL THAT WAY SOMETIMES, TOO!! IT'S FREAKY!
IN FACT, THAT'S WHAT *MY* STORY WAS GOING TO BE ABOUT!
You, too, Tama-chan?!
YES, WELL. EVERYONE KNOWS ABOUT THAT.

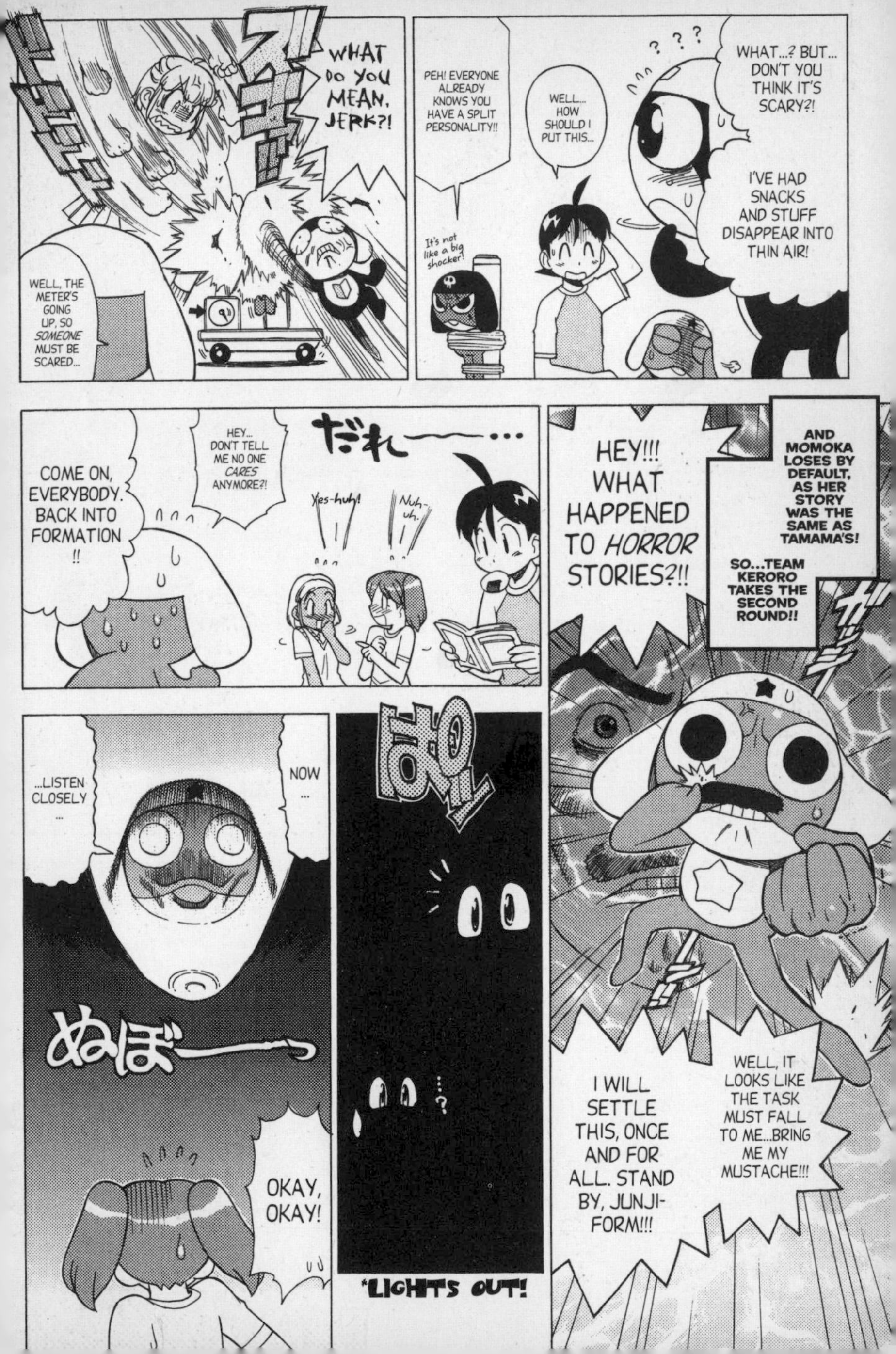

WHAT...? BUT... DON'T YOU THINK IT'S SCARY?!
I'VE HAD SNACKS AND STUFF DISAPPEAR INTO THIN AIR!
WELL... HOW SHOULD I PUT THIS...
PEH! EVERYONE ALREADY KNOWS YOU HAVE A SPLIT PERSONALITY!!
It's not like a big shocker!
WHAT DO YOU MEAN, JERK?!
WELL, THE METER'S GOING UP, SO SOMEONE MUST BE SCARED...
AND MOMOKA LOSES BY DEFAULT, AS HER STORY WAS THE SAME AS TAMAMA'S!
SO...TEAM KERORO TAKES THE SECOND ROUND!!
HEY!!! WHAT HAPPENED TO HORROR STORIES?!!
WELL, IT LOOKS LIKE THE TASK MUST FALL TO ME...BRING ME MY MUSTACHE!!!
I WILL SETTLE THIS, ONCE AND FOR ALL. STAND BY, JUNJI-FORM!!!
HEY... DON'T TELL ME NO ONE CARES ANYMORE?!
だれ——…
Yes-huh!
Nuh-uh.
COME ON, EVERYBODY. BACK INTO FORMATION!!
*LIGHTS OUT!
...?
NOW...
...LISTEN CLOSELY...
ぬぼ——っ
OKAY, OKAY!

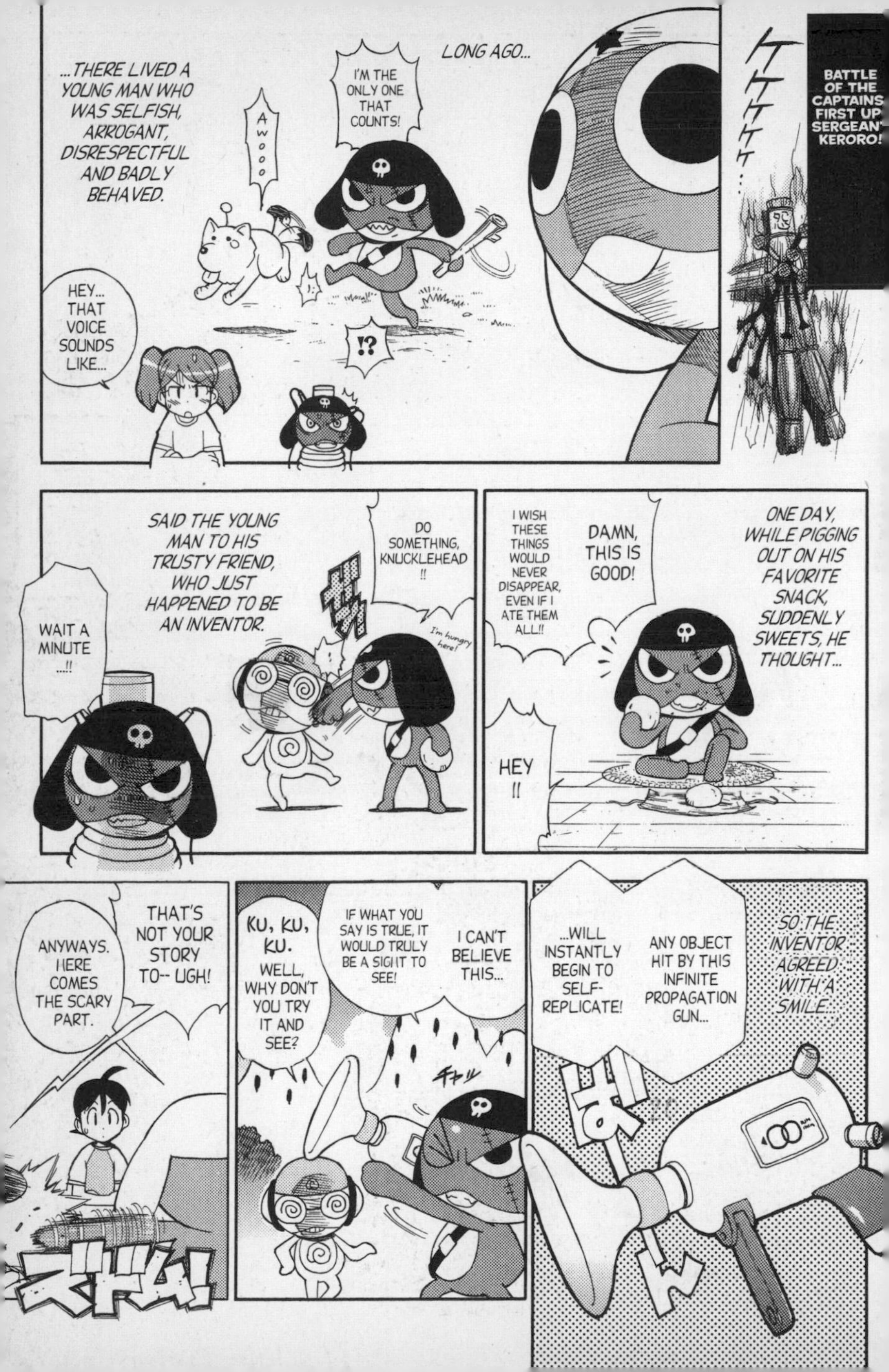
BATTLE OF THE CAPTAINS FIRST UP SERGEANT KERORO!
LONG AGO...
I'M THE ONLY ONE THAT COUNTS!
A W O O O O
...THERE LIVED A YOUNG MAN WHO WAS SELFISH, ARROGANT, DISRESPECTFUL AND BADLY BEHAVED.
!?
HEY... THAT VOICE SOUNDS LIKE...
ONE DAY, WHILE PIGGING OUT ON HIS FAVORITE SNACK, SUDDENLY SWEETS, HE THOUGHT...
DAMN, THIS IS GOOD!
I WISH THESE THINGS WOULD NEVER DISAPPEAR, EVEN IF I ATE THEM ALL!!
HEY !!
DO SOMETHING, KNUCKLEHEAD !!
I'm hungry here!
SAID THE YOUNG MAN TO HIS TRUSTY FRIEND, WHO JUST HAPPENED TO BE AN INVENTOR.
WAIT A MINUTE ....!!
SO THE INVENTOR AGREED WITH A SMILE...
ANY OBJECT HIT BY THIS INFINITE PROPAGATION GUN...
...WILL INSTANTLY BEGIN TO SELF-REPLICATE!
I CAN'T BELIEVE THIS...
IF WHAT YOU SAY IS TRUE, IT WOULD TRULY BE A SIGHT TO SEE!
KU, KU, KU.
WELL, WHY DON'T YOU TRY IT AND SEE?
THAT'S NOT YOUR STORY TO-- UGH!
ANYWAYS. HERE COMES THE SCARY PART.

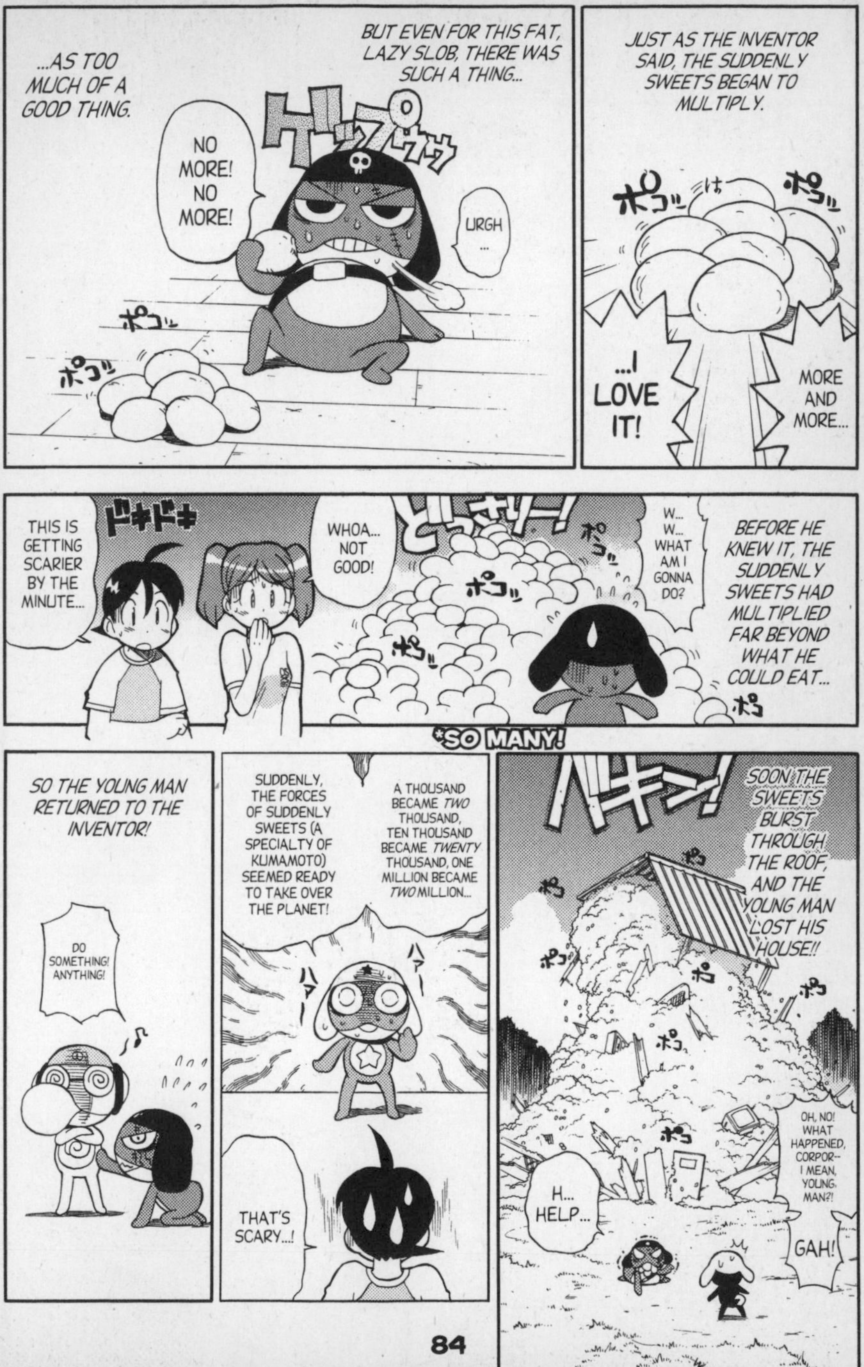
JUST AS THE INVENTOR SAID, THE SUDDENLY SWEETS BEGAN TO MULTIPLY.
ポコッ
は—
ポコッ
MORE AND MORE...
...I LOVE IT!
BUT EVEN FOR THIS FAT, LAZY SLOB, THERE WAS SUCH A THING...
...AS TOO MUCH OF A GOOD THING.
ゲップゥゥ
URGH...
NO MORE! NO MORE!
ポコッ
ポコッ
BEFORE HE KNEW IT, THE SUDDENLY SWEETS HAD MULTIPLIED FAR BEYOND WHAT HE COULD EAT...
W... W... WHAT AM I GONNA DO?
ポコ
ポコッ
ポコッ
ポコッ
WHOA... NOT GOOD!
ドキドキ
THIS IS GETTING SCARIER BY THE MINUTE...
*SO MANY!
SOON THE SWEETS BURST THROUGH THE ROOF, AND THE YOUNG MAN LOST HIS HOUSE!!
OH, NO! WHAT HAPPENED, CORPOR-- I MEAN, YOUNG MAN?!
GAH!
H... HELP...
A THOUSAND BECAME TWO THOUSAND, TEN THOUSAND BECAME TWENTY THOUSAND, ONE MILLION BECAME TWO MILLION...
SUDDENLY, THE FORCES OF SUDDENLY SWEETS (A SPECIALTY OF KUMAMOTO) SEEMED READY TO TAKE OVER THE PLANET!
THAT'S SCARY...!
SO THE YOUNG MAN RETURNED TO THE INVENTOR!
DO SOMETHING! ANYTHING!

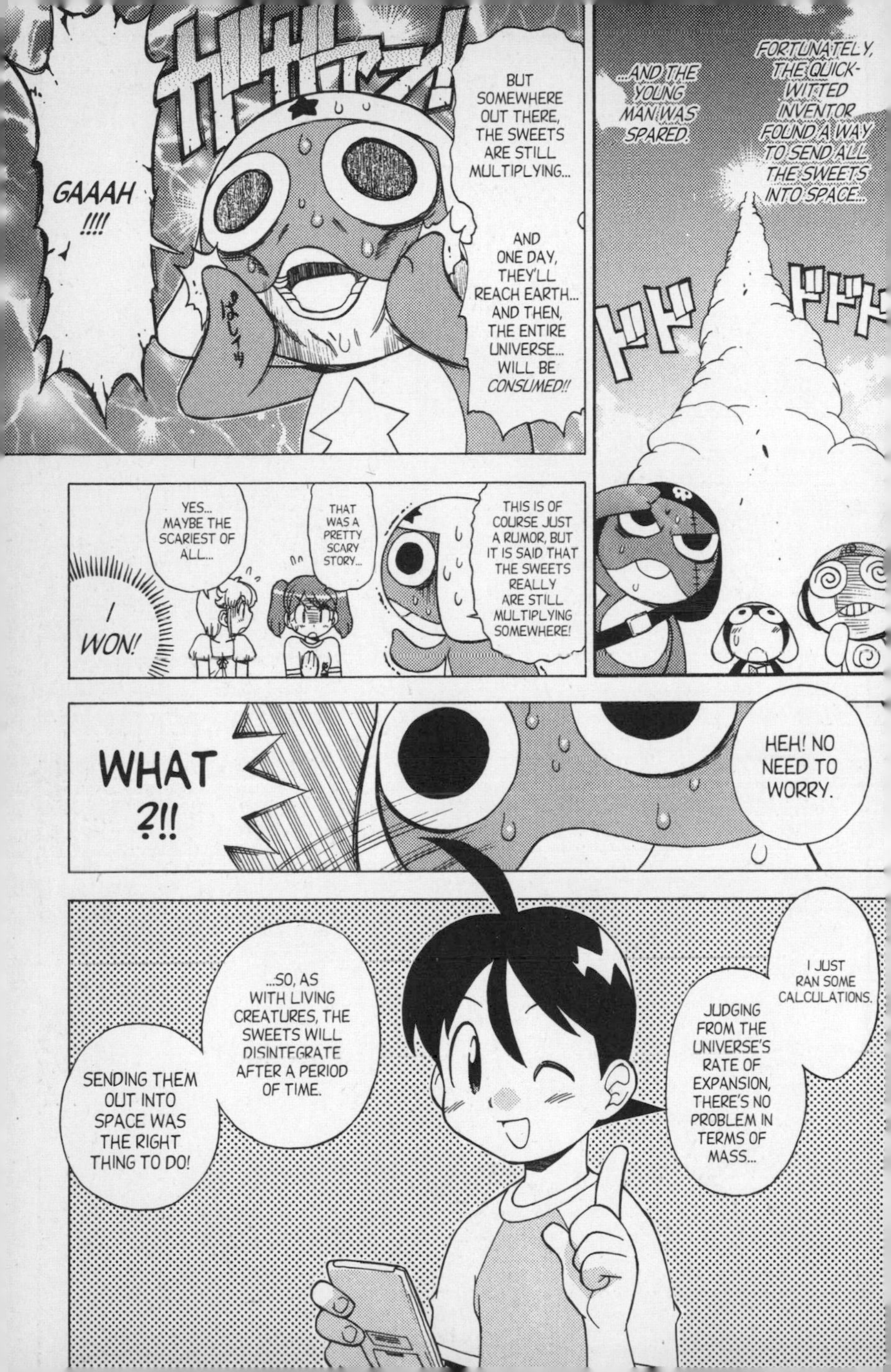
FORTUNATELY, THE QUICK-WITTED INVENTOR FOUND A WAY TO SEND ALL THE SWEETS INTO SPACE...
...AND THE YOUNG MAN WAS SPARED.
ドドド
ドド
BUT SOMEWHERE OUT THERE, THE SWEETS ARE STILL MULTIPLYING...
AND ONE DAY, THEY'LL REACH EARTH... AND THEN, THE ENTIRE UNIVERSE... WILL BE CONSUMED!!
GAAAH !!!!
THIS IS OF COURSE JUST A RUMOR, BUT IT IS SAID THAT THE SWEETS REALLY ARE STILL MULTIPLYING SOMEWHERE!
THAT WAS A PRETTY SCARY STORY...
YES... MAYBE THE SCARIEST OF ALL...
I WON!
HEH! NO NEED TO WORRY.
WHAT ?!!
I JUST RAN SOME CALCULATIONS.
JUDGING FROM THE UNIVERSE'S RATE OF EXPANSION, THERE'S NO PROBLEM IN TERMS OF MASS...
...SO, AS WITH LIVING CREATURES, THE SWEETS WILL DISINTEGRATE AFTER A PERIOD OF TIME.
SENDING THEM OUT INTO SPACE WAS THE RIGHT THING TO DO!

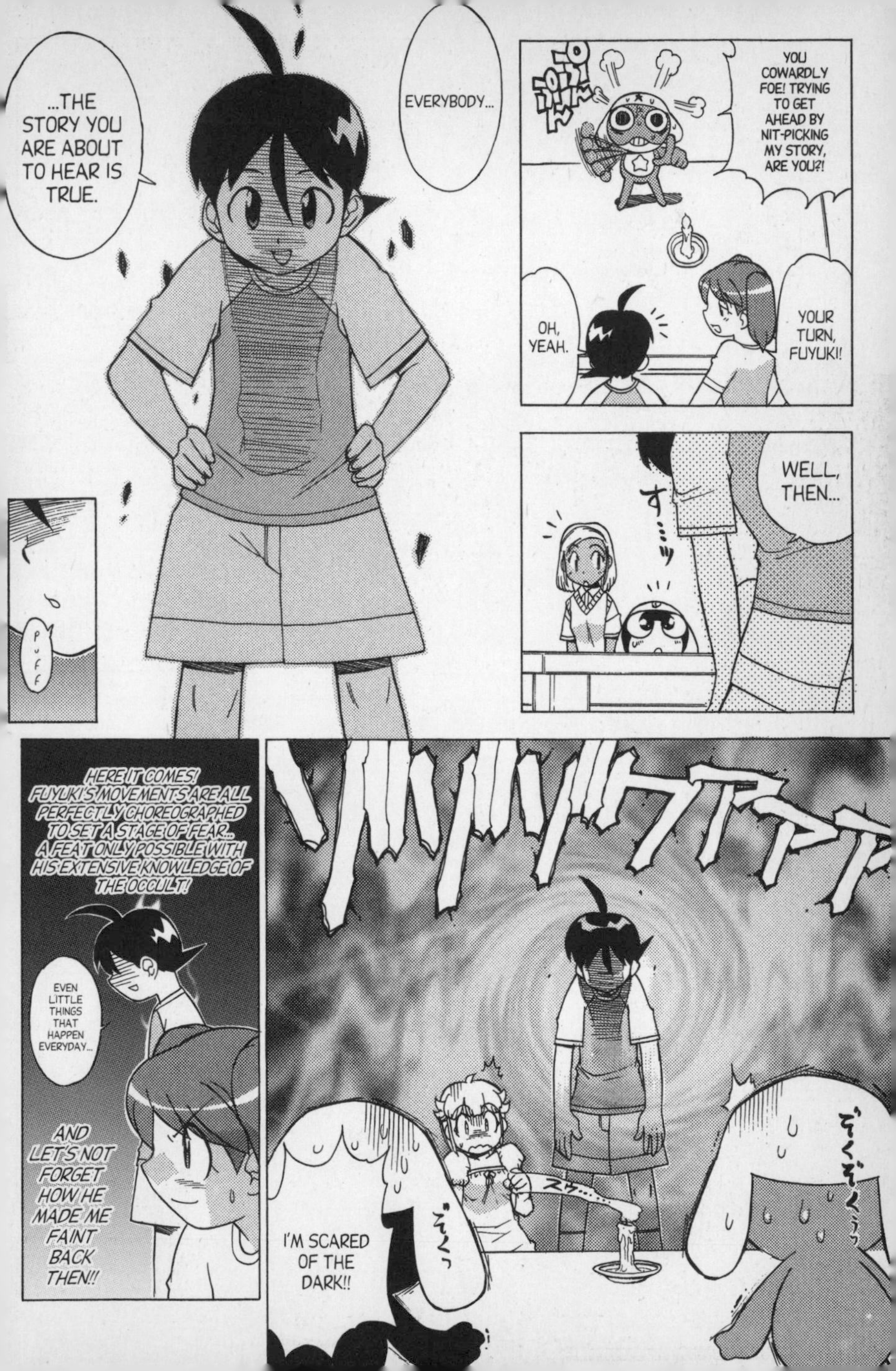
YOU COWARDLY FOE! TRYING TO GET AHEAD BY NIT-PICKING MY STORY, ARE YOU?!
YOUR TURN, FUYUKI!
OH, YEAH.
WELL, THEN...
EVERYBODY...
...THE STORY YOU ARE ABOUT TO HEAR IS TRUE.
puff
I'M SCARED OF THE DARK!!
HERE IT COMES! FUYUKI'S MOVEMENTS ARE ALL PERFECTLY CHOREOGRAPHED TO SET A STAGE OF FEAR... A FEAT ONLY POSSIBLE WITH HIS EXTENSIVE KNOWLEDGE OF THE OCCULT!
EVEN LITTLE THINGS THAT HAPPEN EVERYDAY...
AND LET'S NOT FORGET HOW HE MADE ME FAINT BACK THEN!!

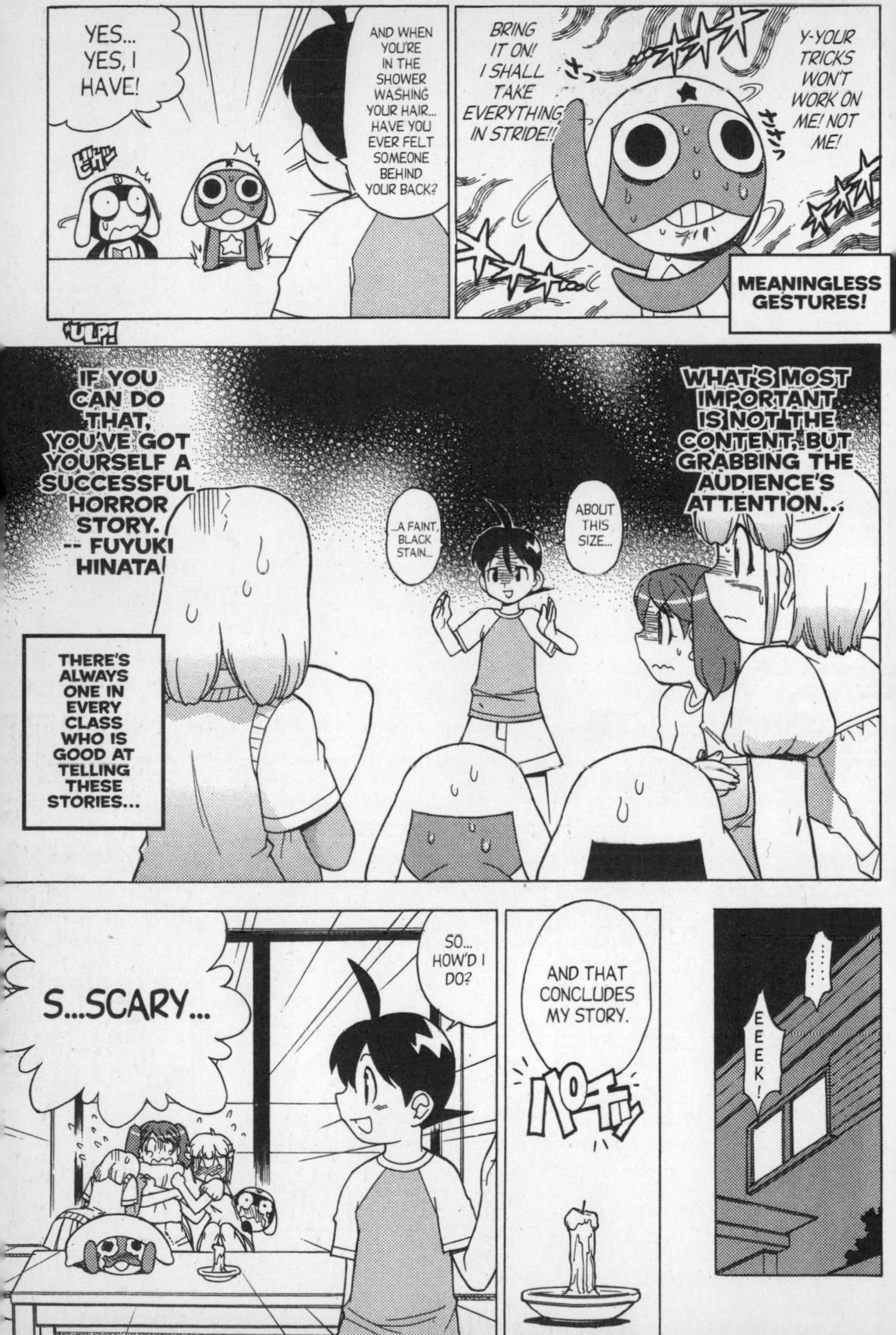

BRING IT ON! I SHALL TAKE EVERYTHING IN STRIDE!!
Y-YOUR TRICKS WON'T WORK ON ME! NOT ME!
MEANINGLESS GESTURES!
AND WHEN YOU'RE IN THE SHOWER WASHING YOUR HAIR... HAVE YOU EVER FELT SOMEONE BEHIND YOUR BACK?
YES... YES, I HAVE!
ULP!
WHAT'S MOST IMPORTANT IS NOT THE CONTENT, BUT GRABBING THE AUDIENCE'S ATTENTION...
ABOUT THIS SIZE...
...A FAINT, BLACK STAIN...
IF YOU CAN DO THAT, YOU'VE GOT YOURSELF A SUCCESSFUL HORROR STORY. -- FUYUKI HINATA
THERE'S ALWAYS ONE IN EVERY CLASS WHO IS GOOD AT TELLING THESE STORIES...
EEEK!
AND THAT CONCLUDES MY STORY.
SO... HOW'D I DO?
S...SCARY...

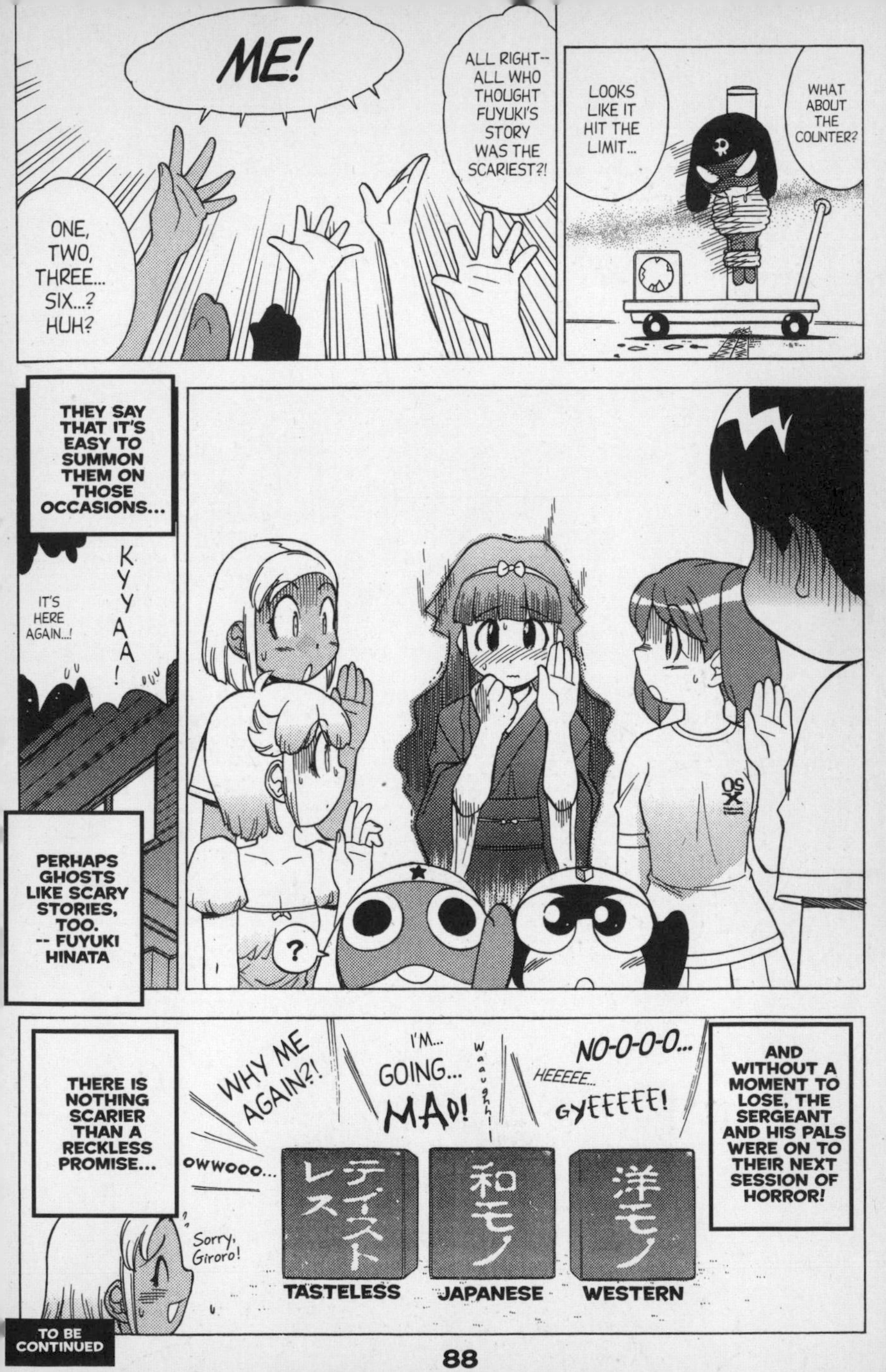

WHAT ABOUT THE COUNTER?
LOOKS LIKE IT HIT THE LIMIT...
ALL RIGHT-- ALL WHO THOUGHT FUYUKI'S STORY WAS THE SCARIEST?!
ME!
ONE, TWO, THREE... SIX...? HUH?
THEY SAY THAT IT'S EASY TO SUMMON THEM ON THOSE OCCASIONS...
KYYAA!
IT'S HERE AGAIN...!
?
PERHAPS GHOSTS LIKE SCARY STORIES, TOO. -- FUYUKI HINATA
AND WITHOUT A MOMENT TO LOSE, THE SERGEANT AND HIS PALS WERE ON TO THEIR NEXT SESSION OF HORROR!
NO-O-O-O...
HEEEEE...
GYEEEEE!
I'M... GOING... MAD!
Waaugh!
WHY ME AGAIN?!
OWWOOO...
THERE IS NOTHING SCARIER THAN A RECKLESS PROMISE...
テイストレス
和モノ
洋モノ
TASTELESS
JAPANESE
WESTERN
Sorry, Giroro!
TO BE CONTINUED

ENCOUNTER XXVI

LADY MOA GROWS UP FAST

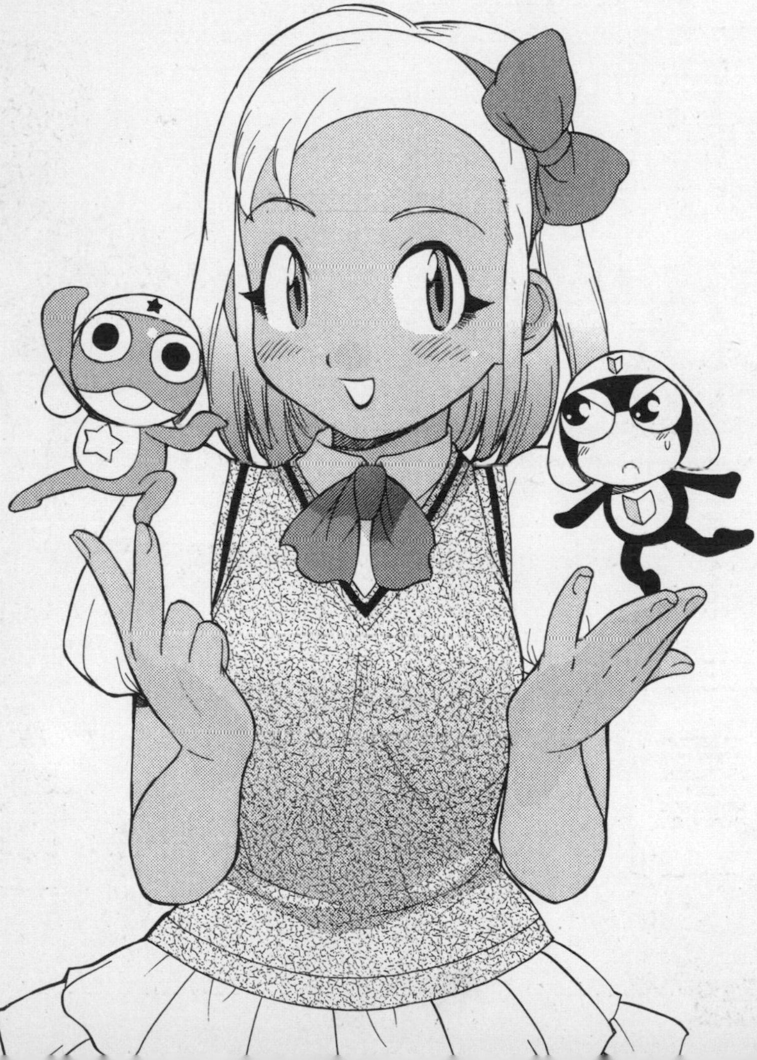

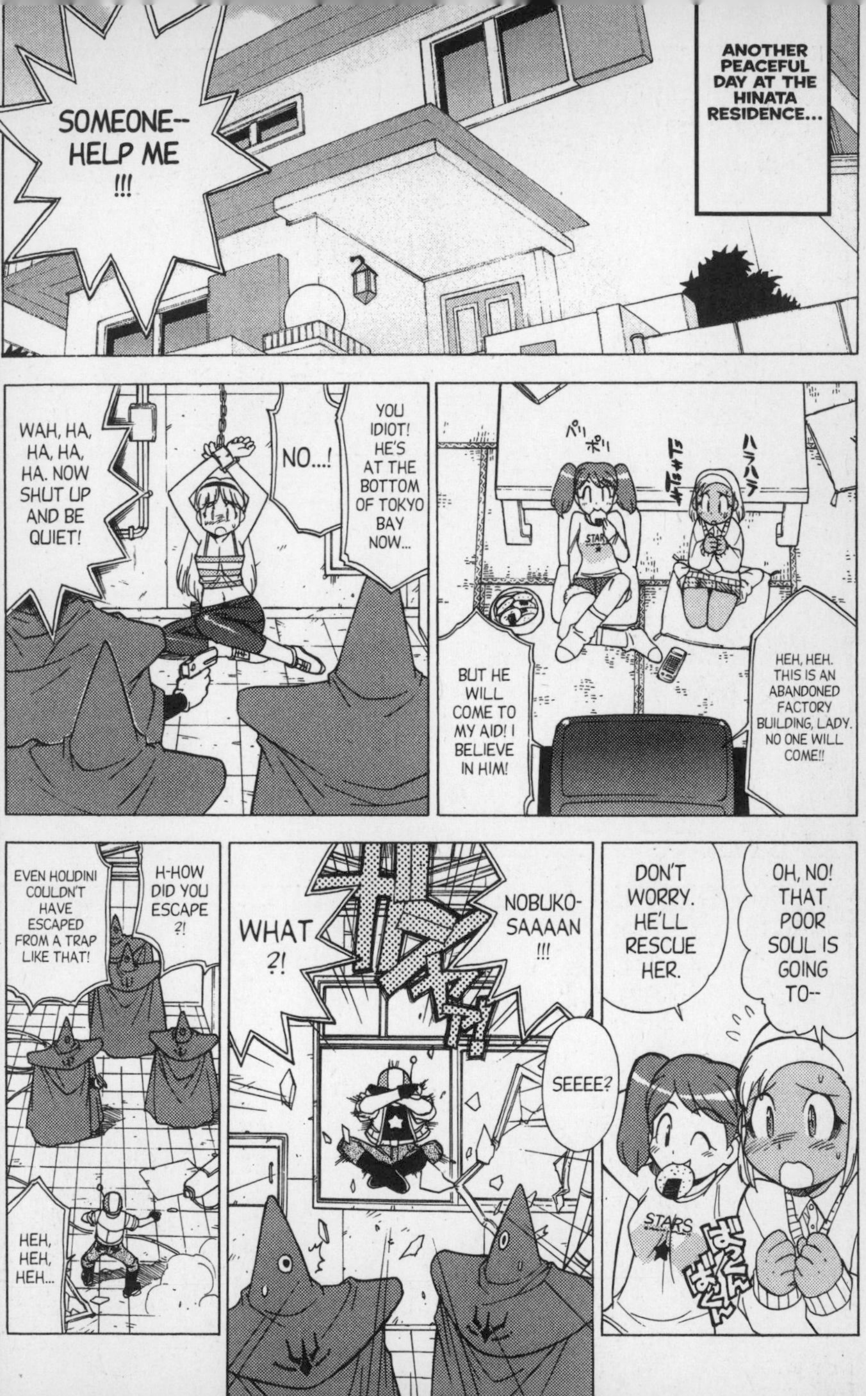
ANOTHER PEACEFUL DAY AT THE HINATA RESIDENCE...
SOMEONE-- HELP ME !!!
HEH, HEH. THIS IS AN ABANDONED FACTORY BUILDING, LADY. NO ONE WILL COME!!
BUT HE WILL COME TO MY AID! I BELIEVE IN HIM!
ハラハラ
パリポリ
STARS
YOU IDIOT! HE'S AT THE BOTTOM OF TOKYO BAY NOW...
NO...!
WAH, HA, HA, HA, HA. NOW SHUT UP AND BE QUIET!
OH, NO! THAT POOR SOUL IS GOING TO--
DON'T WORRY. HE'LL RESCUE HER.
SEEEE?
STARS
NOBUKO-SAAAAN !!!
WHAT ?!
H-HOW DID YOU ESCAPE ?!
EVEN HOUDINI COULDN'T HAVE ESCAPED FROM A TRAP LIKE THAT!
HEH, HEH, HEH...

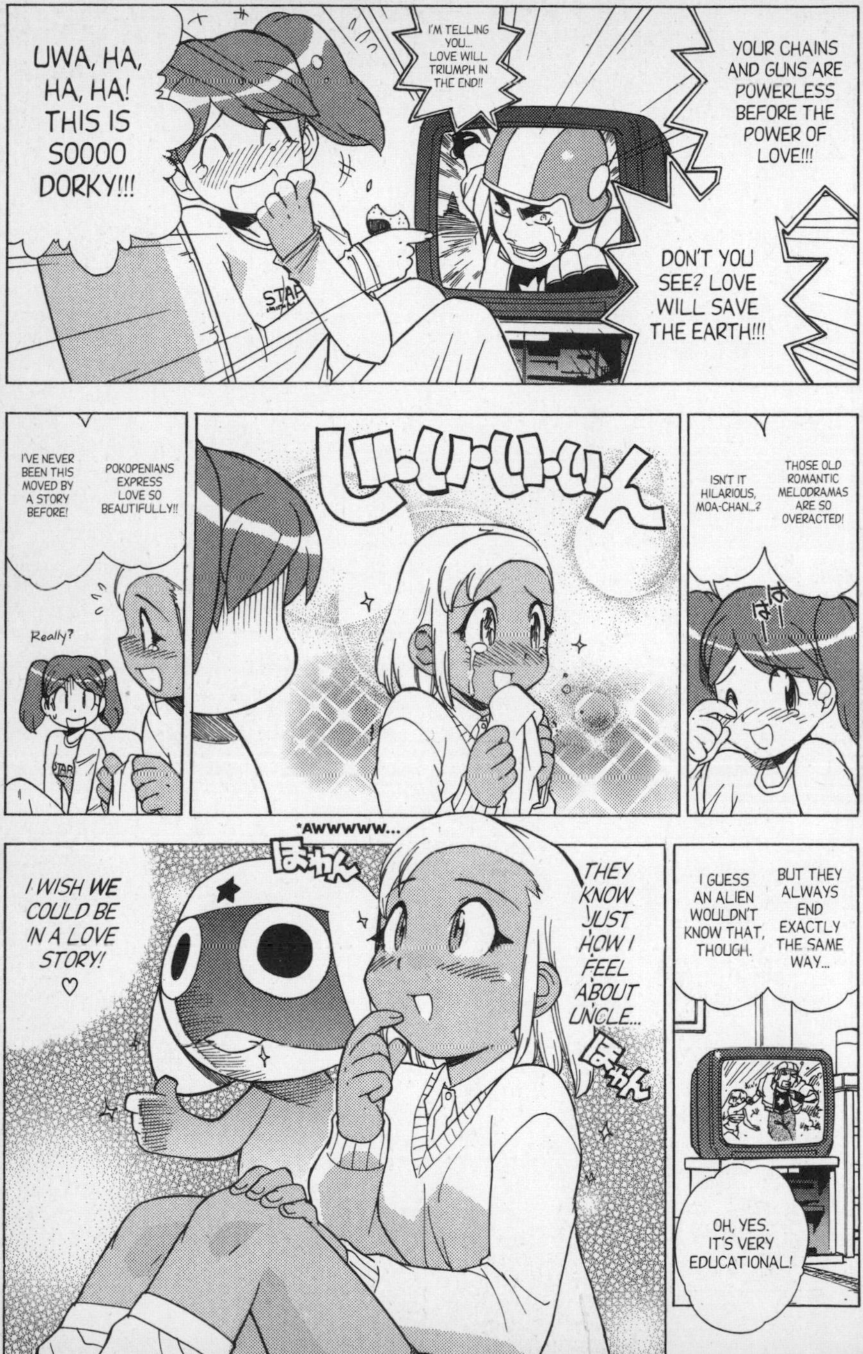
YOUR CHAINS AND GUNS ARE POWERLESS BEFORE THE POWER OF LOVE!!!
I'M TELLING YOU... LOVE WILL TRIUMPH IN THE END!!
DON'T YOU SEE? LOVE WILL SAVE THE EARTH!!!
UWA, HA, HA, HA! THIS IS SOOOO DORKY!!!
THOSE OLD ROMANTIC MELODRAMAS ARE SO OVERACTED!
ISN'T IT HILARIOUS, MOA-CHAN...?
POKOPENIANS EXPRESS LOVE SO BEAUTIFULLY!!
I'VE NEVER BEEN THIS MOVED BY A STORY BEFORE!
Really?
BUT THEY ALWAYS END EXACTLY THE SAME WAY...
I GUESS AN ALIEN WOULDN'T KNOW THAT, THOUGH.
OH, YES. IT'S VERY EDUCATIONAL!
*AWWWWW...
THEY KNOW JUST HOW I FEEL ABOUT UNCLE...
I WISH WE COULD BE IN A LOVE STORY! ♡

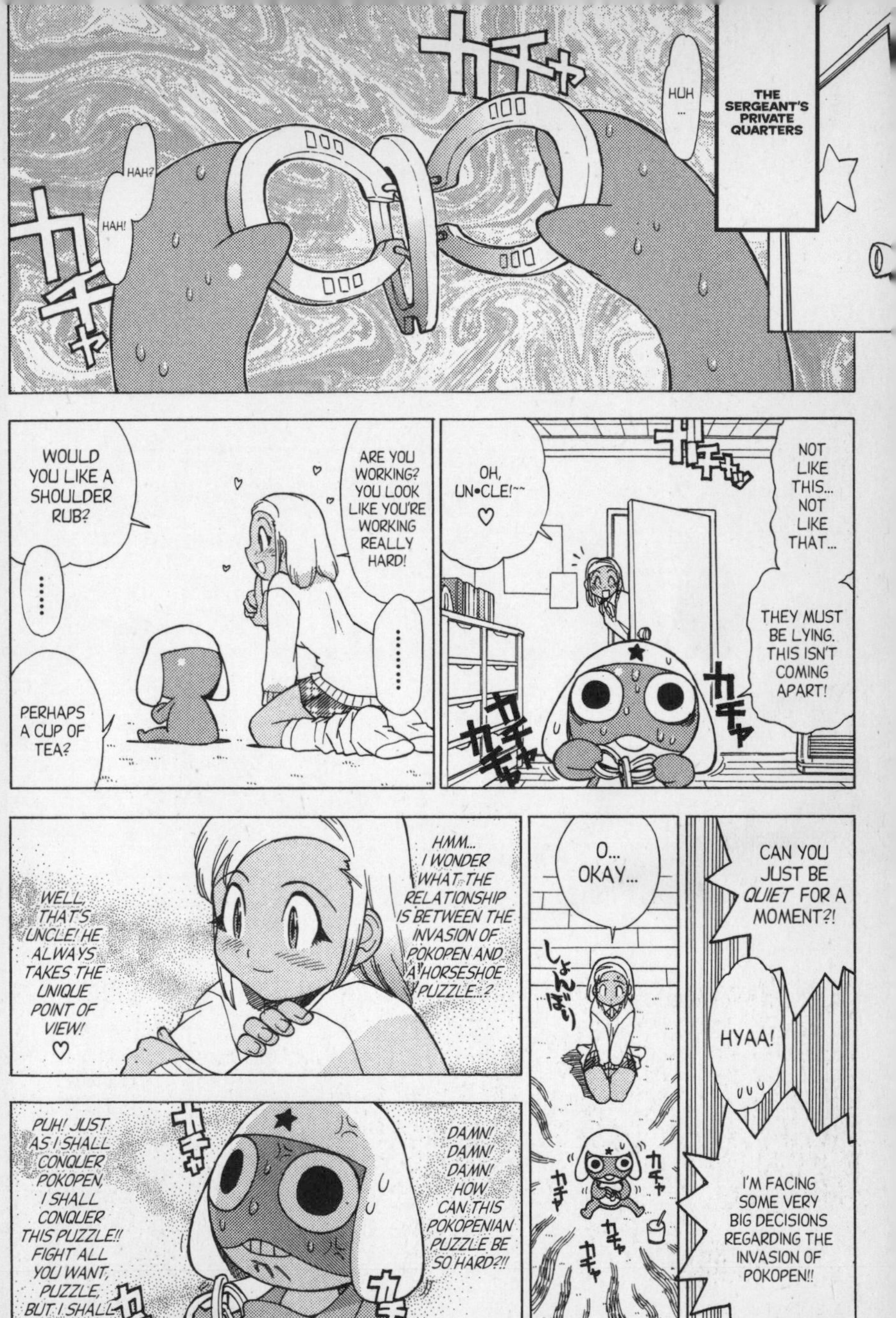
THE SERGEANT'S PRIVATE QUARTERS
カチャ
HUH ...
HAH?
HAH!
カチャ
NOT LIKE THIS... NOT LIKE THAT...
THEY MUST BE LYING. THIS ISN'T COMING APART!
OH, UN•CLE!~~ ♡
カチャ
ARE YOU WORKING? YOU LOOK LIKE YOU'RE WORKING REALLY HARD!
......
WOULD YOU LIKE A SHOULDER RUB?
......
PERHAPS A CUP OF TEA?
CAN YOU JUST BE QUIET FOR A MOMENT?!
HYAA!
I'M FACING SOME VERY BIG DECISIONS REGARDING THE INVASION OF POKOPEN!!
O... OKAY...
しょんぼり
カチャ
HMM... I WONDER WHAT THE RELATIONSHIP IS BETWEEN THE INVASION OF POKOPEN AND A HORSESHOE PUZZLE...?
WELL, THAT'S UNCLE! HE ALWAYS TAKES THE UNIQUE POINT OF VIEW! ♡
DAMN! DAMN! DAMN! HOW CAN THIS POKOPENIAN PUZZLE BE SO HARD?!!
PUH! JUST AS I SHALL CONQUER POKOPEN, I SHALL CONQUER THIS PUZZLE!! FIGHT ALL YOU WANT, PUZZLE, BUT I SHALL PREVAIL...!
カチャ

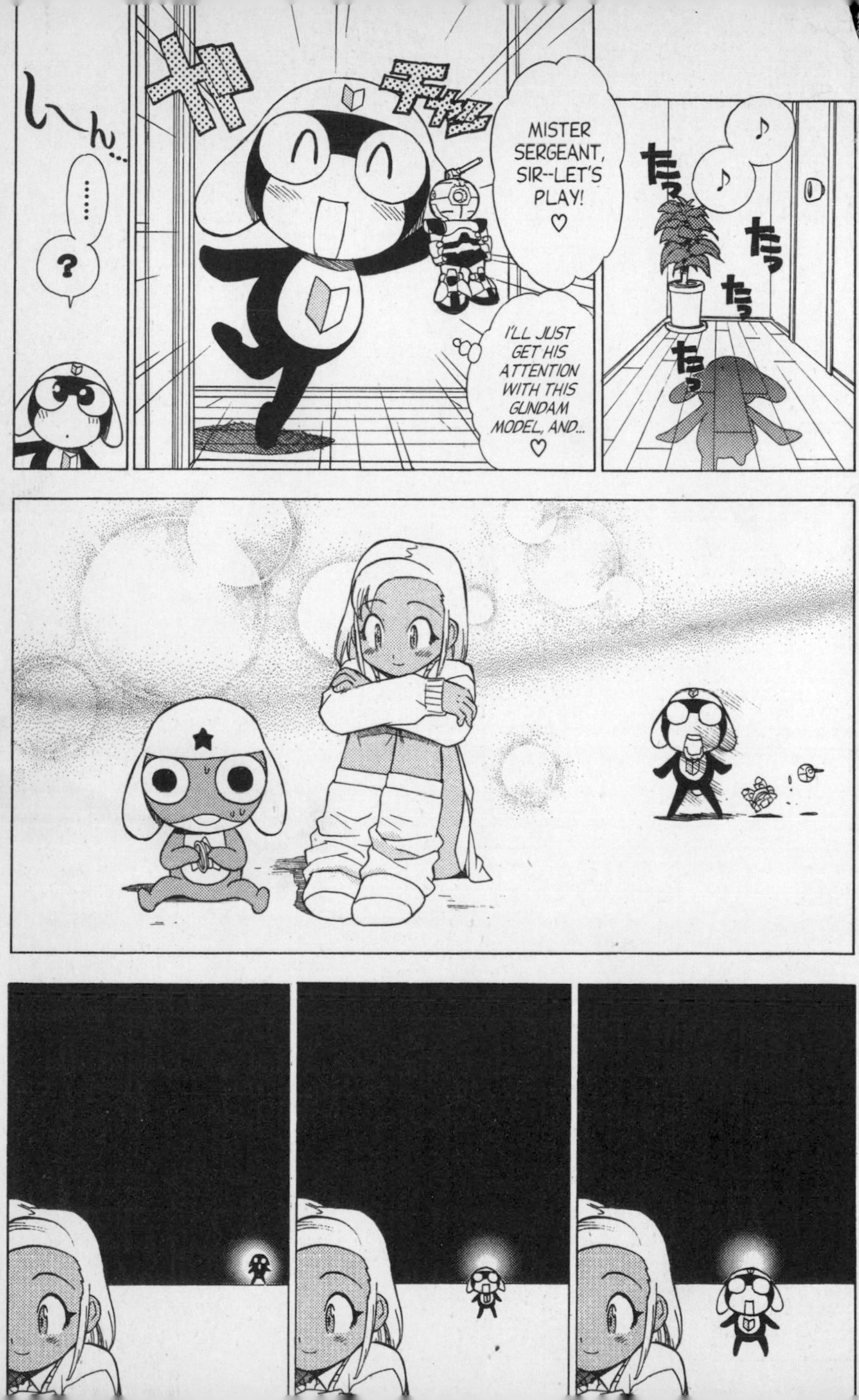
♪
♪
たっ
たっ
たっ
たっ
ガチャ
MISTER SERGEANT, SIR--LET'S PLAY! ♡
I'LL JUST GET HIS ATTENTION WITH THIS GUNDAM MODEL, AND... ♡
し～ん...
......
?

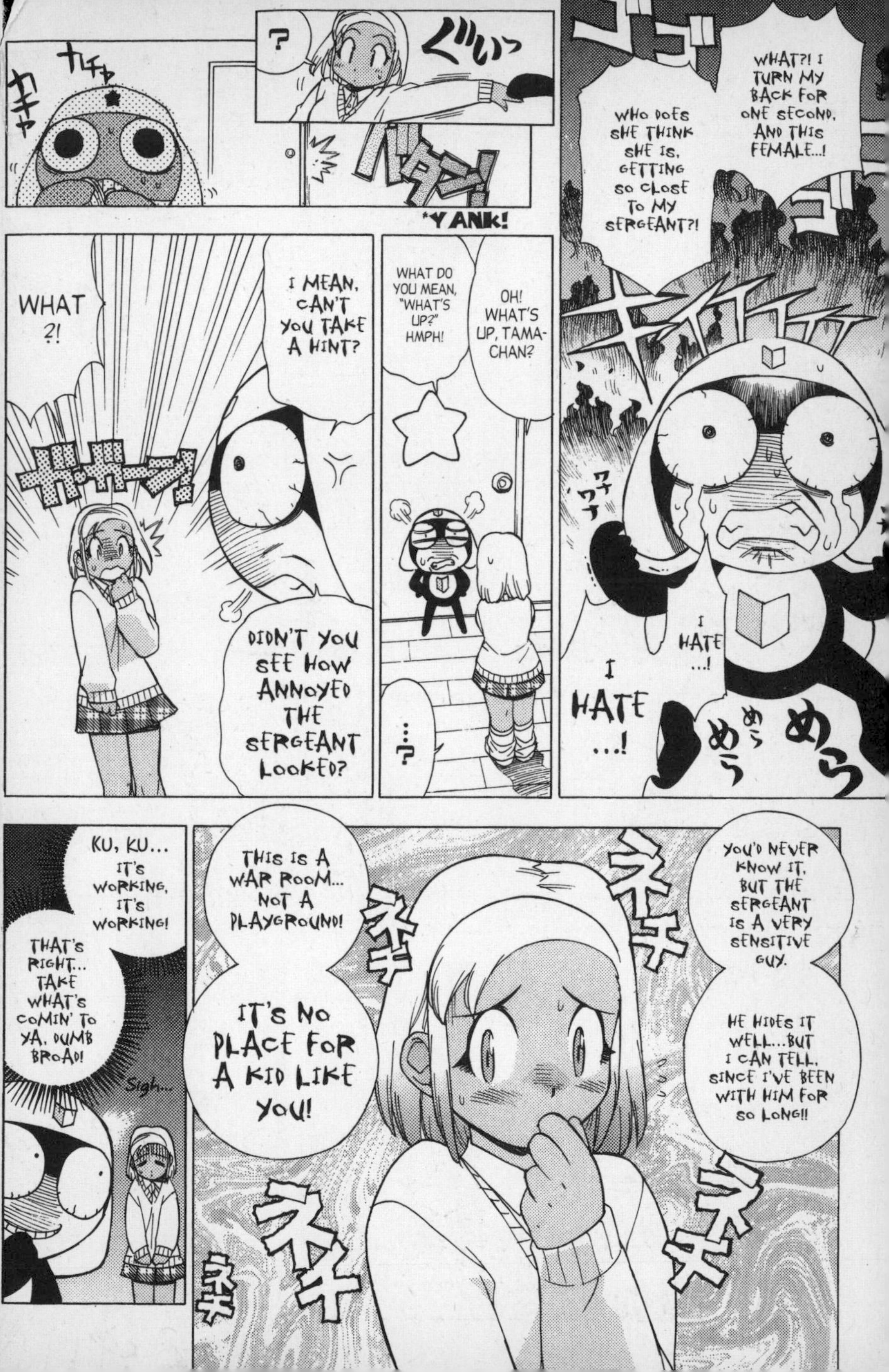
WHAT?! I TURN MY BACK FOR ONE SECOND, AND THIS FEMALE...!
WHO DOES SHE THINK SHE IS, GETTING SO CLOSE TO MY SERGEANT?!
?
*YANK!
OH! WHAT'S UP, TAMA-CHAN?
WHAT DO YOU MEAN, "WHAT'S UP?" HMPH!
...?
I HATE...!
I HATE...!
めらめら
めらめら
I MEAN, CAN'T YOU TAKE A HINT?
DIDN'T YOU SEE HOW ANNOYED THE SERGEANT LOOKED?
WHAT ?!
YOU'D NEVER KNOW IT, BUT THE SERGEANT IS A VERY SENSITIVE GUY.
HE HIDES IT WELL...BUT I CAN TELL, SINCE I'VE BEEN WITH HIM FOR SO LONG!!
THIS IS A WAR ROOM... NOT A PLAYGROUND!
IT'S NO PLACE FOR A KID LIKE YOU!
ネチ
ネチ
ネチ
ネチ
KU, KU... IT'S WORKING, IT'S WORKING!
THAT'S RIGHT... TAKE WHAT'S COMIN' TO YA, DUMB BROAD!
Sigh...

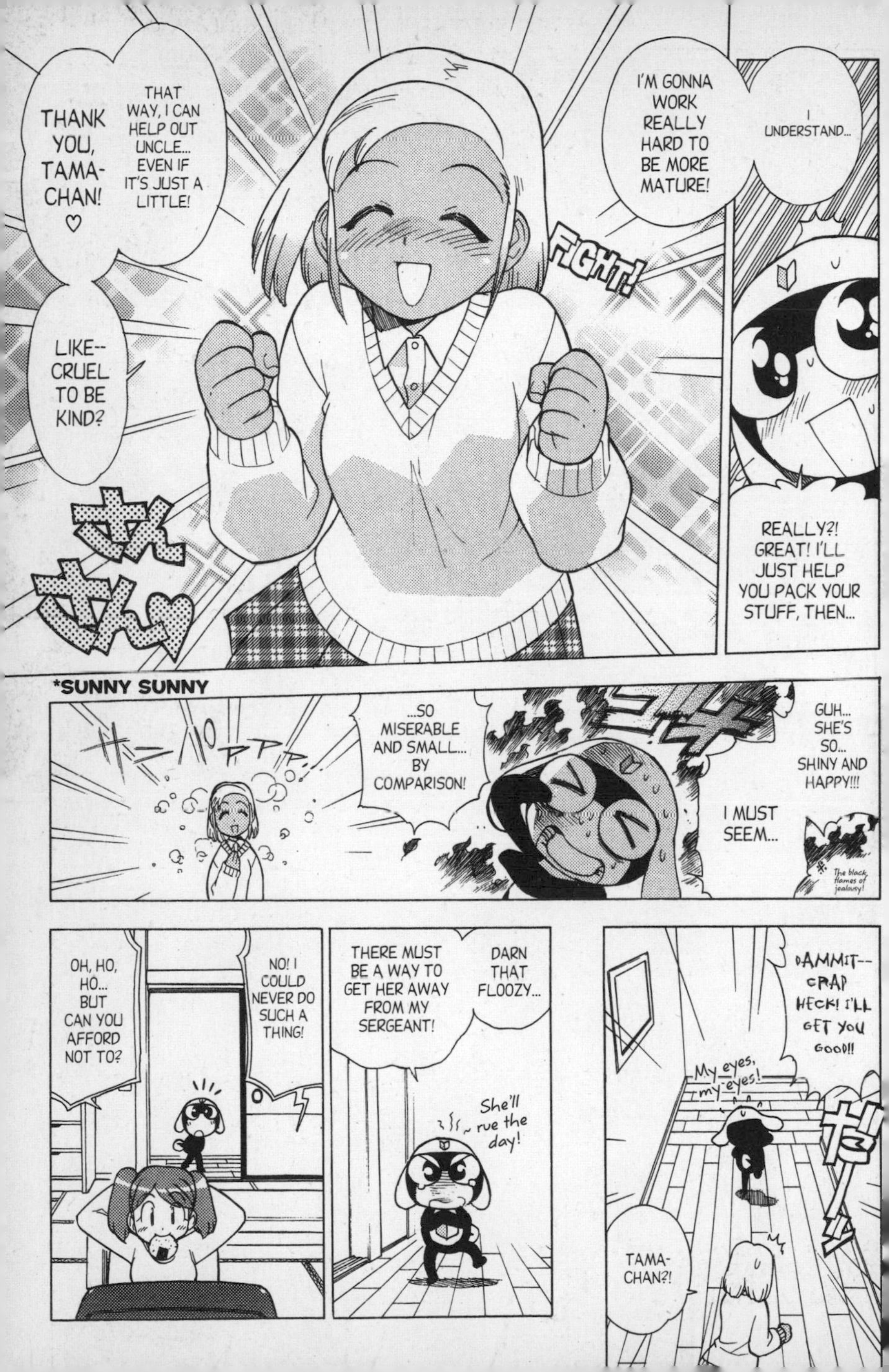
I UNDERSTAND...
REALLY?! GREAT! I'LL JUST HELP YOU PACK YOUR STUFF, THEN...
I'M GONNA WORK REALLY HARD TO BE MORE MATURE!
FIGHT!
THAT WAY, I CAN HELP OUT UNCLE... EVEN IF IT'S JUST A LITTLE!
THANK YOU, TAMA-CHAN! ♡
LIKE--CRUEL TO BE KIND?
*SUNNY SUNNY
GUH... SHE'S SO... SHINY AND HAPPY!!!
I MUST SEEM...
...SO MISERABLE AND SMALL... BY COMPARISON!
The black flames of jealousy!
DAMMIT--CRAP HECK! I'LL GET YOU GOOD!!
My eyes, my eyes!
TAMA-CHAN?!
DARN THAT FLOOZY...
THERE MUST BE A WAY TO GET HER AWAY FROM MY SERGEANT!
She'll rue the day!
NO! I COULD NEVER DO SUCH A THING!
OH, HO, HO... BUT CAN YOU AFFORD NOT TO?

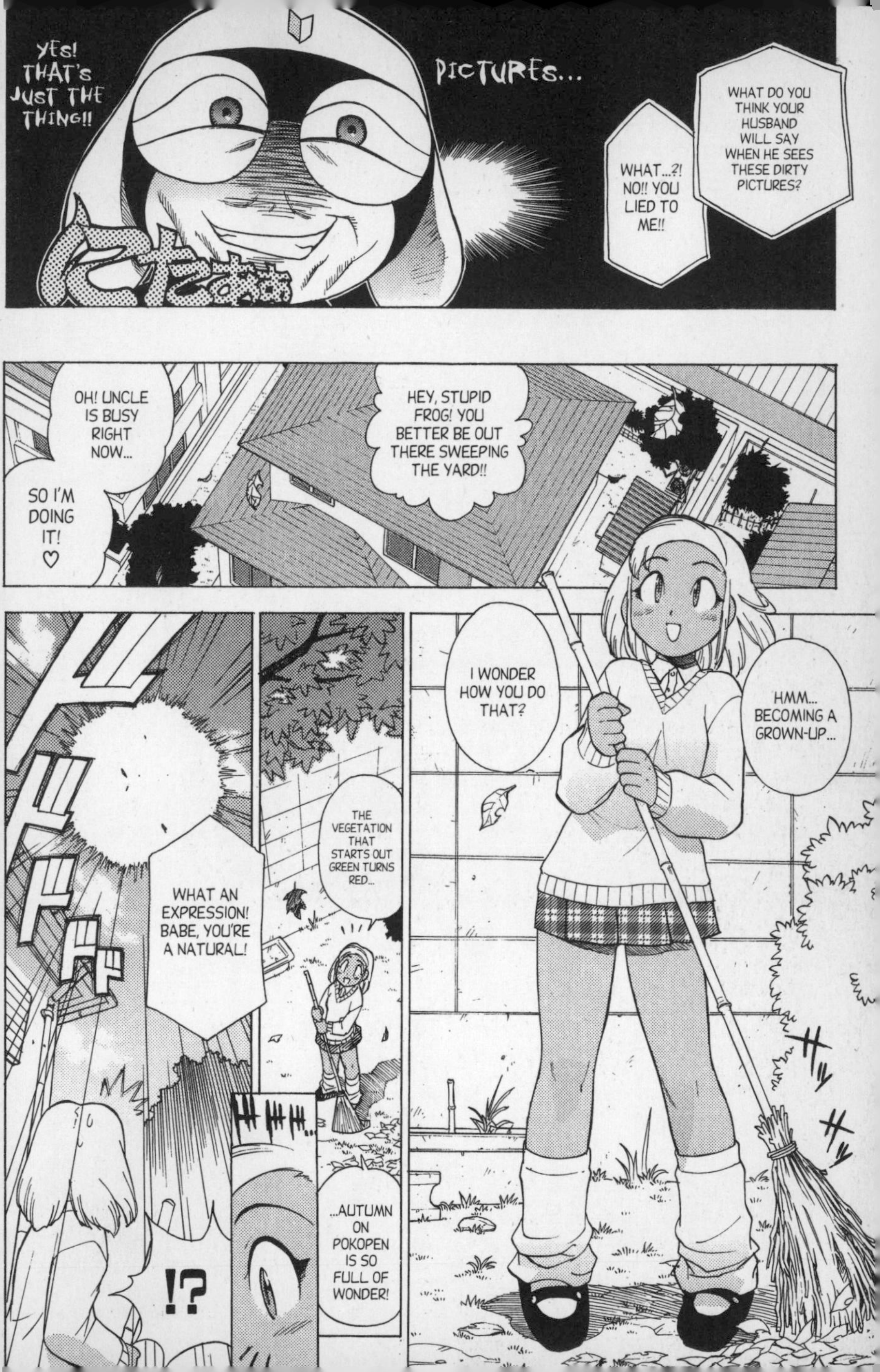
WHAT DO YOU THINK YOUR HUSBAND WILL SAY WHEN HE SEES THESE DIRTY PICTURES?
WHAT...?! NO!! YOU LIED TO ME!!
PICTURES...
YES! THAT'S JUST THE THING!!
HEY, STUPID FROG! YOU BETTER BE OUT THERE SWEEPING THE YARD!!
OH! UNCLE IS BUSY RIGHT NOW...
SO I'M DOING IT! ♡
HMM... BECOMING A GROWN-UP...
I WONDER HOW YOU DO THAT?
THE VEGETATION THAT STARTS OUT GREEN TURNS RED...
...AUTUMN ON POKOPEN IS SO FULL OF WONDER!
WHAT AN EXPRESSION! BABE, YOU'RE A NATURAL!
!?

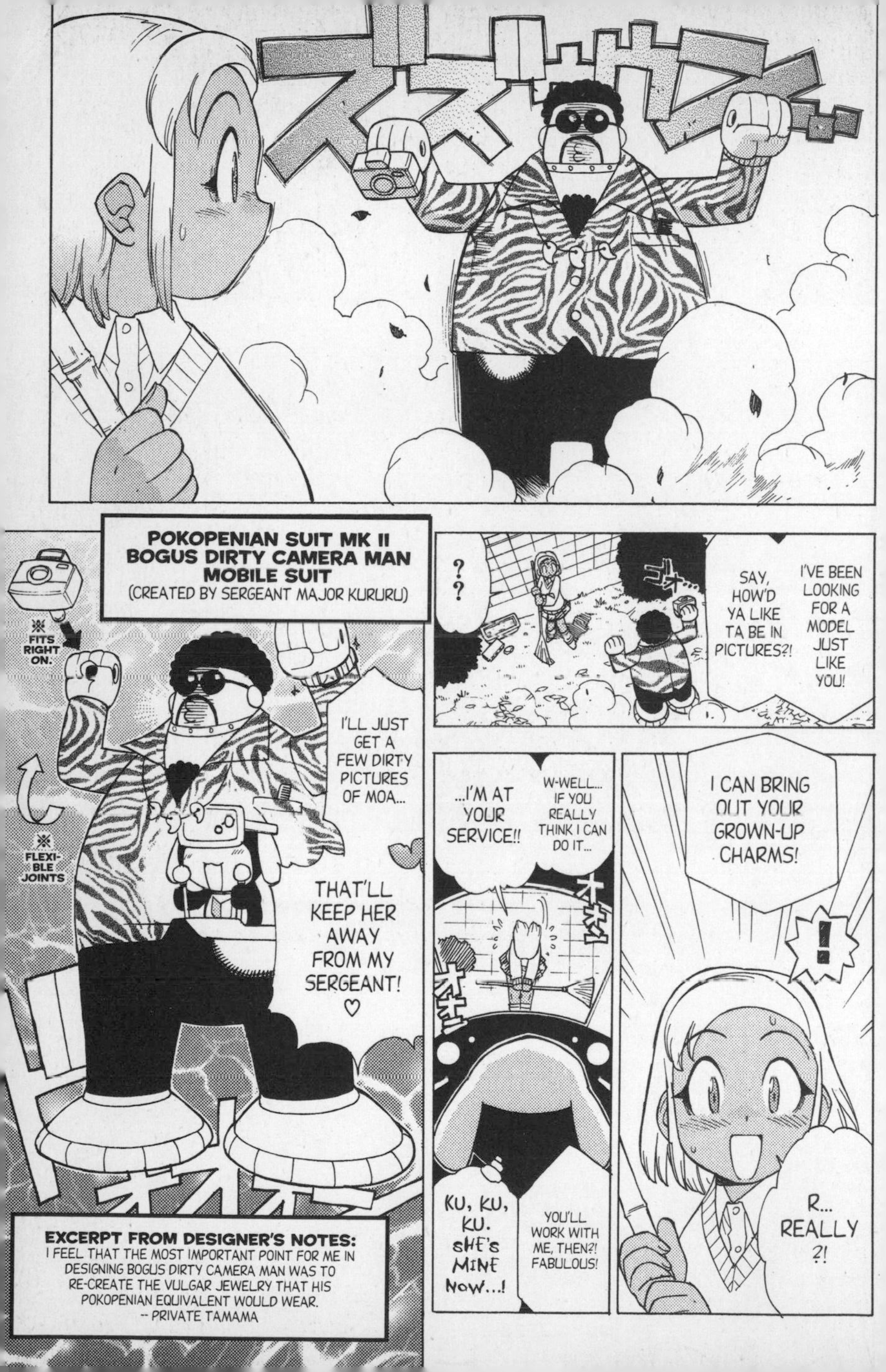
I'VE BEEN LOOKING FOR A MODEL JUST LIKE YOU!
SAY, HOW'D YA LIKE TA BE IN PICTURES?!
??
I CAN BRING OUT YOUR GROWN-UP CHARMS!
!
R... REALLY?!
W-WELL... IF YOU REALLY THINK I CAN DO IT...
...I'M AT YOUR SERVICE!!
YOU'LL WORK WITH ME, THEN?! FABULOUS!
KU, KU, KU. SHE'S MINE NOW...!
POKOPENIAN SUIT MK II
BOGUS DIRTY CAMERA MAN
MOBILE SUIT
(CREATED BY SERGEANT MAJOR KURURU)
※ FITS RIGHT ON.
※ FLEXI-BLE JOINTS
I'LL JUST GET A FEW DIRTY PICTURES OF MOA...
THAT'LL KEEP HER AWAY FROM MY SERGEANT! ♡
EXCERPT FROM DESIGNER'S NOTES:
I FEEL THAT THE MOST IMPORTANT POINT FOR ME IN DESIGNING BOGUS DIRTY CAMERA MAN WAS TO RE-CREATE THE VULGAR JEWELRY THAT HIS POKOPENIAN EQUIVALENT WOULD WEAR.
-- PRIVATE TAMAMA

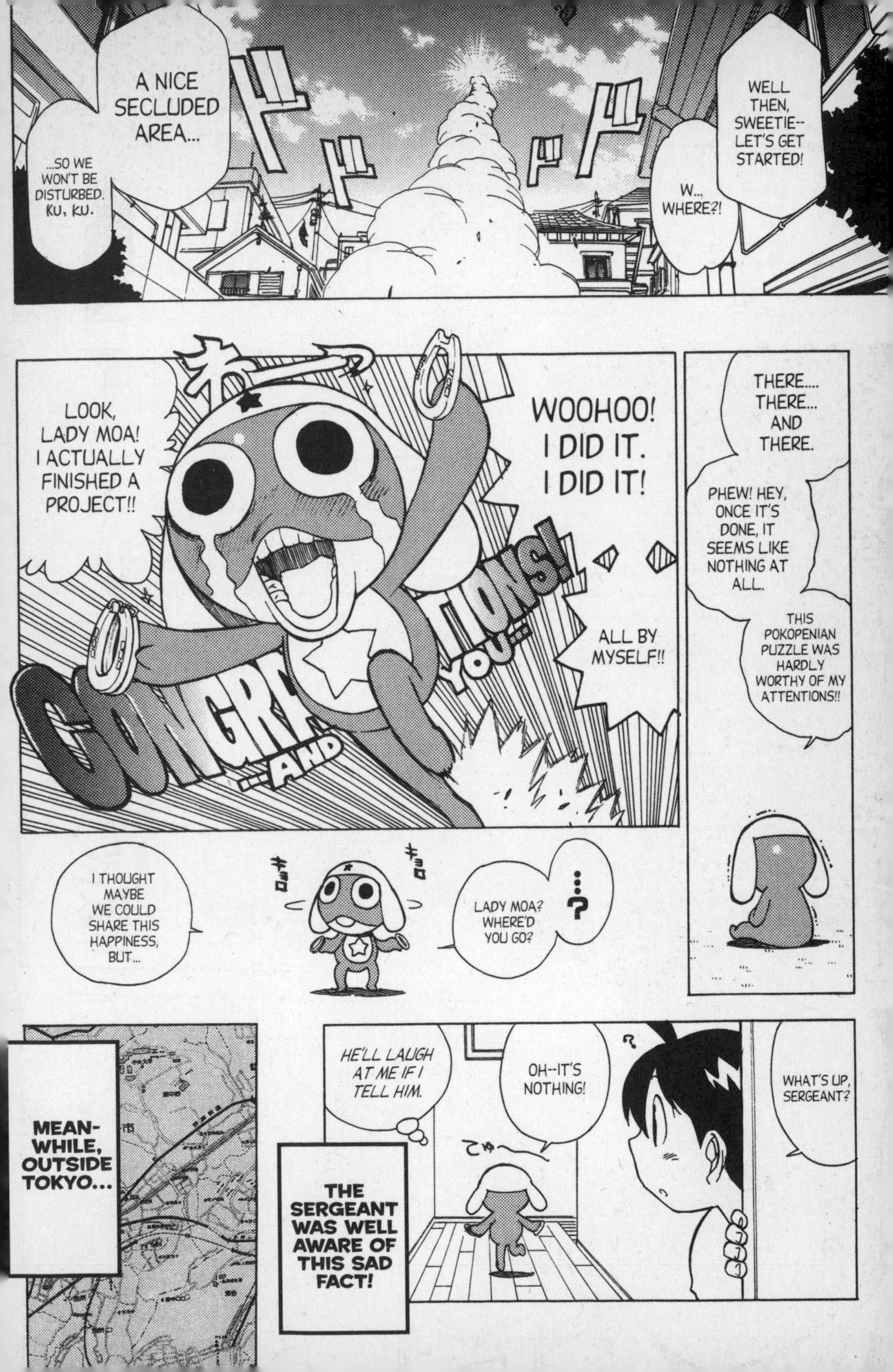
WELL THEN, SWEETIE-- LET'S GET STARTED!
W... WHERE?!
A NICE SECLUDED AREA...
...SO WE WON'T BE DISTURBED. KU, KU.
THERE.... THERE... AND THERE.
PHEW! HEY, ONCE IT'S DONE, IT SEEMS LIKE NOTHING AT ALL.
THIS POKOPENIAN PUZZLE WAS HARDLY WORTHY OF MY ATTENTIONS!!
WOOHOO! I DID IT. I DID IT!
LOOK, LADY MOA! I ACTUALLY FINISHED A PROJECT!!
ALL BY MYSELF!!
CONGRA...TIONS!!
...AND YOU...
...?
LADY MOA? WHERE'D YOU GO?
I THOUGHT MAYBE WE COULD SHARE THIS HAPPINESS, BUT...
WHAT'S UP, SERGEANT?
OH--IT'S NOTHING!
HE'LL LAUGH AT ME IF I TELL HIM.
THE SERGEANT WAS WELL AWARE OF THIS SAD FACT!
MEAN-WHILE, OUTSIDE TOKYO...

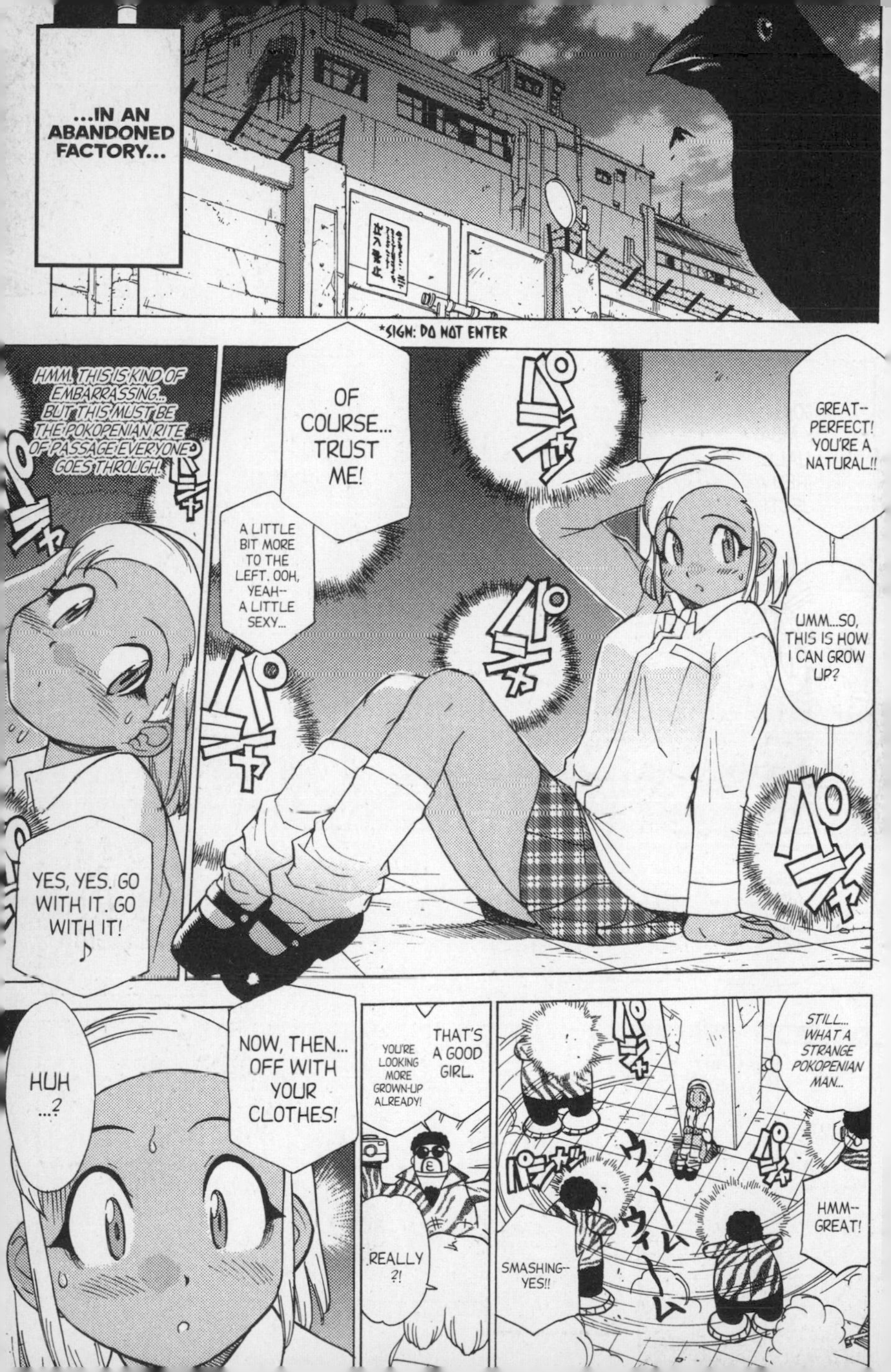

...IN AN ABANDONED FACTORY...
*SIGN: DO NOT ENTER
GREAT-- PERFECT! YOU'RE A NATURAL!!
UMM...SO, THIS IS HOW I CAN GROW UP?
OF COURSE... TRUST ME!
A LITTLE BIT MORE TO THE LEFT. OOH, YEAH-- A LITTLE SEXY...
HMM. THIS IS KIND OF EMBARRASSING... BUT THIS MUST BE THE POKOPENIAN RITE OF PASSAGE EVERYONE GOES THROUGH.
YES, YES. GO WITH IT. GO WITH IT! ♪
STILL... WHAT A STRANGE POKOPENIAN MAN...
HMM-- GREAT!
SMASHING-- YES!!
THAT'S A GOOD GIRL..
YOU'RE LOOKING MORE GROWN-UP ALREADY!
REALLY ?!
NOW, THEN... OFF WITH YOUR CLOTHES!
HUH ...?

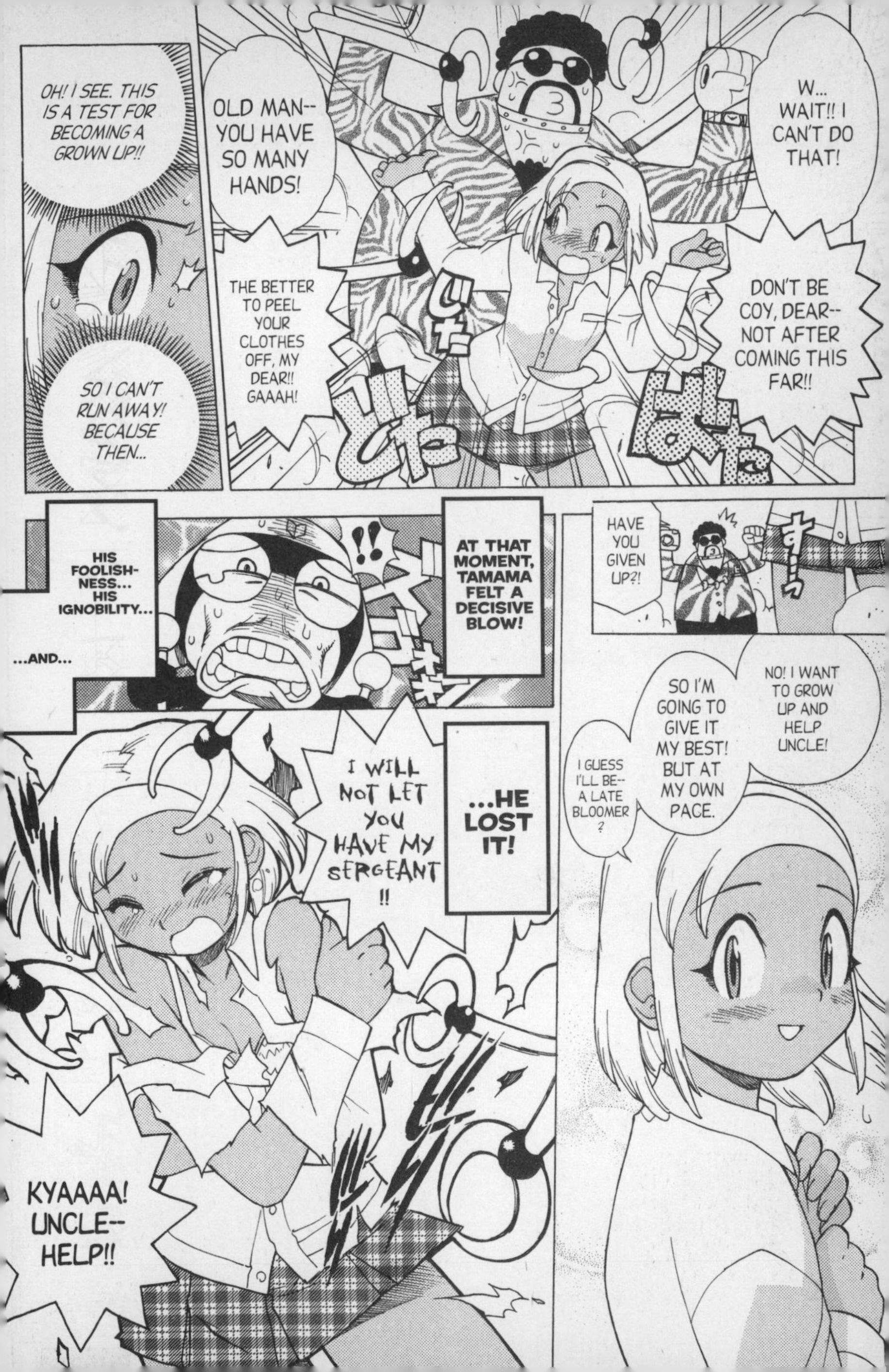
W... WAIT!! I CAN'T DO THAT!
OLD MAN-- YOU HAVE SO MANY HANDS!
DON'T BE COY, DEAR-- NOT AFTER COMING THIS FAR!!
THE BETTER TO PEEL YOUR CLOTHES OFF, MY DEAR!! GAAAH!
OH! I SEE. THIS IS A TEST FOR BECOMING A GROWN UP!!
SO I CAN'T RUN AWAY! BECAUSE THEN...
HAVE YOU GIVEN UP?!
NO! I WANT TO GROW UP AND HELP UNCLE!
SO I'M GOING TO GIVE IT MY BEST! BUT AT MY OWN PACE.
I GUESS I'LL BE-- A LATE BLOOMER?
AT THAT MOMENT, TAMAMA FELT A DECISIVE BLOW!
HIS FOOLISHNESS... HIS IGNOBILITY...
...AND...
...HE LOST IT!
I WILL NOT LET YOU HAVE MY SERGEANT!!
KYAAAA! UNCLE-- HELP!!

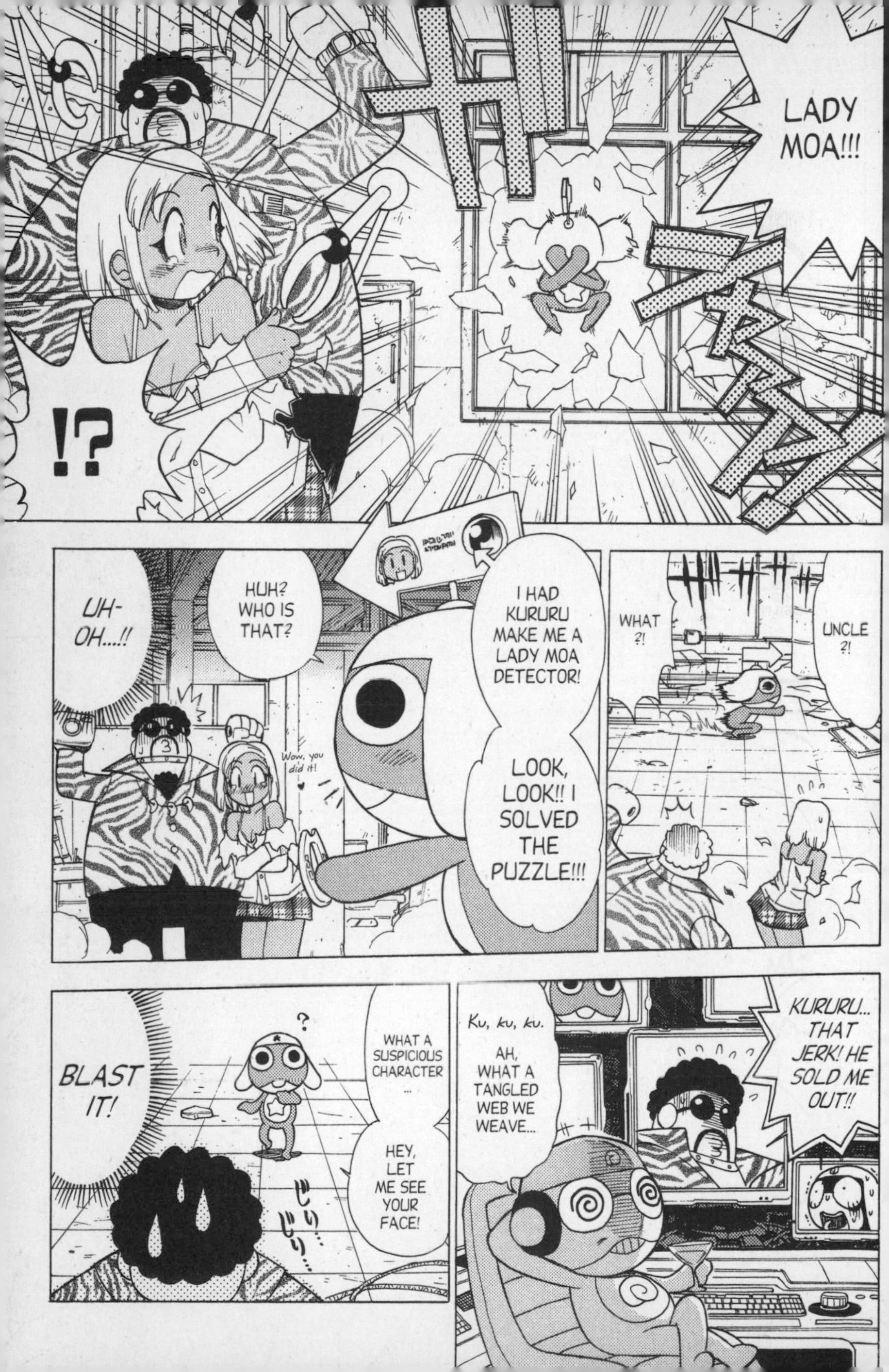
LADY MOA!!!
!?
UNCLE ?!
WHAT ?!
I HAD KURURU MAKE ME A LADY MOA DETECTOR!
LOOK, LOOK!! I SOLVED THE PUZZLE!!!
HUH? WHO IS THAT?
Wow, you did it!
UH-OH...!!
KURURU... THAT JERK! HE SOLD ME OUT!!
Ku, ku, ku.
AH, WHAT A TANGLED WEB WE WEAVE...
WHAT A SUSPICIOUS CHARACTER ...
HEY, LET ME SEE YOUR FACE!
BLAST IT!

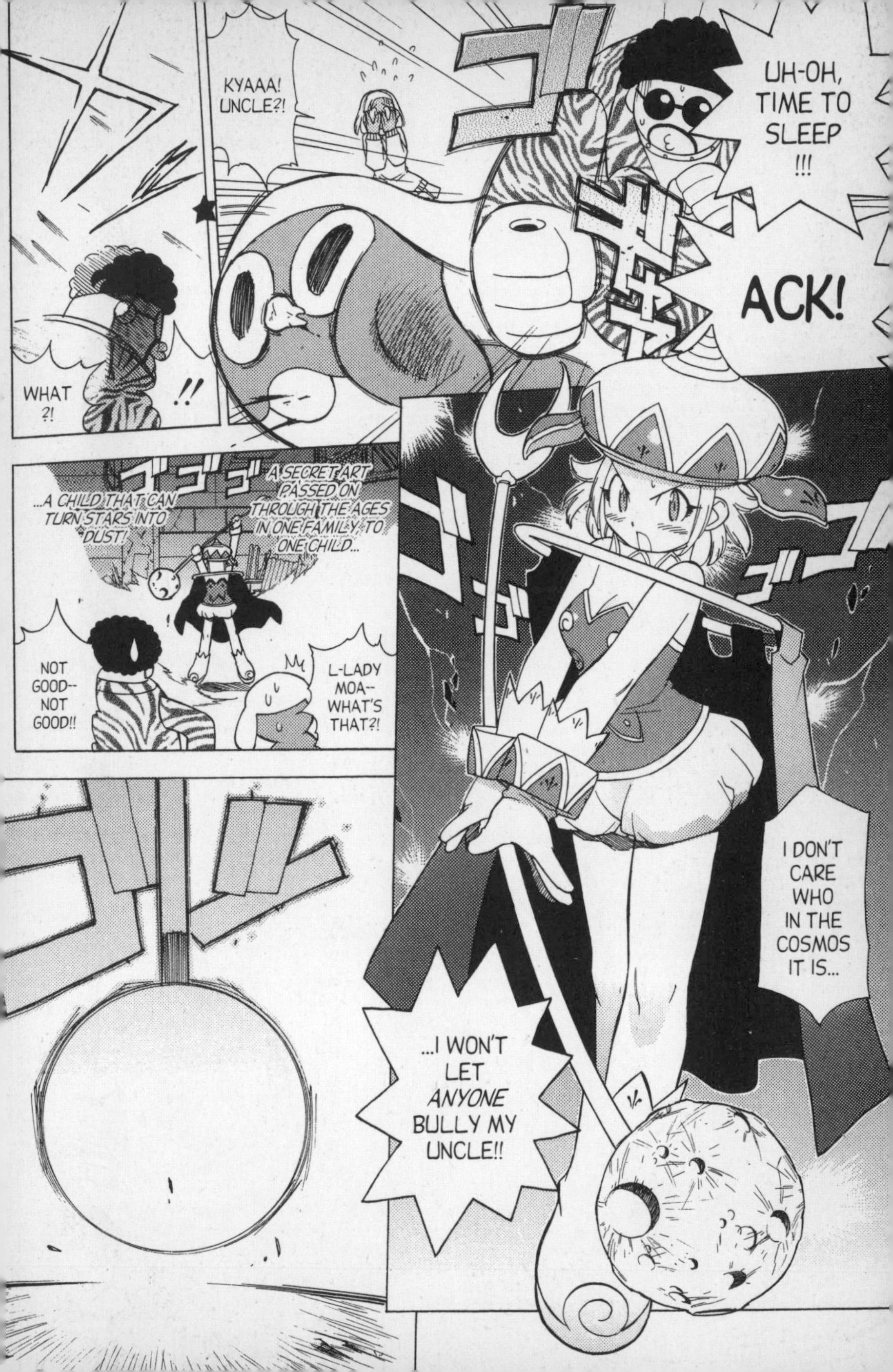
UH-OH, TIME TO SLEEP !!!
KYAAA! UNCLE?!
ACK!
!!
WHAT ?!
A SECRET ART PASSED ON THROUGH THE AGES IN ONE FAMILY, TO ONE CHILD...
...A CHILD THAT CAN TURN STARS INTO DUST!
L-LADY MOA-- WHAT'S THAT?!
NOT GOOD-- NOT GOOD!!
I DON'T CARE WHO IN THE COSMOS IT IS...
...I WON'T LET *ANYONE* BULLY MY UNCLE!!

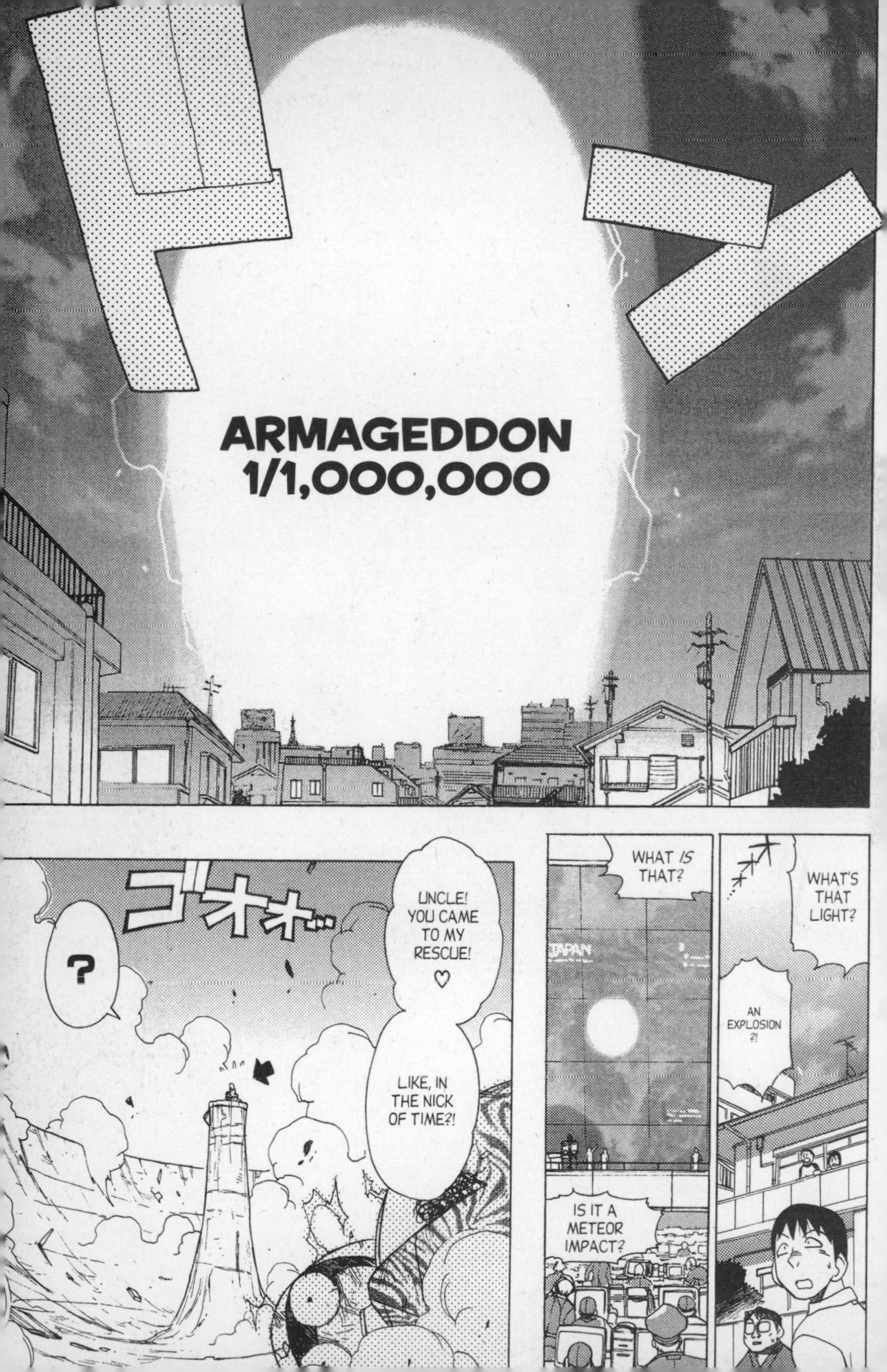
ARMAGEDDON
1/1,000,000
WHAT'S THAT LIGHT?
AN EXPLOSION ?!
WHAT *IS* THAT?
IS IT A METEOR IMPACT?
UNCLE! YOU CAME TO MY RESCUE! ♡
LIKE, IN THE NICK OF TIME?!
?

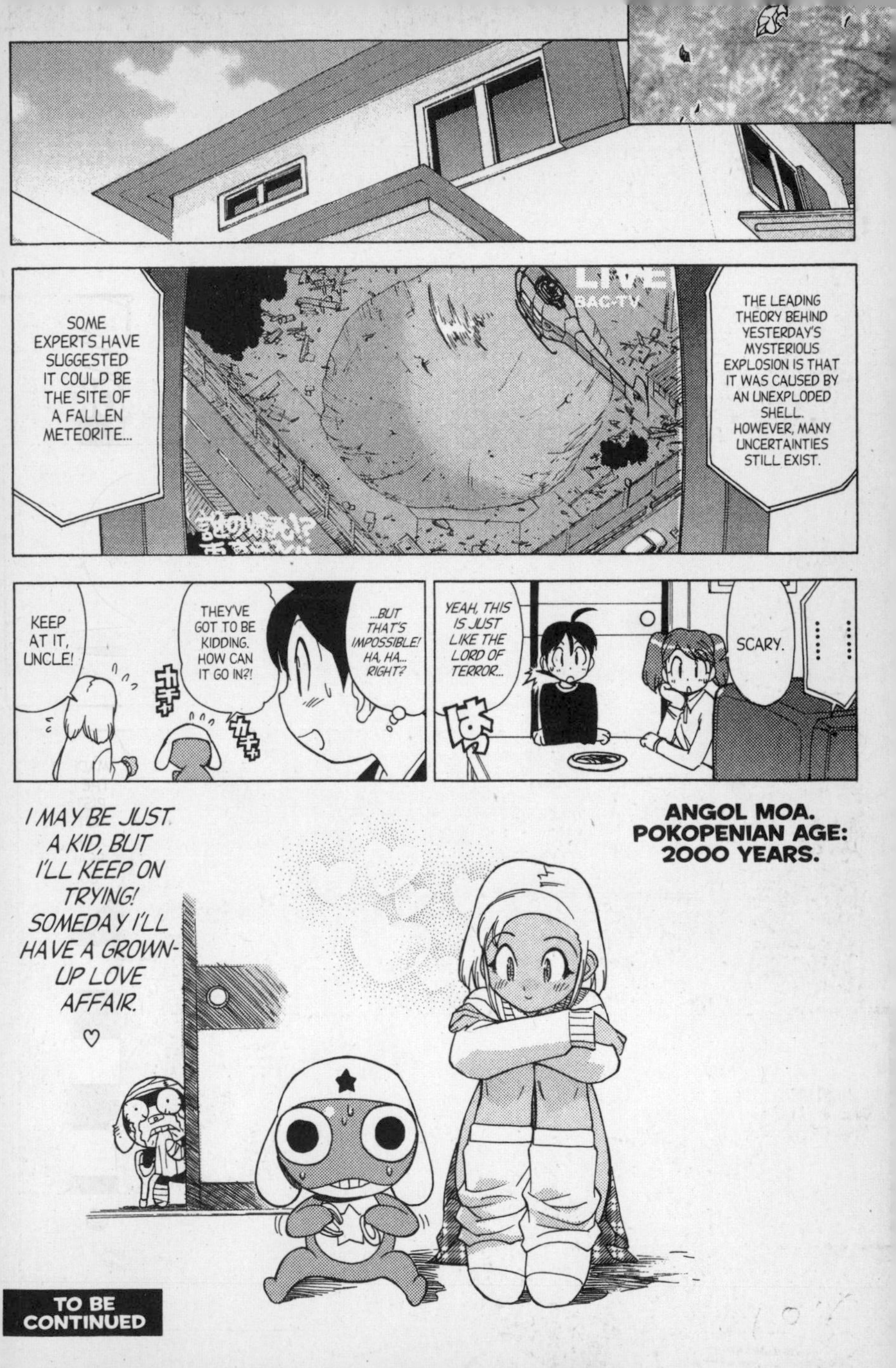
LIVE
BAC-TV
THE LEADING THEORY BEHIND YESTERDAY'S MYSTERIOUS EXPLOSION IS THAT IT WAS CAUSED BY AN UNEXPLODED SHELL. HOWEVER, MANY UNCERTAINTIES STILL EXIST.
SOME EXPERTS HAVE SUGGESTED IT COULD BE THE SITE OF A FALLEN METEORITE...
......
SCARY.
YEAH, THIS IS JUST LIKE THE LORD OF TERROR...
は
...BUT THAT'S IMPOSSIBLE! HA, HA... RIGHT?
THEY'VE GOT TO BE KIDDING. HOW CAN IT GO IN?!
KEEP AT IT, UNCLE!
ANGOL MOA. POKOPENIAN AGE: 2000 YEARS.
I MAY BE JUST A KID, BUT I'LL KEEP ON TRYING! SOMEDAY I'LL HAVE A GROWN-UP LOVE AFFAIR. ♡
TO BE CONTINUED

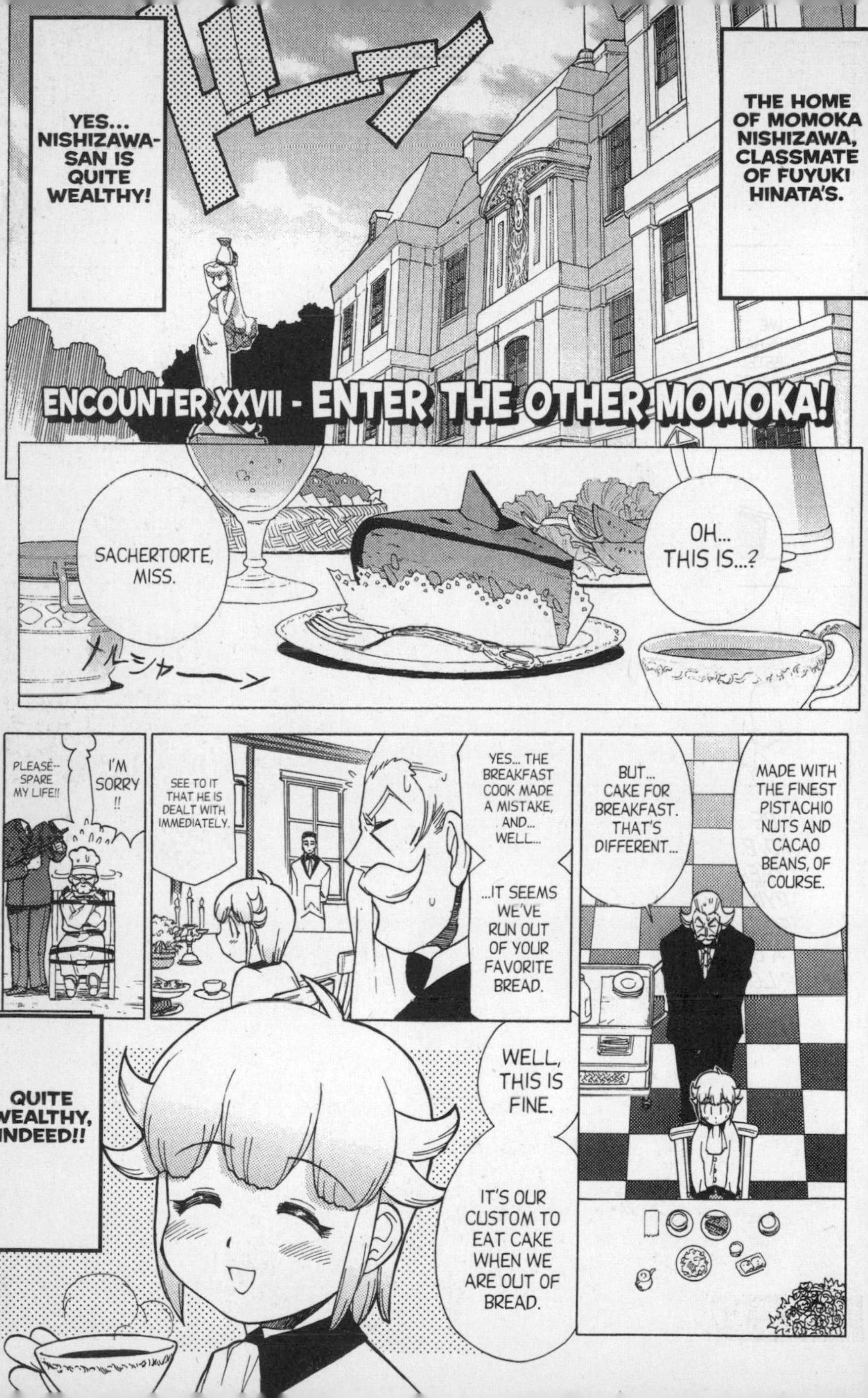
THE HOME OF MOMOKA NISHIZAWA, CLASSMATE OF FUYUKI HINATA'S.
YES... NISHIZAWA-SAN IS QUITE WEALTHY!
ENCOUNTER XXVII - ENTER THE OTHER MOMOKA!
OH... THIS IS...?
SACHERTORTE, MISS.
MADE WITH THE FINEST PISTACHIO NUTS AND CACAO BEANS, OF COURSE.
BUT... CAKE FOR BREAKFAST. THAT'S DIFFERENT...
YES... THE BREAKFAST COOK MADE A MISTAKE, AND... WELL...
...IT SEEMS WE'VE RUN OUT OF YOUR FAVORITE BREAD.
SEE TO IT THAT HE IS DEALT WITH IMMEDIATELY.
I'M SORRY !!
PLEASE-- SPARE MY LIFE!!
WELL, THIS IS FINE.
IT'S OUR CUSTOM TO EAT CAKE WHEN WE ARE OUT OF BREAD.
QUITE WEALTHY, INDEED!!

ENCOUNTER XXVII

ENTER THE OTHER MOMOKA!

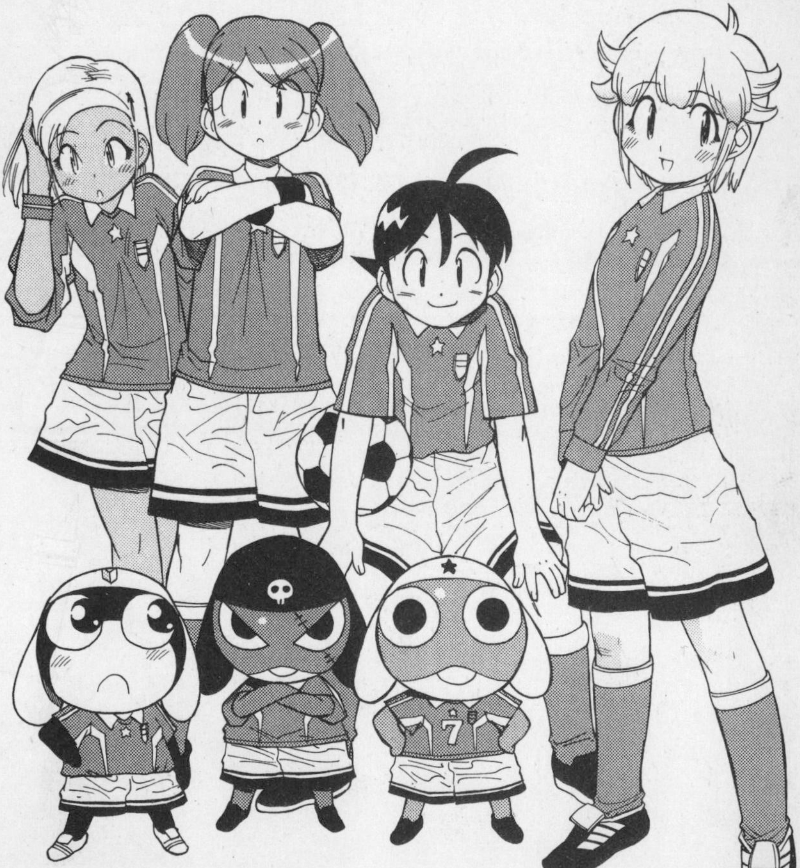

7

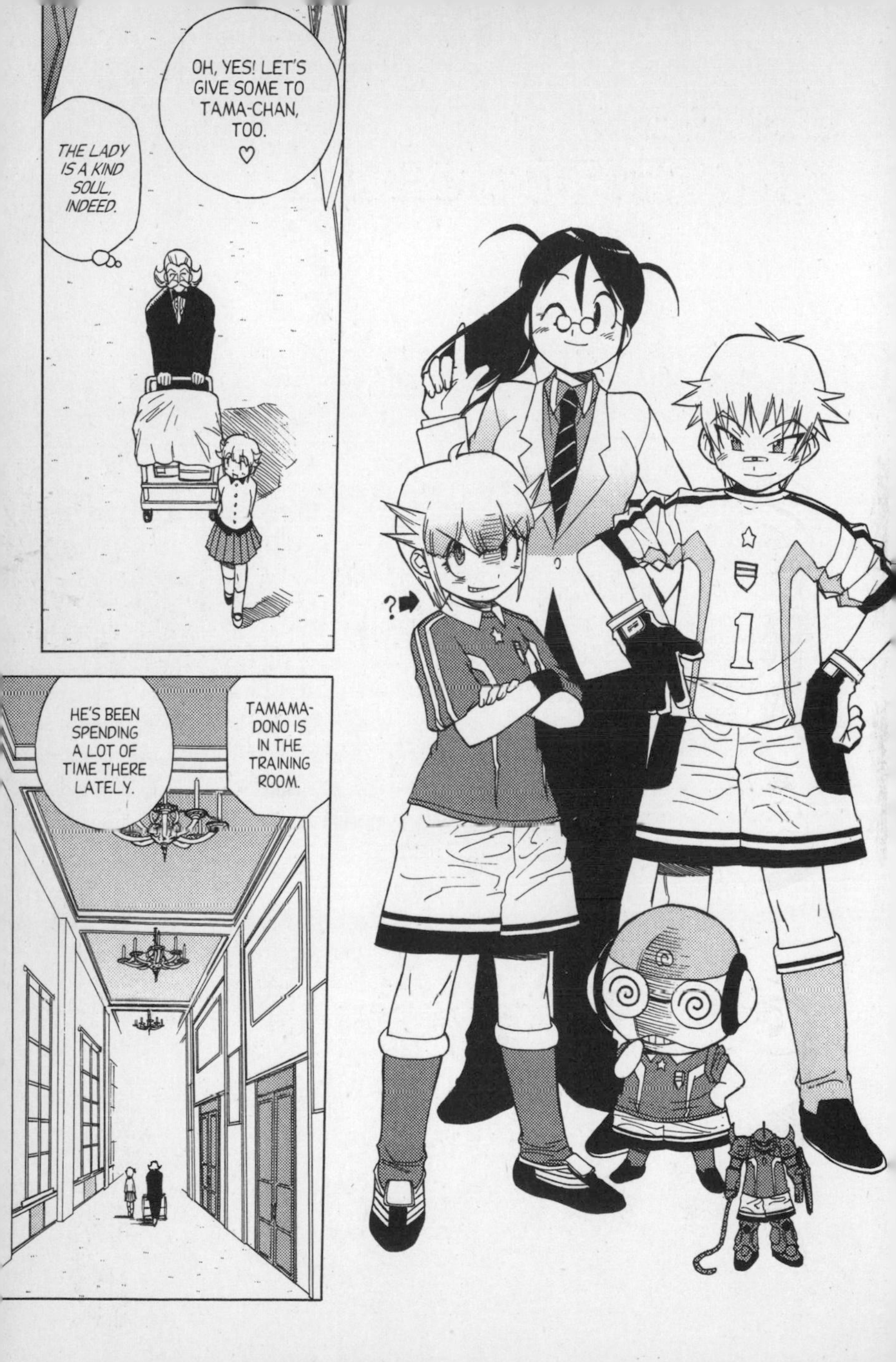
OH, YES! LET'S GIVE SOME TO TAMA-CHAN, TOO. ♡
THE LADY IS A KIND SOUL, INDEED.
TAMAMA-DONO IS IN THE TRAINING ROOM.
HE'S BEEN SPENDING A LOT OF TIME THERE LATELY.

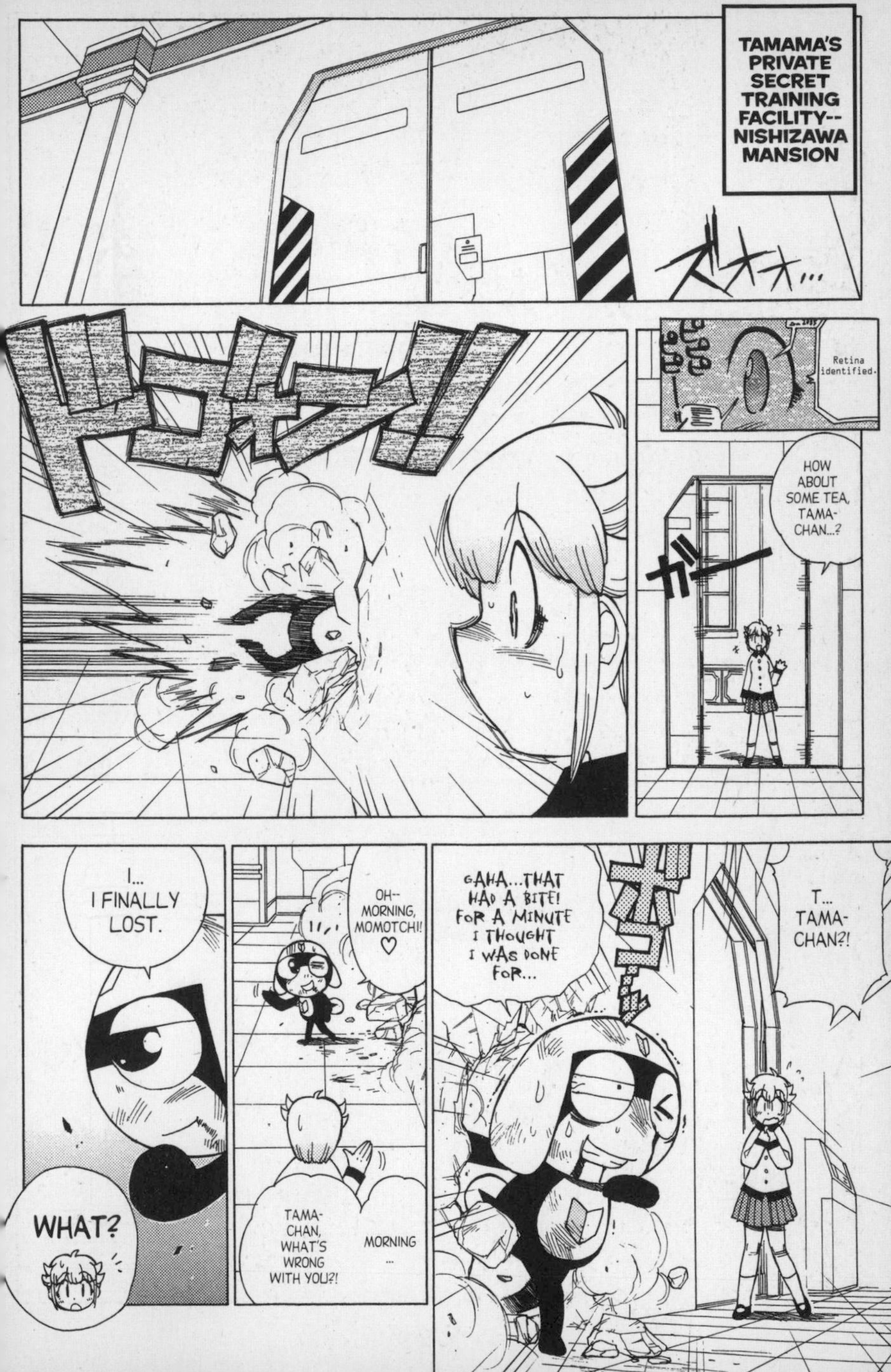
TAMAMA'S PRIVATE SECRET TRAINING FACILITY--NISHIZAWA MANSION
Retina identified.
HOW ABOUT SOME TEA, TAMA-CHAN...?
T... TAMA-CHAN?!
GAHA...THAT HAD A BITE! FOR A MINUTE I THOUGHT I WAS DONE FOR...
OH-- MORNING, MOMOTCHI! ♡
MORNING ...
TAMA-CHAN, WHAT'S WRONG WITH YOU?!
I... I FINALLY LOST.
WHAT?

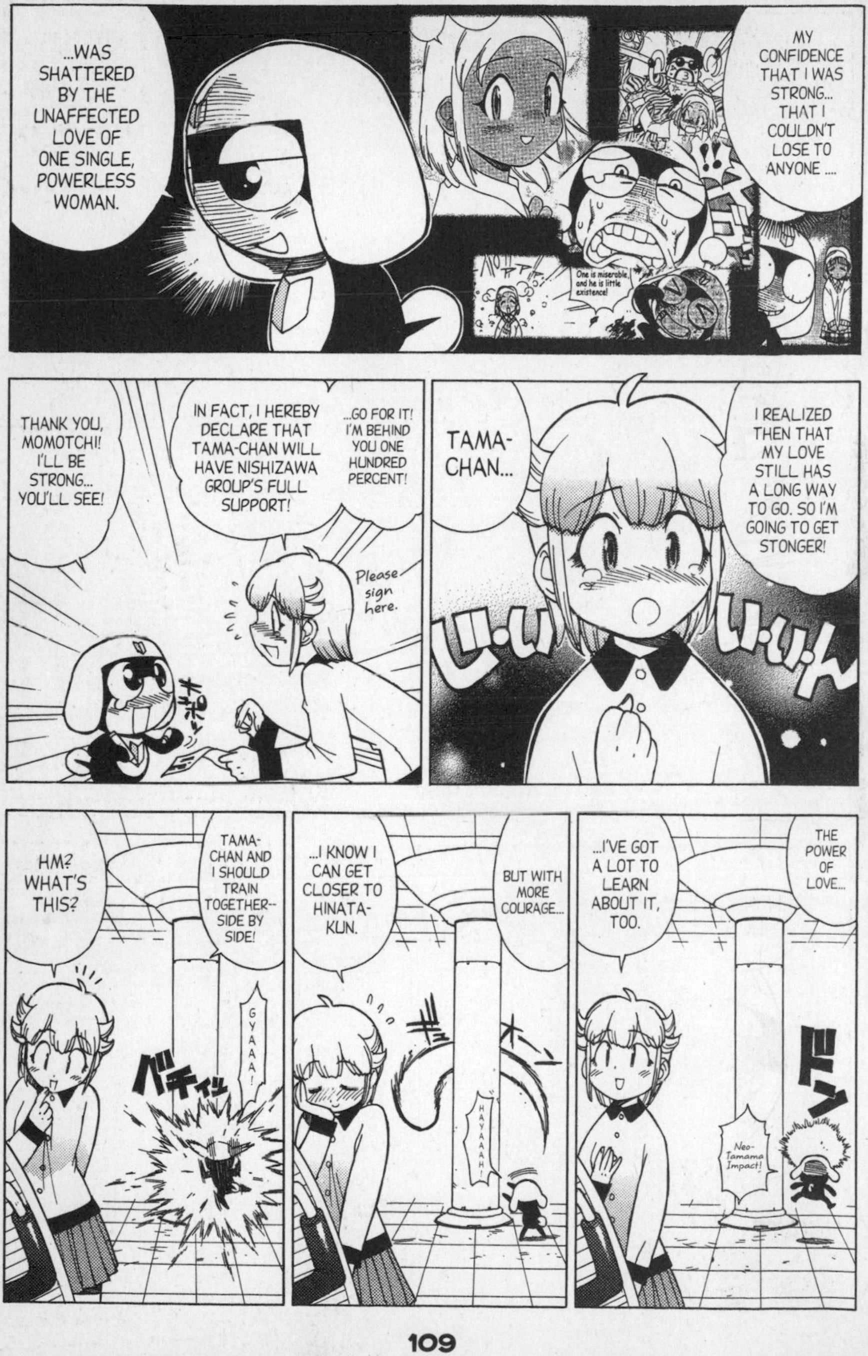
MY CONFIDENCE THAT I WAS STRONG... THAT I COULDN'T LOSE TO ANYONE ....
One is miserable, and he is little existence!
...WAS SHATTERED BY THE UNAFFECTED LOVE OF ONE SINGLE, POWERLESS WOMAN.
I REALIZED THEN THAT MY LOVE STILL HAS A LONG WAY TO GO. SO I'M GOING TO GET STONGER!
TAMA-CHAN...
...GO FOR IT! I'M BEHIND YOU ONE HUNDRED PERCENT!
IN FACT, I HEREBY DECLARE THAT TAMA-CHAN WILL HAVE NISHIZAWA GROUP'S FULL SUPPORT!
Please sign here.
THANK YOU, MOMOTCHI! I'LL BE STRONG... YOU'LL SEE!
THE POWER OF LOVE...
...I'VE GOT A LOT TO LEARN ABOUT IT, TOO.
Neo-Tamama Impact!
BUT WITH MORE COURAGE...
...I KNOW I CAN GET CLOSER TO HINATA-KUN.
HAYAAAH!
TAMA-CHAN AND I SHOULD TRAIN TOGETHER--SIDE BY SIDE!
GYAAA!
HM? WHAT'S THIS?

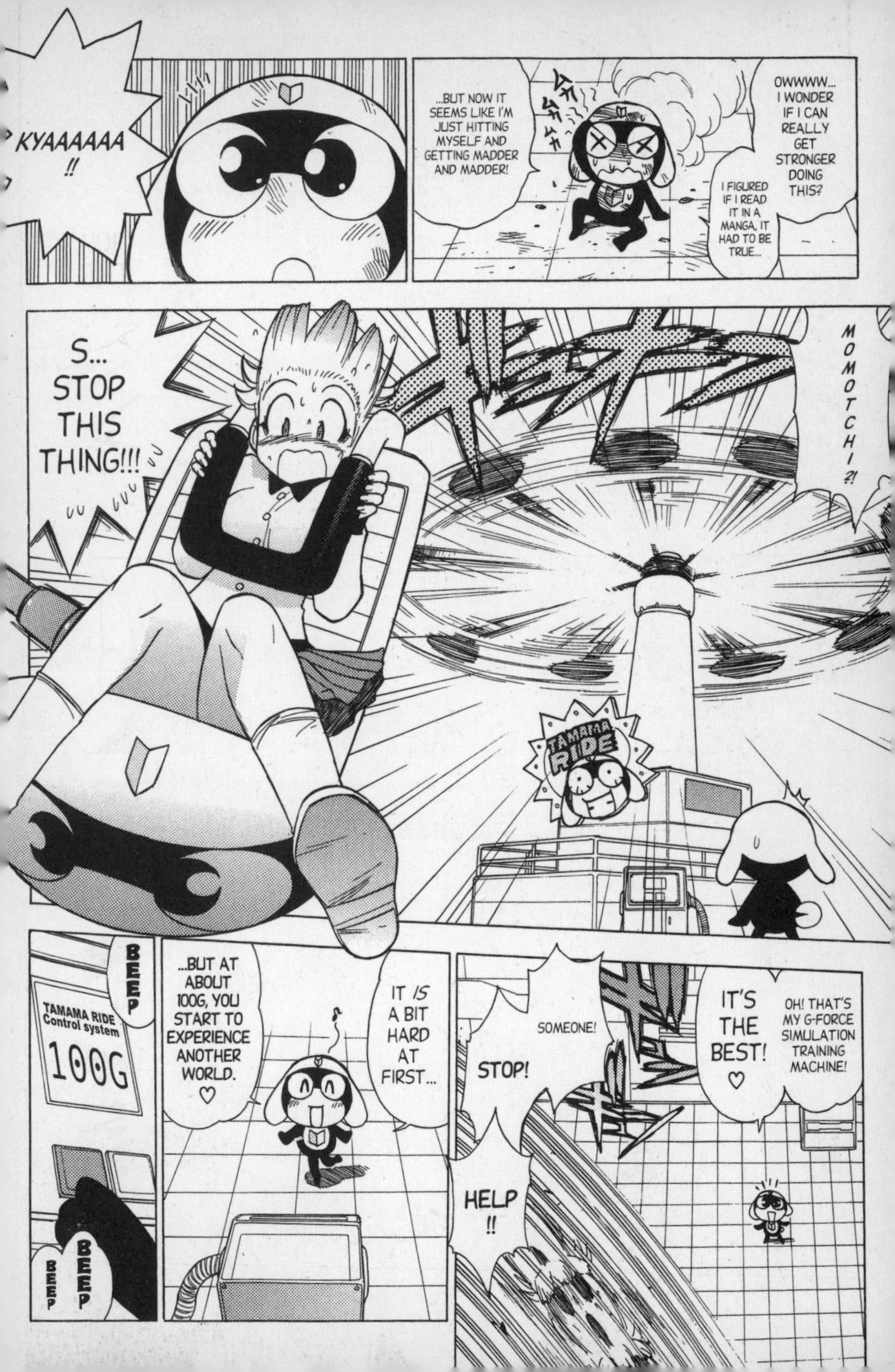
OWWWW... I WONDER IF I CAN REALLY GET STRONGER DOING THIS?
I FIGURED IF I READ IT IN A MANGA, IT HAD TO BE TRUE...
...BUT NOW IT SEEMS LIKE I'M JUST HITTING MYSELF AND GETTING MADDER AND MADDER!
KYAAAAAA!!
MOMOTCHI?!
S... STOP THIS THING!!!
TAMAMA RIDE
OH! THAT'S MY G-FORCE SIMULATION TRAINING MACHINE!
IT'S THE BEST! ♡
SOMEONE!
STOP!
HELP!!
IT *IS* A BIT HARD AT FIRST...
...BUT AT ABOUT 100G, YOU START TO EXPERIENCE ANOTHER WORLD. ♡
BEEP
TAMAMA RIDE Control system
100G
BEEP
BEEP

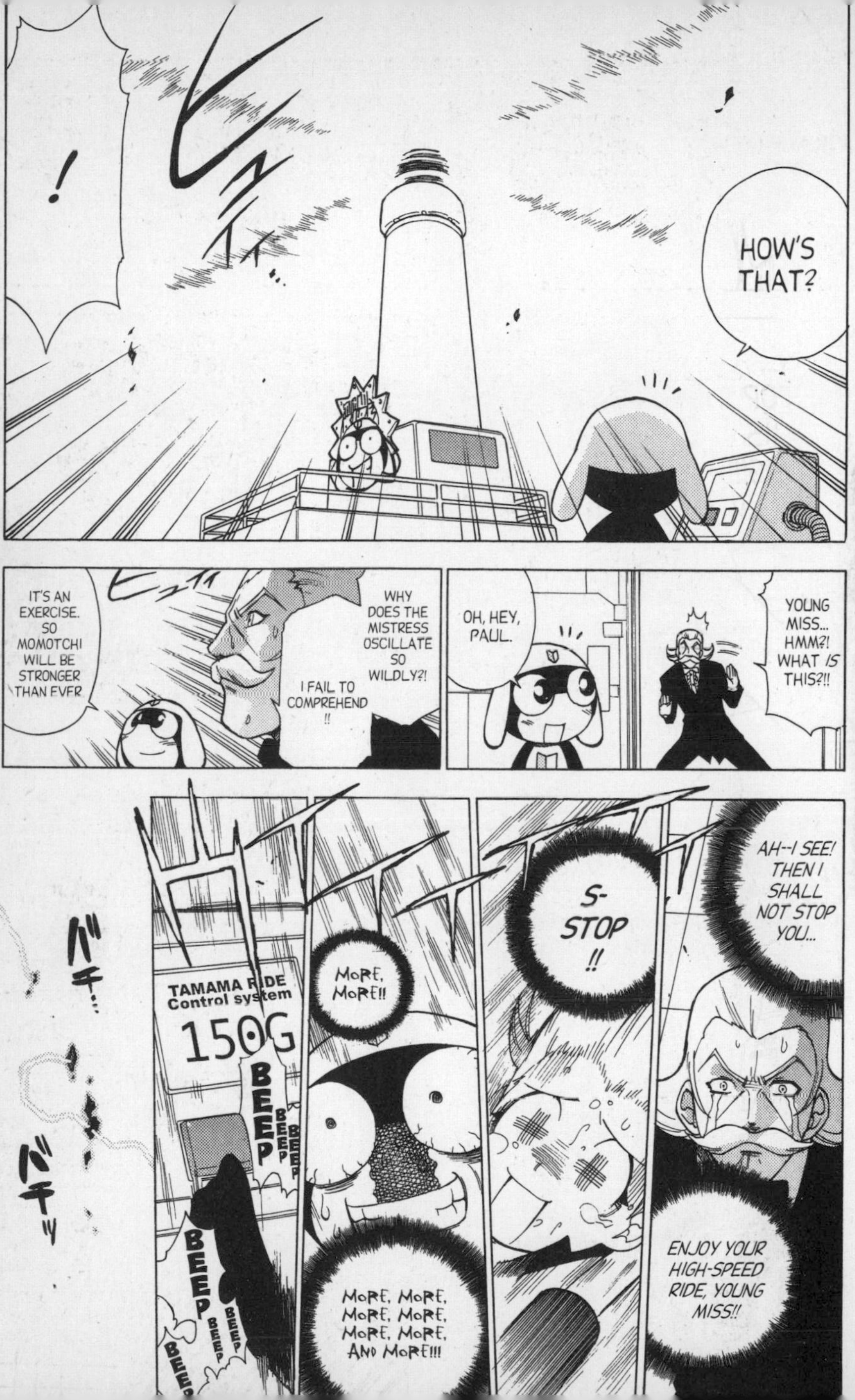
HOW'S THAT?
!
YOUNG MISS... HMM?! WHAT IS THIS?!!
OH, HEY, PAUL.
WHY DOES THE MISTRESS OSCILLATE SO WILDLY?!
I FAIL TO COMPREHEND !!
IT'S AN EXERCISE. SO MOMOTCHI WILL BE STRONGER THAN EVER
AH--I SEE! THEN I SHALL NOT STOP YOU...
ENJOY YOUR HIGH-SPEED RIDE, YOUNG MISS!!
S-STOP !!
MORE, MORE!!
MORE, MORE, MORE, MORE, MORE, MORE, AND MORE!!!
TAMAMA RIDE Control system
150G
BEEP BEEP BEEP
BEEP BEEP BEEP
バチ…
バチッ

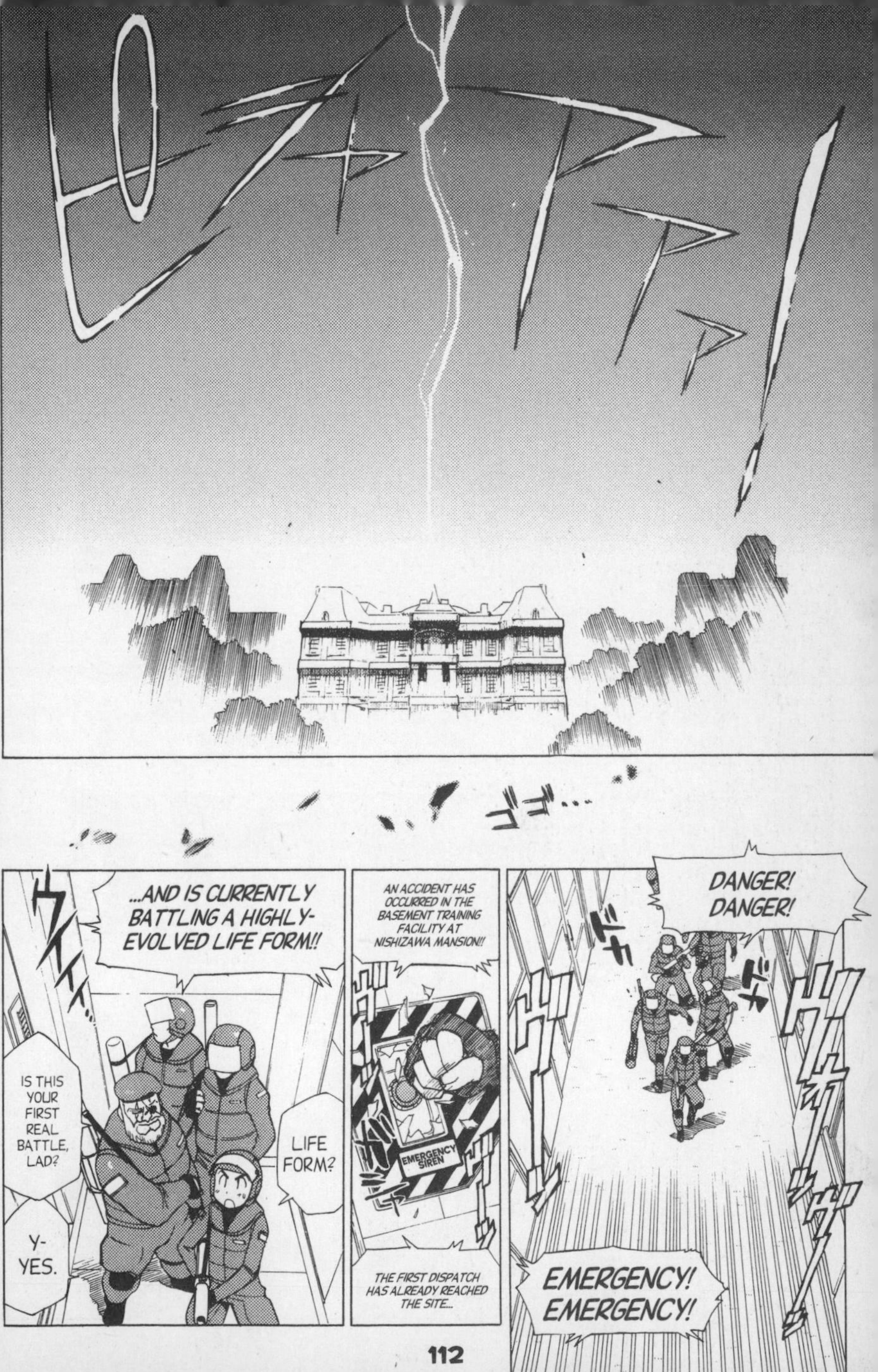
ゴゴ…
DANGER! DANGER!
EMERGENCY! EMERGENCY!
AN ACCIDENT HAS OCCURRED IN THE BASEMENT TRAINING FACILITY AT NISHIZAWA MANSION!!
EMERGENCY SIREN
THE FIRST DISPATCH HAS ALREADY REACHED THE SITE...
...AND IS CURRENTLY BATTLING A HIGHLY-EVOLVED LIFE FORM!!
LIFE FORM?
IS THIS YOUR FIRST REAL BATTLE, LAD?
Y-YES.

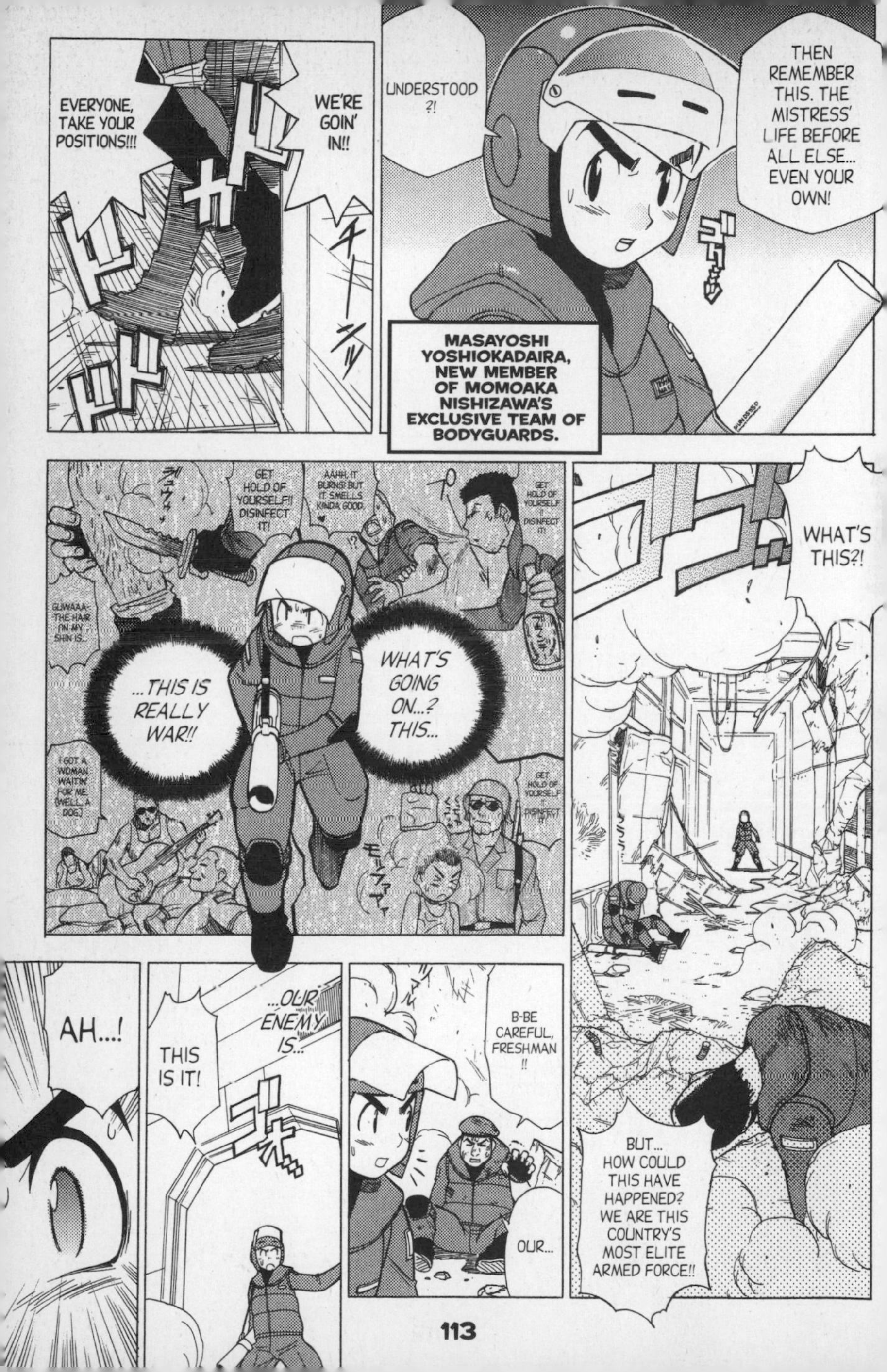
THEN REMEMBER THIS. THE MISTRESS' LIFE BEFORE ALL ELSE... EVEN YOUR OWN!
UNDERSTOOD ?!
MASAYOSHI YOSHIOKADAIRA, NEW MEMBER OF MOMOAKA NISHIZAWA'S EXCLUSIVE TEAM OF BODYGUARDS.
WE'RE GOIN' IN!!
EVERYONE, TAKE YOUR POSITIONS!!!
WHAT'S THIS?!
GET HOLD OF YOURSELF!! DISINFECT IT!
AAHH, IT BURNS! BUT IT SMELLS KINDA GOOD.
GET HOLD OF YOURSELF!! DISINFECT IT!
GUWAAA- THE HAIR ON MY SHIN IS...
WHAT'S GOING ON...? THIS...
...THIS IS REALLY WAR!!
I GOT A WOMAN WAITIN' FOR ME. (WELL, A DOG)
GET HOLD OF YOURSELF!! DISINFECT IT!
BUT... HOW COULD THIS HAVE HAPPENED? WE ARE THIS COUNTRY'S MOST ELITE ARMED FORCE!!
B-BE CAREFUL, FRESHMAN!!
OUR...
...OUR ENEMY IS...
THIS IS IT!
AH...!

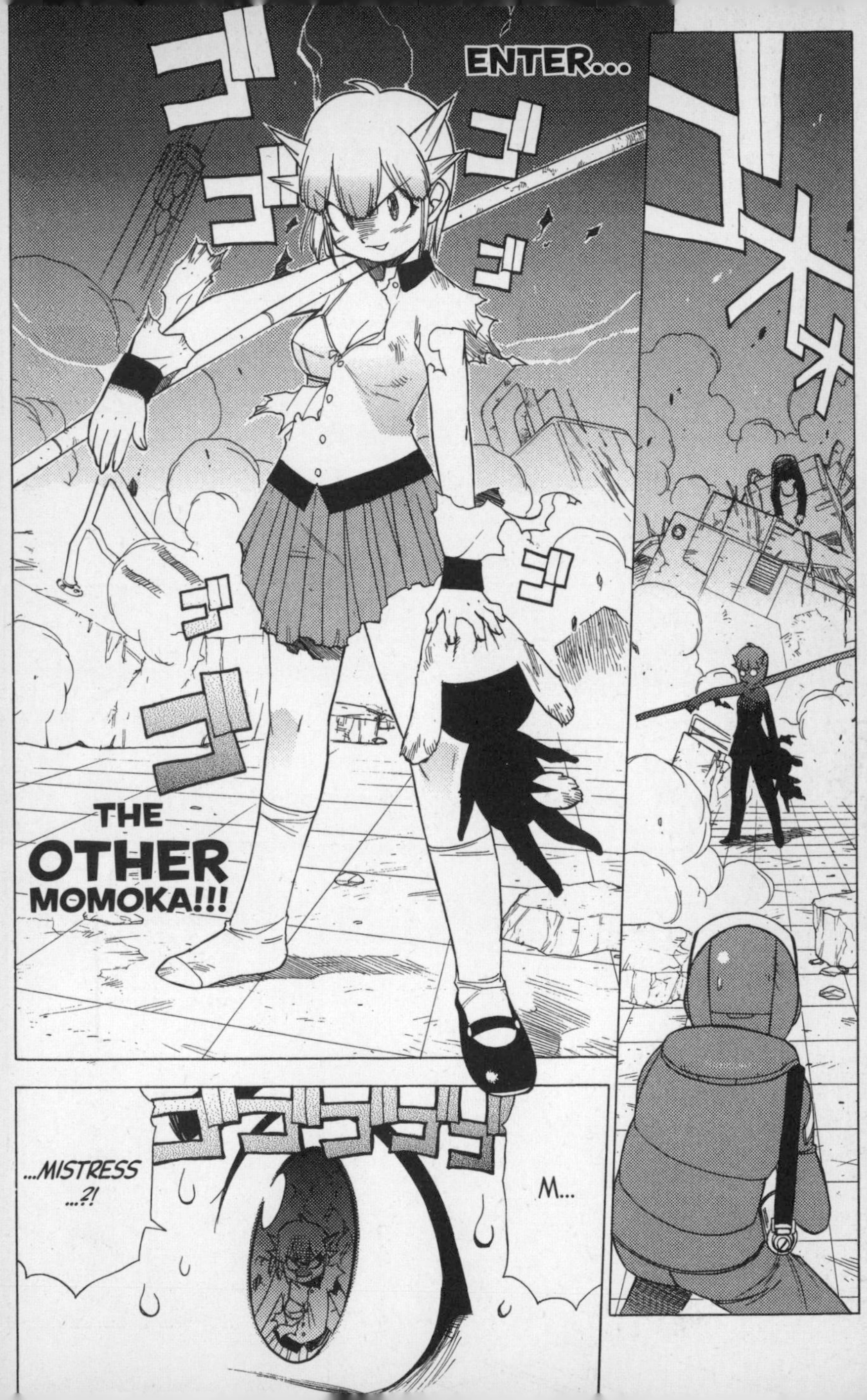

ENTER...
THE OTHER MOMOKA!!!
M...
...MISTRESS ...?!

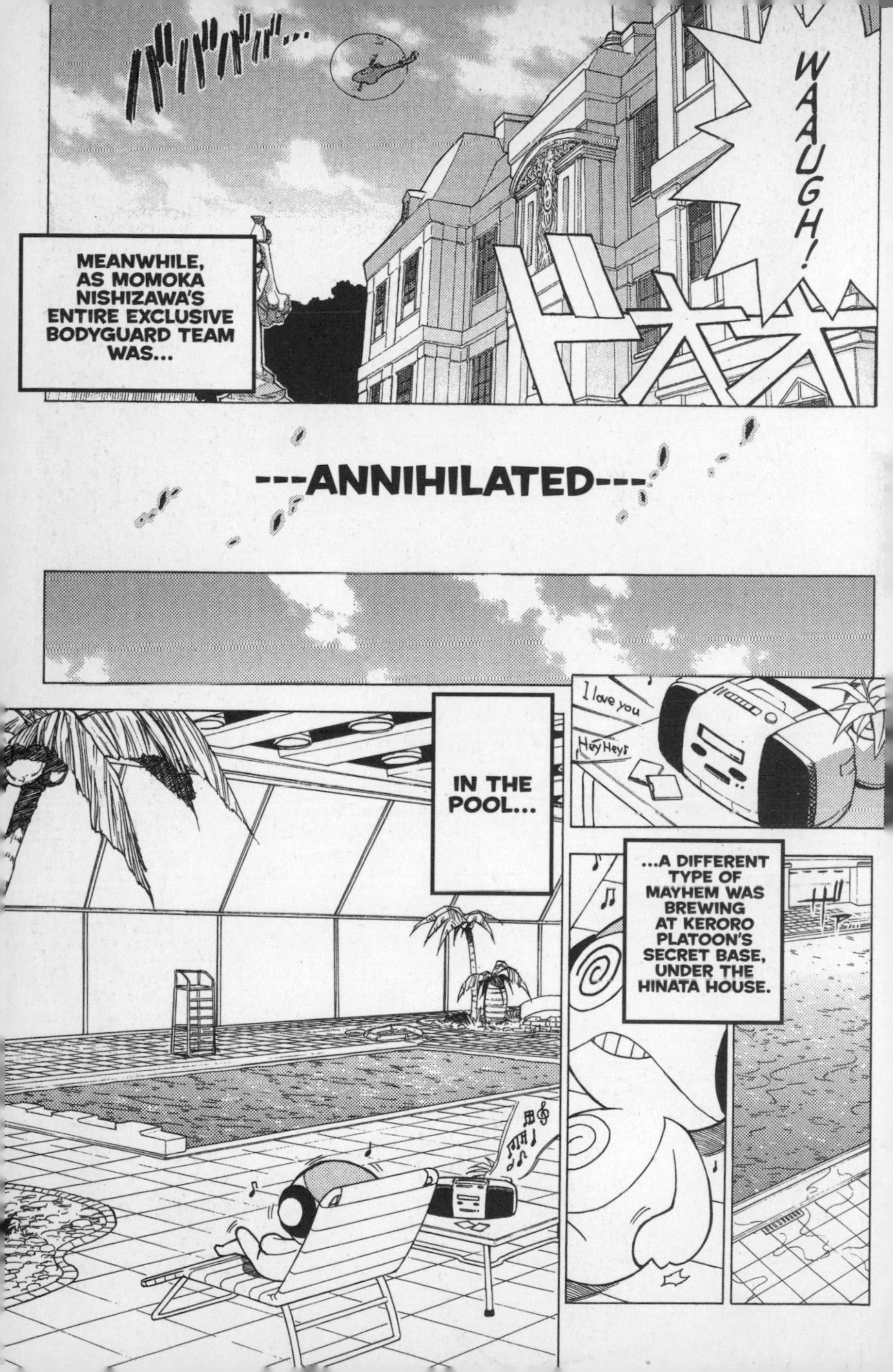
WAAUGH!
MEANWHILE, AS MOMOKA NISHIZAWA'S ENTIRE EXCLUSIVE BODYGUARD TEAM WAS...
---ANNIHILATED---
I love you
Hey Hey
IN THE POOL...
...A DIFFERENT TYPE OF MAYHEM WAS BREWING AT KERORO PLATOON'S SECRET BASE, UNDER THE HINATA HOUSE.

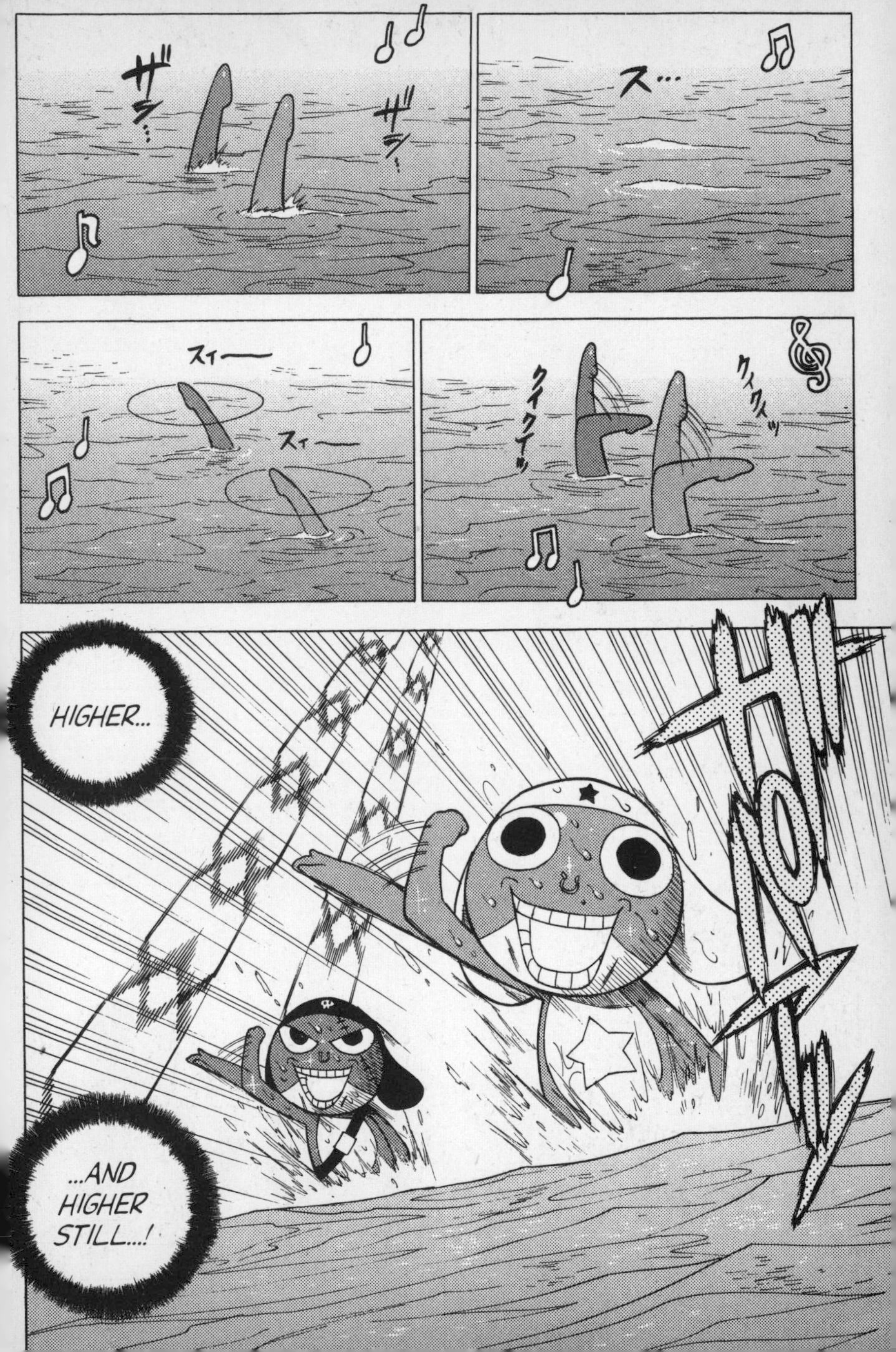
ザブ…
ザブ
ス…
スィー
スィー
クイクイッ
クイクイッ
HIGHER...
...AND HIGHER STILL...!

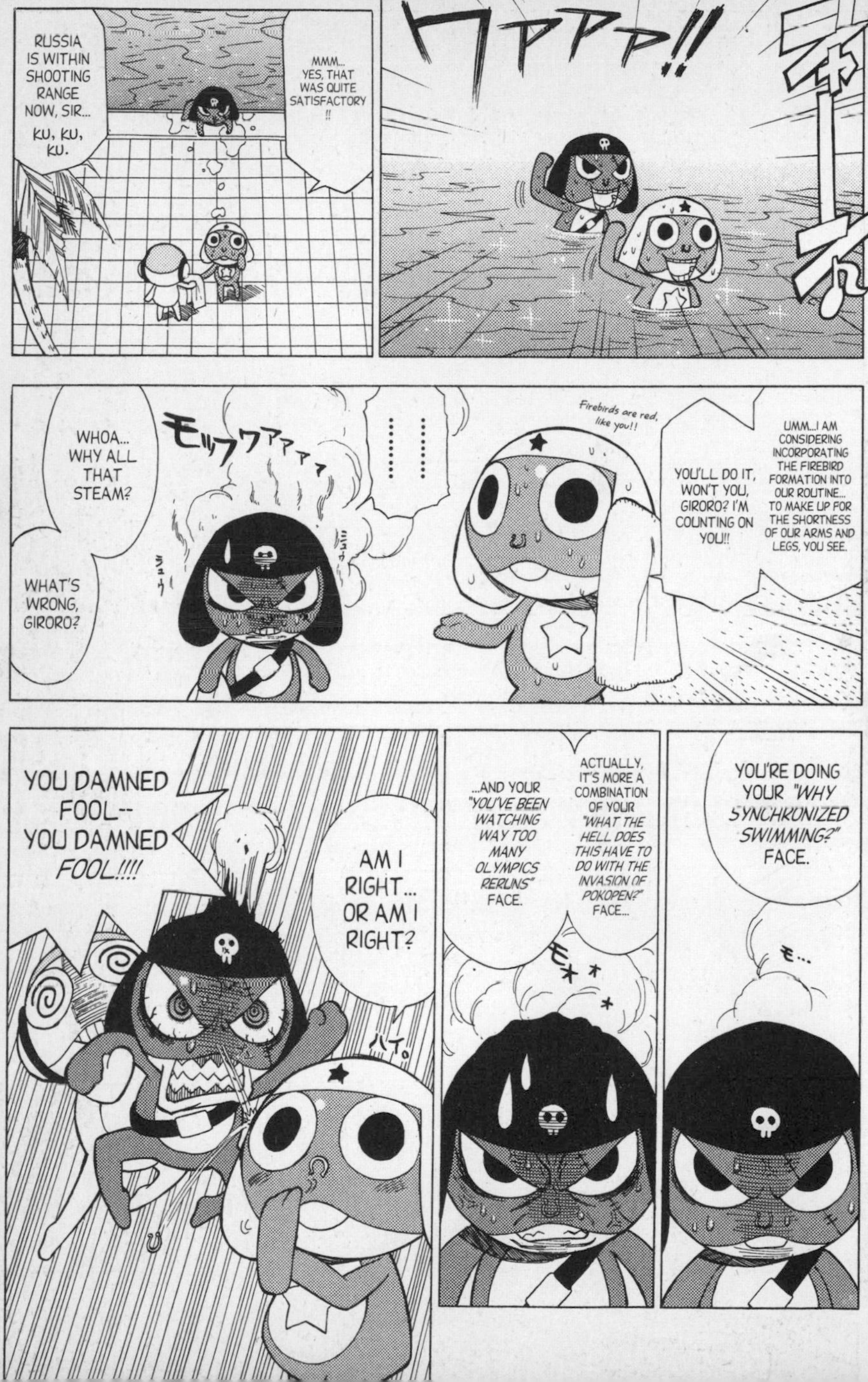
MMM... YES, THAT WAS QUITE SATISFACTORY !!
RUSSIA IS WITHIN SHOOTING RANGE NOW, SIR...
KU, KU, KU.
UMM...I AM CONSIDERING INCORPORATING THE FIREBIRD FORMATION INTO OUR ROUTINE... TO MAKE UP FOR THE SHORTNESS OF OUR ARMS AND LEGS, YOU SEE.
YOU'LL DO IT, WON'T YOU, GIRORO? I'M COUNTING ON YOU!!
Firebirds are red, like you!!
......
WHOA... WHY ALL THAT STEAM?
WHAT'S WRONG, GIRORO?
YOU'RE DOING YOUR "WHY SYNCHRONIZED SWIMMING?" FACE.
ACTUALLY, IT'S MORE A COMBINATION OF YOUR "WHAT THE HELL DOES THIS HAVE TO DO WITH THE INVASION OF POKOPEN?" FACE...
...AND YOUR "YOU'VE BEEN WATCHING WAY TOO MANY OLYMPICS RERUNS" FACE.
AM I RIGHT... OR AM I RIGHT?
YOU DAMNED FOOL-- YOU DAMNED FOOL!!!!

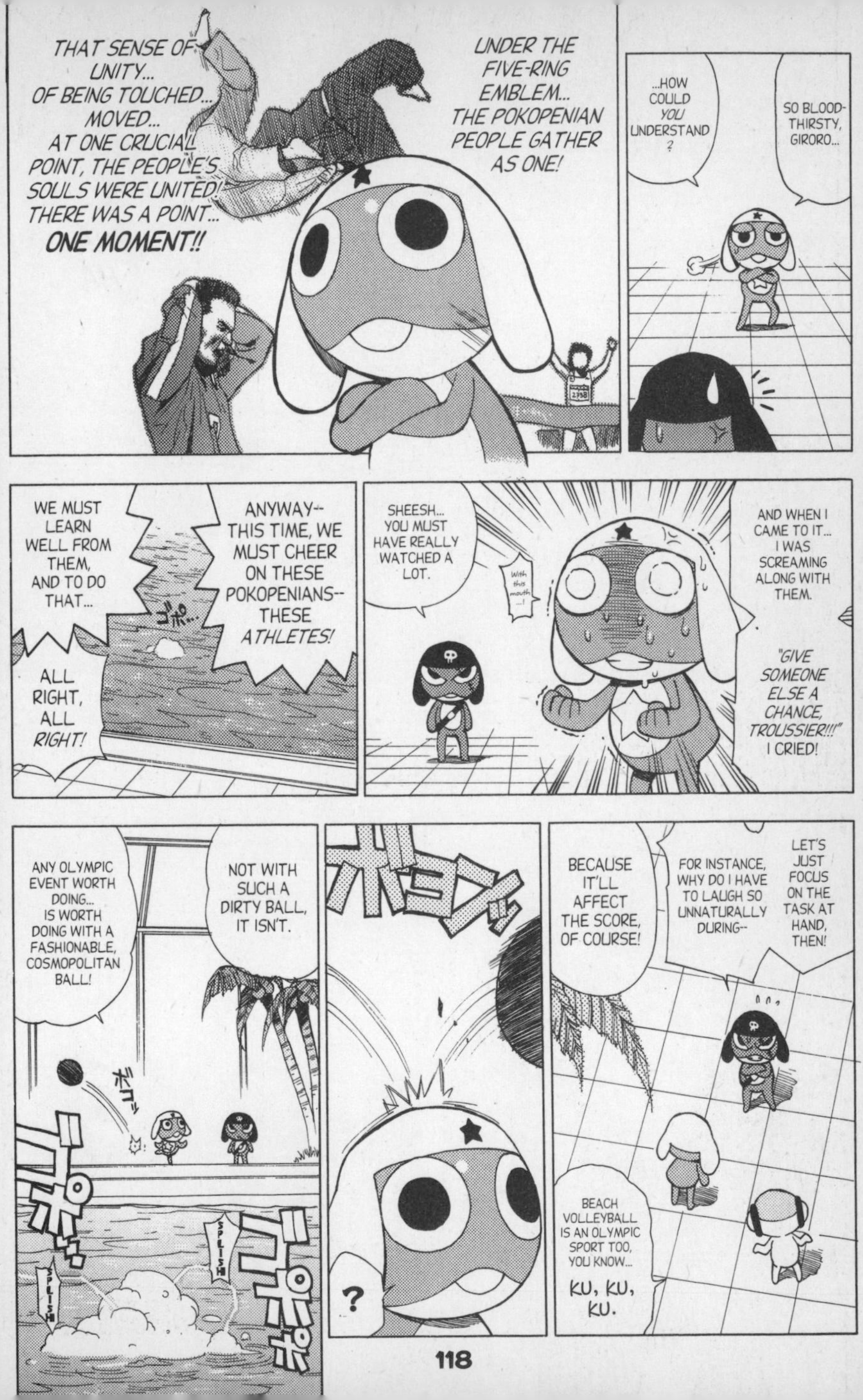
...HOW COULD YOU UNDERSTAND?
SO BLOOD-THIRSTY, GIRORO...
UNDER THE FIVE-RING EMBLEM... THE POKOPENIAN PEOPLE GATHER AS ONE!
THAT SENSE OF UNITY... OF BEING TOUCHED... MOVED... AT ONE CRUCIAL POINT, THE PEOPLE'S SOULS WERE UNITED! THERE WAS A POINT... ONE MOMENT!!
AND WHEN I CAME TO IT... I WAS SCREAMING ALONG WITH THEM.
"GIVE SOMEONE ELSE A CHANCE, TROUSSIER!!!" I CRIED!
SHEESH... YOU MUST HAVE REALLY WATCHED A LOT.
With this mouth...!
ANYWAY-- THIS TIME, WE MUST CHEER ON THESE POKOPENIANS-- THESE ATHLETES!
WE MUST LEARN WELL FROM THEM, AND TO DO THAT...
ALL RIGHT, ALL RIGHT!
LET'S JUST FOCUS ON THE TASK AT HAND, THEN!
FOR INSTANCE, WHY DO I HAVE TO LAUGH SO UNNATURALLY DURING--
BECAUSE IT'LL AFFECT THE SCORE, OF COURSE!
BEACH VOLLEYBALL IS AN OLYMPIC SPORT TOO, YOU KNOW...
KU, KU, KU.
?
NOT WITH SUCH A DIRTY BALL, IT ISN'T.
ANY OLYMPIC EVENT WORTH DOING... IS WORTH DOING WITH A FASHIONABLE, COSMOPOLITAN BALL!
SPLISH
SPLISH

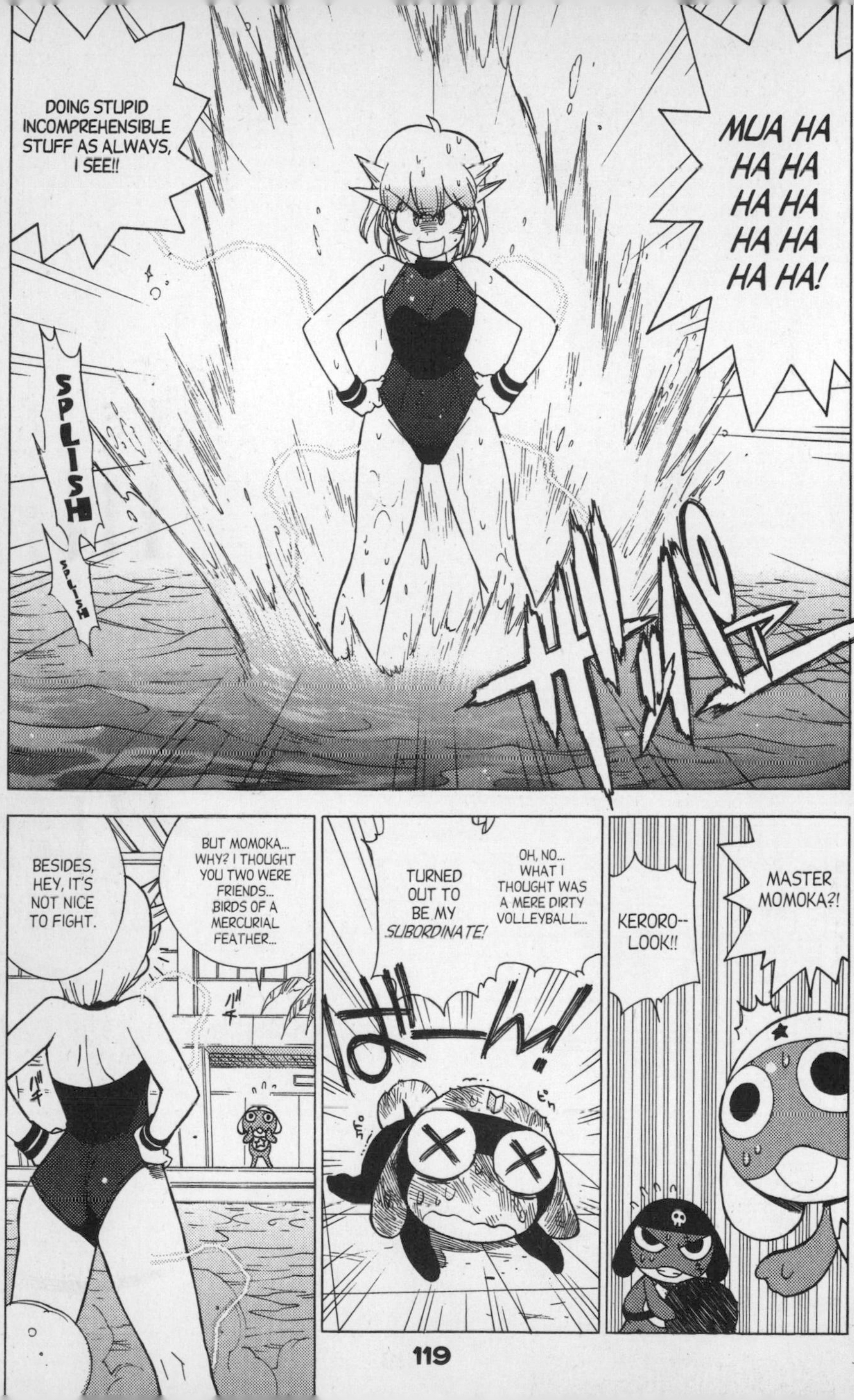
MUA HA HA HA HA HA HA HA HA HA!
DOING STUPID INCOMPREHENSIBLE STUFF AS ALWAYS, I SEE!!
SPLISH
SPLISH
MASTER MOMOKA?!
KERORO-- LOOK!!
OH, NO... WHAT I THOUGHT WAS A MERE DIRTY VOLLEYBALL...
TURNED OUT TO BE MY SUBORDINATE!
BUT MOMOKA... WHY? I THOUGHT YOU TWO WERE FRIENDS... BIRDS OF A MERCURIAL FEATHER...
BESIDES, HEY, IT'S NOT NICE TO FIGHT.

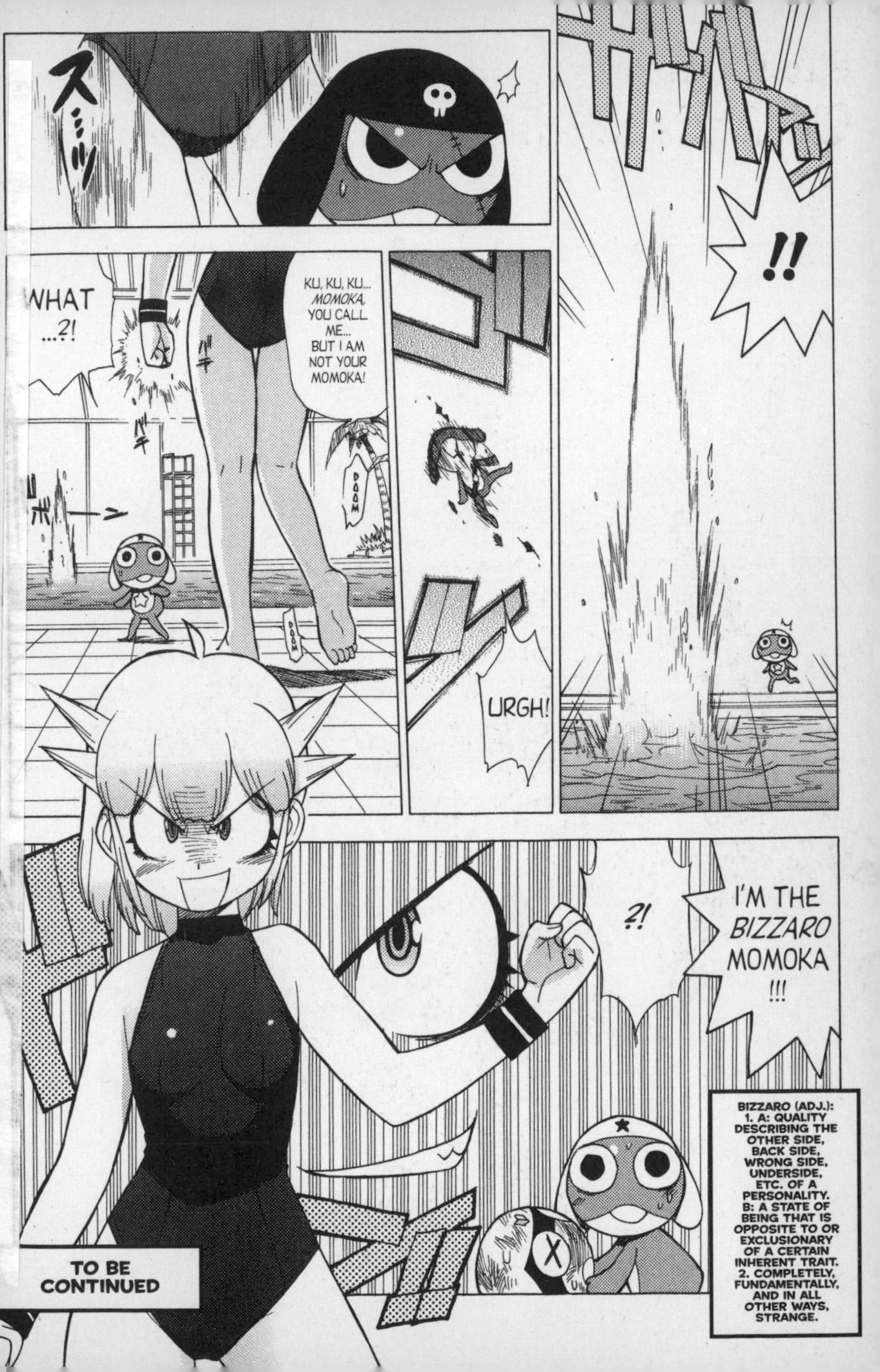

ス
WHAT ...?!
KU, KU, KU... MOMOKA, YOU CALL ME... BUT I AM NOT YOUR MOMOKA!
DOOM
DOOM
URGH!
!!
?!
I'M THE BIZZARO MOMOKA !!!
BIZZARO (ADJ.): 1. A: QUALITY DESCRIBING THE OTHER SIDE, BACK SIDE, WRONG SIDE, UNDERSIDE, ETC. OF A PERSONALITY. B: A STATE OF BEING THAT IS OPPOSITE TO OR EXCLUSIONARY OF A CERTAIN INHERENT TRAIT. 2. COMPLETELY, FUNDAMENTALLY, AND IN ALL OTHER WAYS, STRANGE.
TO BE CONTINUED

ENCOUNTER XXVIII

MOMOKA PLATOON STRIKES BACK

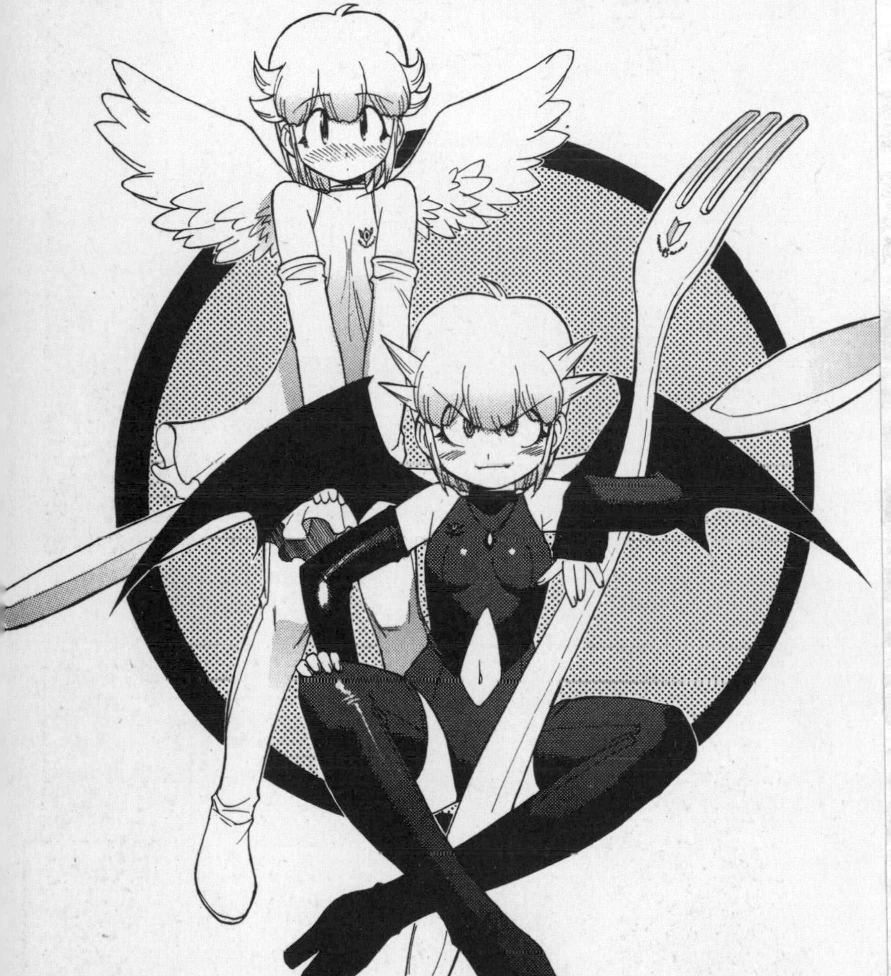

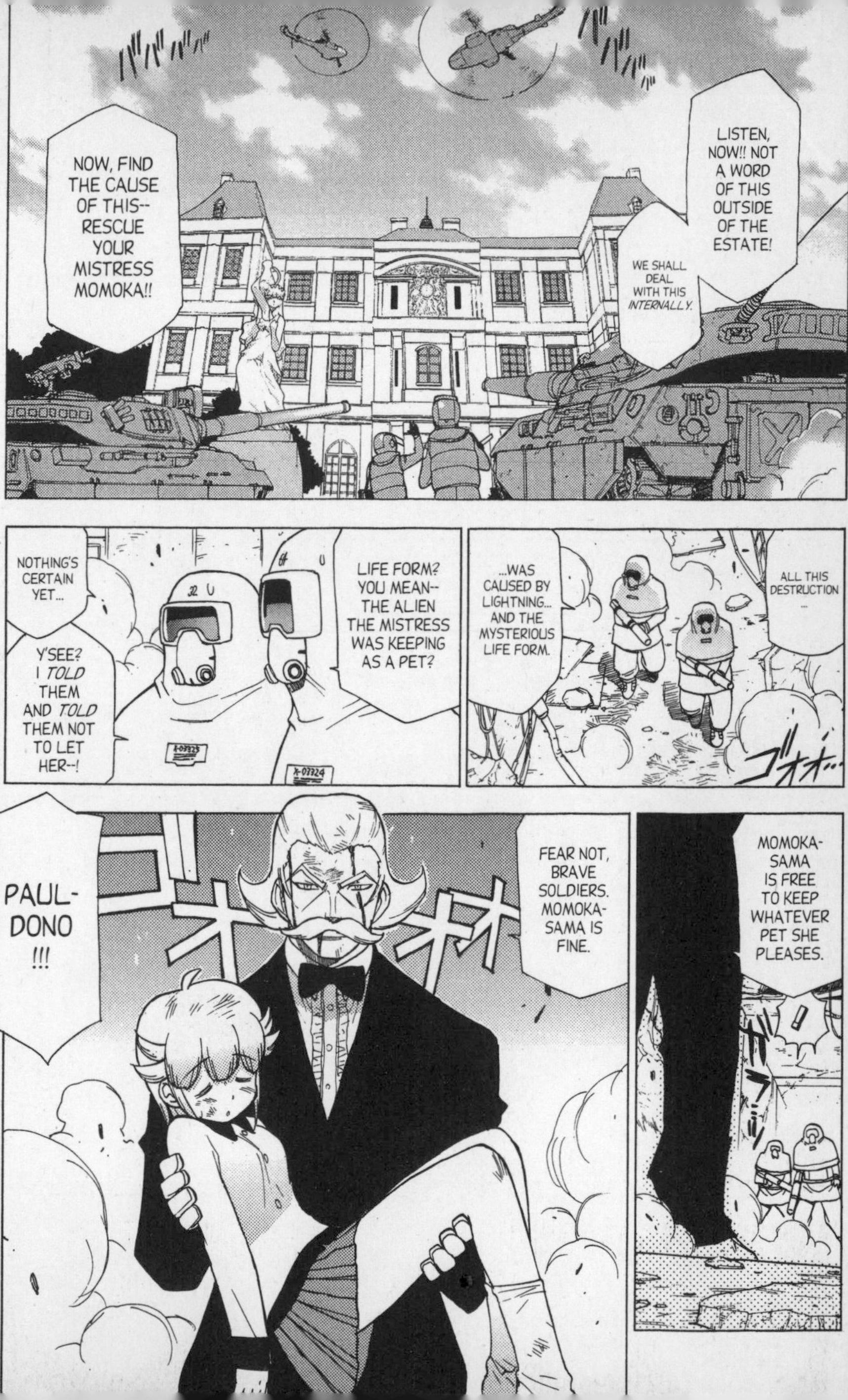
LISTEN, NOW!! NOT A WORD OF THIS OUTSIDE OF THE ESTATE!
WE SHALL DEAL WITH THIS *INTERNALLY*.
NOW, FIND THE CAUSE OF THIS-- RESCUE YOUR MISTRESS MOMOKA!!
ALL THIS DESTRUCTION ...
...WAS CAUSED BY LIGHTNING... AND THE MYSTERIOUS LIFE FORM.
LIFE FORM? YOU MEAN-- THE ALIEN THE MISTRESS WAS KEEPING AS A PET?
NOTHING'S CERTAIN YET...
Y'SEE? I *TOLD* THEM AND *TOLD* THEM NOT TO LET HER--!
MOMOKA-SAMA IS FREE TO KEEP WHATEVER PET SHE PLEASES.
FEAR NOT, BRAVE SOLDIERS. MOMOKA-SAMA IS FINE.
PAUL-DONO !!!

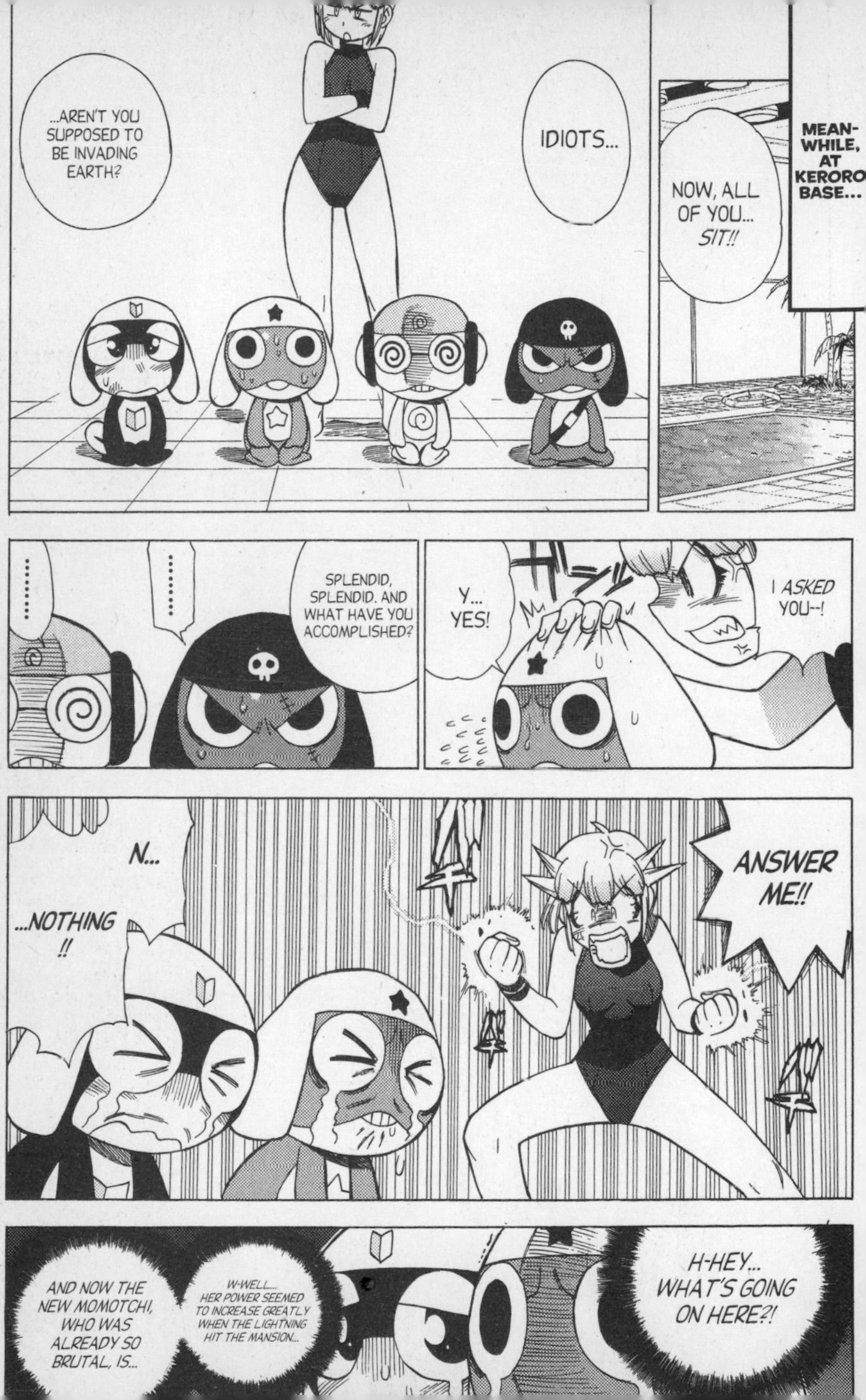
MEAN-WHILE, AT KERORO BASE...
NOW, ALL OF YOU... SIT!!
IDIOTS...
...AREN'T YOU SUPPOSED TO BE INVADING EARTH?
I ASKED YOU--!
Y... YES!
SPLENDID, SPLENDID. AND WHAT HAVE YOU ACCOMPLISHED?
....
....
ANSWER ME!!
N...
...NOTHING!!
H-HEY... WHAT'S GOING ON HERE?!
W-WELL... HER POWER SEEMED TO INCREASE GREATLY WHEN THE LIGHTNING HIT THE MANSION...
AND NOW THE NEW MOMOTCHI, WHO WAS ALREADY SO BRUTAL, IS...

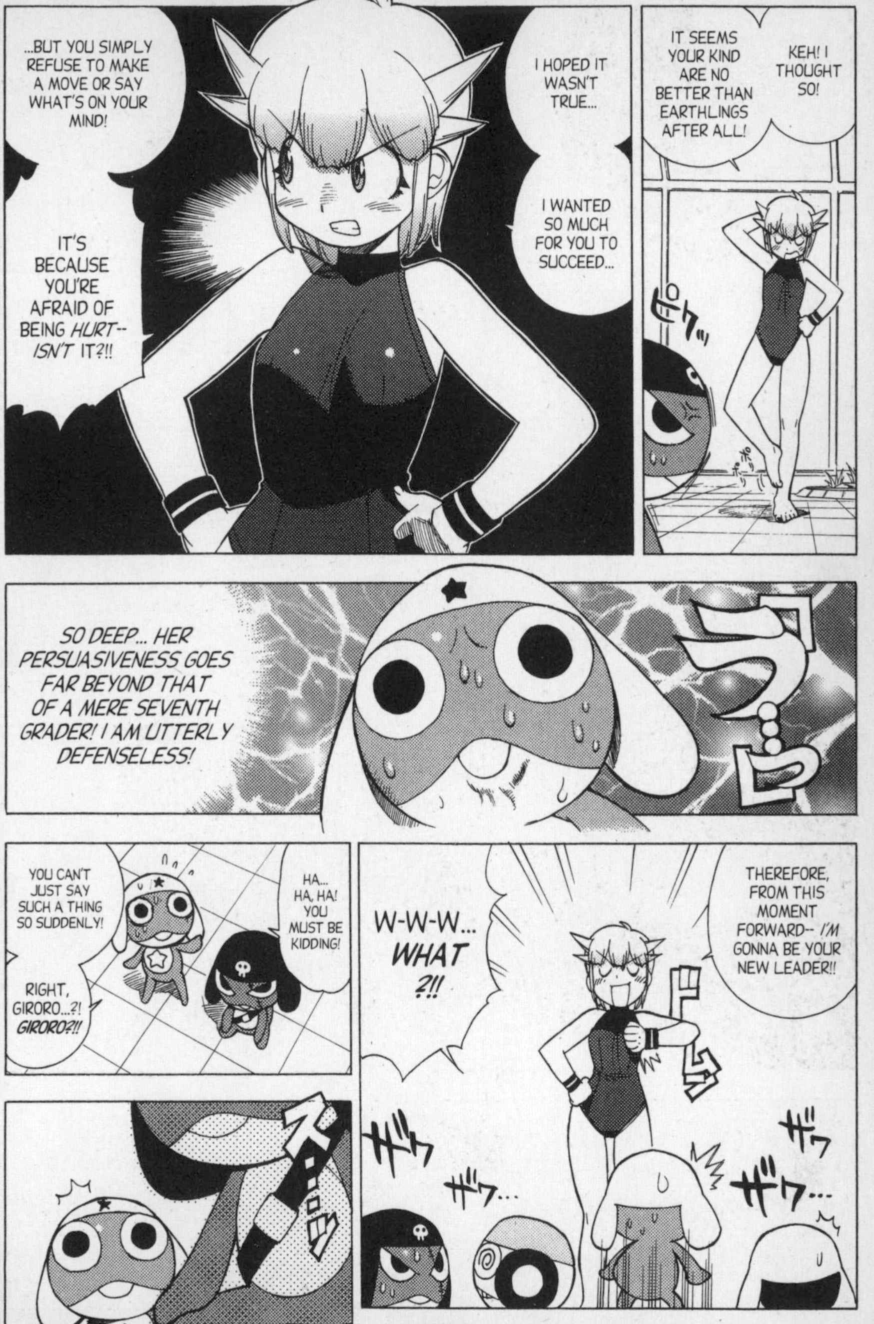
KEH! I THOUGHT SO!
IT SEEMS YOUR KIND ARE NO BETTER THAN EARTHLINGS AFTER ALL!
I HOPED IT WASN'T TRUE...
I WANTED SO MUCH FOR YOU TO SUCCEED...
...BUT YOU SIMPLY REFUSE TO MAKE A MOVE OR SAY WHAT'S ON YOUR MIND!
IT'S BECAUSE YOU'RE AFRAID OF BEING *HURT*-- *ISN'T* IT?!!
SO DEEP... HER PERSUASIVENESS GOES FAR BEYOND THAT OF A MERE SEVENTH GRADER! I AM UTTERLY DEFENSELESS!
THEREFORE, FROM THIS MOMENT FORWARD-- *I'M* GONNA BE YOUR NEW LEADER!!
W-W-W... *WHAT ?!!*
HA... HA, HA! YOU MUST BE KIDDING!
YOU CAN'T JUST SAY SUCH A THING SO SUDDENLY!
RIGHT, GIRORO...?! *GIRORO?!!*

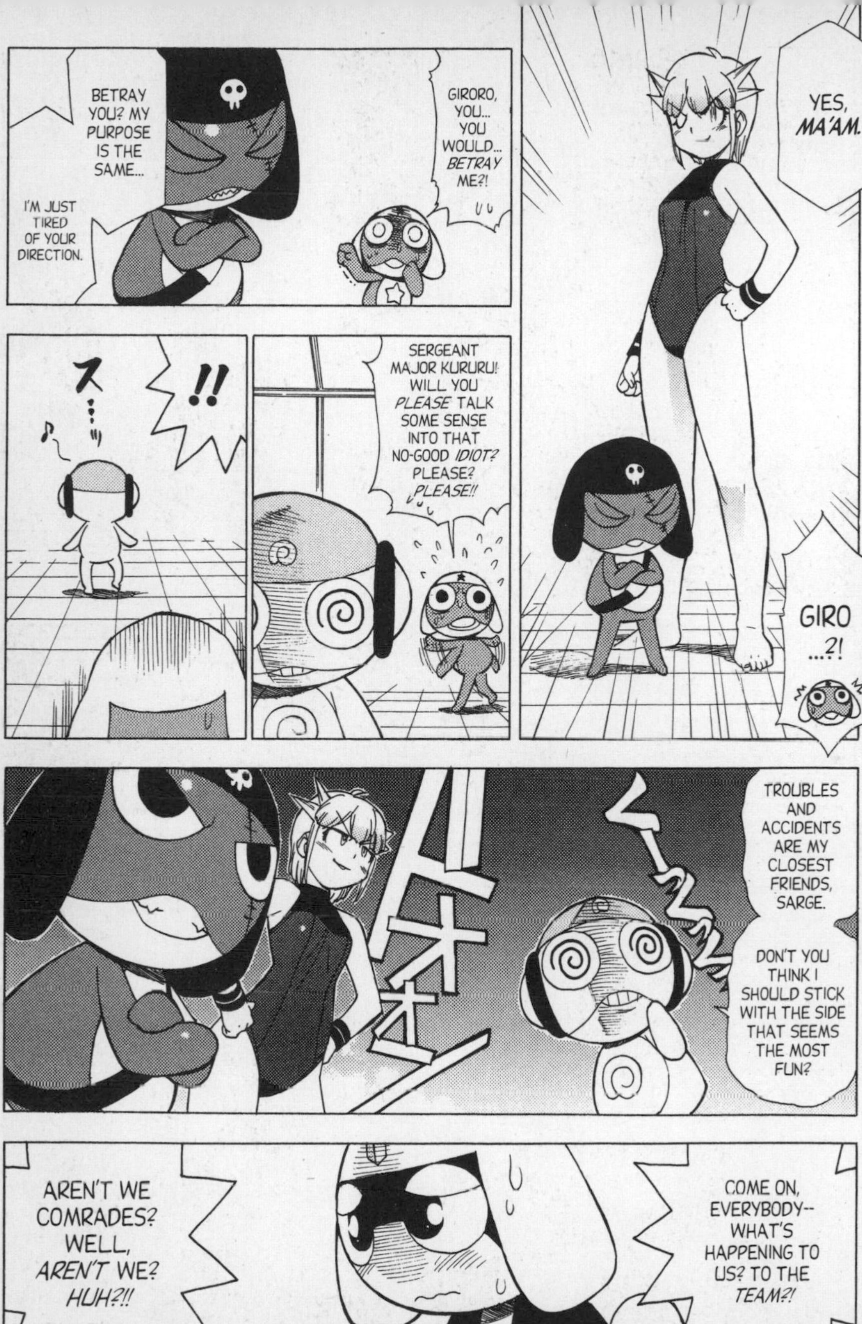
GIRORO, YOU... YOU WOULD... BETRAY ME?!
BETRAY YOU? MY PURPOSE IS THE SAME...
I'M JUST TIRED OF YOUR DIRECTION.
YES, MA'AM.
GIRO ...?!
SERGEANT MAJOR KURURU! WILL YOU PLEASE TALK SOME SENSE INTO THAT NO-GOOD IDIOT? PLEASE? PLEASE!!
!!
ス
TROUBLES AND ACCIDENTS ARE MY CLOSEST FRIENDS, SARGE.
DON'T YOU THINK I SHOULD STICK WITH THE SIDE THAT SEEMS THE MOST FUN?
COME ON, EVERYBODY-- WHAT'S HAPPENING TO US? TO THE TEAM?!
AREN'T WE COMRADES? WELL, AREN'T WE? HUH?!!

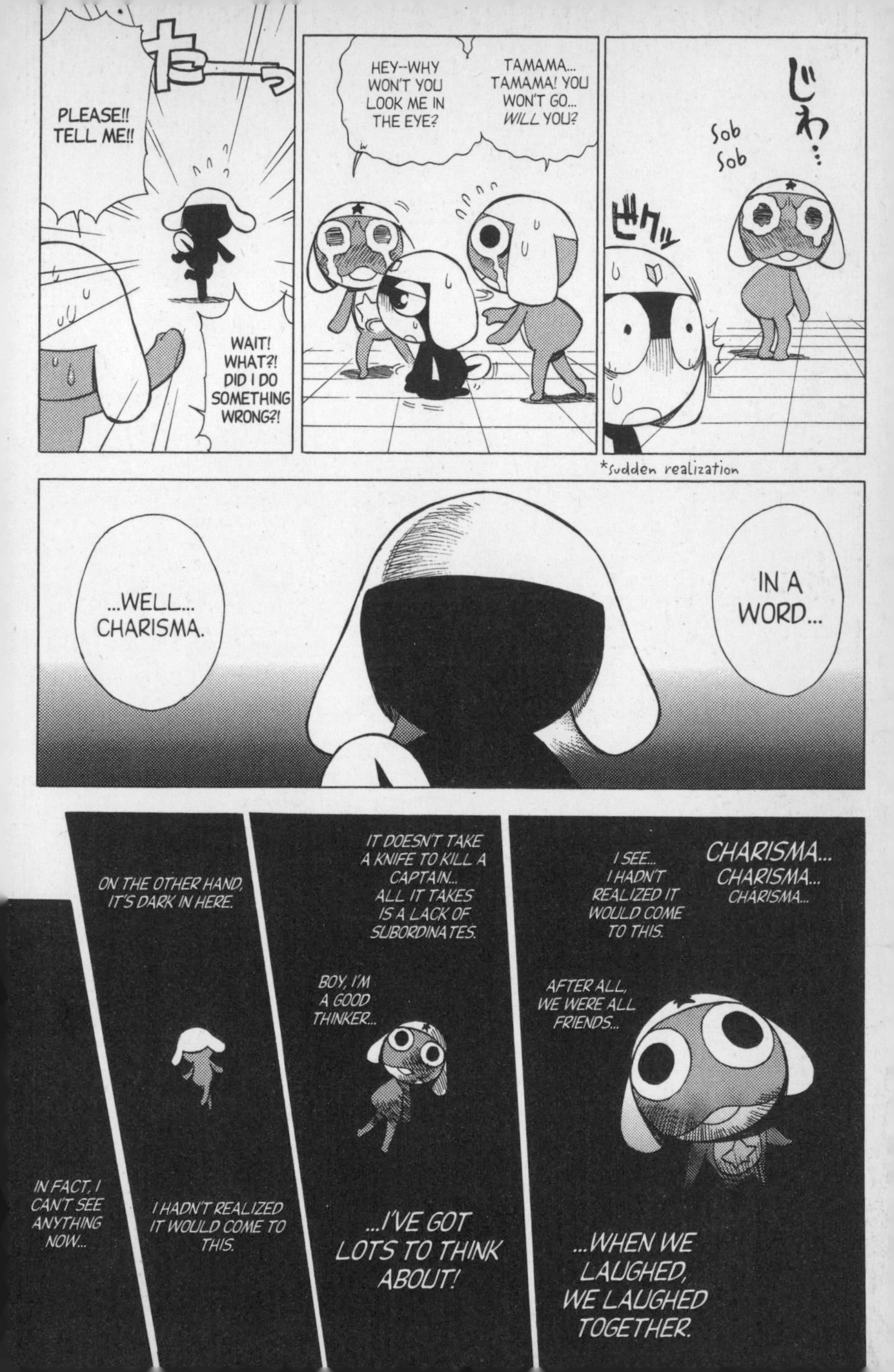
じわ…
Sob
Sob
ビクッ
*sudden realization
TAMAMA... TAMAMA! YOU WON'T GO... *WILL* YOU?
HEY--WHY WON'T YOU LOOK ME IN THE EYE?
たっ
PLEASE!! TELL ME!!
WAIT! WHAT?! DID I DO SOMETHING WRONG?!
IN A WORD...
...WELL... CHARISMA.
CHARISMA... CHARISMA... CHARISMA...
I SEE... I HADN'T REALIZED IT WOULD COME TO THIS.
AFTER ALL, WE WERE ALL FRIENDS...
...WHEN WE LAUGHED, WE LAUGHED TOGETHER.
IT DOESN'T TAKE A KNIFE TO KILL A CAPTAIN... ALL IT TAKES IS A LACK OF SUBORDINATES.
BOY, I'M A GOOD THINKER...
...I'VE GOT LOTS TO THINK ABOUT!
ON THE OTHER HAND, IT'S DARK IN HERE.
I HADN'T REALIZED IT WOULD COME TO THIS.
IN FACT, I CAN'T SEE ANYTHING NOW...

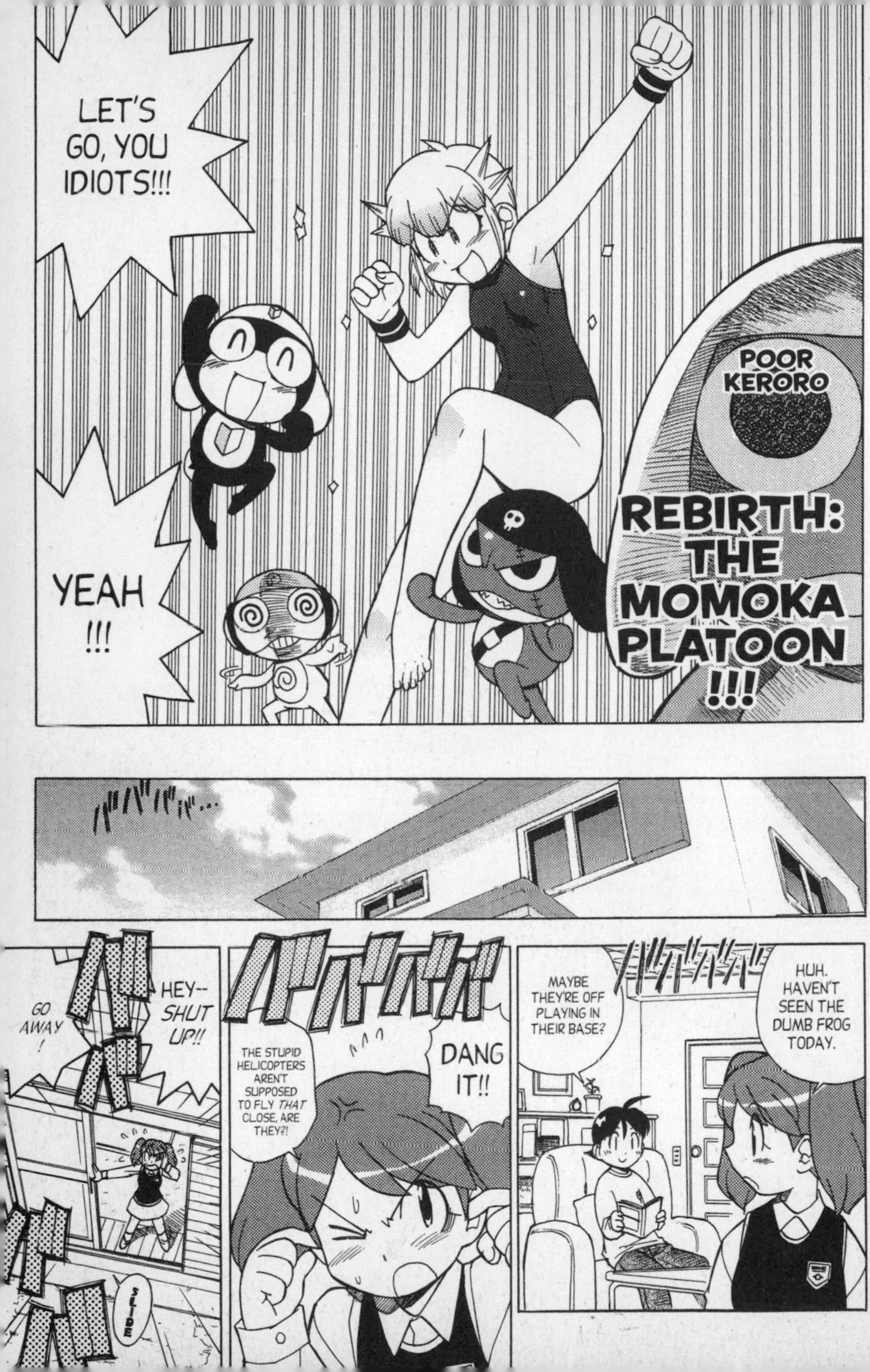
LET'S GO, YOU IDIOTS!!!
POOR KERORO
REBIRTH: THE MOMOKA PLATOON !!!
YEAH !!!
HUH. HAVEN'T SEEN THE DUMB FROG TODAY.
MAYBE THEY'RE OFF PLAYING IN THEIR BASE?
DANG IT!!
THE STUPID HELICOPTERS AREN'T SUPPOSED TO FLY THAT CLOSE, ARE THEY?!
HEY-- SHUT UP!!
GO AWAY!
SLIDE

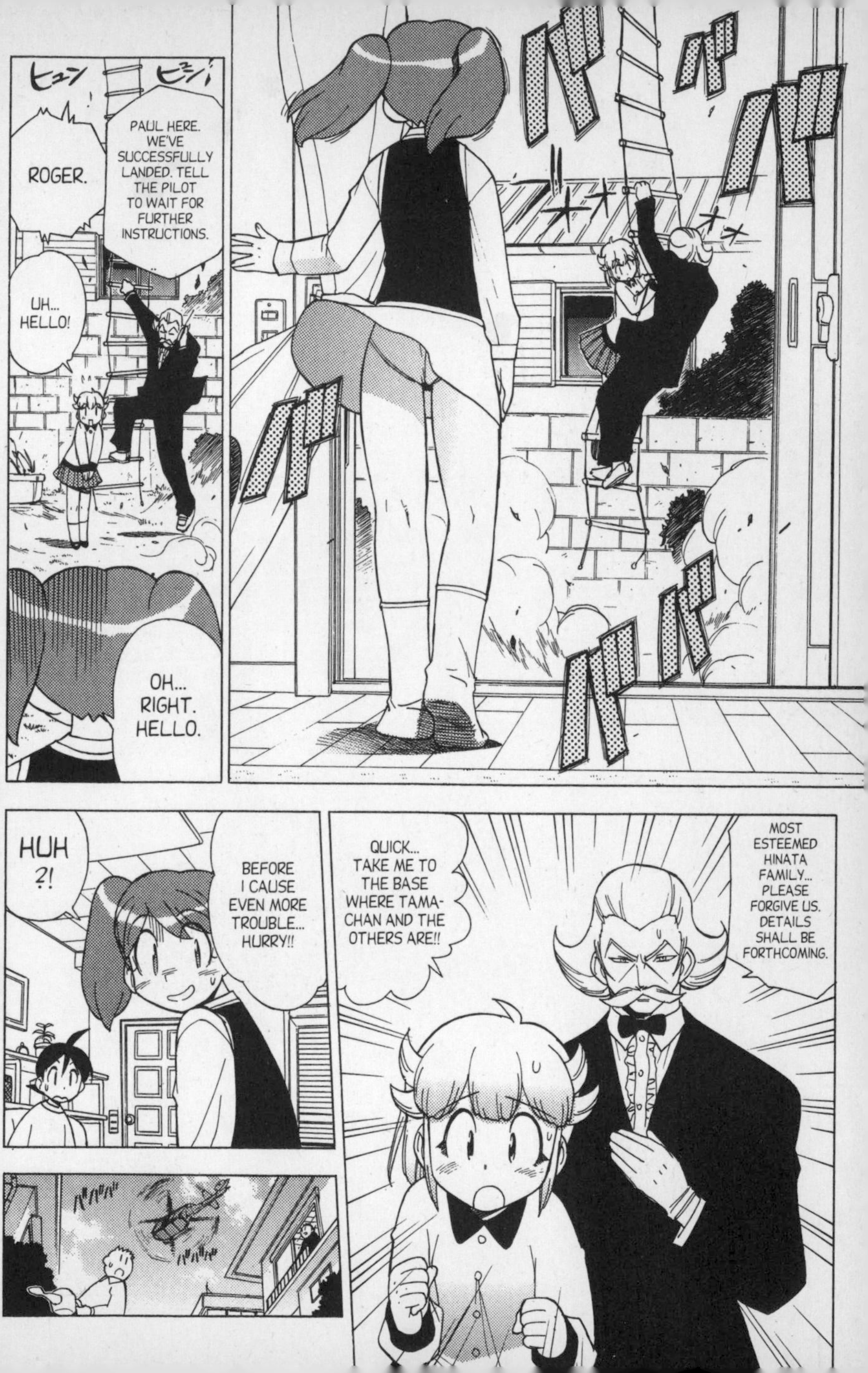
PAUL HERE. WE'VE SUCCESSFULLY LANDED. TELL THE PILOT TO WAIT FOR FURTHER INSTRUCTIONS.
ROGER.
UH... HELLO!
OH... RIGHT. HELLO.
MOST ESTEEMED HINATA FAMILY... PLEASE FORGIVE US. DETAILS SHALL BE FORTHCOMING.
QUICK... TAKE ME TO THE BASE WHERE TAMA-CHAN AND THE OTHERS ARE!!
BEFORE I CAUSE EVEN MORE TROUBLE... HURRY!!
HUH ?!

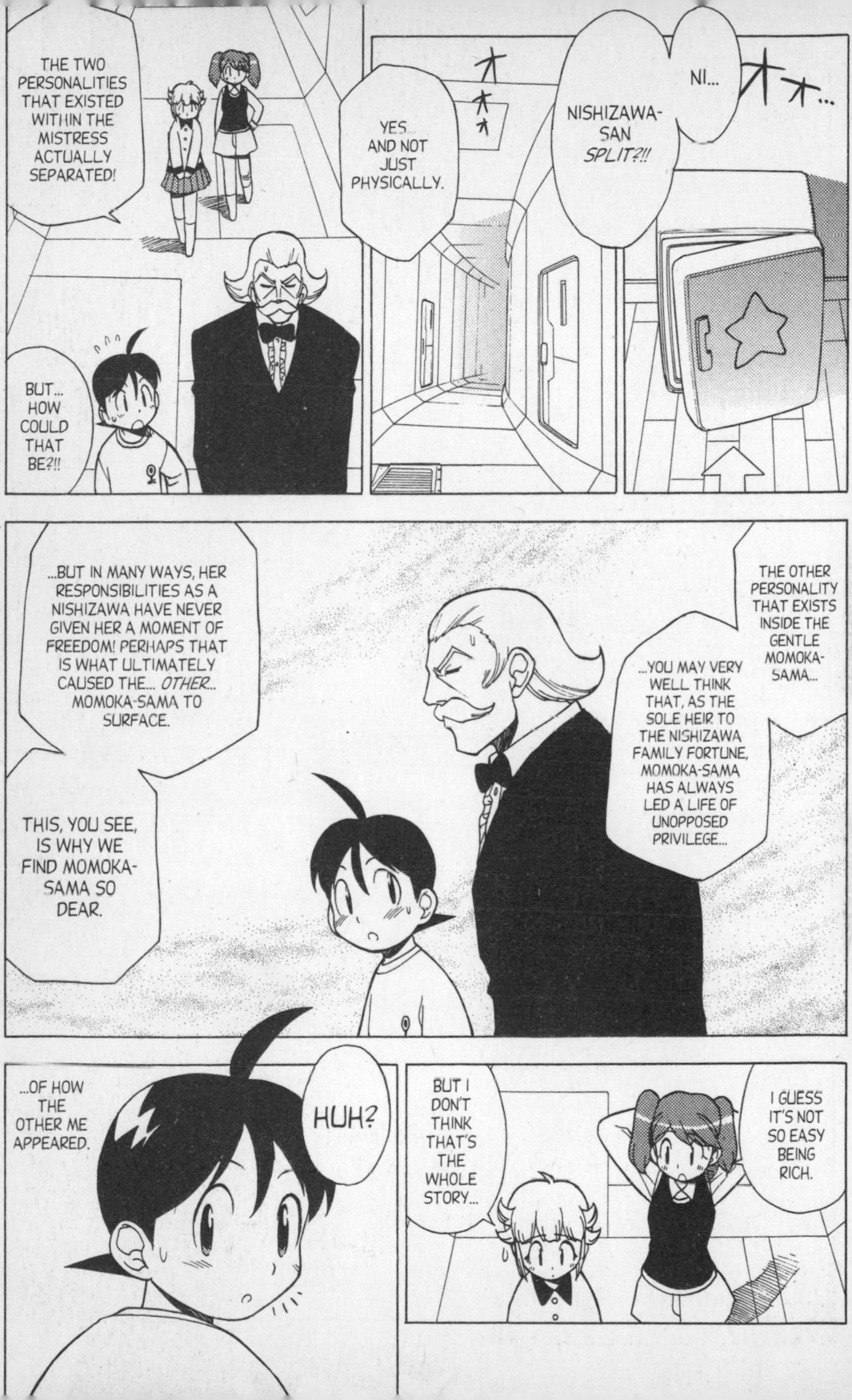
NI...
NISHIZAWA-SAN *SPLIT?!!*
YES... AND NOT JUST PHYSICALLY.
THE TWO PERSONALITIES THAT EXISTED WITHIN THE MISTRESS ACTUALLY SEPARATED!
BUT... HOW COULD THAT BE?!!
THE OTHER PERSONALITY THAT EXISTS INSIDE THE GENTLE MOMOKA-SAMA...
...YOU MAY VERY WELL THINK THAT, AS THE SOLE HEIR TO THE NISHIZAWA FAMILY FORTUNE, MOMOKA-SAMA HAS ALWAYS LED A LIFE OF UNOPPOSED PRIVILEGE...
...BUT IN MANY WAYS, HER RESPONSIBILITIES AS A NISHIZAWA HAVE NEVER GIVEN HER A MOMENT OF FREEDOM! PERHAPS THAT IS WHAT ULTIMATELY CAUSED THE... *OTHER*... MOMOKA-SAMA TO SURFACE.
THIS, YOU SEE, IS WHY WE FIND MOMOKA-SAMA SO DEAR.
I GUESS IT'S NOT SO EASY BEING RICH.
BUT I DON'T THINK THAT'S THE WHOLE STORY...
HUH?
...OF HOW THE OTHER ME APPEARED.

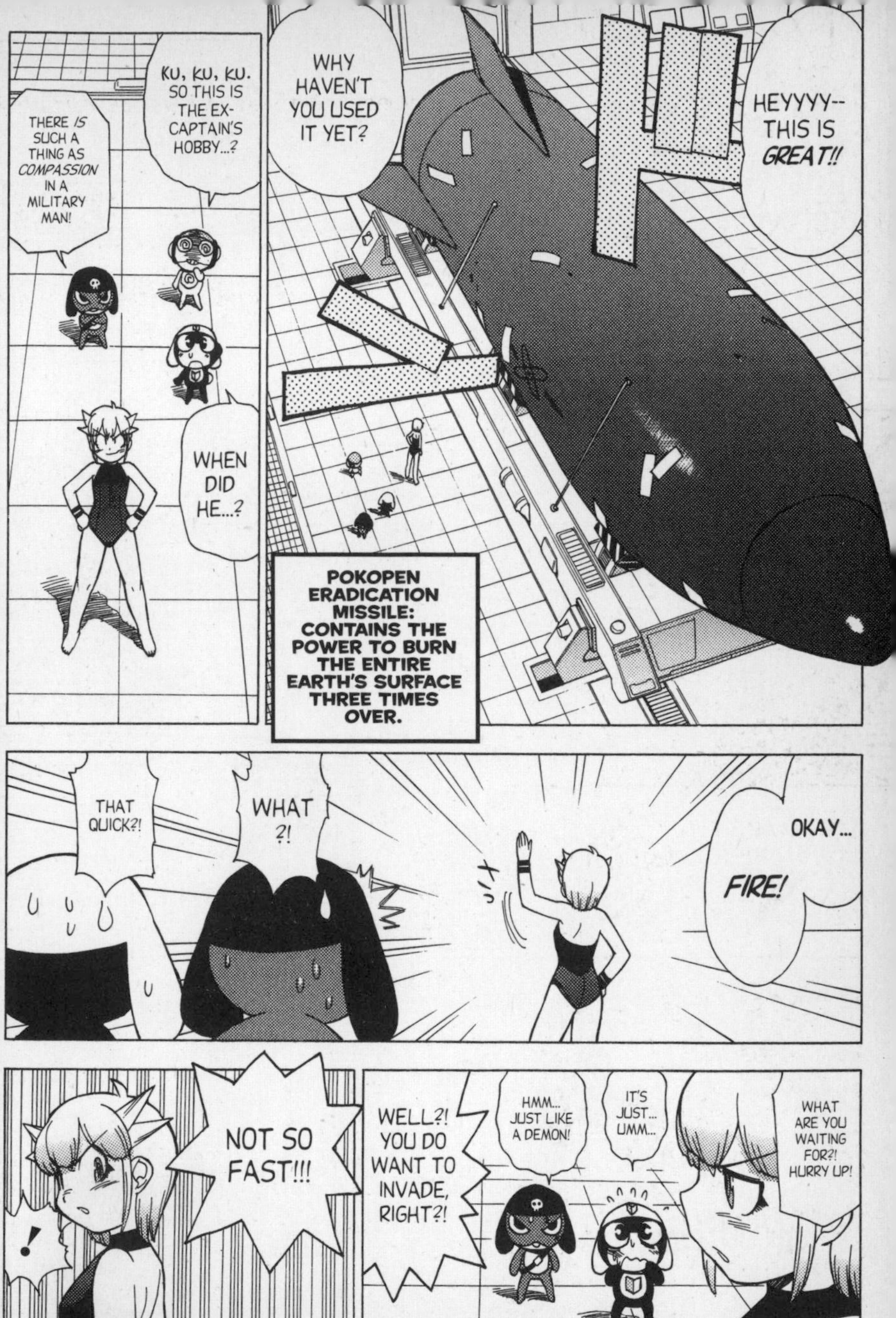
HEYYYY-- THIS IS *GREAT!!*
WHY HAVEN'T YOU USED IT YET?
POKOPEN ERADICATION MISSILE: CONTAINS THE POWER TO BURN THE ENTIRE EARTH'S SURFACE THREE TIMES OVER.
KU, KU, KU. SO THIS IS THE EX-CAPTAIN'S HOBBY...?
THERE *IS* SUCH A THING AS *COMPASSION* IN A MILITARY MAN!
WHEN DID HE...?
OKAY... *FIRE!*
WHAT?!
THAT QUICK?!
WHAT ARE YOU WAITING FOR?! HURRY UP!
IT'S JUST... UMM...
HMM... JUST LIKE A DEMON!
WELL?! YOU DO WANT TO INVADE, RIGHT?!
NOT SO FAST!!!
!

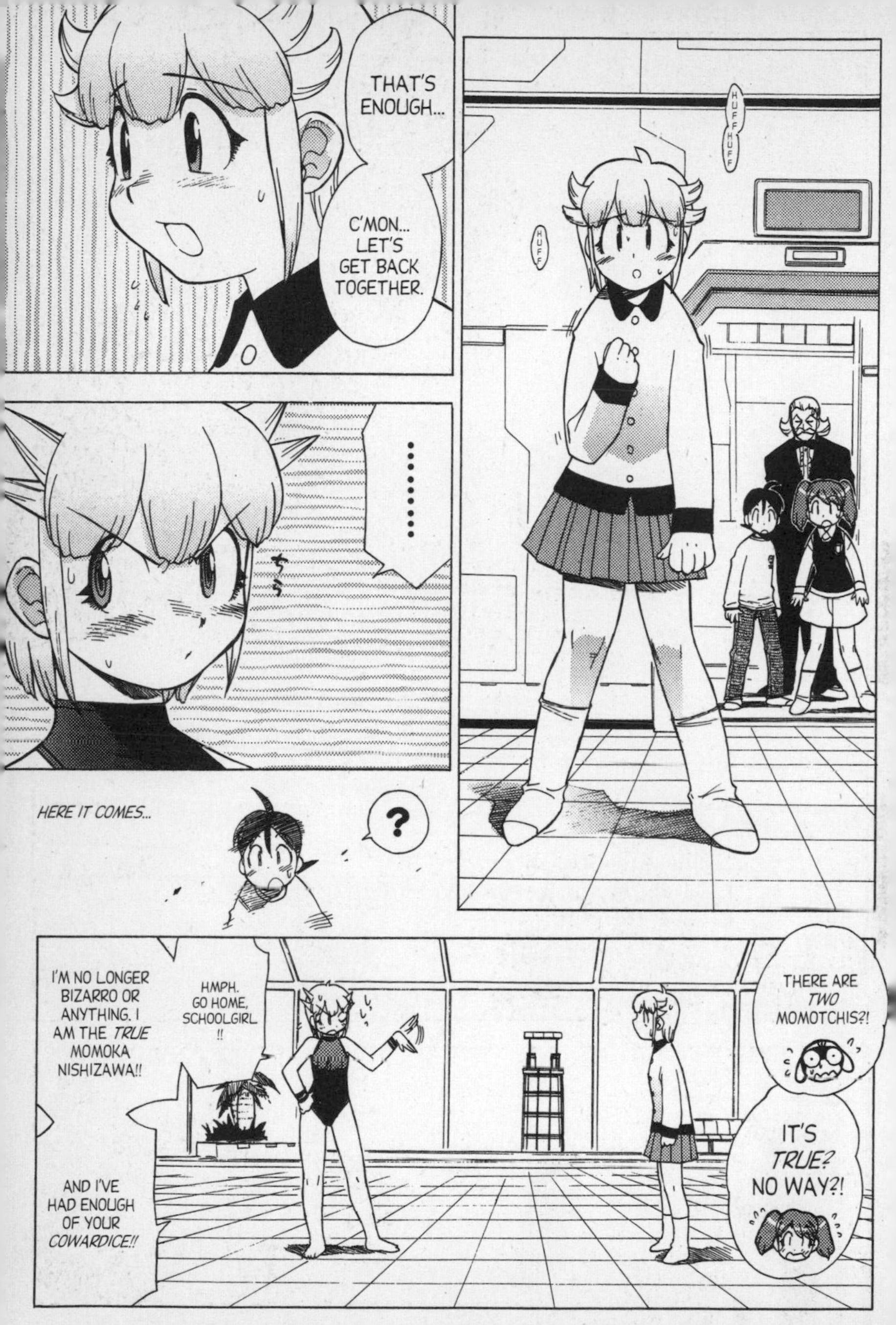
THAT'S ENOUGH...
C'MON... LET'S GET BACK TOGETHER.
HUFF HUFF
HUFF
....
HERE IT COMES...
?
THERE ARE TWO MOMOTCHIS?!
IT'S TRUE? NO WAY?!
HMPH. GO HOME, SCHOOLGIRL!!
I'M NO LONGER BIZARRO OR ANYTHING. I AM THE TRUE MOMOKA NISHIZAWA!!
AND I'VE HAD ENOUGH OF YOUR COWARDICE!!

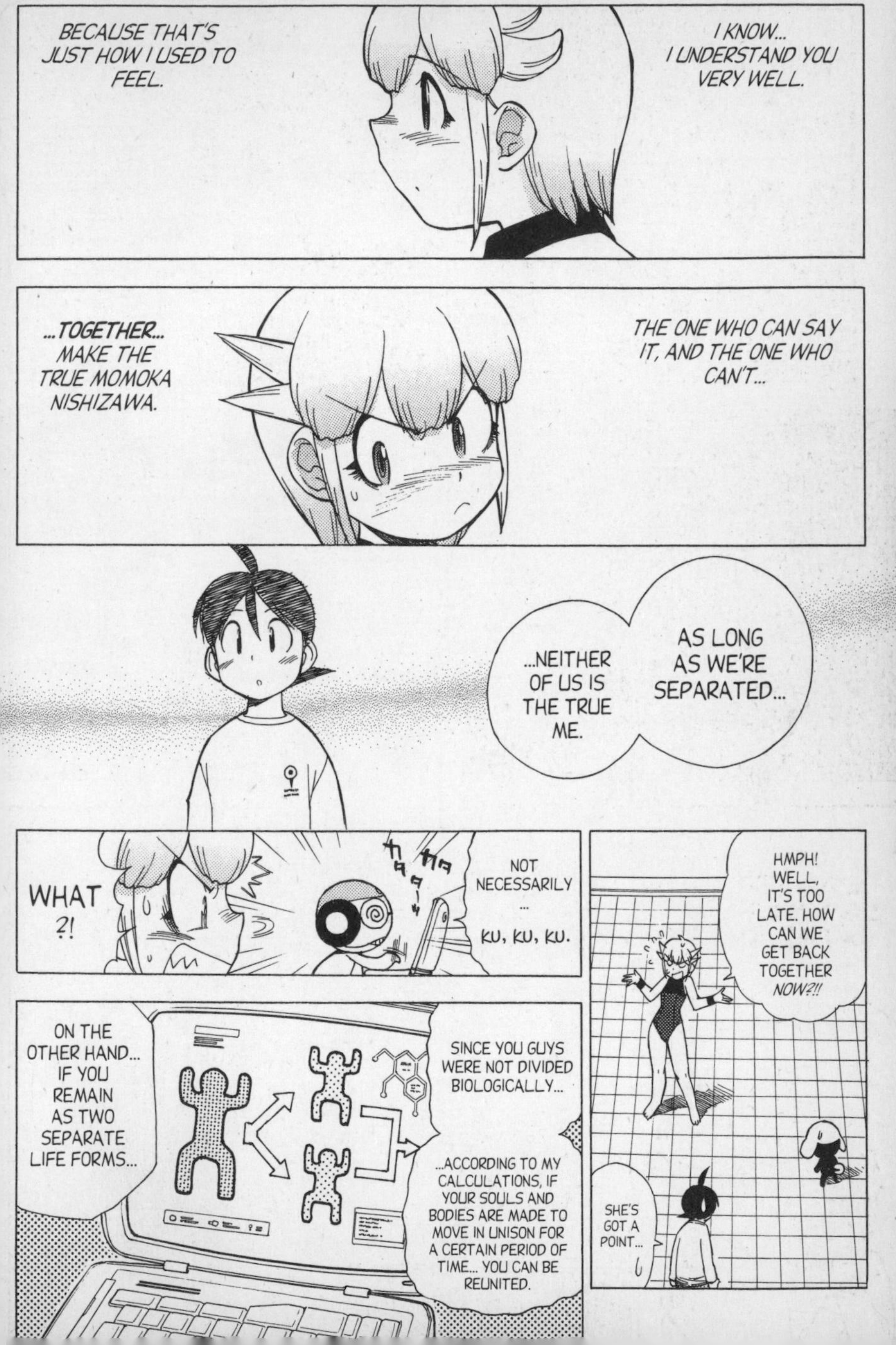
I KNOW... I UNDERSTAND YOU VERY WELL.
BECAUSE THAT'S JUST HOW I USED TO FEEL.
THE ONE WHO CAN SAY IT, AND THE ONE WHO CAN'T...
...TOGETHER... MAKE THE TRUE MOMOKA NISHIZAWA.
AS LONG AS WE'RE SEPARATED...
...NEITHER OF US IS THE TRUE ME.
HMPH! WELL, IT'S TOO LATE. HOW CAN WE GET BACK TOGETHER NOW?!!
SHE'S GOT A POINT...
NOT NECESSARILY ... KU, KU, KU.
WHAT ?!
SINCE YOU GUYS WERE NOT DIVIDED BIOLOGICALLY...
...ACCORDING TO MY CALCULATIONS, IF YOUR SOULS AND BODIES ARE MADE TO MOVE IN UNISON FOR A CERTAIN PERIOD OF TIME... YOU CAN BE REUNITED.
ON THE OTHER HAND... IF YOU REMAIN AS TWO SEPARATE LIFE FORMS...

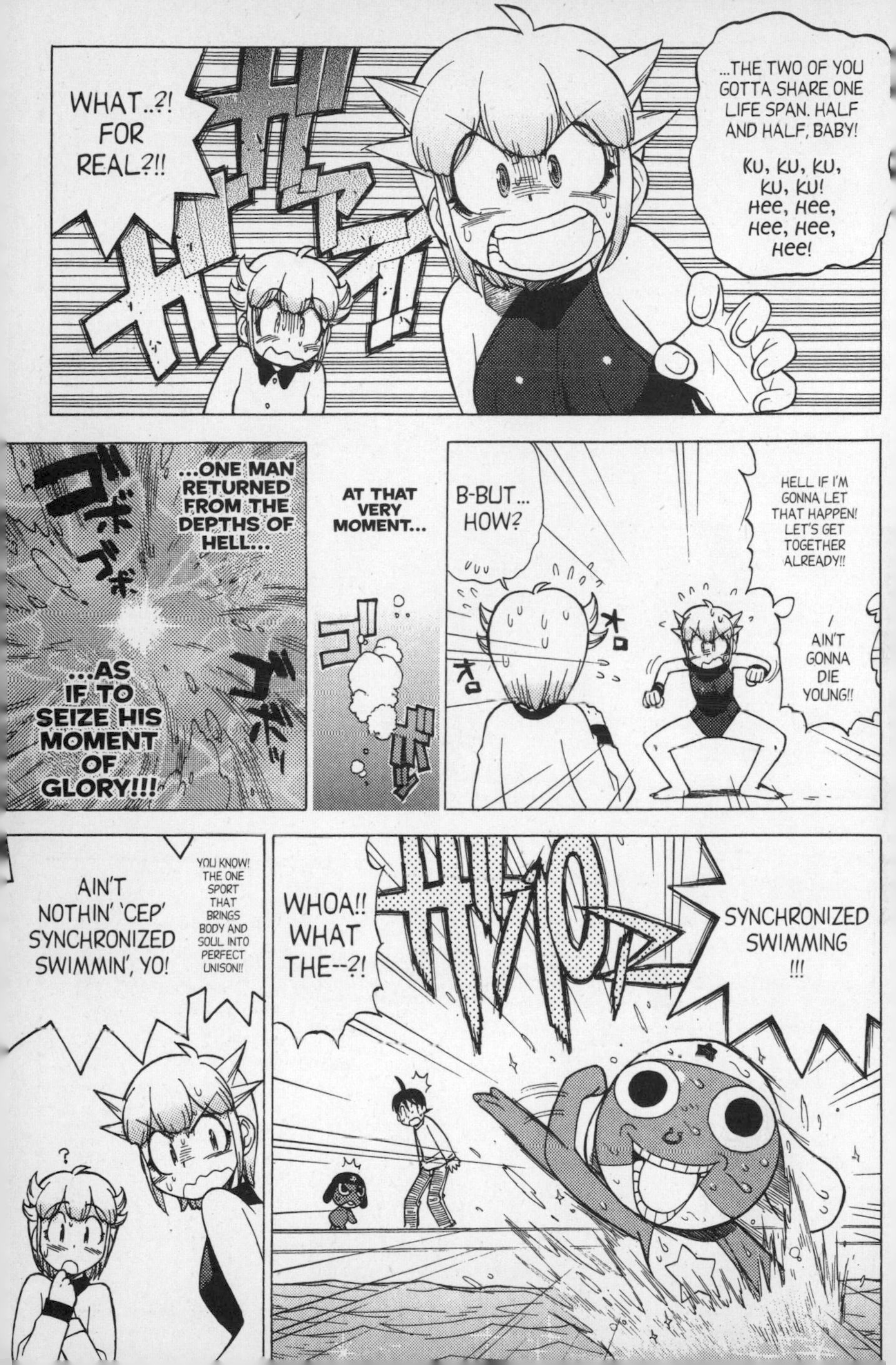
...THE TWO OF YOU GOTTA SHARE ONE LIFE SPAN. HALF AND HALF, BABY!
KU, KU, KU, KU, KU! HEE, HEE, HEE, HEE, HEE!
WHAT..?! FOR REAL?!!
HELL IF I'M GONNA LET THAT HAPPEN! LET'S GET TOGETHER ALREADY!!
I AIN'T GONNA DIE YOUNG!!
B-BUT... HOW?
AT THAT VERY MOMENT...
...ONE MAN RETURNED FROM THE DEPTHS OF HELL...
...AS IF TO SEIZE HIS MOMENT OF GLORY!!!
SYNCHRONIZED SWIMMING !!!
WHOA!! WHAT THE--?!
YOU KNOW! THE ONE SPORT THAT BRINGS BODY AND SOUL INTO PERFECT UNISON!!
AIN'T NOTHIN' 'CEP' SYNCHRONIZED SWIMMIN', YO!

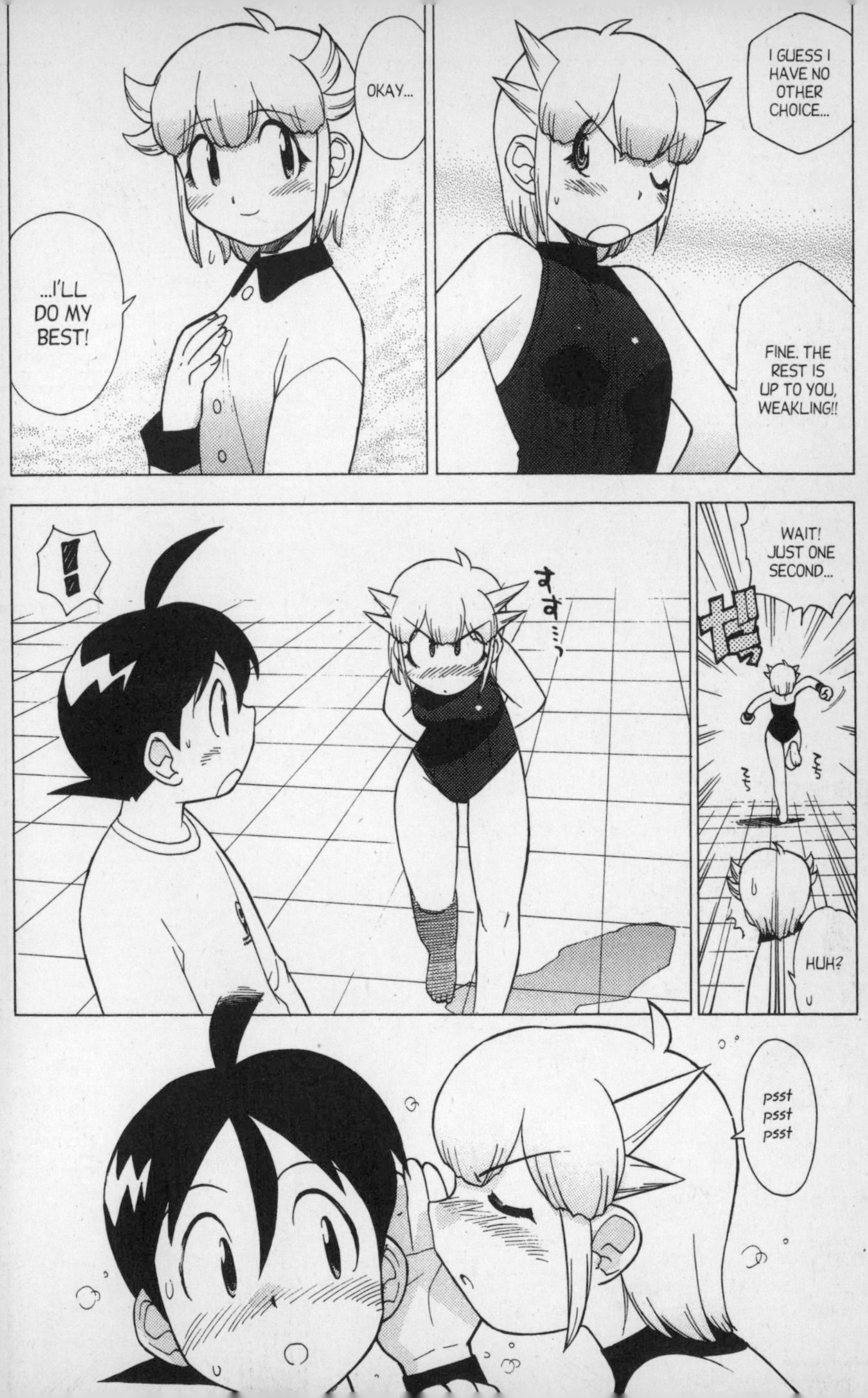
I GUESS I HAVE NO OTHER CHOICE...
FINE. THE REST IS UP TO YOU, WEAKLING!!
OKAY...
...I'LL DO MY BEST!
WAIT! JUST ONE SECOND...
HUH?
!!
すす...
psst
psst
psst

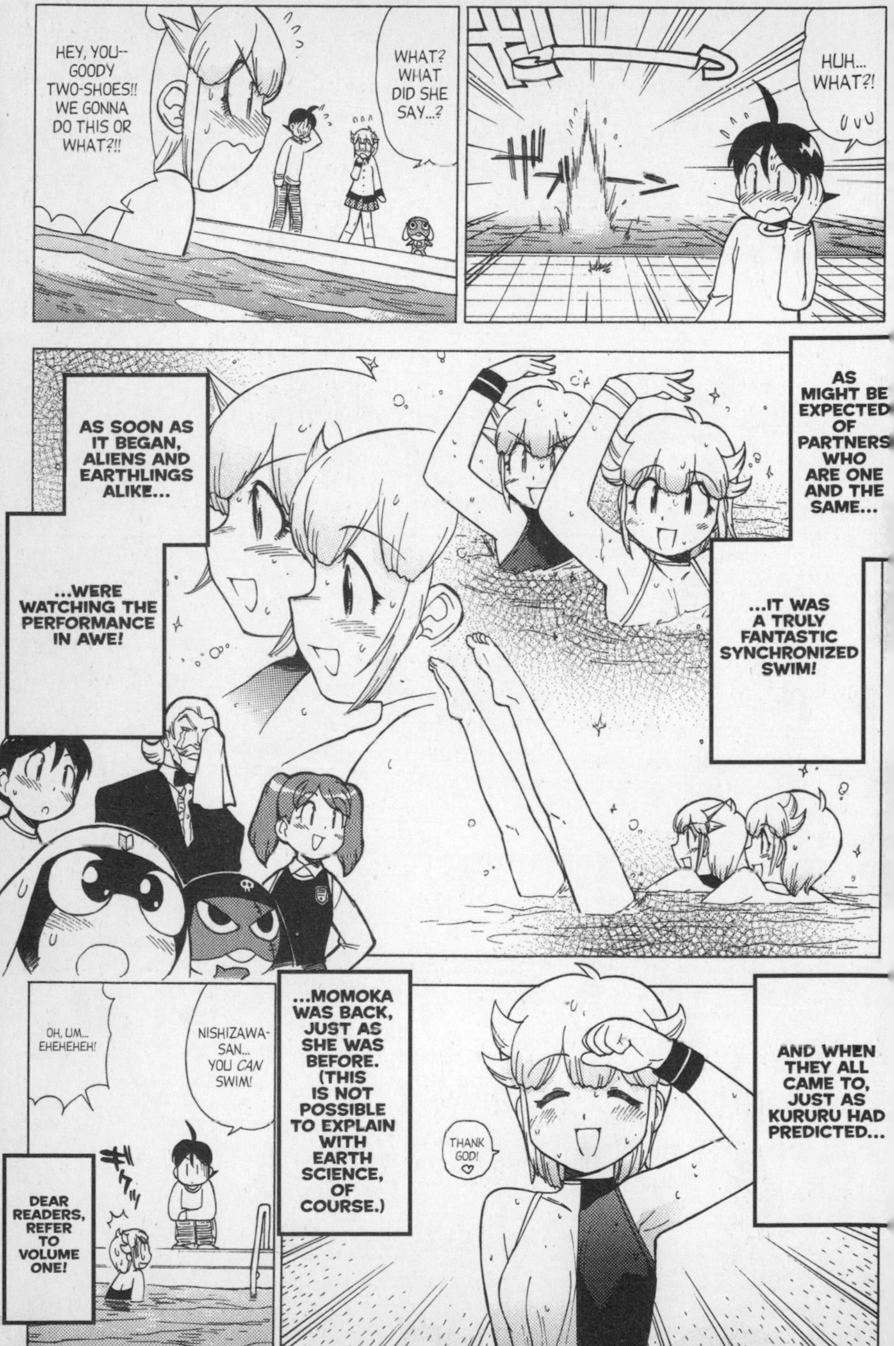

HUH... WHAT?!
HEY, YOU-- GOODY TWO-SHOES!! WE GONNA DO THIS OR WHAT?!!
WHAT? WHAT DID SHE SAY...?
AS MIGHT BE EXPECTED OF PARTNERS WHO ARE ONE AND THE SAME...
...IT WAS A TRULY FANTASTIC SYNCHRONIZED SWIM!
AS SOON AS IT BEGAN, ALIENS AND EARTHLINGS ALIKE...
...WERE WATCHING THE PERFORMANCE IN AWE!
AND WHEN THEY ALL CAME TO, JUST AS KURURU HAD PREDICTED...
THANK GOD! ♡
...MOMOKA WAS BACK, JUST AS SHE WAS BEFORE. (THIS IS NOT POSSIBLE TO EXPLAIN WITH EARTH SCIENCE, OF COURSE.)
NISHIZAWA-SAN... YOU *CAN* SWIM!
OH, UM... EHEHEHEH!
DEAR READERS, REFER TO VOLUME ONE!

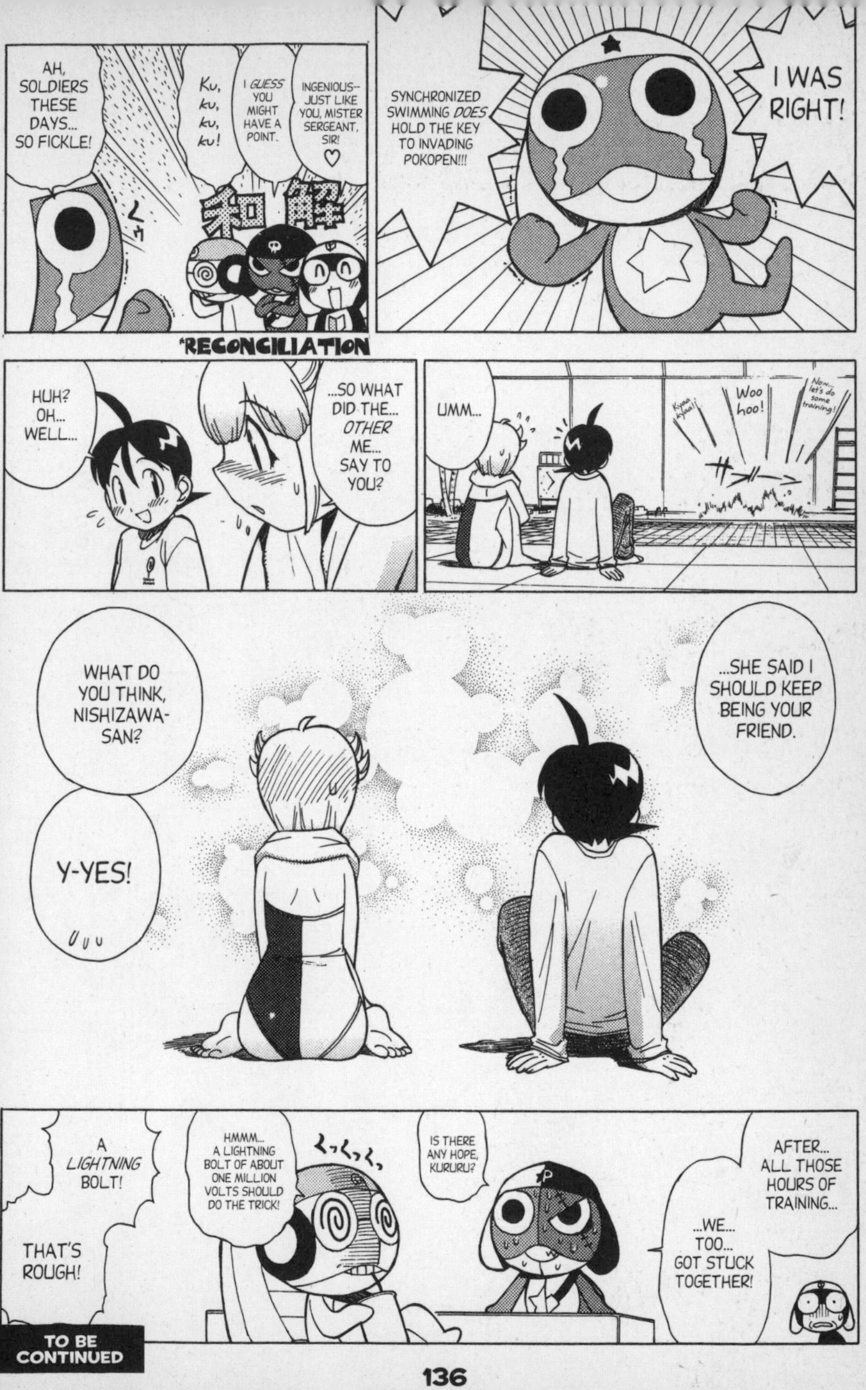

I WAS RIGHT!
SYNCHRONIZED SWIMMING *DOES* HOLD THE KEY TO INVADING POKOPEN!!!
INGENIOUS-- JUST LIKE YOU, MISTER SERGEANT, SIR! ♡
I *GUESS* YOU MIGHT HAVE A POINT.
Ku, ku, ku, ku!
AH, SOLDIERS THESE DAYS... SO FICKLE!
ムゥ
和解
*RECONCILIATION
Now... let's do some training!
Woo hoo!
Kyaa kyaa!!
UMM...
...SO WHAT DID THE... *OTHER* ME... SAY TO YOU?
HUH? OH... WELL...
...SHE SAID I SHOULD KEEP BEING YOUR FRIEND.
WHAT DO YOU THINK, NISHIZAWA-SAN?
Y-YES!
AFTER... ALL THOSE HOURS OF TRAINING...
...WE... TOO... GOT STUCK TOGETHER!
IS THERE ANY HOPE, KURURU?
HMMM... A LIGHTNING BOLT OF ABOUT ONE MILLION VOLTS SHOULD DO THE TRICK!
くっくっくっ
A *LIGHTNING* BOLT!
THAT'S ROUGH!
TO BE CONTINUED

ENCOUNTER XXIX

A VERY KERORO CHRISTMAS

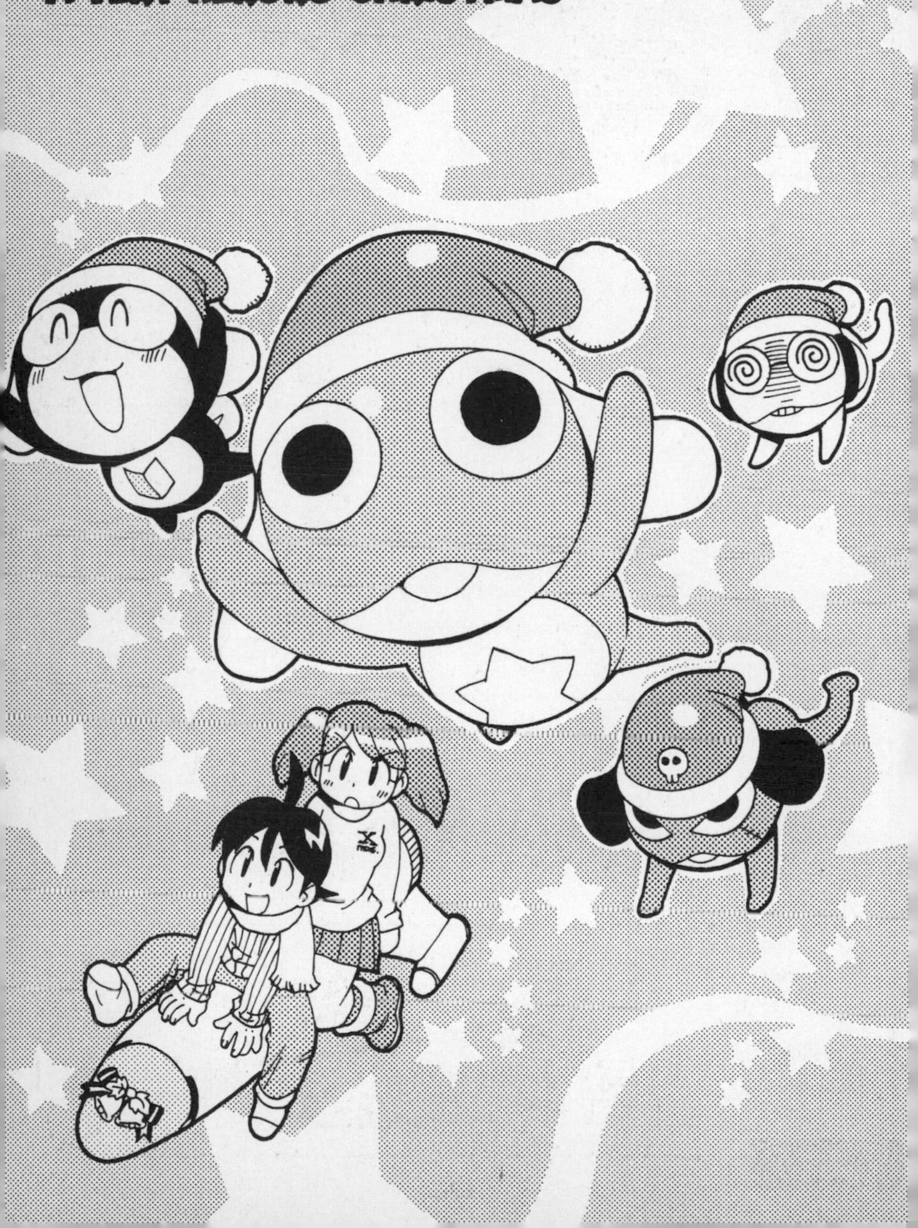

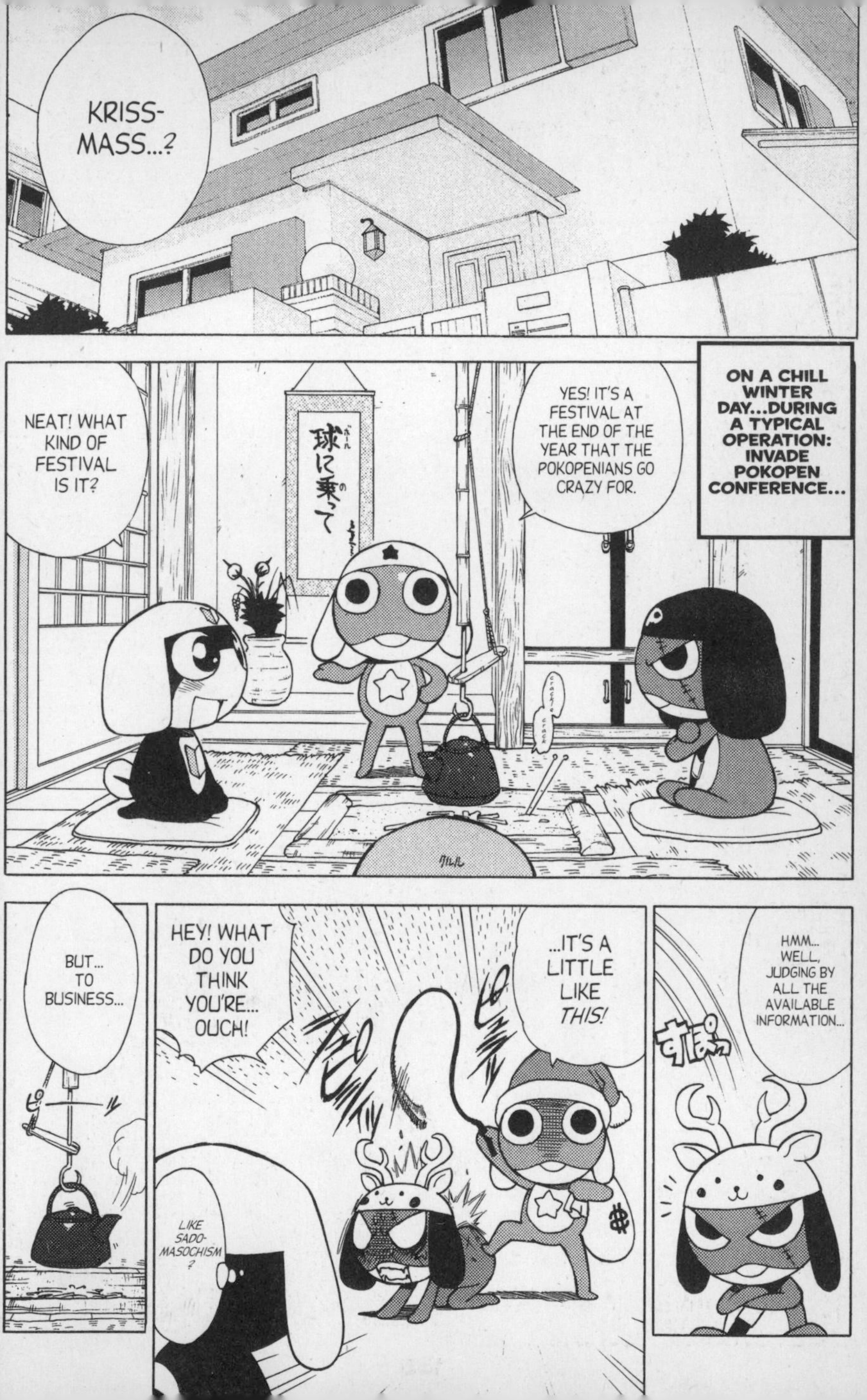
KRISS-MASS...?
ON A CHILL WINTER DAY...DURING A TYPICAL OPERATION: INVADE POKOPEN CONFERENCE...
YES! IT'S A FESTIVAL AT THE END OF THE YEAR THAT THE POKOPENIANS GO CRAZY FOR.
球に乗って
NEAT! WHAT KIND OF FESTIVAL IS IT?
HMM... WELL, JUDGING BY ALL THE AVAILABLE INFORMATION...
すぽっ
...IT'S A LITTLE LIKE THIS!
HEY! WHAT DO YOU THINK YOU'RE... OUCH!
LIKE SADO-MASOCHISM?
BUT... TO BUSINESS...

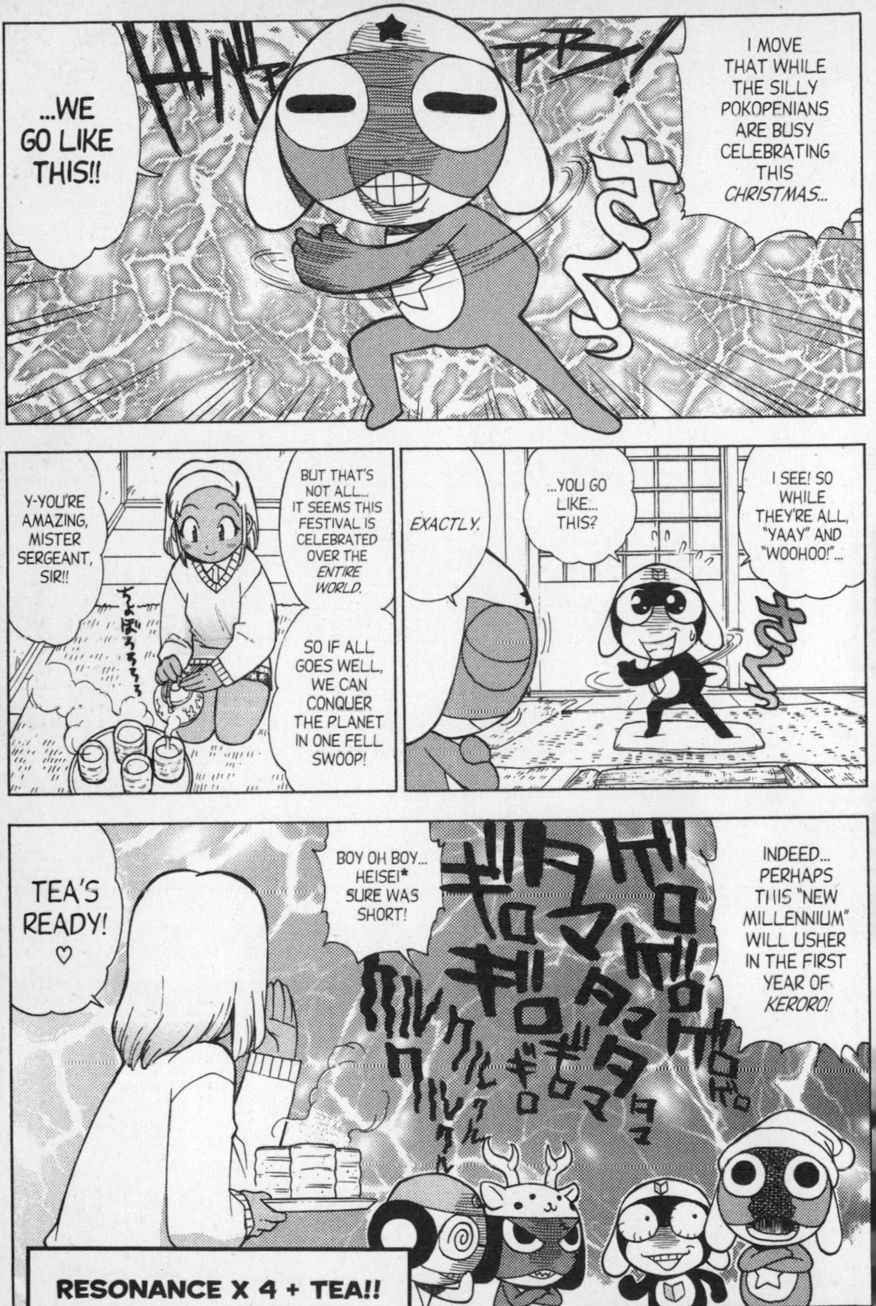
I MOVE THAT WHILE THE SILLY POKOPENIANS ARE BUSY CELEBRATING THIS *CHRISTMAS*...
...WE GO LIKE THIS!!
I SEE! SO WHILE THEY'RE ALL, "YAAY" AND "WOOHOO!"...
...YOU GO LIKE... THIS?
EXACTLY.
BUT THAT'S NOT ALL... IT SEEMS THIS FESTIVAL IS CELEBRATED OVER THE *ENTIRE WORLD.*
SO IF ALL GOES WELL, WE CAN CONQUER THE PLANET IN ONE FELL SWOOP!
Y-YOU'RE AMAZING, MISTER SERGEANT, SIR!!
INDEED... PERHAPS THIS "NEW MILLENNIUM" WILL USHER IN THE FIRST YEAR OF *KERORO!*
BOY OH BOY... HEISEI* SURE WAS SHORT!
TEA'S READY! ♡
RESONANCE X 4 + TEA!!

*NAME OF THE CURRENT JAPANESE ERA; 2004 IS HEISEI 16.

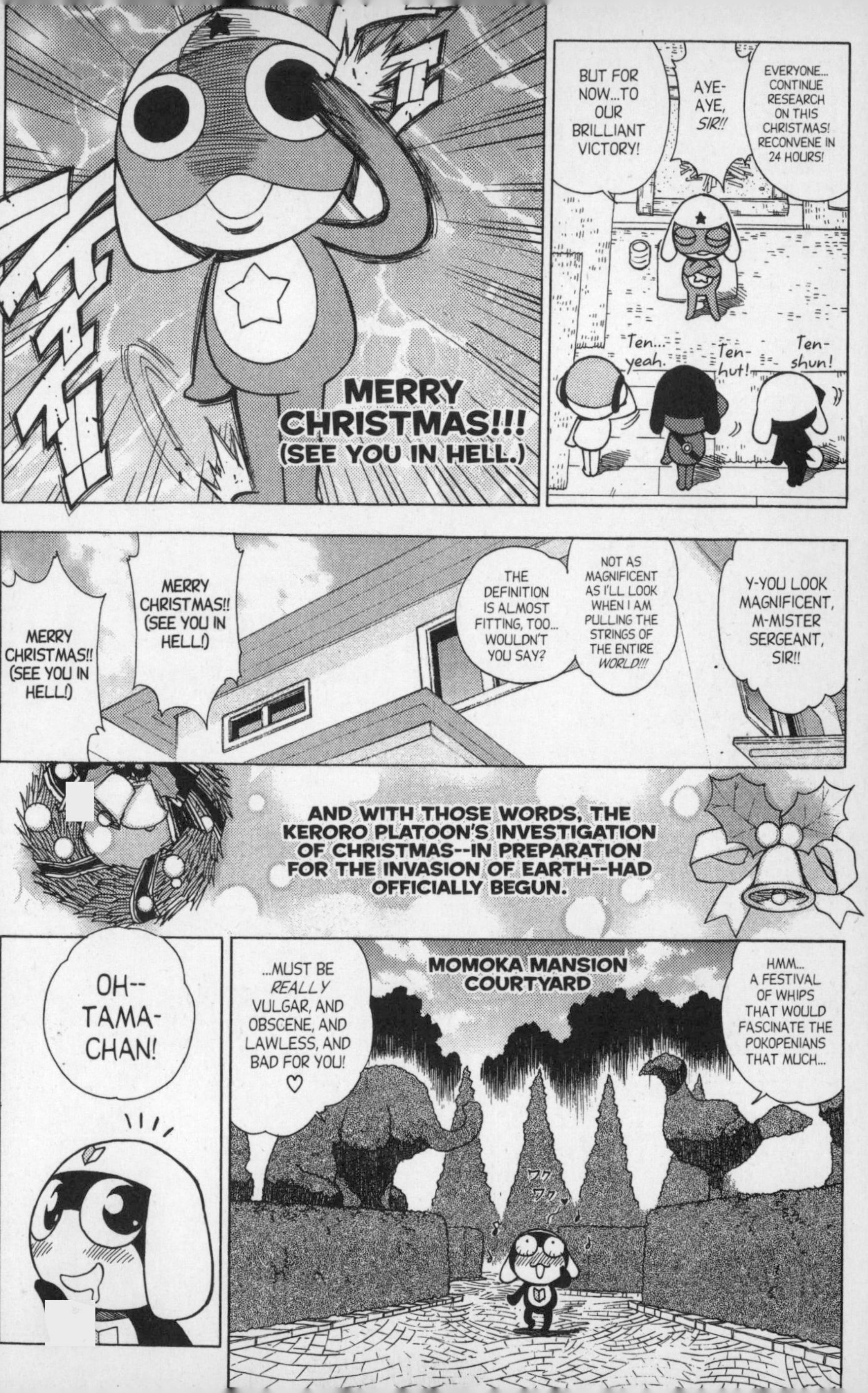
EVERYONE... CONTINUE RESEARCH ON THIS CHRISTMAS! RECONVENE IN 24 HOURS!
AYE-AYE, SIR!!
BUT FOR NOW...TO OUR BRILLIANT VICTORY!
Ten-shun!
Ten-hut!
Ten... yeah.
MERRY CHRISTMAS!!! (SEE YOU IN HELL.)
Y-YOU LOOK MAGNIFICENT, M-MISTER SERGEANT, SIR!!
NOT AS MAGNIFICENT AS I'LL LOOK WHEN I AM PULLING THE STRINGS OF THE ENTIRE WORLD!!!
THE DEFINITION IS ALMOST FITTING, TOO... WOULDN'T YOU SAY?
MERRY CHRISTMAS!! (SEE YOU IN HELL!)
MERRY CHRISTMAS!! (SEE YOU IN HELL!)
AND WITH THOSE WORDS, THE KERORO PLATOON'S INVESTIGATION OF CHRISTMAS--IN PREPARATION FOR THE INVASION OF EARTH--HAD OFFICIALLY BEGUN.
HMM... A FESTIVAL OF WHIPS THAT WOULD FASCINATE THE POKOPENIANS THAT MUCH...
MOMOKA MANSION COURTYARD
...MUST BE REALLY VULGAR, AND OBSCENE, AND LAWLESS, AND BAD FOR YOU! ♡
OH-- TAMA-CHAN!

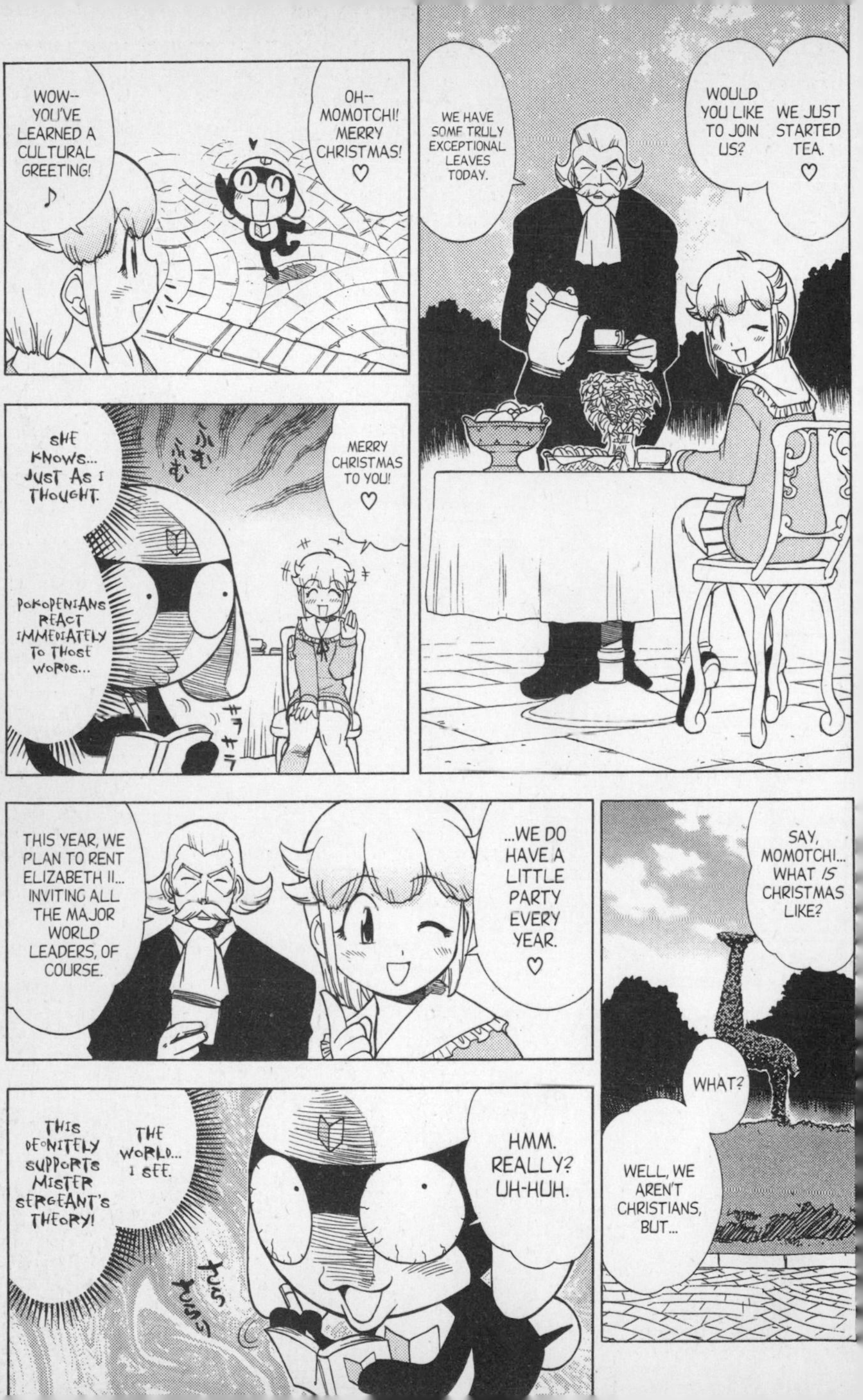
WE JUST STARTED TEA. ♡
WOULD YOU LIKE TO JOIN US?
WE HAVE SOME TRULY EXCEPTIONAL LEAVES TODAY.
OH-- MOMOTCHI! MERRY CHRISTMAS! ♡
WOW-- YOU'VE LEARNED A CULTURAL GREETING! ♪
MERRY CHRISTMAS TO YOU! ♡
ふむ ふむ
SHE KNOWS... JUST AS I THOUGHT.
POKOPENIANS REACT IMMEDIATELY TO THOSE WORDS...
キラキラ
SAY, MOMOTCHI... WHAT *IS* CHRISTMAS LIKE?
WHAT?
WELL, WE AREN'T CHRISTIANS, BUT...
...WE DO HAVE A LITTLE PARTY EVERY YEAR. ♡
THIS YEAR, WE PLAN TO RENT ELIZABETH II... INVITING ALL THE MAJOR WORLD LEADERS, OF COURSE.
HMM. REALLY? UH-HUH.
THE WORLD... I SEE.
THIS DEFINITELY SUPPORTS MISTER SERGEANT'S THEORY!

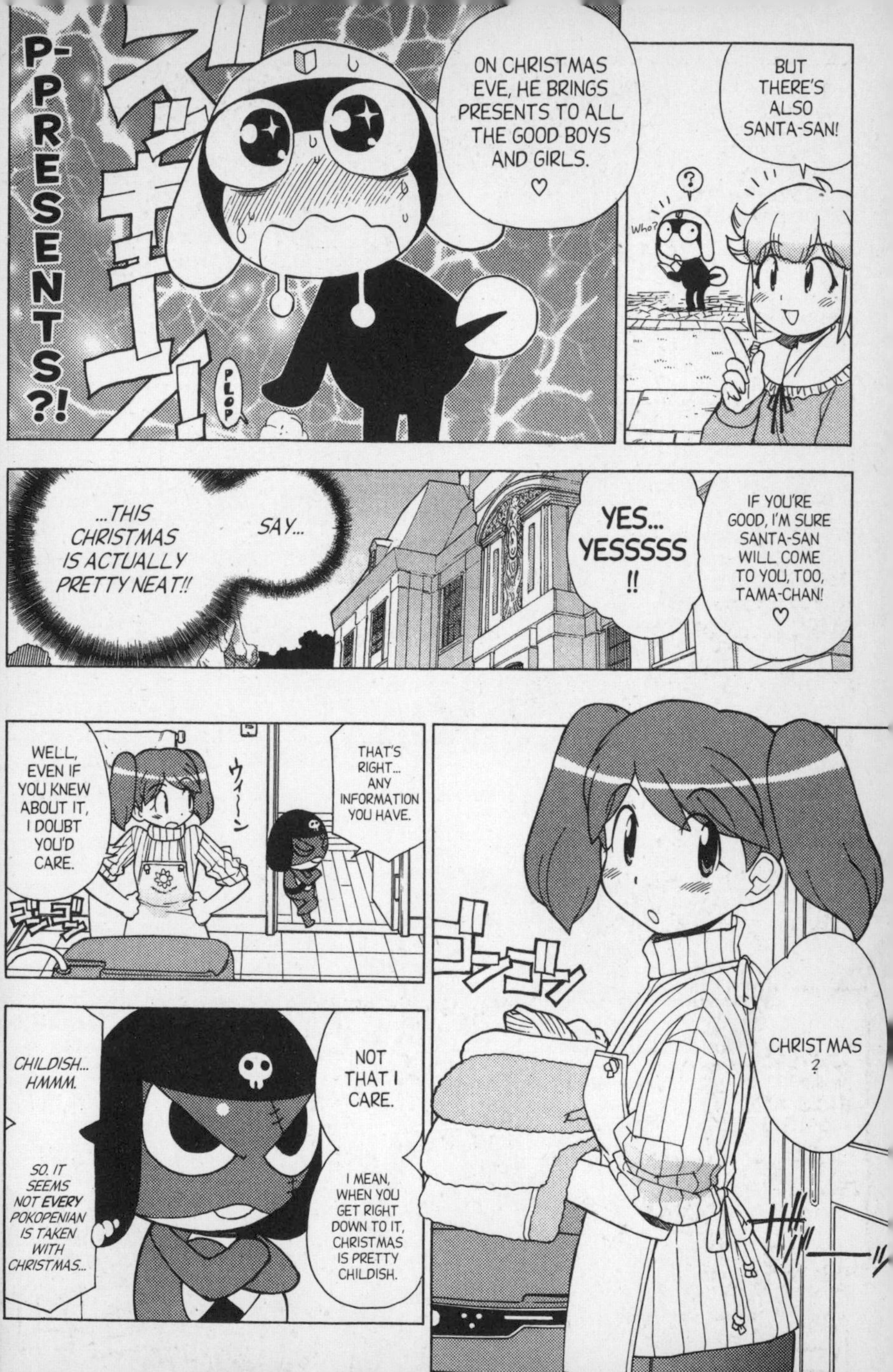
BUT THERE'S ALSO SANTA-SAN!
Who?
ON CHRISTMAS EVE, HE BRINGS PRESENTS TO ALL THE GOOD BOYS AND GIRLS. ♡
P-PRESENTS?!
PLOP
IF YOU'RE GOOD, I'M SURE SANTA-SAN WILL COME TO YOU, TOO, TAMA-CHAN! ♡
YES... YESSSSS !!
SAY...
...THIS CHRISTMAS IS ACTUALLY PRETTY NEAT!!
CHRISTMAS?
THAT'S RIGHT... ANY INFORMATION YOU HAVE.
WELL, EVEN IF YOU KNEW ABOUT IT, I DOUBT YOU'D CARE.
NOT THAT I CARE.
I MEAN, WHEN YOU GET RIGHT DOWN TO IT, CHRISTMAS IS PRETTY CHILDISH.
CHILDISH... HMMM.
SO. IT SEEMS NOT EVERY POKOPENIAN IS TAKEN WITH CHRISTMAS...

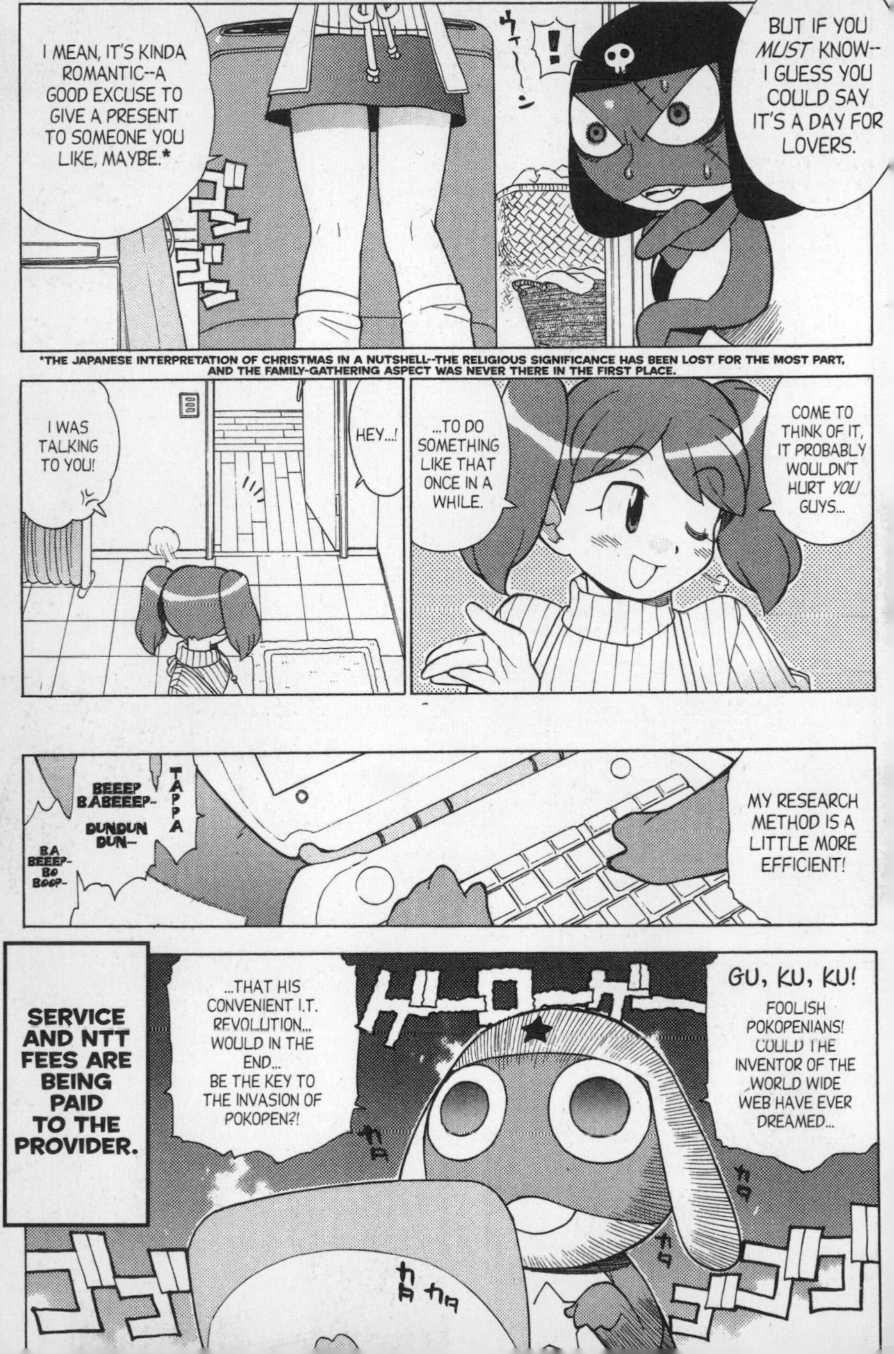
BUT IF YOU *MUST* KNOW-- I GUESS YOU COULD SAY IT'S A DAY FOR LOVERS.
I MEAN, IT'S KINDA ROMANTIC--A GOOD EXCUSE TO GIVE A PRESENT TO SOMEONE YOU LIKE, MAYBE.*
*THE JAPANESE INTERPRETATION OF CHRISTMAS IN A NUTSHELL--THE RELIGIOUS SIGNIFICANCE HAS BEEN LOST FOR THE MOST PART, AND THE FAMILY-GATHERING ASPECT WAS NEVER THERE IN THE FIRST PLACE.
COME TO THINK OF IT, IT PROBABLY WOULDN'T HURT *YOU* GUYS...
...TO DO SOMETHING LIKE THAT ONCE IN A WHILE.
HEY...!
I WAS TALKING TO YOU!
MY RESEARCH METHOD IS A LITTLE MORE EFFICIENT!
TAPPA
BEEEP BABEEEP-
DUNDUN DUN--
BA BEEEP-BO BOOP-
GU, KU, KU!
FOOLISH POKOPENIANS! COULD THE INVENTOR OF THE WORLD WIDE WEB HAVE EVER DREAMED...
...THAT HIS CONVENIENT I.T. REVOLUTION... WOULD IN THE END... BE THE KEY TO THE INVASION OF POKOPEN?!
SERVICE AND NTT FEES ARE BEING PAID TO THE PROVIDER.

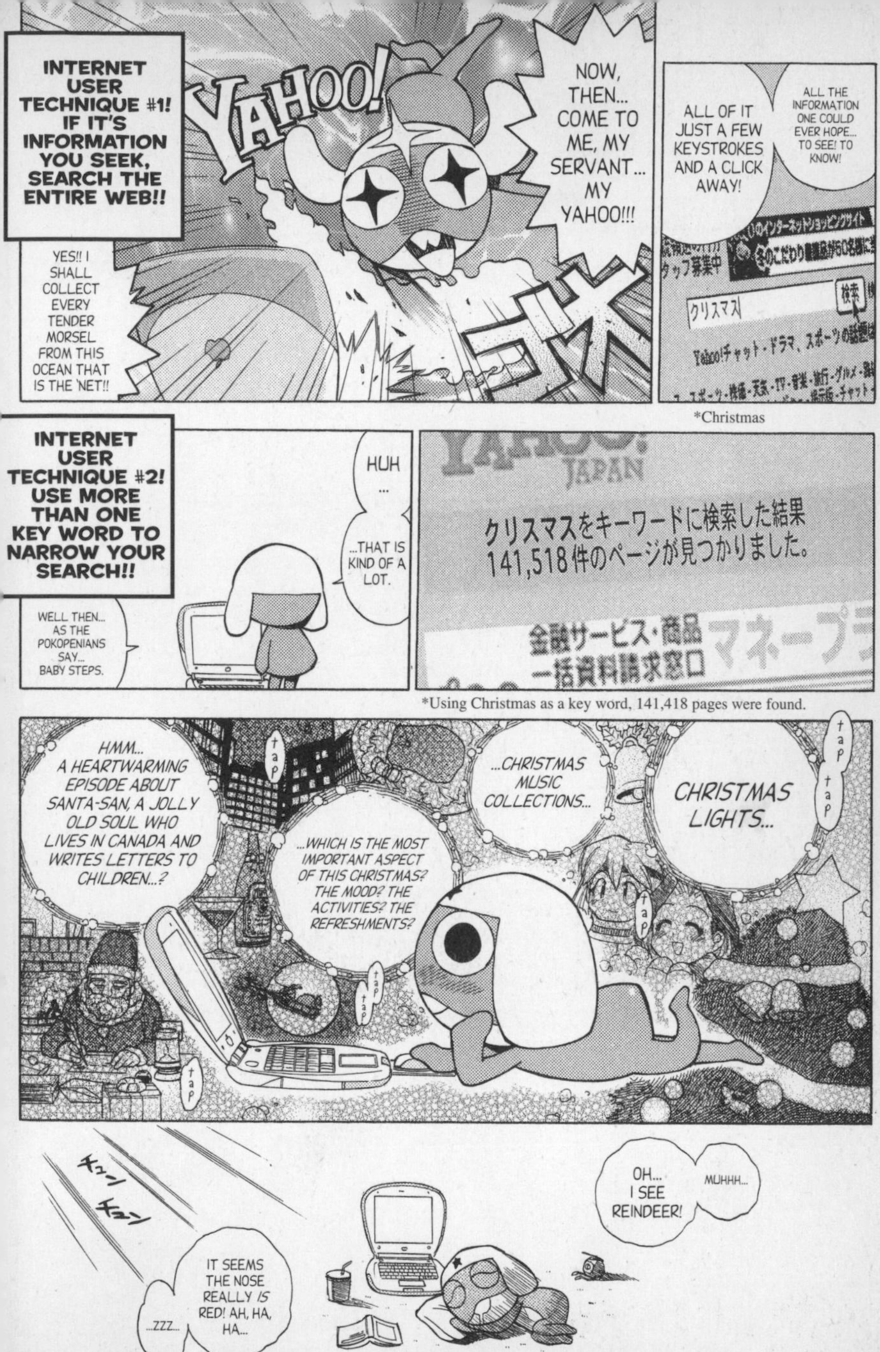
INTERNET USER TECHNIQUE #1! IF IT'S INFORMATION YOU SEEK, SEARCH THE ENTIRE WEB!!
YAHOO!
NOW, THEN... COME TO ME, MY SERVANT... MY YAHOO!!!
YES!! I SHALL COLLECT EVERY TENDER MORSEL FROM THIS OCEAN THAT IS THE 'NET!!
ALL OF IT JUST A FEW KEYSTROKES AND A CLICK AWAY!
ALL THE INFORMATION ONE COULD EVER HOPE... TO SEE! TO KNOW!
クリスマス
検索
INTERNET USER TECHNIQUE #2! USE MORE THAN ONE KEY WORD TO NARROW YOUR SEARCH!!
HUH ...
...THAT IS KIND OF A LOT.
WELL THEN... AS THE POKOPENIANS SAY... BABY STEPS.
JAPAN
クリスマスをキーワードに検索した結果
141,518件のページが見つかりました。
金融サービス・商品
一括資料請求窓口
HMM... A HEARTWARMING EPISODE ABOUT SANTA-SAN, A JOLLY OLD SOUL WHO LIVES IN CANADA AND WRITES LETTERS TO CHILDREN...?
...WHICH IS THE MOST IMPORTANT ASPECT OF THIS CHRISTMAS? THE MOOD? THE ACTIVITIES? THE REFRESHMENTS?
...CHRISTMAS MUSIC COLLECTIONS...
CHRISTMAS LIGHTS...
tap tap
チュン
チュン
OH... I SEE REINDEER!
MUHHH...
IT SEEMS THE NOSE REALLY IS RED! AH, HA, HA...
...ZZZ...

*Christmas

*Using Christmas as a key word, 141,418 pages were found.

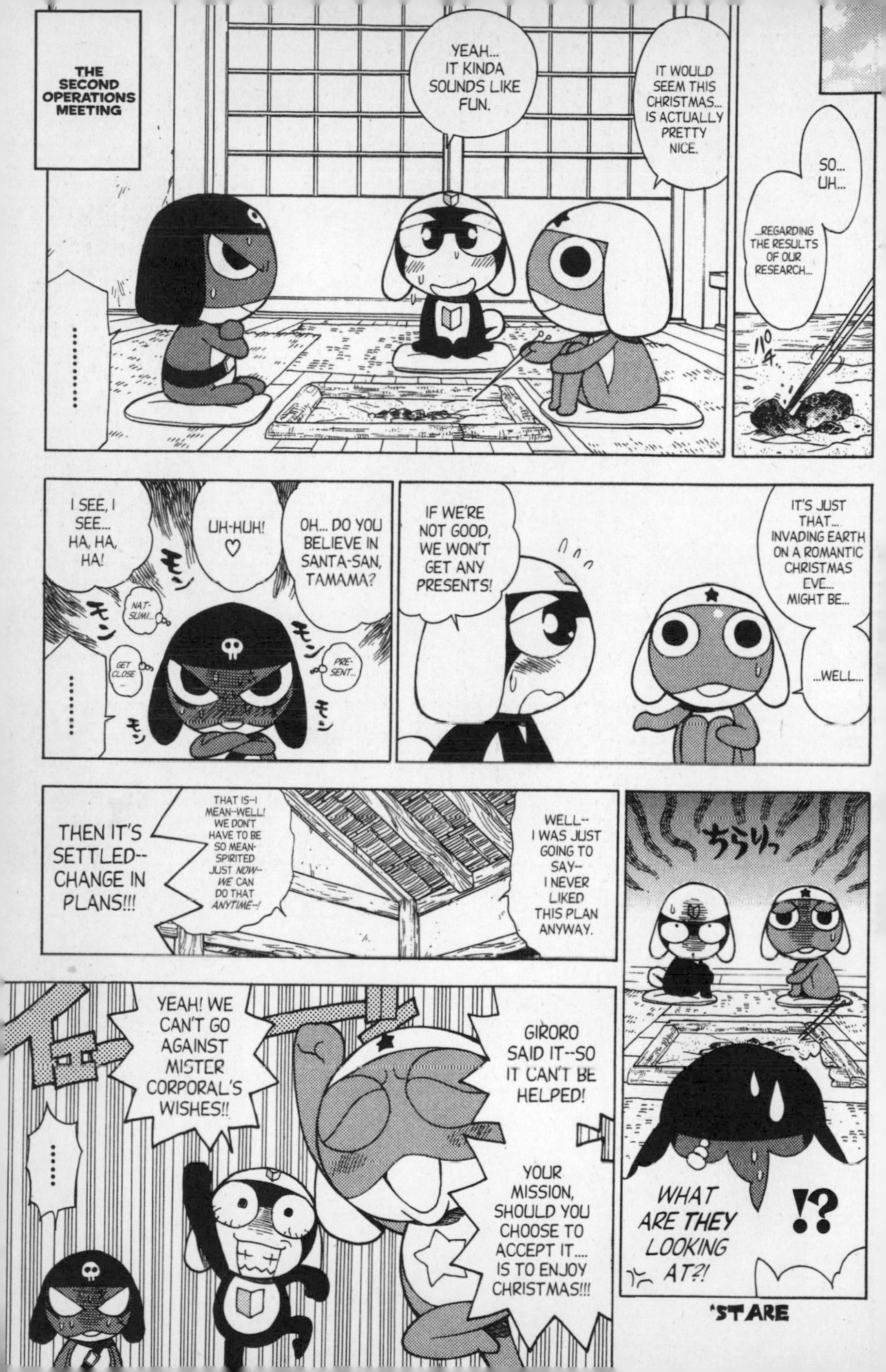
THE SECOND OPERATIONS MEETING
SO... UH...
...REGARDING THE RESULTS OF OUR RESEARCH...
IT WOULD SEEM THIS CHRISTMAS... IS ACTUALLY PRETTY NICE.
YEAH... IT KINDA SOUNDS LIKE FUN.
....
IT'S JUST THAT... INVADING EARTH ON A ROMANTIC CHRISTMAS EVE... MIGHT BE...
...WELL...
IF WE'RE NOT GOOD, WE WON'T GET ANY PRESENTS!
OH... DO YOU BELIEVE IN SANTA-SAN, TAMAMA?
UH-HUH! ♡
I SEE, I SEE... HA, HA, HA!
PRE-SENT...
NAT-SUMI...
GET CLOSE...
モン
....
ちらりっ
WHAT ARE THEY LOOKING AT?!
!?
*STARE
WELL-- I WAS JUST GOING TO SAY-- I NEVER LIKED THIS PLAN ANYWAY.
THAT IS--I MEAN--WELL! WE DON'T HAVE TO BE SO MEAN-SPIRITED JUST NOW--WE CAN DO THAT ANYTIME--!
THEN IT'S SETTLED-- CHANGE IN PLANS!!!
GIRORO SAID IT--SO IT CAN'T BE HELPED!
YOUR MISSION, SHOULD YOU CHOOSE TO ACCEPT IT.... IS TO ENJOY CHRISTMAS!!!
YEAH! WE CAN'T GO AGAINST MISTER CORPORAL'S WISHES!!
......

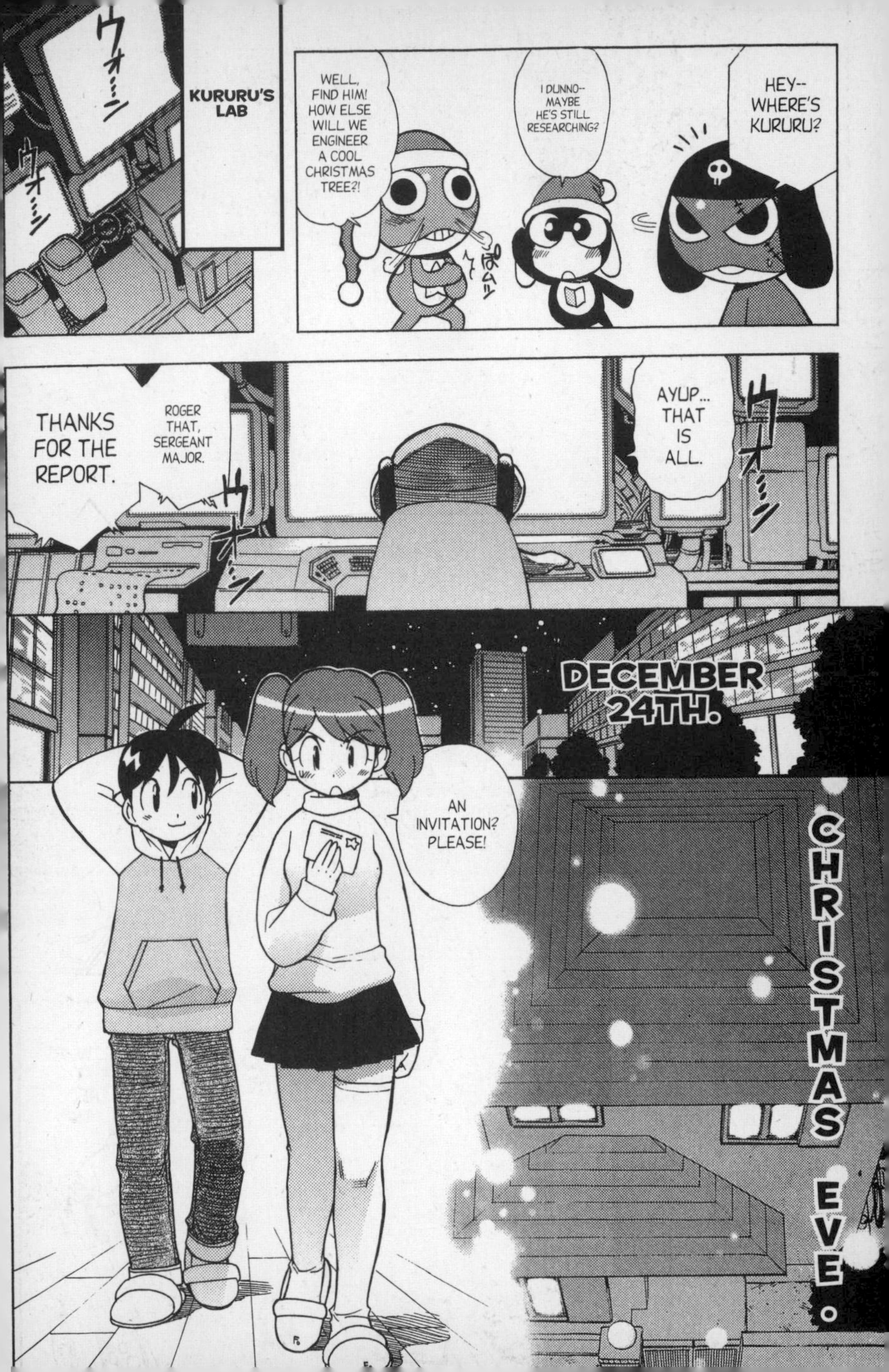
HEY-- WHERE'S KURURU?
I DUNNO-- MAYBE HE'S STILL RESEARCHING?
WELL, FIND HIM! HOW ELSE WILL WE ENGINEER A COOL CHRISTMAS TREE?!
KURURU'S LAB
AYUP... THAT IS ALL.
ROGER THAT, SERGEANT MAJOR.
THANKS FOR THE REPORT.
DECEMBER 24TH.
CHRISTMAS EVE.
AN INVITATION? PLEASE!

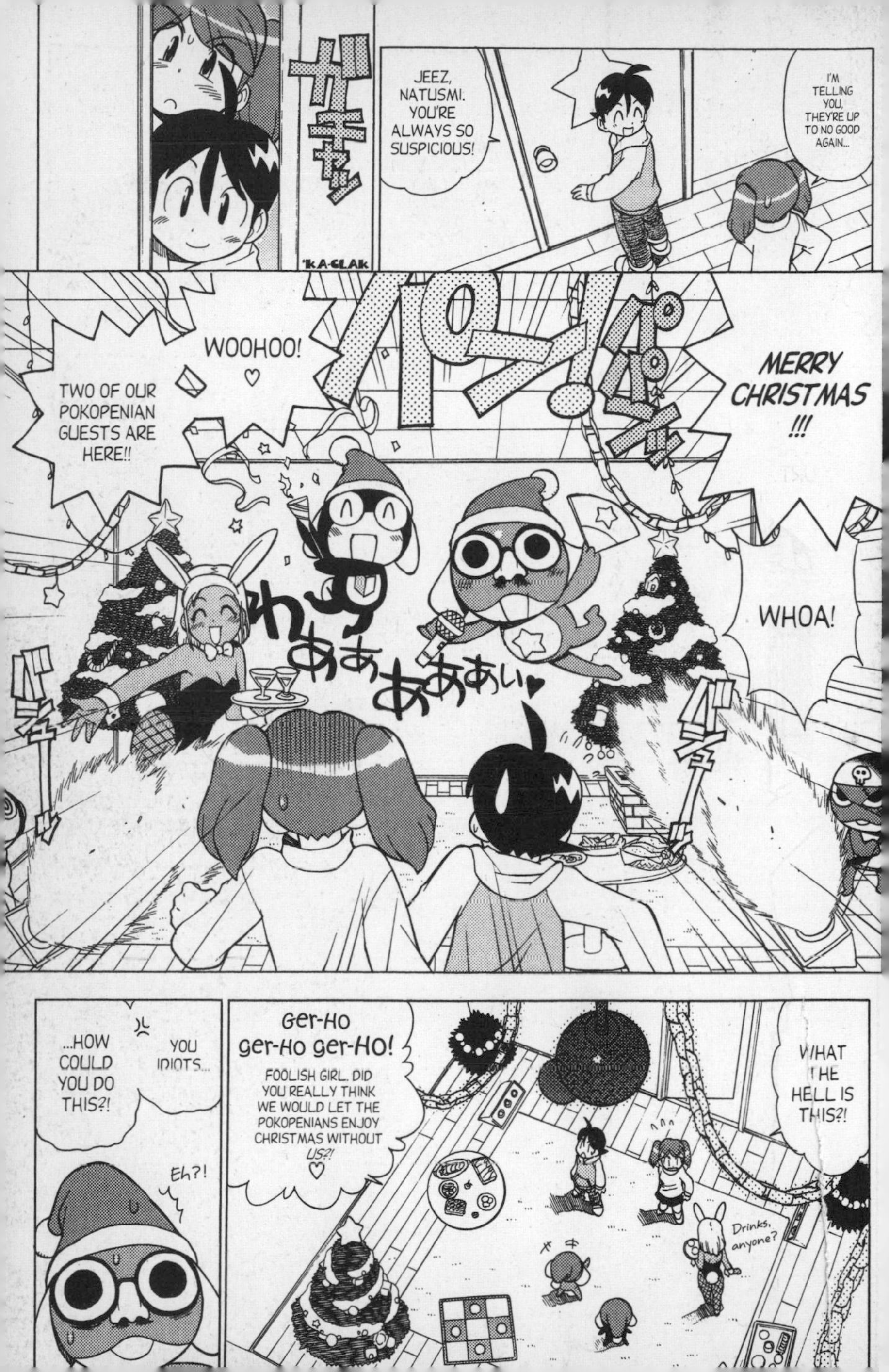
I'M TELLING YOU, THEY'RE UP TO NO GOOD AGAIN...
JEEZ, NATUSMI. YOU'RE ALWAYS SO SUSPICIOUS!
*KA-CLAK
MERRY CHRISTMAS !!!
WOOHOO!
TWO OF OUR POKOPENIAN GUESTS ARE HERE!!
WHOA!
WHAT THE HELL IS THIS?!
Ger-Ho ger-Ho ger-HO!
FOOLISH GIRL. DID YOU REALLY THINK WE WOULD LET THE POKOPENIANS ENJOY CHRISTMAS WITHOUT US?!
Drinks, anyone?
YOU IDIOTS...
...HOW COULD YOU DO THIS?!
Eh?!

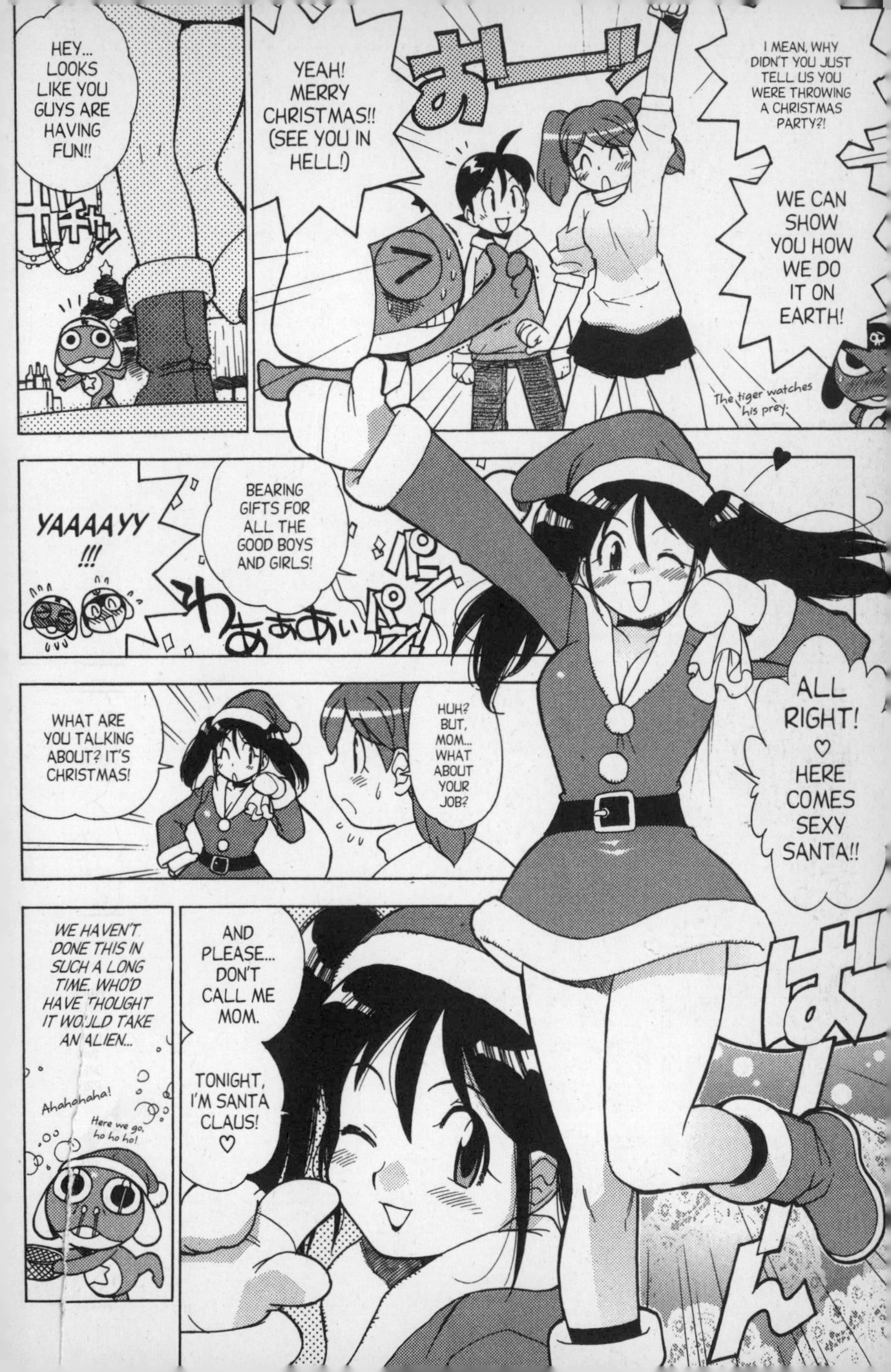

I MEAN, WHY DIDN'T YOU JUST TELL US YOU WERE THROWING A CHRISTMAS PARTY?!
WE CAN SHOW YOU HOW WE DO IT ON EARTH!
The tiger watches his prey.
おーーッ
YEAH! MERRY CHRISTMAS!! (SEE YOU IN HELL!)
HEY... LOOKS LIKE YOU GUYS ARE HAVING FUN!!
ALL RIGHT! ♡ HERE COMES SEXY SANTA!!
BEARING GIFTS FOR ALL THE GOOD BOYS AND GIRLS!
わあああい
YAAAAYY !!!
HUH? BUT, MOM... WHAT ABOUT YOUR JOB?
WHAT ARE YOU TALKING ABOUT? IT'S CHRISTMAS!
AND PLEASE... DON'T CALL ME MOM.
TONIGHT, I'M SANTA CLAUS! ♡
WE HAVEN'T DONE THIS IN SUCH A LONG TIME. WHO'D HAVE THOUGHT IT WOULD TAKE AN ALIEN...
Ahahahaha!
Here we go, ho ho ho!

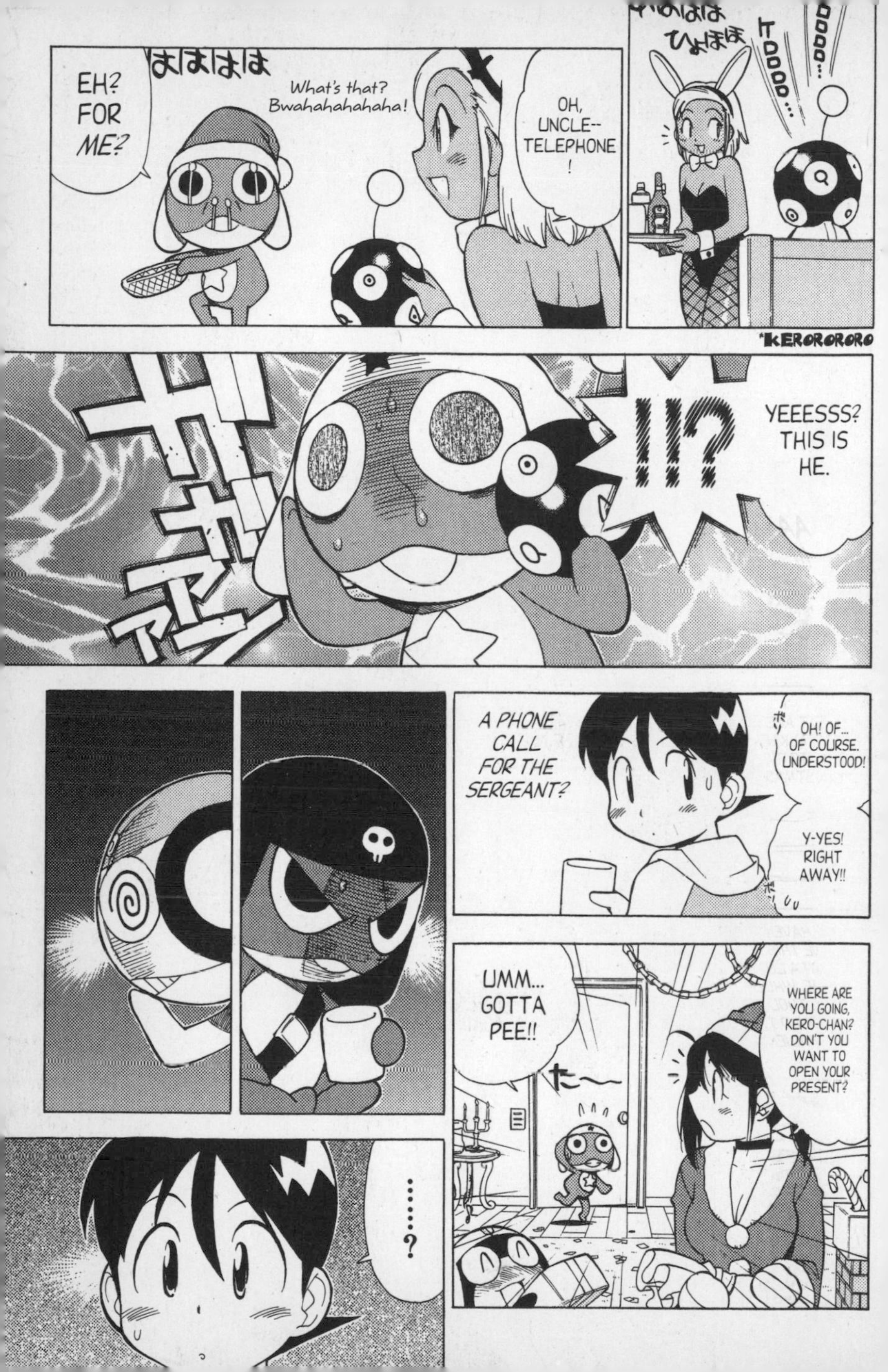
*KERORORORO
OH, UNCLE--TELEPHONE!
What's that? Bwahahahahaha!
EH? FOR ME?
YEEESSS? THIS IS HE.
!!?
OH! OF... OF COURSE. UNDERSTOOD!
Y-YES! RIGHT AWAY!!
A PHONE CALL FOR THE SERGEANT?
WHERE ARE YOU GOING, KERO-CHAN? DON'T YOU WANT TO OPEN YOUR PRESENT?
UMM... GOTTA PEE!!
た~~
......?

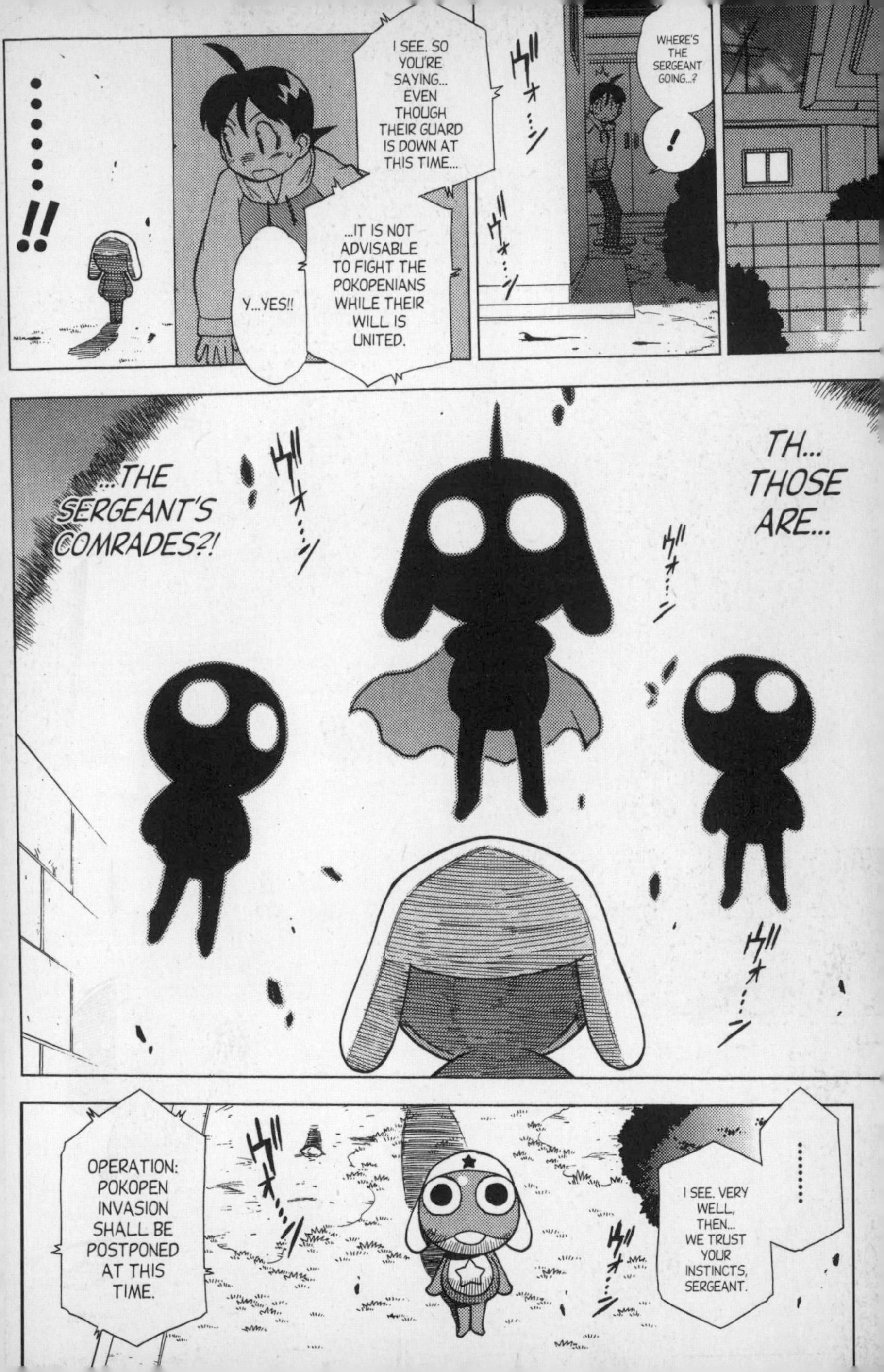
WHERE'S THE SERGEANT GOING...?
!
I SEE. SO YOU'RE SAYING... EVEN THOUGH THEIR GUARD IS DOWN AT THIS TIME...
...IT IS NOT ADVISABLE TO FIGHT THE POKOPENIANS WHILE THEIR WILL IS UNITED.
Y...YES!!
......!!
TH... THOSE ARE...
...THE SERGEANT'S COMRADES?!
......
I SEE. VERY WELL, THEN... WE TRUST YOUR INSTINCTS, SERGEANT.
OPERATION: POKOPEN INVASION SHALL BE POSTPONED AT THIS TIME.

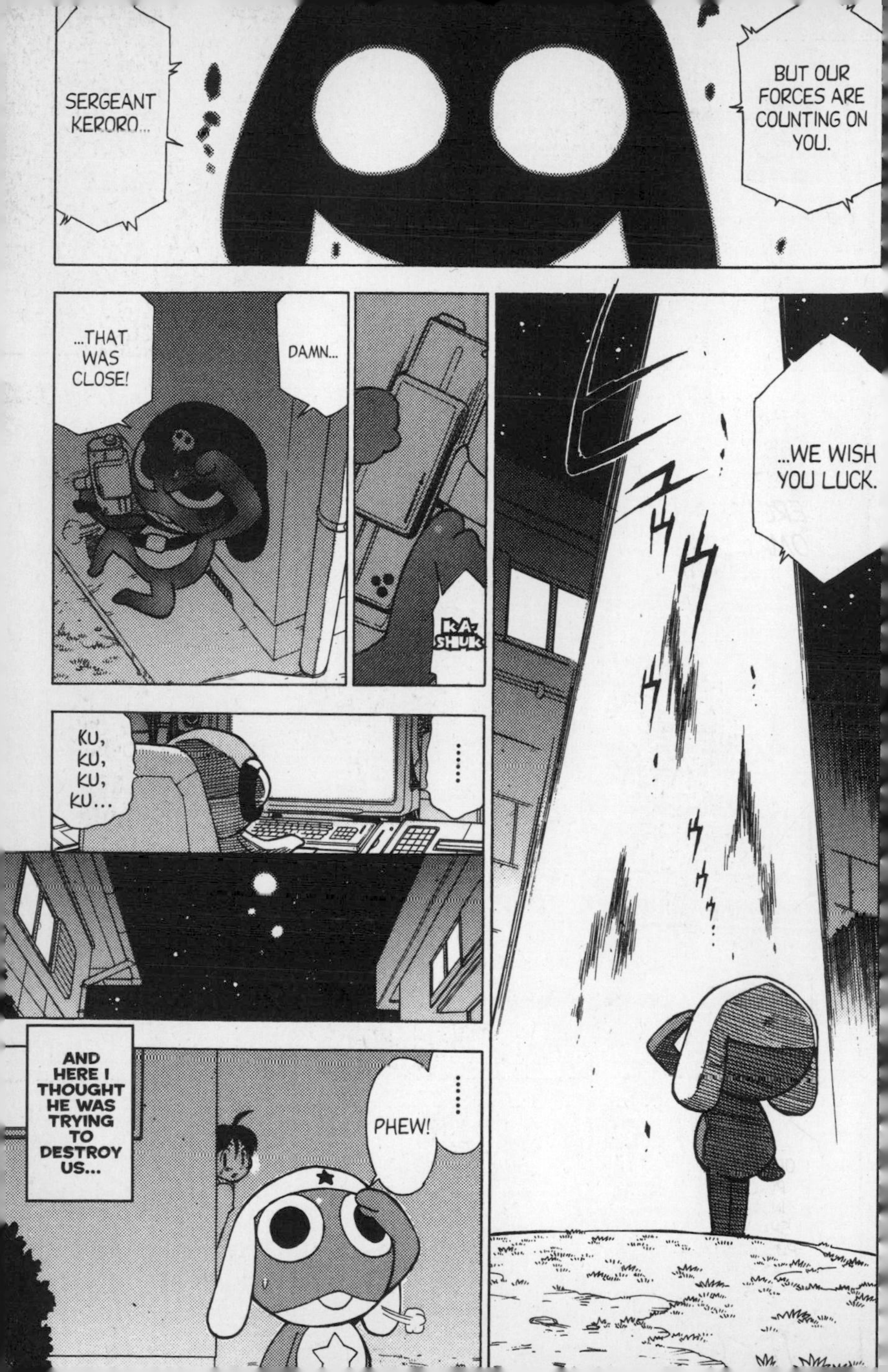

BUT OUR FORCES ARE COUNTING ON YOU.
SERGEANT KERORO...
...WE WISH YOU LUCK.
DAMN...
KA-SHUK
...THAT WAS CLOSE!
......
KU, KU, KU, KU...
......
PHEW!
AND HERE I THOUGHT HE WAS TRYING TO DESTROY US...

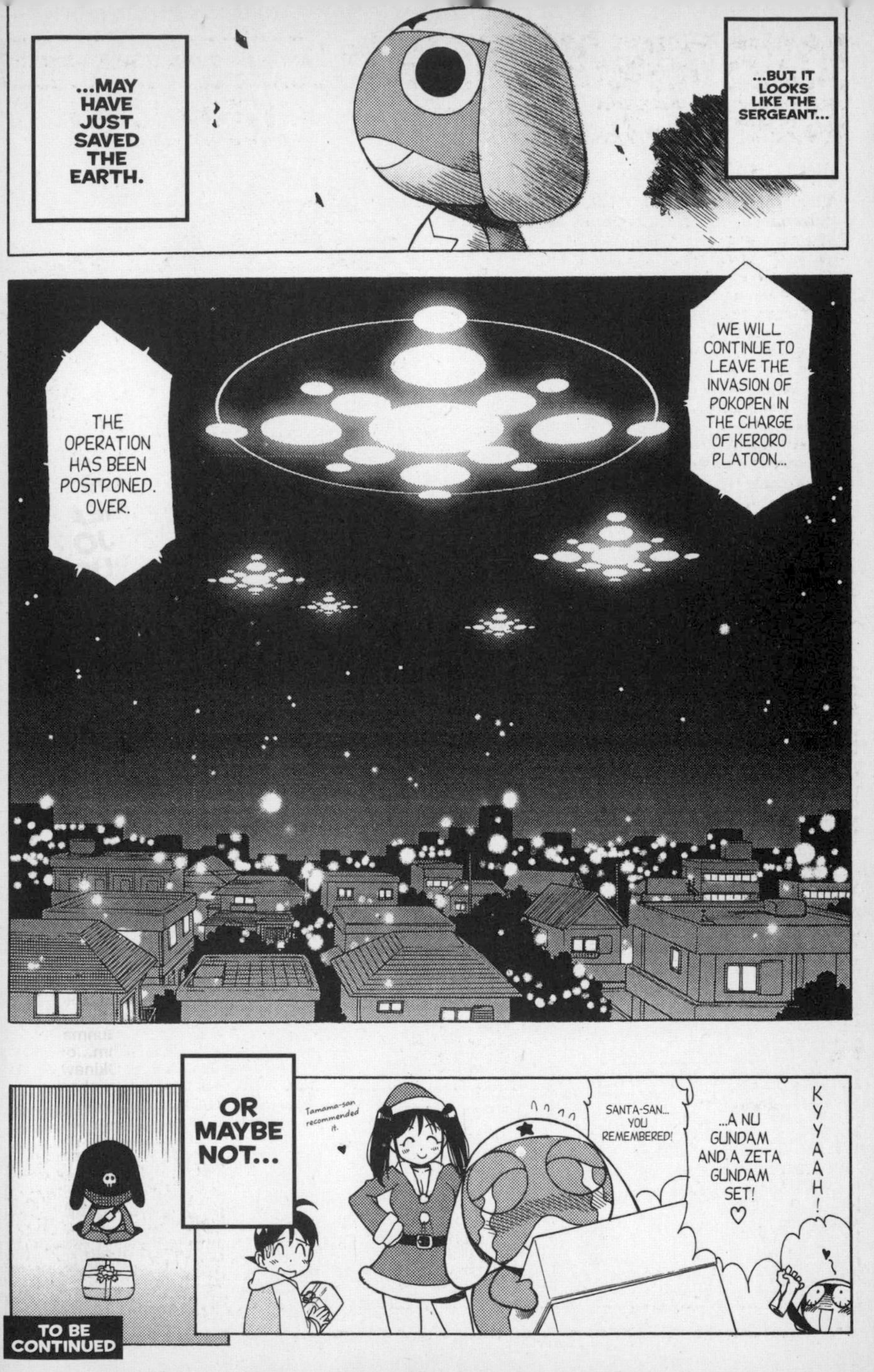
...BUT IT LOOKS LIKE THE SERGEANT...
...MAY HAVE JUST SAVED THE EARTH.
WE WILL CONTINUE TO LEAVE THE INVASION OF POKOPEN IN THE CHARGE OF KERORO PLATOON...
THE OPERATION HAS BEEN POSTPONED. OVER.
KYYAAH!
...A NU GUNDAM AND A ZETA GUNDAM SET! ♡
SANTA-SAN... YOU REMEMBERED!
Tamama-san recommended it.
OR MAYBE NOT...
TO BE CONTINUED

BOGUS DEVELOPMENT DIARY

PHASE 1: CONFIRMATION OF SETTINGS

ALL ABOUT SERGEANT MAJOR KURURU

KRR-04Q

Sergeant Major Kururu Edition

WHY HIM?!

Of all the characters in "Sgt. Frog," the one we decided to release when the time was most ripe was Sergeant Major Kururu! When Sergeant Major Kururu was introduced in the middle of the Second Volume, he was definitely the least favorite alien, owing to his selfishness, weirdness, and yellowness. However, here in Volume Three, it is not an overstatement to say that almost all the stories were able to progress solely thanks to the numerous devices that Kururu invented. Whatever the reader's impression of Kururu may have been, for the author of this work, his presence must have carried a certain amount of weight.

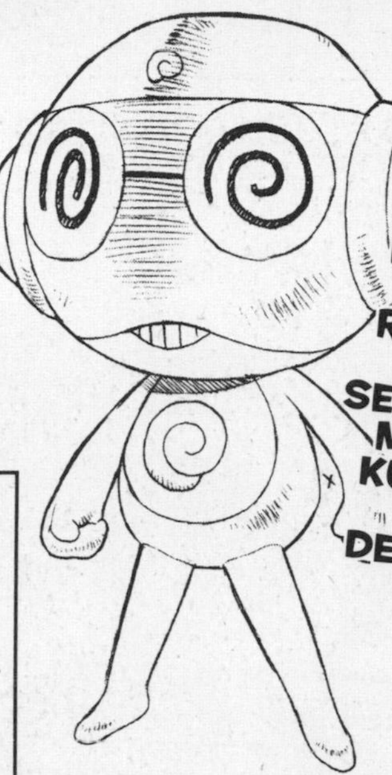

MG (MONDAY GRADE.) SERIES NUMBER ONE! RELEASE OF SERGEANT MAJOR KURURU IS DECIDED!!

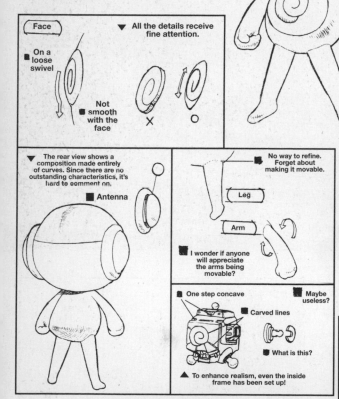

Face
▼ All the details receive fine attention.
■ On a loose swivel
■ Not smooth with the face

▼ The rear view shows a composition made entirely of curves. Since there are no outstanding characteristics, it's hard to comment on.
■ Antenna

■ No way to refine. Forget about making it movable.
Leg
Arm
■ I wonder if anyone will appreciate the arms being movable?

■ One step concave
■ Maybe useless?
■ Carved lines
■ What is this?
▲ To enhance realism, even the inside frame has been set up!

Though the first in this series has already been decided, we don't expect others to follow. However, we have already received a landslide of your wishes and comments!

- Let's stop this silliness right now. (Heaven's Door, Tokyo)
- I don't think I'll buy it. (Thighbone, Gunma)
- It's like...hmm...okay. (Runta-kun, Okinawa)
- If N-Natsumi-chan's figure comes with it, I'll buy it! I'll buy three! (Anonymous, Tokyo)

MONDAY GRADE KRR-04Q SERGEANT MAJOR KURURU

- Sold by Kadokawa Publishing, Toy Operations Department
- 4,800 yen (without tax)
- Release Date not specified
- Plastic Kit
- Scale 1:144; overall height approx. 4 mm

※ This product sold only on Planet Keron. There are no plans for Earth sales. We thank you for your understanding.

SUMOMO PROLOGUE

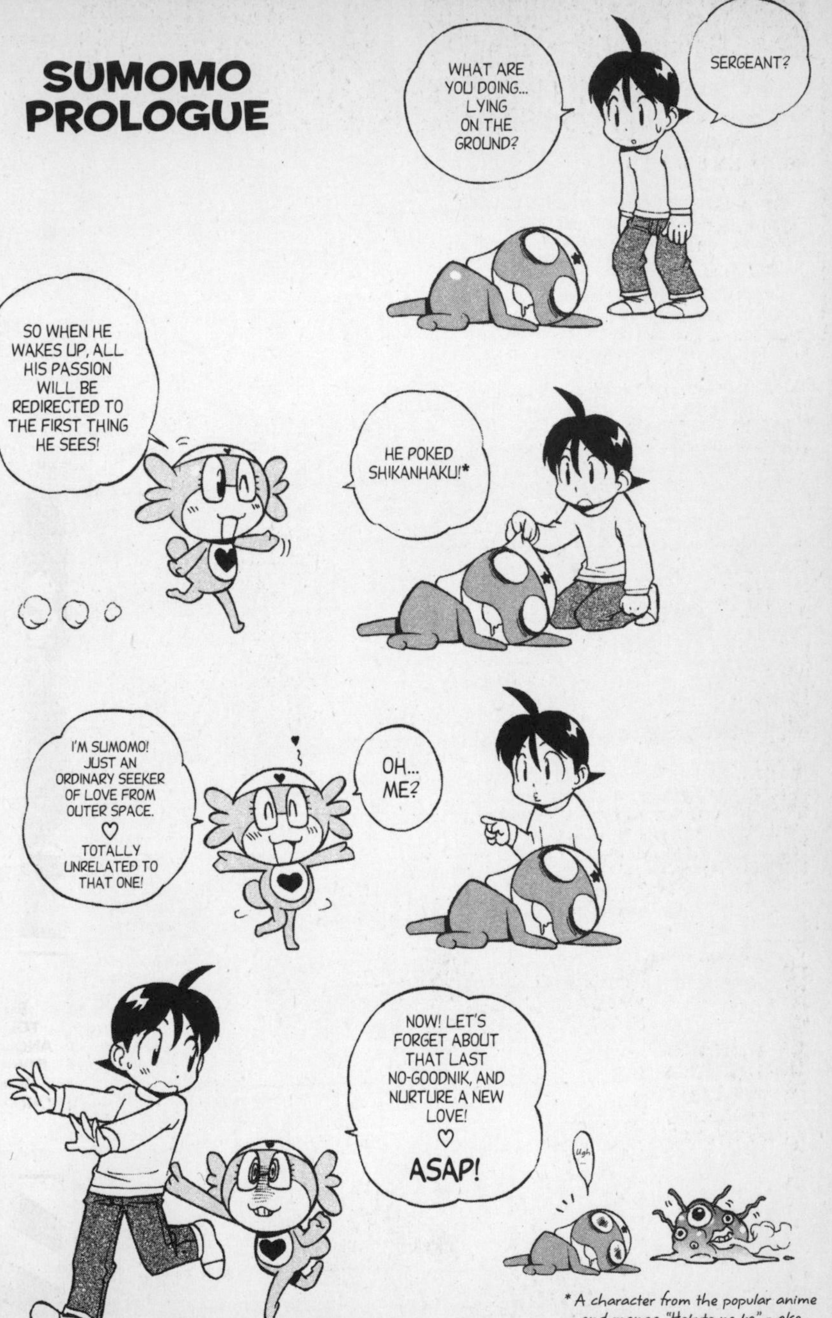
SERGEANT?
WHAT ARE YOU DOING... LYING ON THE GROUND?
HE POKED SHIKANHAKU!*
SO WHEN HE WAKES UP, ALL HIS PASSION WILL BE REDIRECTED TO THE FIRST THING HE SEES!
OH... ME?
I'M SUMOMO! JUST AN ORDINARY SEEKER OF LOVE FROM OUTER SPACE. ♡ TOTALLY UNRELATED TO THAT ONE!
NOW! LET'S FORGET ABOUT THAT LAST NO-GOODNIK, AND NURTURE A NEW LOVE! ♡ ASAP!
Ugh

* A character from the popular anime and manga "Hokuto no ke" - also known as "Fist of the North Star"

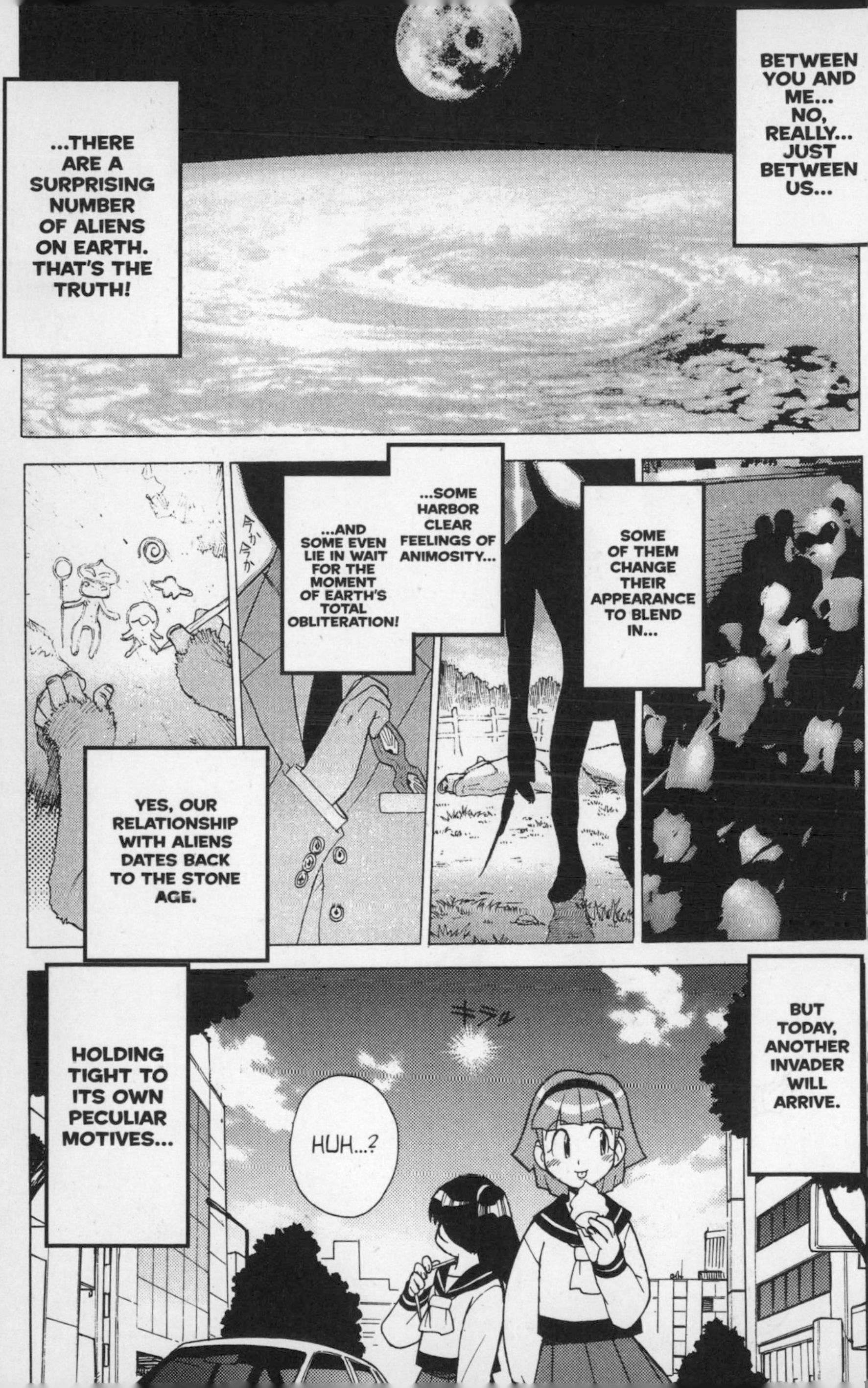
BETWEEN YOU AND ME... NO, REALLY... JUST BETWEEN US...
...THERE ARE A SURPRISING NUMBER OF ALIENS ON EARTH. THAT'S THE TRUTH!
SOME OF THEM CHANGE THEIR APPEARANCE TO BLEND IN...
...SOME HARBOR CLEAR FEELINGS OF ANIMOSITY...
...AND SOME EVEN LIE IN WAIT FOR THE MOMENT OF EARTH'S TOTAL OBLITERATION!
今か今か
YES, OUR RELATIONSHIP WITH ALIENS DATES BACK TO THE STONE AGE.
BUT TODAY, ANOTHER INVADER WILL ARRIVE.
キラッ
HUH...?
HOLDING TIGHT TO ITS OWN PECULIAR MOTIVES...

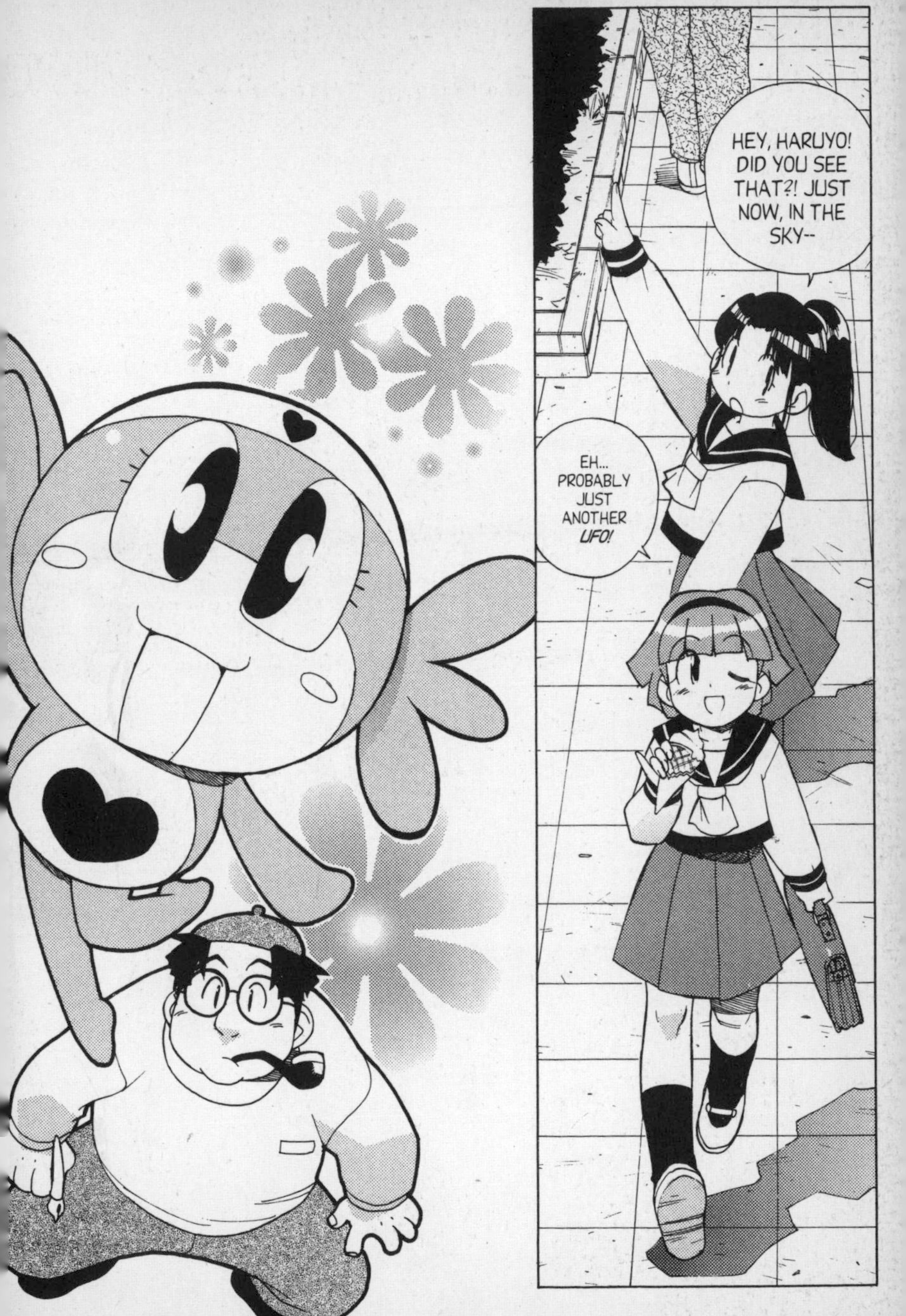
HEY, HARUYO! DID YOU SEE THAT?! JUST NOW, IN THE SKY--
EH... PROBABLY JUST ANOTHER *UFO!*

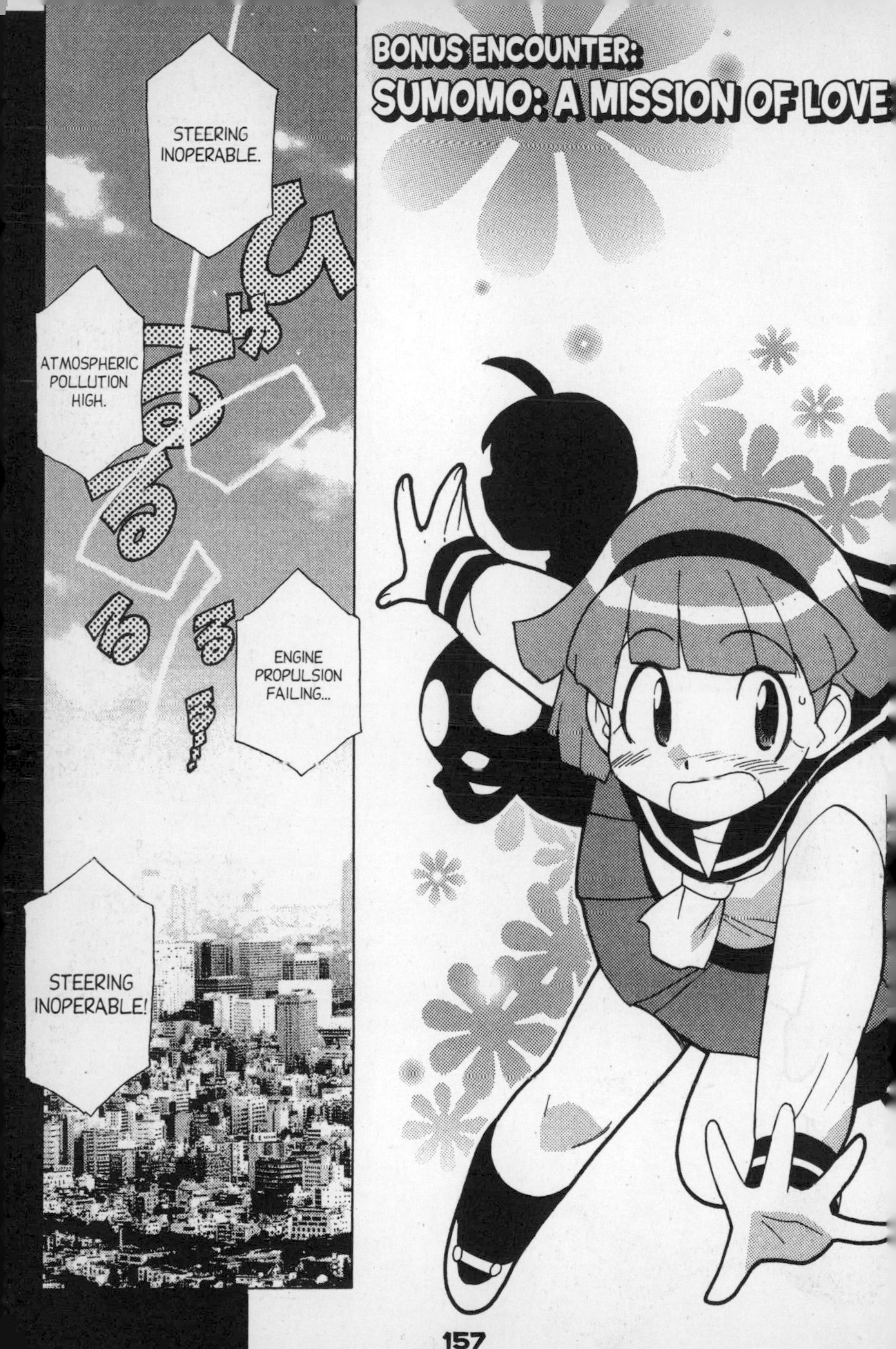
BONUS ENCOUNTER:
SUMOMO: A MISSION OF LOVE
STEERING INOPERABLE.
ATMOSPHERIC POLLUTION HIGH.
ENGINE PROPULSION FAILING...
STEERING INOPERABLE!

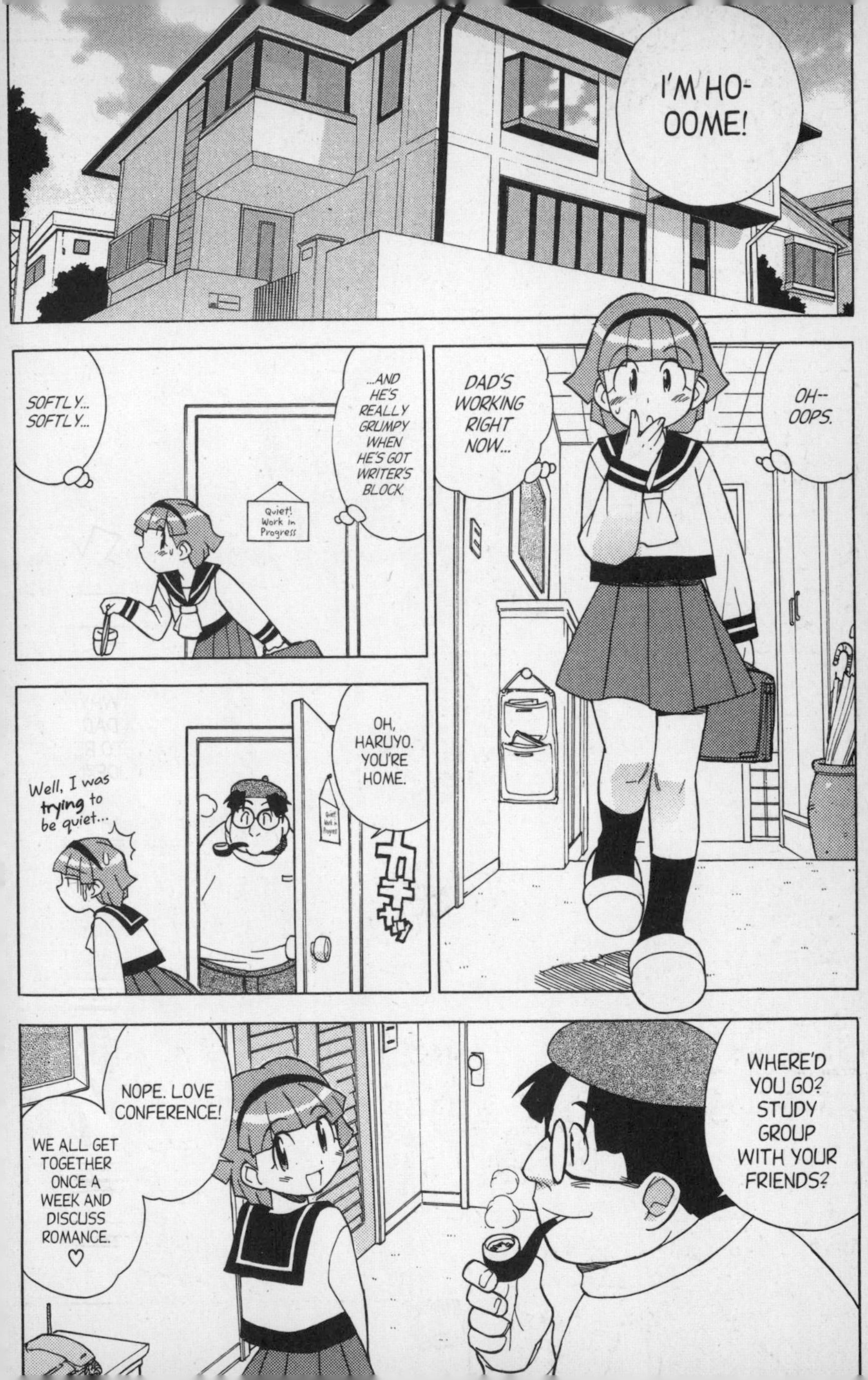
I'M HO-OOME!
OH-- OOPS.
DAD'S WORKING RIGHT NOW...
...AND HE'S REALLY GRUMPY WHEN HE'S GOT WRITER'S BLOCK.
Quiet! Work in Progress
SOFTLY... SOFTLY...
OH, HARUYO. YOU'RE HOME.
Well, I was **trying** to be quiet...
WHERE'D YOU GO? STUDY GROUP WITH YOUR FRIENDS?
NOPE. LOVE CONFERENCE!
WE ALL GET TOGETHER ONCE A WEEK AND DISCUSS ROMANCE. ♡

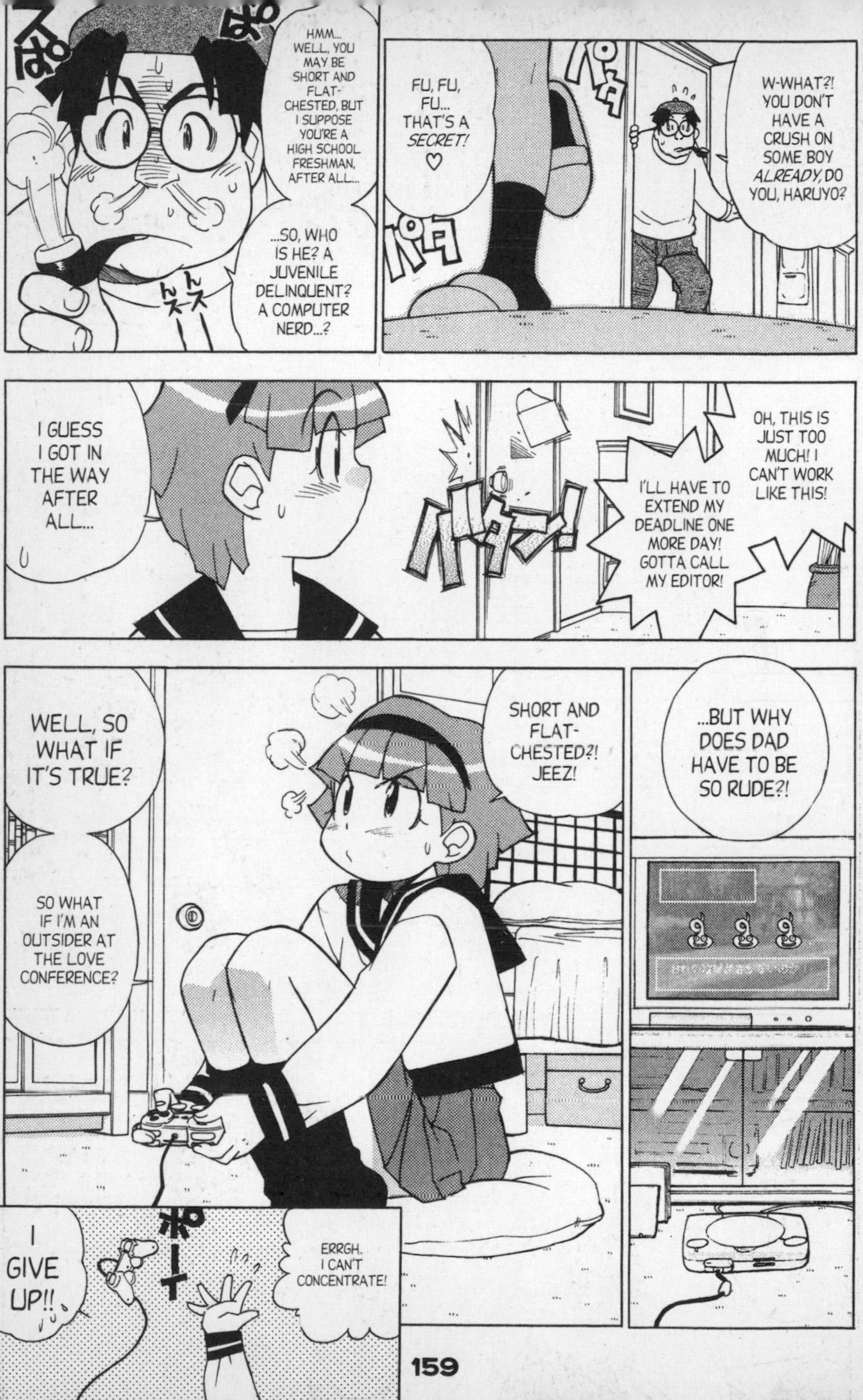
W-WHAT?! YOU DON'T HAVE A CRUSH ON SOME BOY *ALREADY,* DO YOU, HARUYO?
FU, FU, FU... THAT'S A *SECRET!* ♡
HMM... WELL, YOU MAY BE SHORT AND FLAT-CHESTED, BUT I SUPPOSE YOU'RE A HIGH SCHOOL FRESHMAN, AFTER ALL...
...SO, WHO IS HE? A JUVENILE DELINQUENT? A COMPUTER NERD...?
OH, THIS IS JUST TOO MUCH! I CAN'T WORK LIKE THIS!
I'LL HAVE TO EXTEND MY DEADLINE ONE MORE DAY! GOTTA CALL MY EDITOR!
I GUESS I GOT IN THE WAY AFTER ALL...
...BUT WHY DOES DAD HAVE TO BE SO RUDE?!
SHORT AND FLAT-CHESTED?! JEEZ!
WELL, SO WHAT IF IT'S TRUE?
SO WHAT IF I'M AN OUTSIDER AT THE LOVE CONFERENCE?
ERRGH. I CAN'T CONCENTRATE!
I GIVE UP!!

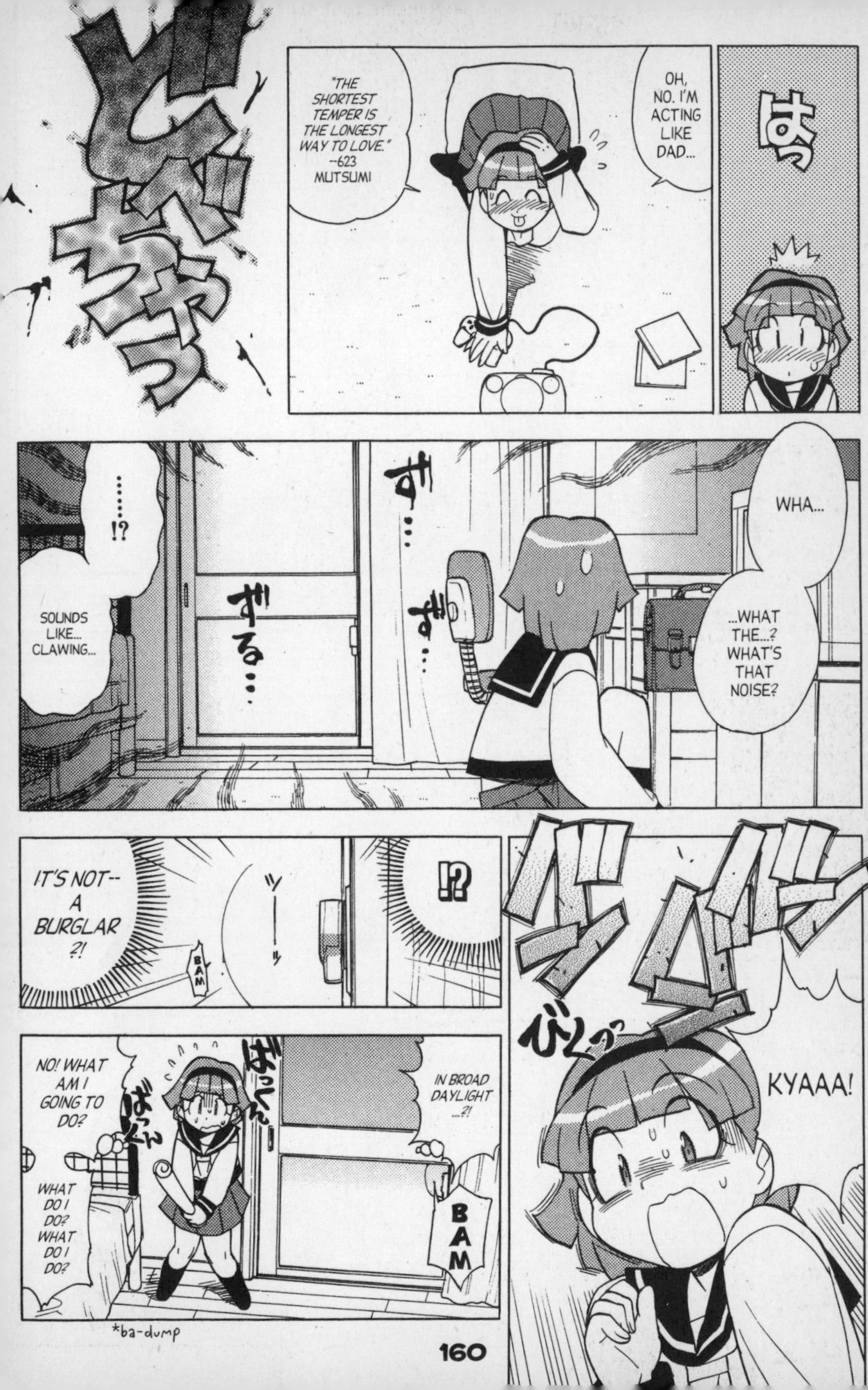

OH, NO. I'M ACTING LIKE DAD...
"THE SHORTEST TEMPER IS THE LONGEST WAY TO LOVE." --623 MUTSUMI
WHA...
...WHAT THE...? WHAT'S THAT NOISE?
......!?
SOUNDS LIKE... CLAWING...
KYAAA!
!?
BAM
IT'S NOT-- A BURGLAR?!
IN BROAD DAYLIGHT ...?!
BAM
NO! WHAT AM I GOING TO DO?
WHAT DO I DO? WHAT DO I DO?
*ba-dump

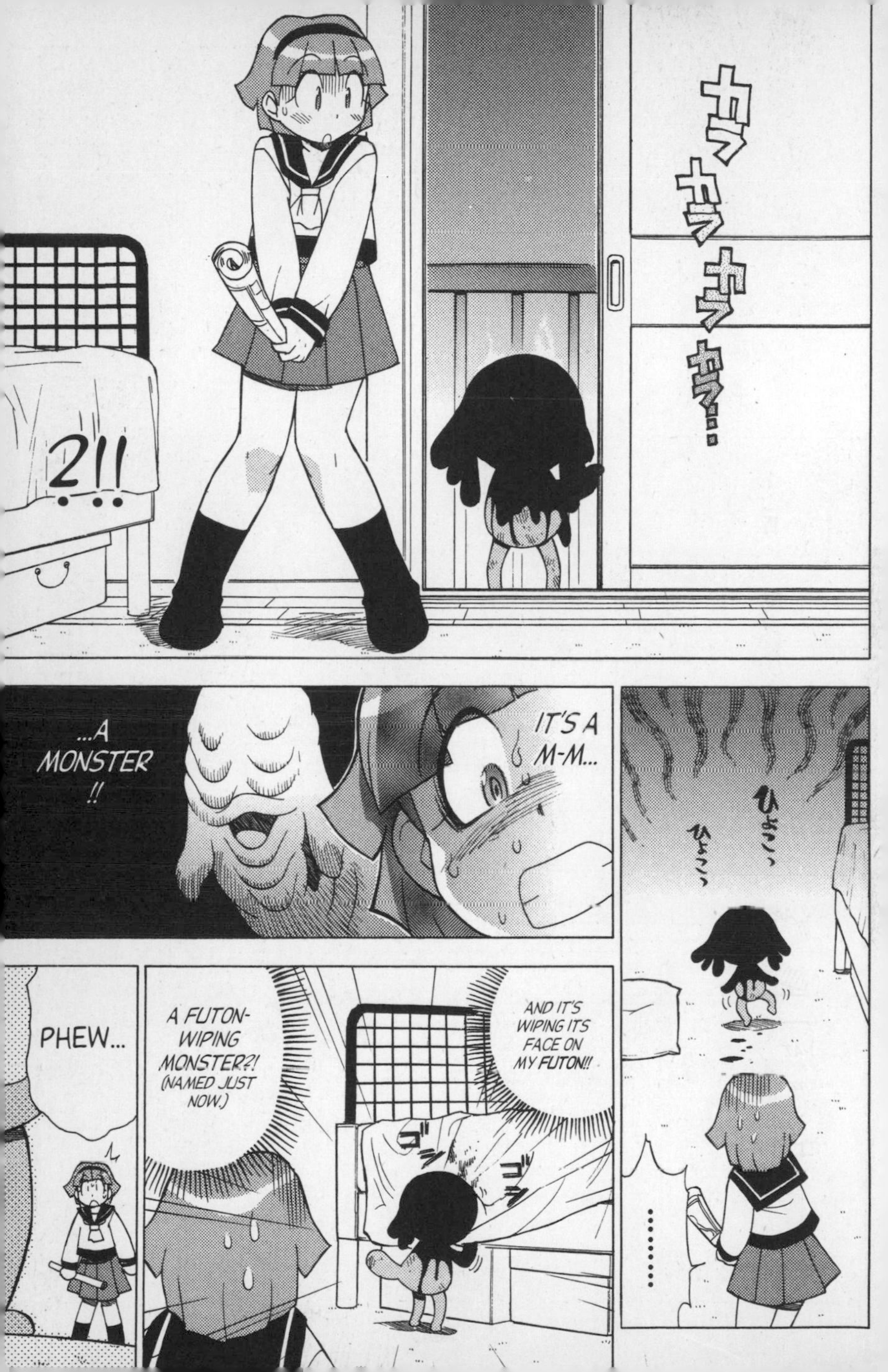
カラカラカラカラ!!
?!!
IT'S A M-M...
...A MONSTER !!
ひょこっ ひょこっ
......
AND IT'S WIPING ITS FACE ON MY FUTON!!
ゴシ ゴシ
A FUTON-WIPING MONSTER?! (NAMED JUST NOW.)
PHEW...

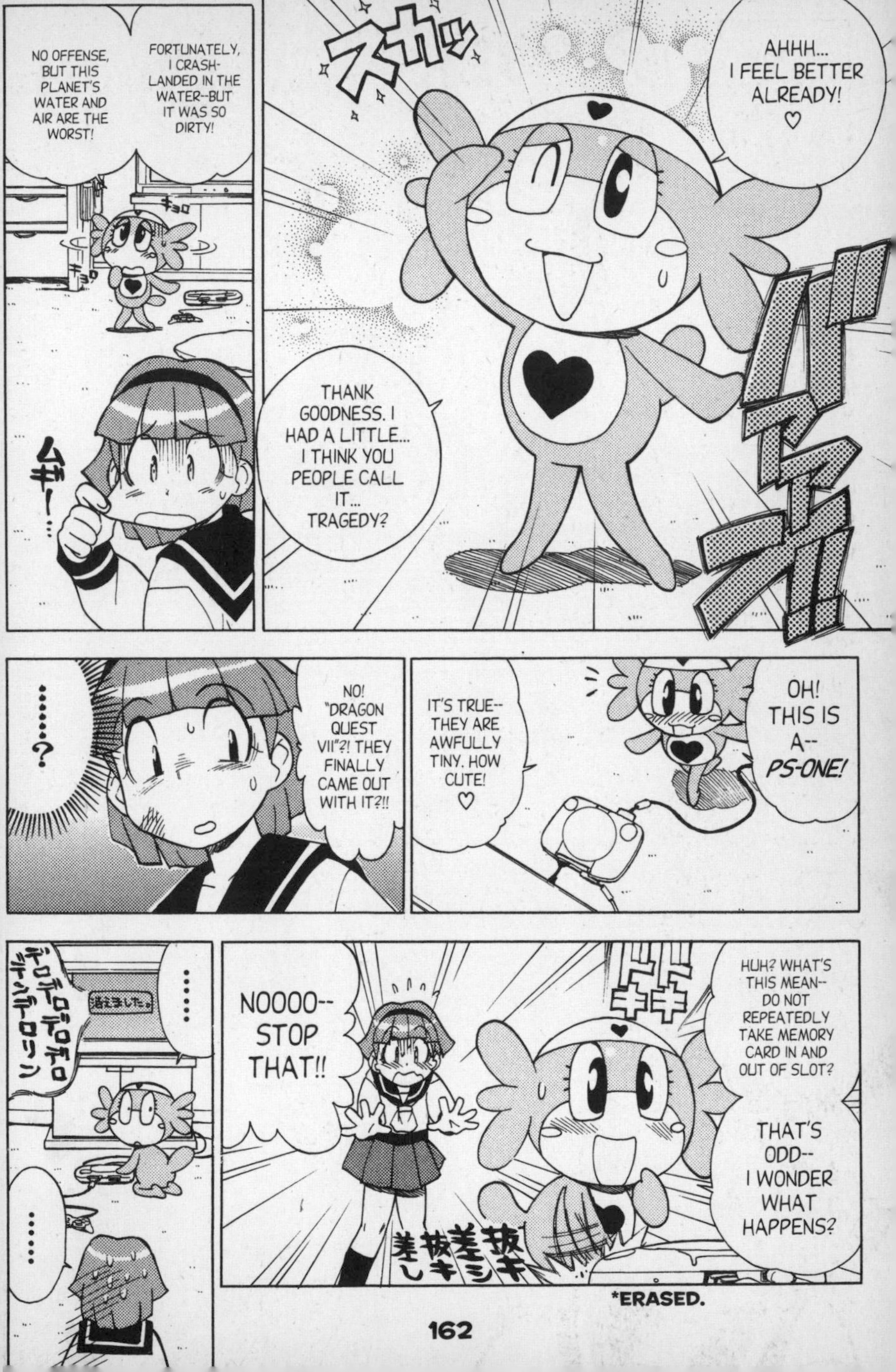
スカッ
AHHH... I FEEL BETTER ALREADY! ♡
THANK GOODNESS. I HAD A LITTLE... I THINK YOU PEOPLE CALL IT... TRAGEDY?
FORTUNATELY, I CRASH-LANDED IN THE WATER--BUT IT WAS SO DIRTY!
NO OFFENSE, BUT THIS PLANET'S WATER AND AIR ARE THE WORST!
キョロ
キョロ
ムギー…
OH! THIS IS A-- PS-ONE!
IT'S TRUE-- THEY ARE AWFULLY TINY. HOW CUTE! ♡
NO! "DRAGON QUEST VII"?! THEY FINALLY CAME OUT WITH IT?!!
......?
HUH? WHAT'S THIS MEAN-- DO NOT REPEATEDLY TAKE MEMORY CARD IN AND OUT OF SLOT?
THAT'S ODD-- I WONDER WHAT HAPPENS?
NOOOO-- STOP THAT!!
抜キ差シ抜キ差シ
......
消えました。*
デロデロデロデロデンデロリン
......

*ERASED.

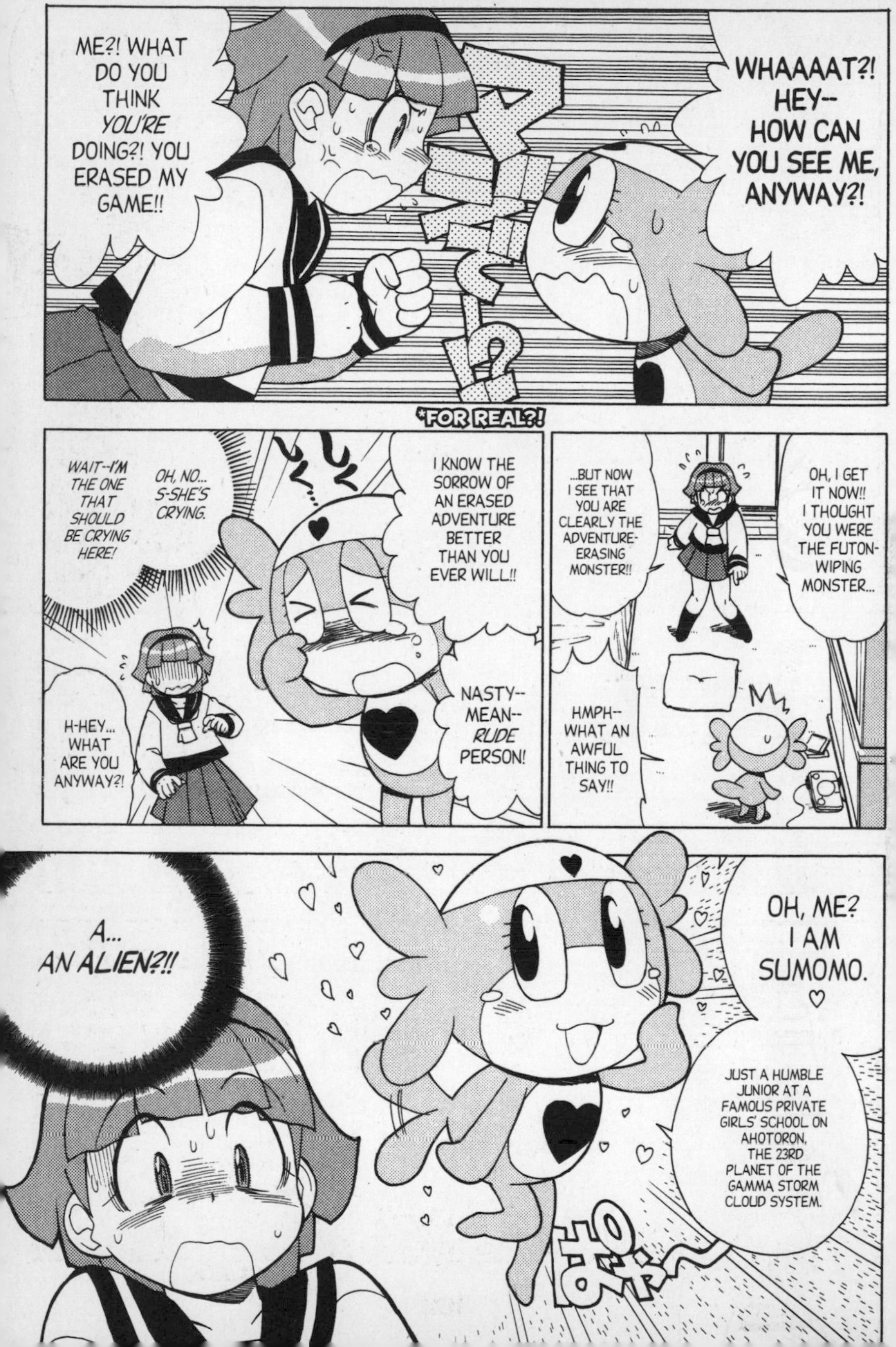
WHAAAAT?! HEY-- HOW CAN YOU SEE ME, ANYWAY?!
ME?! WHAT DO YOU THINK *YOU'RE* DOING?! YOU ERASED MY GAME!!
*FOR REAL?!
OH, I GET IT NOW!! I THOUGHT YOU WERE THE FUTON-WIPING MONSTER...
...BUT NOW I SEE THAT YOU ARE CLEARLY THE ADVENTURE-ERASING MONSTER!!
HMPH-- WHAT AN AWFUL THING TO SAY!!
I KNOW THE SORROW OF AN ERASED ADVENTURE BETTER THAN YOU EVER WILL!!
NASTY-- MEAN-- *RUDE* PERSON!
OH, NO... S-SHE'S CRYING.
WAIT--I'M THE ONE THAT SHOULD BE CRYING HERE!
H-HEY... WHAT ARE YOU ANYWAY?!
OH, ME? I AM SUMOMO. ♡
JUST A HUMBLE JUNIOR AT A FAMOUS PRIVATE GIRLS' SCHOOL ON AHOTORON, THE 23RD PLANET OF THE GAMMA STORM CLOUD SYSTEM.
A... AN ALIEN?!!

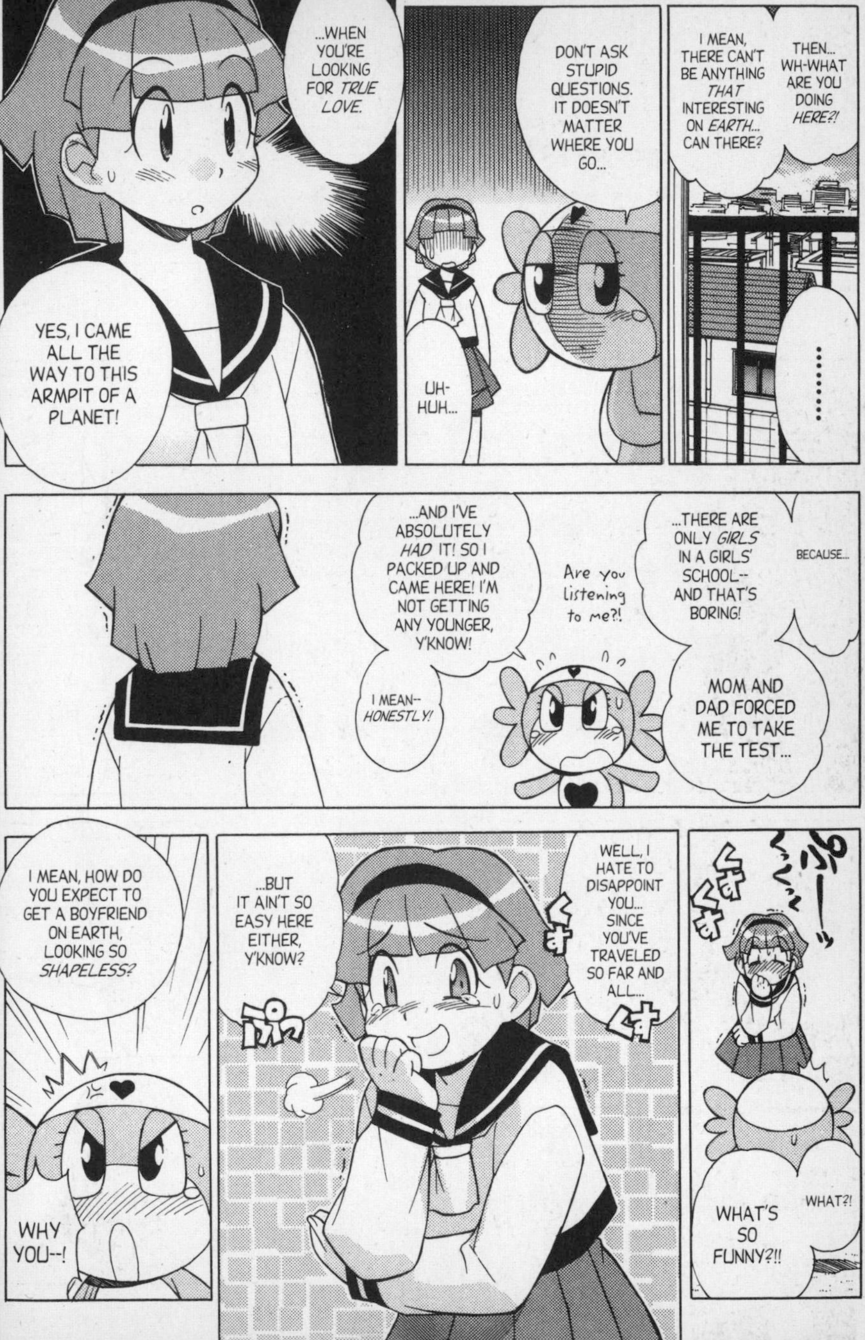
THEN... WH-WHAT ARE YOU DOING *HERE?!*
I MEAN, THERE CAN'T BE ANYTHING *THAT* INTERESTING ON *EARTH*... CAN THERE?
....
DON'T ASK STUPID QUESTIONS. IT DOESN'T MATTER WHERE YOU GO...
UH-HUH...
...WHEN YOU'RE LOOKING FOR *TRUE LOVE.*
YES, I CAME ALL THE WAY TO THIS ARMPIT OF A PLANET!
BECAUSE...
...THERE ARE ONLY *GIRLS* IN A GIRLS' SCHOOL-- AND THAT'S BORING!
MOM AND DAD FORCED ME TO TAKE THE TEST...
Are you listening to me?!
...AND I'VE ABSOLUTELY *HAD* IT! SO I PACKED UP AND CAME HERE! I'M NOT GETTING ANY YOUNGER, Y'KNOW!
I MEAN-- *HONESTLY!*
WHAT?!
WHAT'S SO FUNNY?!!
WELL, I HATE TO DISAPPOINT YOU... SINCE YOU'VE TRAVELED SO FAR AND ALL...
...BUT IT AIN'T SO EASY HERE EITHER, Y'KNOW?
I MEAN, HOW DO YOU EXPECT TO GET A BOYFRIEND ON EARTH, LOOKING SO *SHAPELESS?*
WHY YOU--!

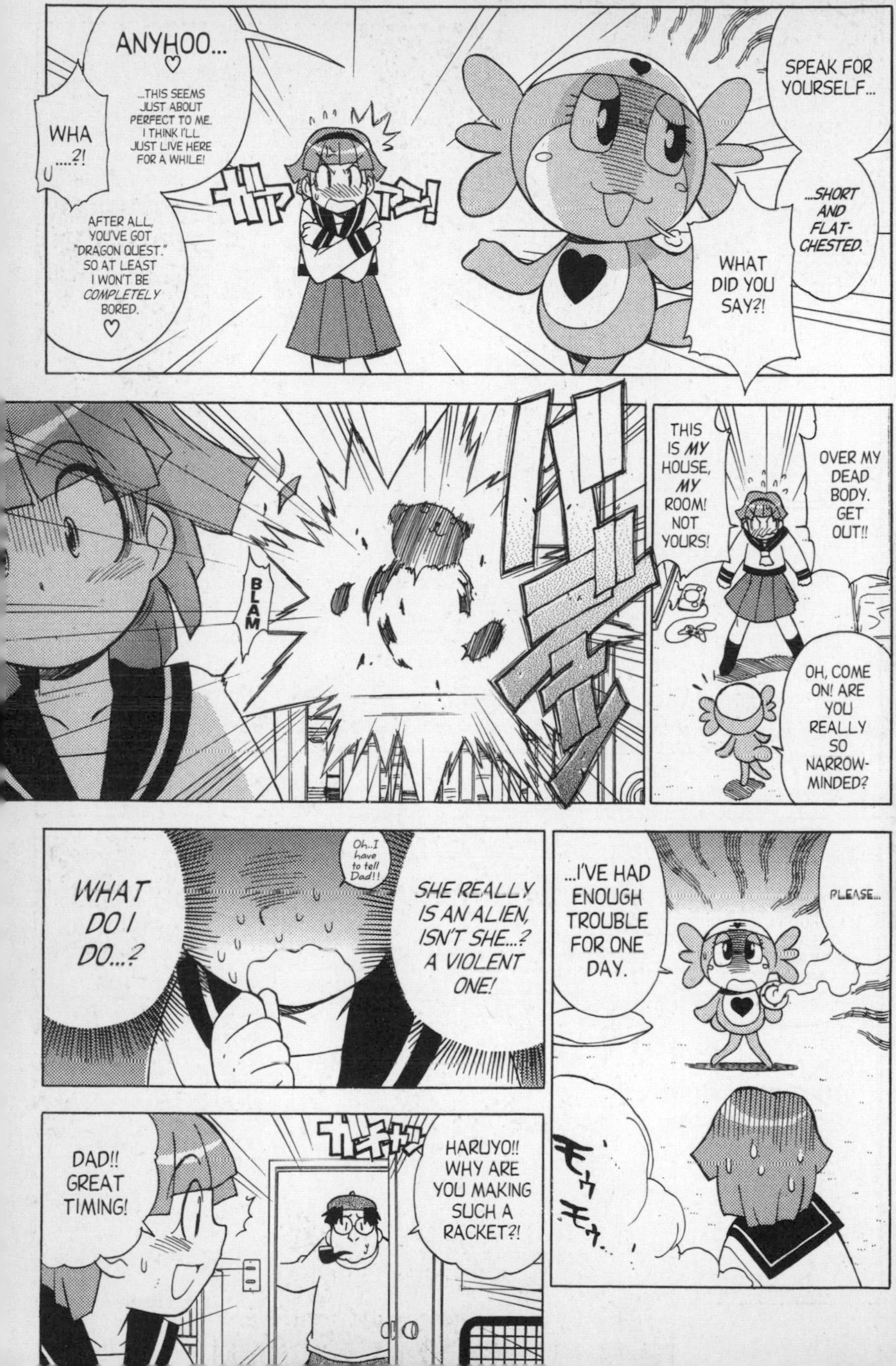
SPEAK FOR YOURSELF...
...SHORT AND FLAT-CHESTED.
WHAT DID YOU SAY?!
ANYHOO... ♡
...THIS SEEMS JUST ABOUT PERFECT TO ME. I THINK I'LL JUST LIVE HERE FOR A WHILE!
AFTER ALL, YOU'VE GOT "DRAGON QUEST." SO AT LEAST I WON'T BE COMPLETELY BORED. ♡
WHA ...?!
OVER MY DEAD BODY. GET OUT!!
THIS IS MY HOUSE, MY ROOM! NOT YOURS!
OH, COME ON! ARE YOU REALLY SO NARROW-MINDED?
BLAM
PLEASE...
...I'VE HAD ENOUGH TROUBLE FOR ONE DAY.
SHE REALLY IS AN ALIEN, ISN'T SHE...? A VIOLENT ONE!
Oh..I have to tell Dad!!
WHAT DO I DO...?
HARUYO!! WHY ARE YOU MAKING SUCH A RACKET?!
DAD!! GREAT TIMING!

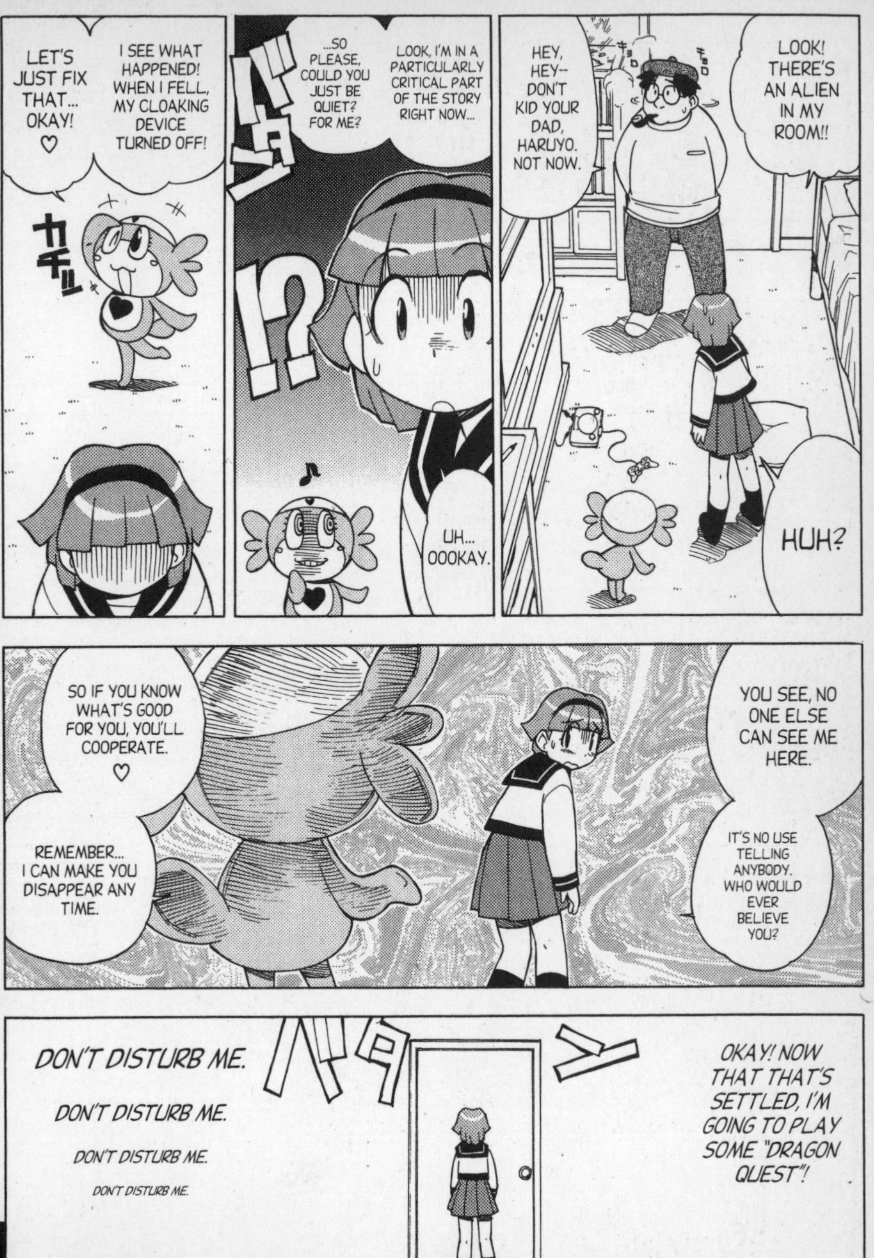
LOOK! THERE'S AN ALIEN IN MY ROOM!!
HEY, HEY-- DON'T KID YOUR DAD, HARUYO. NOT NOW.
HUH?
LOOK, I'M IN A PARTICULARLY CRITICAL PART OF THE STORY RIGHT NOW...
...SO PLEASE, COULD YOU JUST BE QUIET? FOR ME?
!?
UH... OOOKAY.
I SEE WHAT HAPPENED! WHEN I FELL, MY CLOAKING DEVICE TURNED OFF!
LET'S JUST FIX THAT... OKAY! ♡
YOU SEE, NO ONE ELSE CAN SEE ME HERE.
IT'S NO USE TELLING ANYBODY. WHO WOULD EVER BELIEVE YOU?
SO IF YOU KNOW WHAT'S GOOD FOR YOU, YOU'LL COOPERATE. ♡
REMEMBER... I CAN MAKE YOU DISAPPEAR ANY TIME.
OKAY! NOW THAT THAT'S SETTLED, I'M GOING TO PLAY SOME "DRAGON QUEST"!
DON'T DISTURB ME.
DON'T DISTURB ME.
DON'T DISTURB ME.
DON'T DISTURB ME.

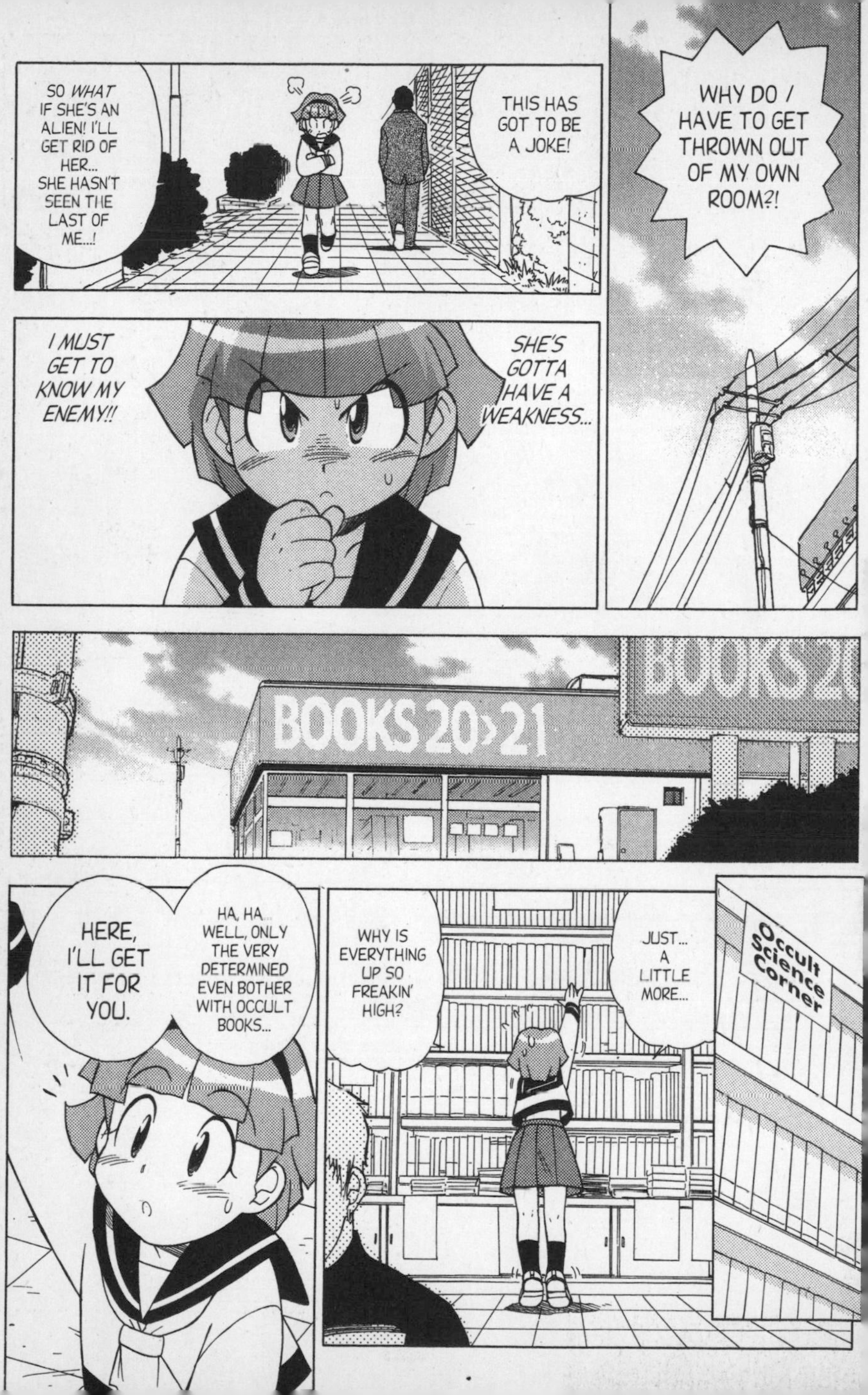

WHY DO I HAVE TO GET THROWN OUT OF MY OWN ROOM?!
THIS HAS GOT TO BE A JOKE!
SO WHAT IF SHE'S AN ALIEN! I'LL GET RID OF HER... SHE HASN'T SEEN THE LAST OF ME...!
SHE'S GOTTA HAVE A WEAKNESS...
I MUST GET TO KNOW MY ENEMY!!
BOOKS 20>21
Occult Science Corner
JUST... A LITTLE MORE...
WHY IS EVERYTHING UP SO FREAKIN' HIGH?
HA, HA... WELL, ONLY THE VERY DETERMINED EVEN BOTHER WITH OCCULT BOOKS...
HERE, I'LL GET IT FOR YOU.

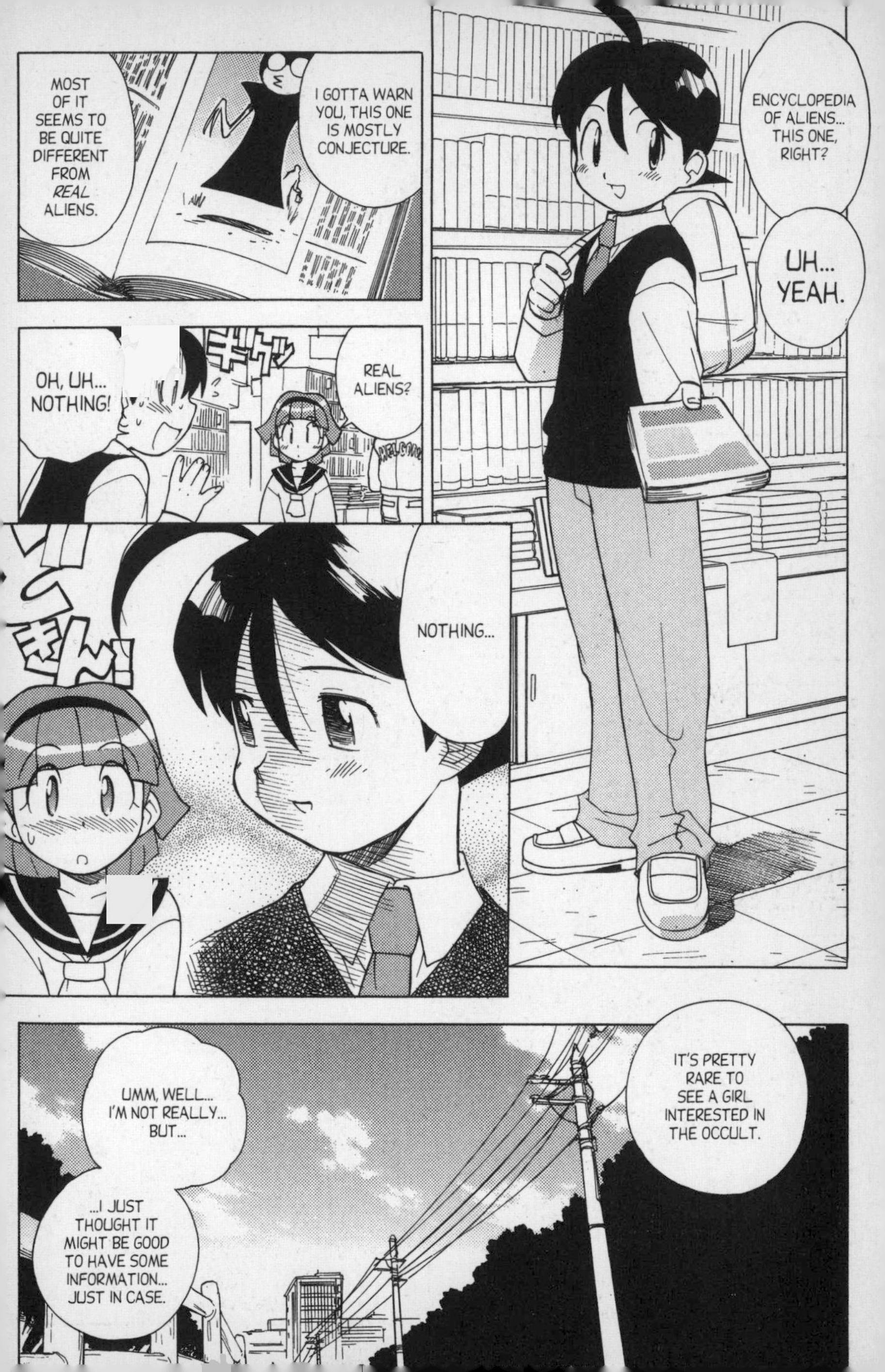

ENCYCLOPEDIA OF ALIENS... THIS ONE, RIGHT?
UH... YEAH.
I GOTTA WARN YOU, THIS ONE IS MOSTLY CONJECTURE.
MOST OF IT SEEMS TO BE QUITE DIFFERENT FROM *REAL* ALIENS.
REAL ALIENS?
OH, UH... NOTHING!
NOTHING...
IT'S PRETTY RARE TO SEE A GIRL INTERESTED IN THE OCCULT.
UMM, WELL... I'M NOT REALLY... BUT...
...I JUST THOUGHT IT MIGHT BE GOOD TO HAVE SOME INFORMATION... JUST IN CASE.

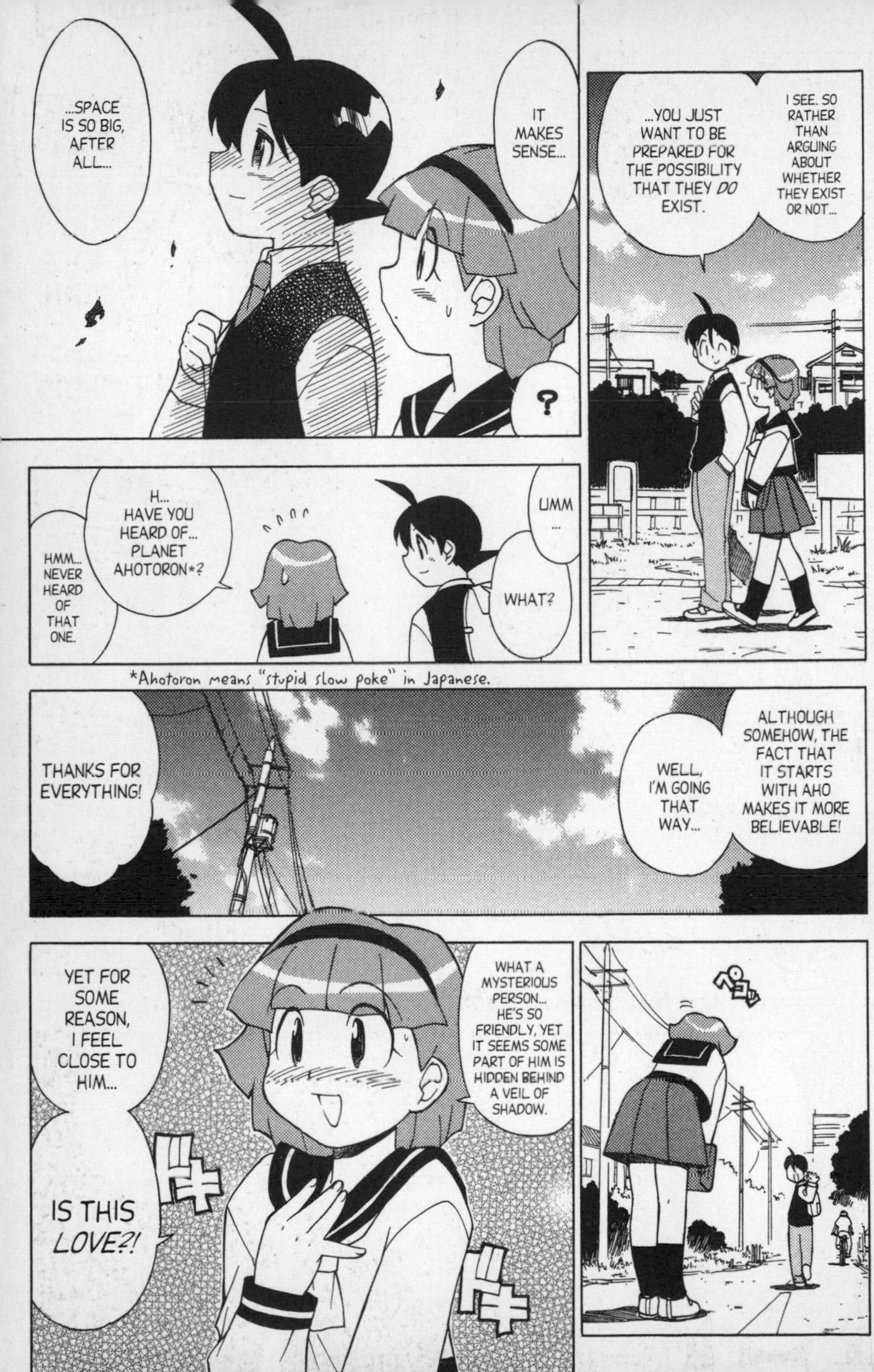
I SEE. SO RATHER THAN ARGUING ABOUT WHETHER THEY EXIST OR NOT...
...YOU JUST WANT TO BE PREPARED FOR THE POSSIBILITY THAT THEY *DO* EXIST.
IT MAKES SENSE...
?
...SPACE IS SO BIG, AFTER ALL...
UMM ...
WHAT?
H... HAVE YOU HEARD OF... PLANET AHOTORON*?
HMM... NEVER HEARD OF THAT ONE.
ALTHOUGH SOMEHOW, THE FACT THAT IT STARTS WITH AHO MAKES IT MORE BELIEVABLE!
WELL, I'M GOING THAT WAY...
THANKS FOR EVERYTHING!
WHAT A MYSTERIOUS PERSON... HE'S SO FRIENDLY, YET IT SEEMS SOME PART OF HIM IS HIDDEN BEHIND A VEIL OF SHADOW.
YET FOR SOME REASON, I FEEL CLOSE TO HIM...
ドキ
IS THIS *LOVE*?!
ドキ

*Ahotoron means "stupid slow poke" in Japanese.

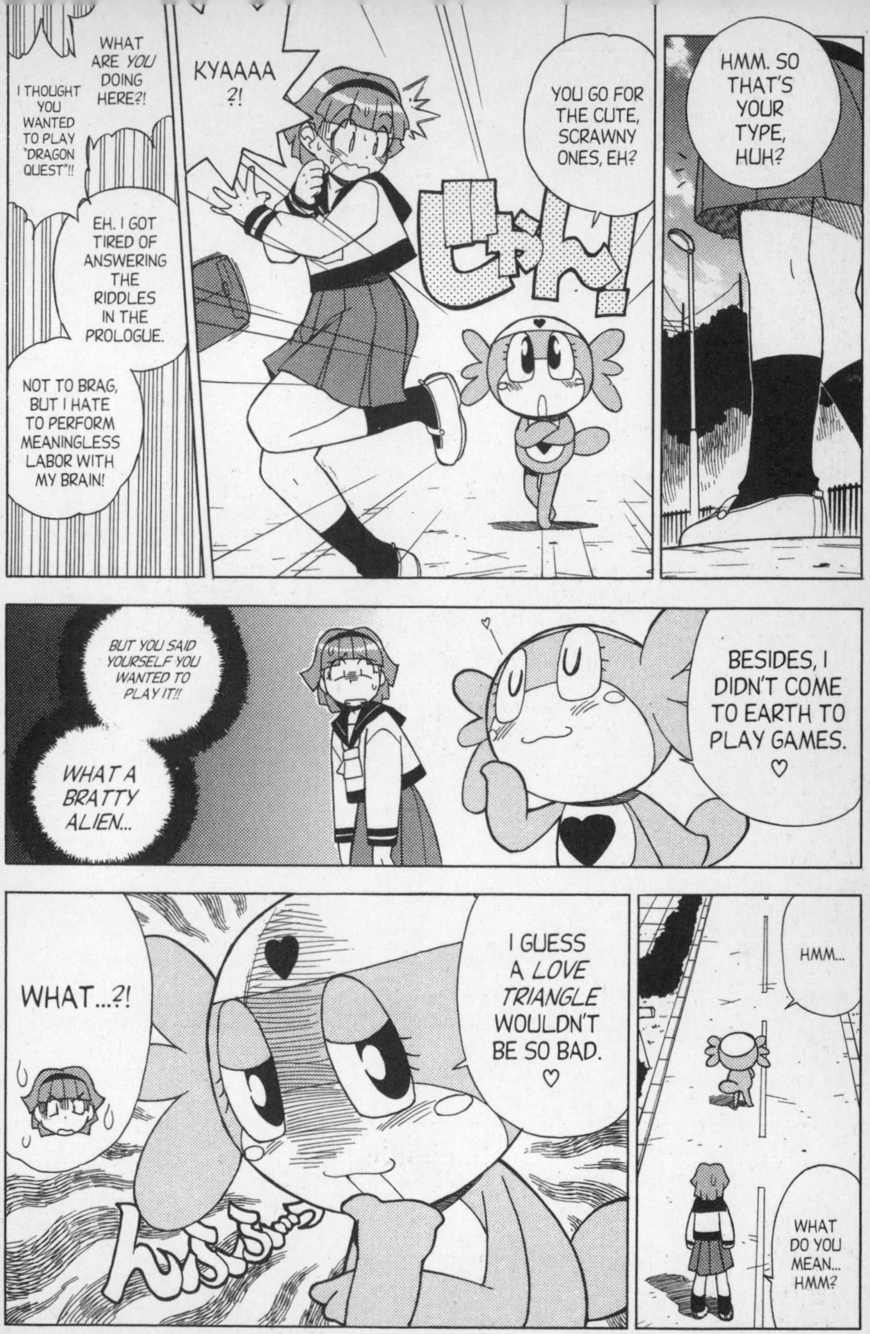
HMM. SO THAT'S YOUR TYPE, HUH?
YOU GO FOR THE CUTE, SCRAWNY ONES, EH?
じゃん!
KYAAAA ?!
WHAT ARE *YOU* DOING HERE?!
I THOUGHT YOU WANTED TO PLAY "DRAGON QUEST"!!
EH. I GOT TIRED OF ANSWERING THE RIDDLES IN THE PROLOGUE.
NOT TO BRAG, BUT I HATE TO PERFORM MEANINGLESS LABOR WITH MY BRAIN!
BESIDES, I DIDN'T COME TO EARTH TO PLAY GAMES. ♡
BUT YOU SAID YOURSELF YOU WANTED TO PLAY IT!!
WHAT A BRATTY ALIEN...
HMM...
WHAT DO YOU MEAN... HMM?
I GUESS A *LOVE TRIANGLE* WOULDN'T BE SO BAD. ♡
WHAT...?!

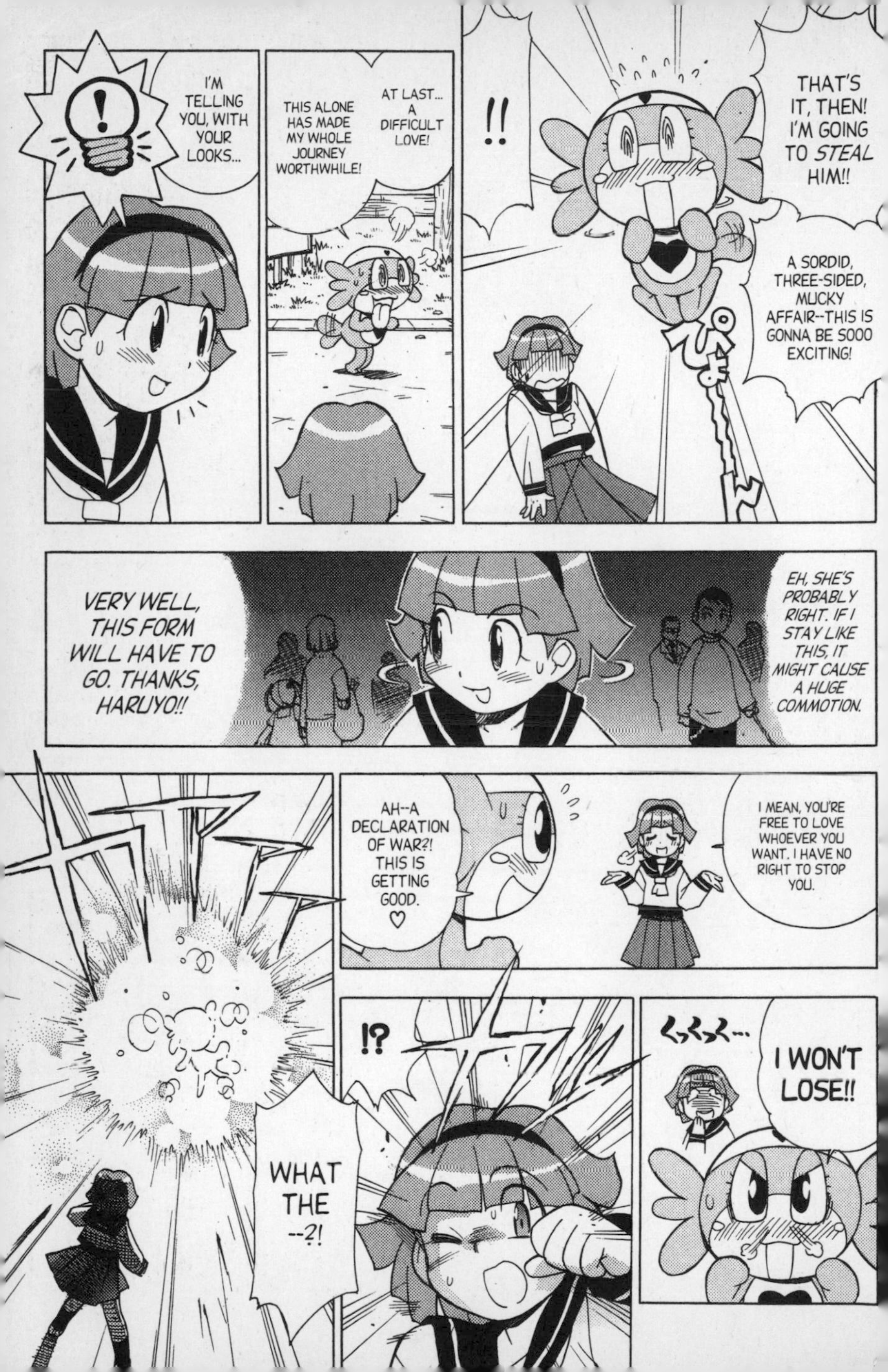
THAT'S IT, THEN! I'M GOING TO *STEAL* HIM!!
A SORDID, THREE-SIDED, MUCKY AFFAIR--THIS IS GONNA BE SOOO EXCITING!
!!
AT LAST... A DIFFICULT LOVE!
THIS ALONE HAS MADE MY WHOLE JOURNEY WORTHWHILE!
I'M TELLING YOU, WITH YOUR LOOKS...
EH, SHE'S PROBABLY RIGHT. IF I STAY LIKE THIS, IT MIGHT CAUSE A HUGE COMMOTION.
VERY WELL, THIS FORM WILL HAVE TO GO. THANKS, HARUYO!!
I MEAN, YOU'RE FREE TO LOVE WHOEVER YOU WANT. I HAVE NO RIGHT TO STOP YOU.
AH--A DECLARATION OF WAR?! THIS IS GETTING GOOD. ♡
くっくっく…
I WON'T LOSE!!
!?
WHAT THE --?!

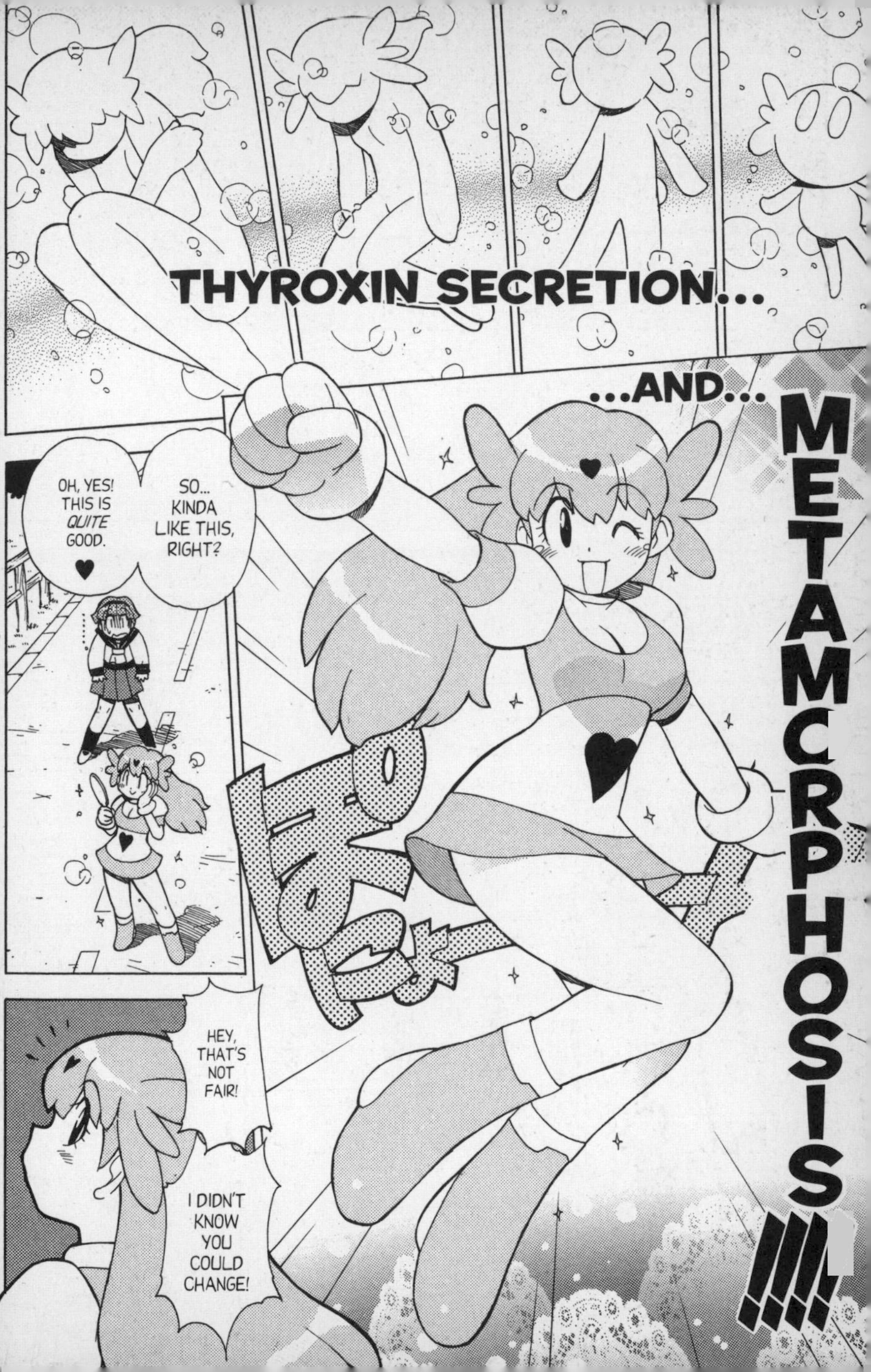
THYROXIN SECRETION...
...AND...
METAMORPHOSIS!!!!
SO... KINDA LIKE THIS, RIGHT?
OH, YES! THIS IS *QUITE* GOOD. ♥
HEY, THAT'S NOT FAIR!
I DIDN'T KNOW YOU COULD CHANGE!

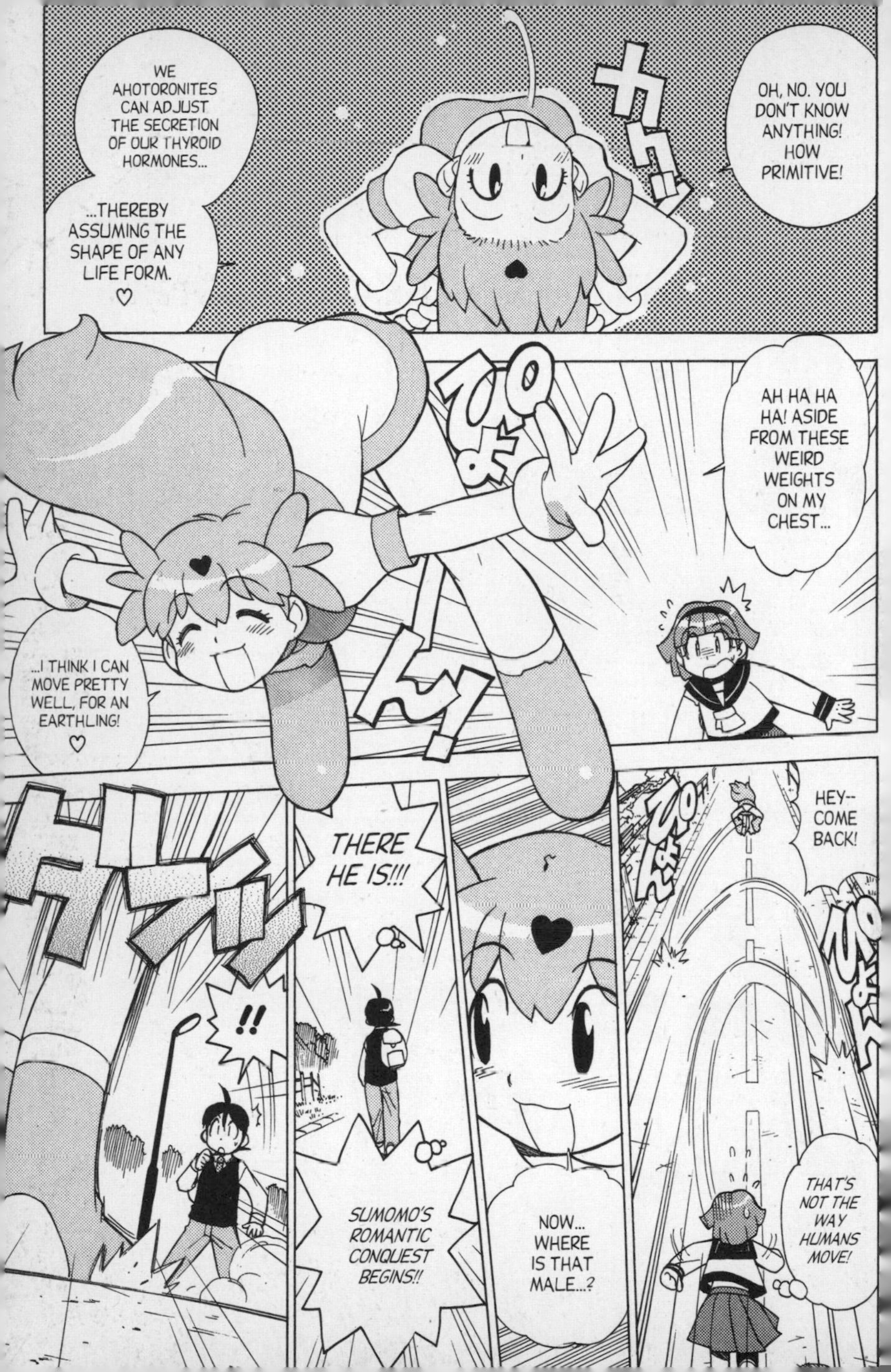

OH, NO. YOU DON'T KNOW ANYTHING! HOW PRIMITIVE!
WE AHOTORONITES CAN ADJUST THE SECRETION OF OUR THYROID HORMONES...
...THEREBY ASSUMING THE SHAPE OF ANY LIFE FORM. ♡
AH HA HA HA! ASIDE FROM THESE WEIRD WEIGHTS ON MY CHEST...
...I THINK I CAN MOVE PRETTY WELL, FOR AN EARTHLING! ♡
HEY-- COME BACK!
THAT'S NOT THE WAY HUMANS MOVE!
NOW... WHERE IS THAT MALE...?
THERE HE IS!!!
SUMOMO'S ROMANTIC CONQUEST BEGINS!!
!!

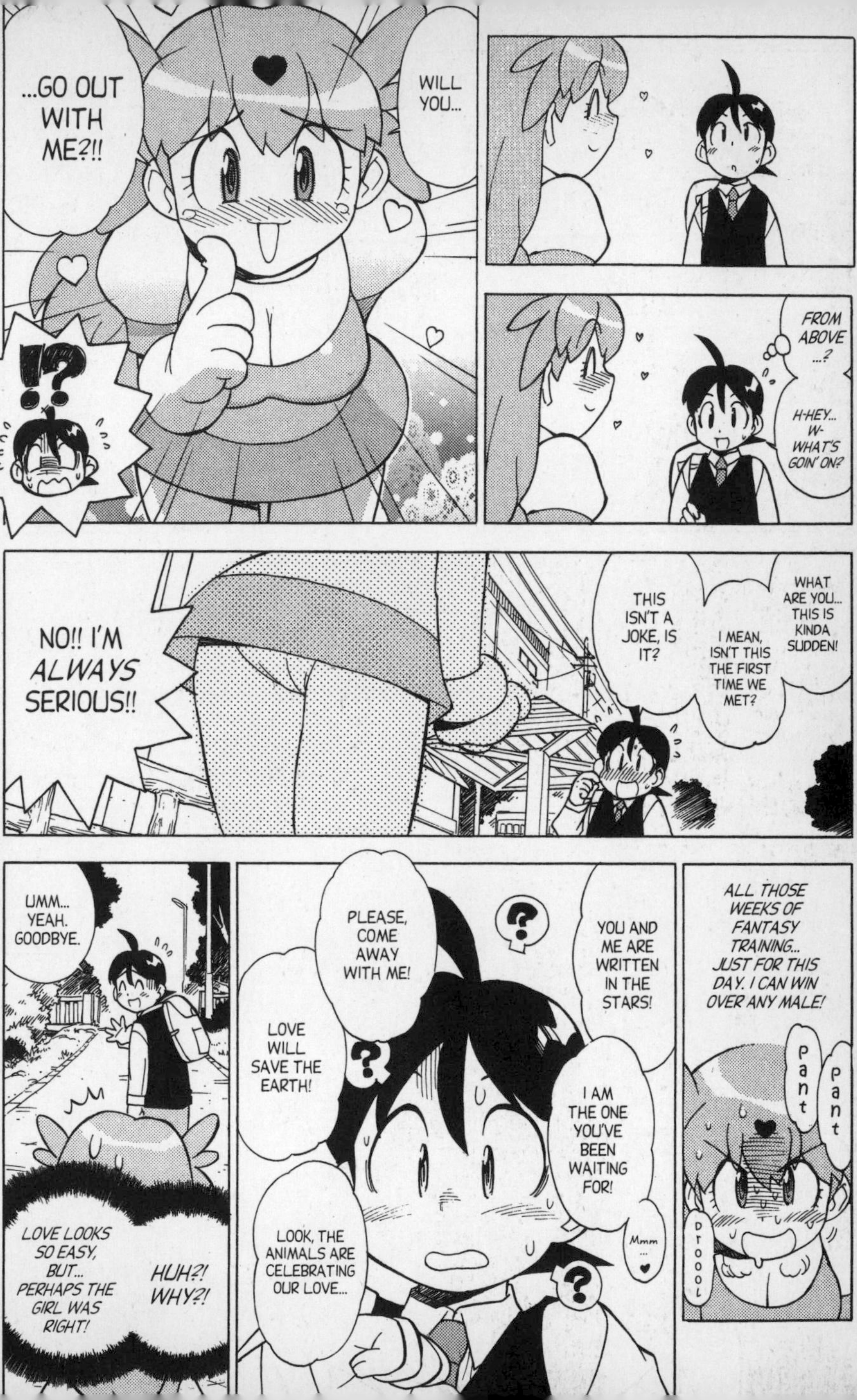
FROM ABOVE ...?
H-HEY... W-WHAT'S GOIN' ON?
WILL YOU...
...GO OUT WITH ME?!!
!?
WHAT ARE YOU... THIS IS KINDA SUDDEN!
I MEAN, ISN'T THIS THE FIRST TIME WE MET?
THIS ISN'T A JOKE, IS IT?
NO!! I'M ALWAYS SERIOUS!!
ALL THOSE WEEKS OF FANTASY TRAINING... JUST FOR THIS DAY. I CAN WIN OVER ANY MALE!
Pant
Pant
Droool
YOU AND ME ARE WRITTEN IN THE STARS!
PLEASE, COME AWAY WITH ME!
LOVE WILL SAVE THE EARTH!
I AM THE ONE YOU'VE BEEN WAITING FOR!
Mmm ...
LOOK, THE ANIMALS ARE CELEBRATING OUR LOVE...
UMM... YEAH. GOODBYE.
HUH?! WHY?!
LOVE LOOKS SO EASY, BUT... PERHAPS THE GIRL WAS RIGHT!

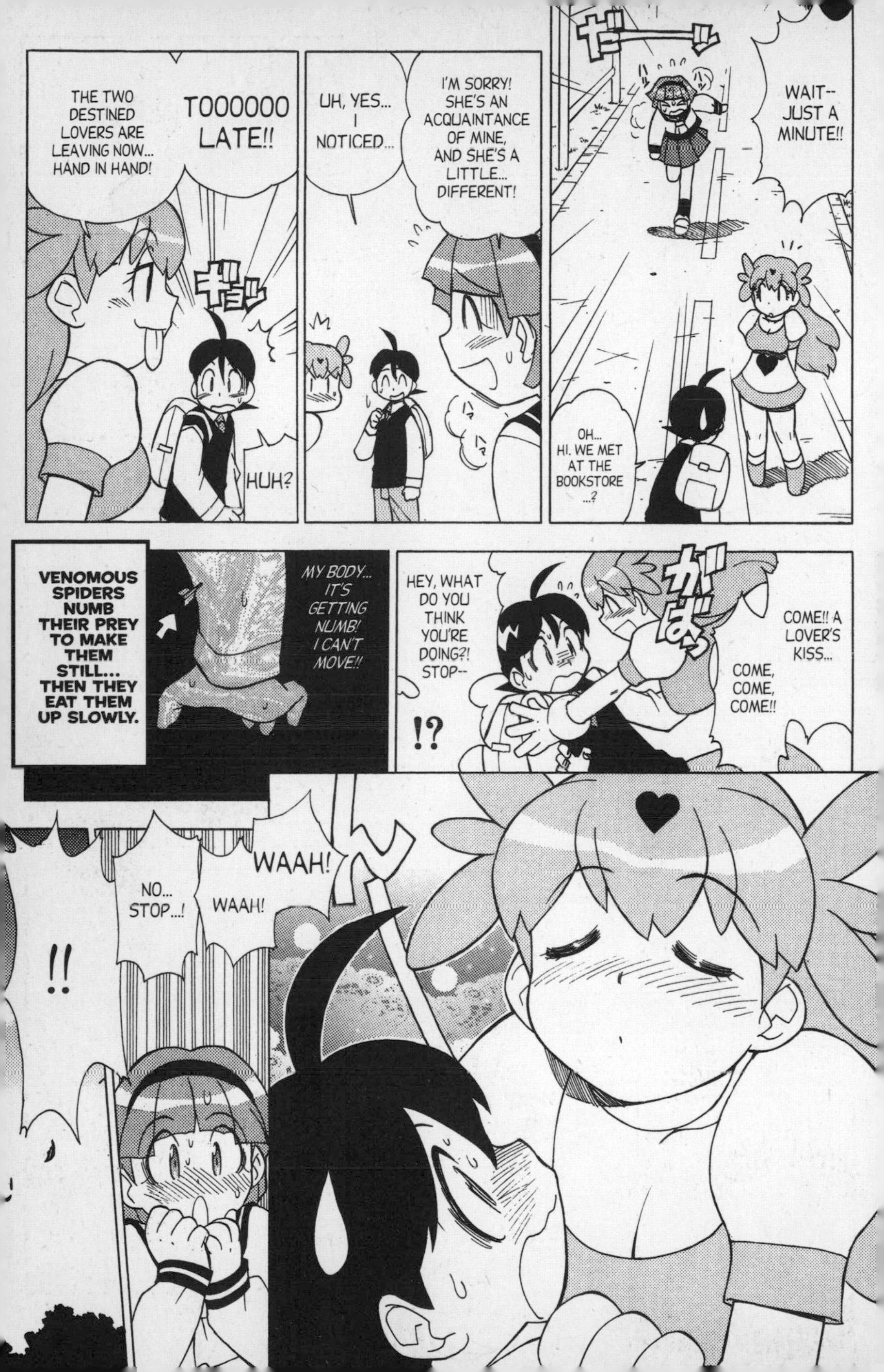
WAIT-- JUST A MINUTE!!
OH... HI. WE MET AT THE BOOKSTORE ...?
I'M SORRY! SHE'S AN ACQUAINTANCE OF MINE, AND SHE'S A LITTLE... DIFFERENT!
UH, YES... I NOTICED...
TOOOOOO LATE!!
THE TWO DESTINED LOVERS ARE LEAVING NOW... HAND IN HAND!
HUH?
COME!! A LOVER'S KISS...
COME, COME, COME!!
HEY, WHAT DO YOU THINK YOU'RE DOING?! STOP--
!?
MY BODY... IT'S GETTING NUMB! I CAN'T MOVE!!
VENOMOUS SPIDERS NUMB THEIR PREY TO MAKE THEM STILL... THEN THEY EAT THEM UP SLOWLY.
WAAH!
WAAH!
NO... STOP...!
!!

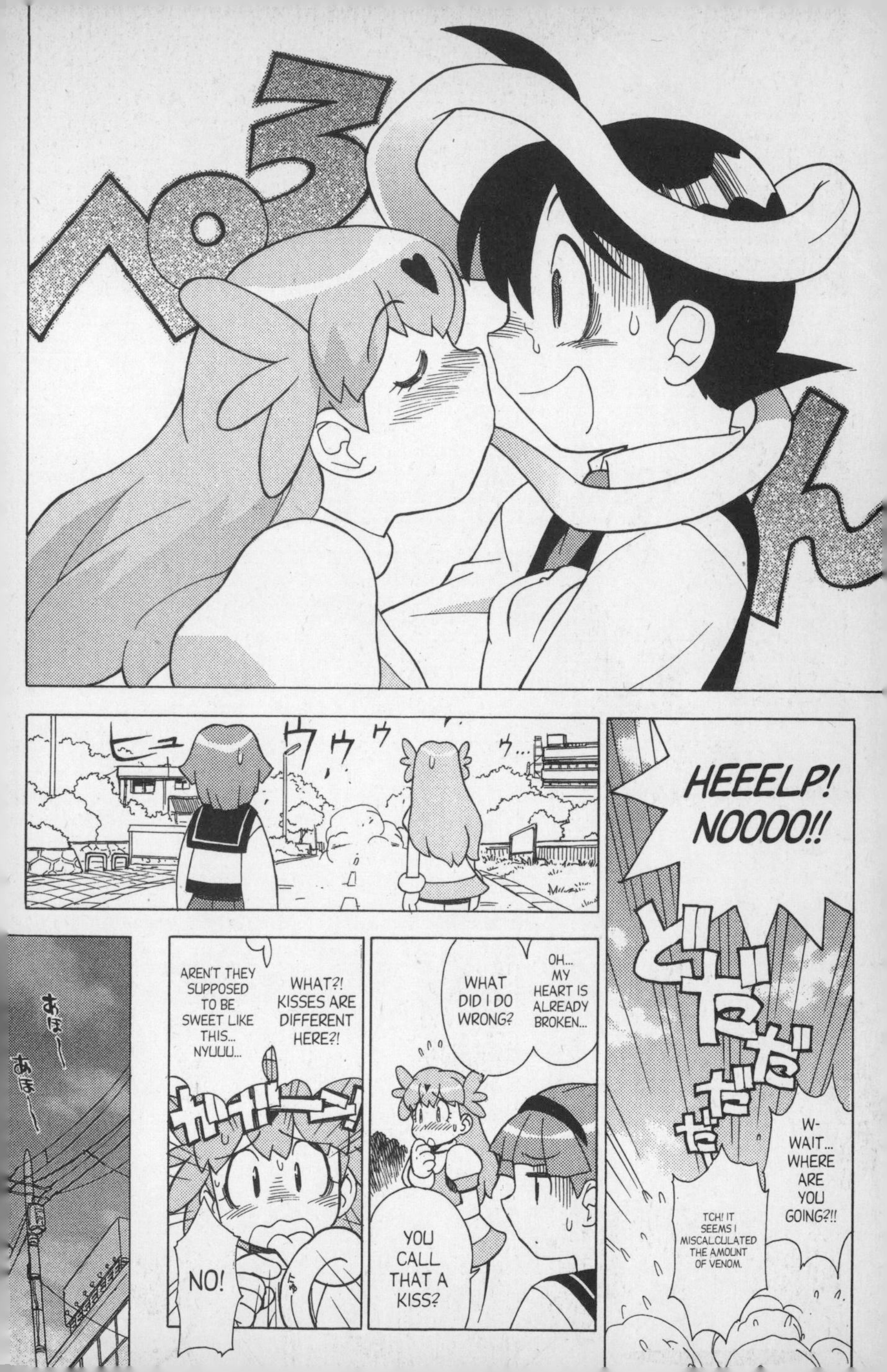
HEEELP! NOOOO!!
ヒュウウウウ…
どだだだだ
W-WAIT... WHERE ARE YOU GOING?!!
TCH! IT SEEMS I MISCALCULATED THE AMOUNT OF VENOM.
OH... MY HEART IS ALREADY BROKEN...
WHAT DID I DO WRONG?
YOU CALL THAT A KISS?
WHAT?! KISSES ARE DIFFERENT HERE?!
AREN'T THEY SUPPOSED TO BE SWEET LIKE THIS... NYUUU...
NO!
あほー
あほー

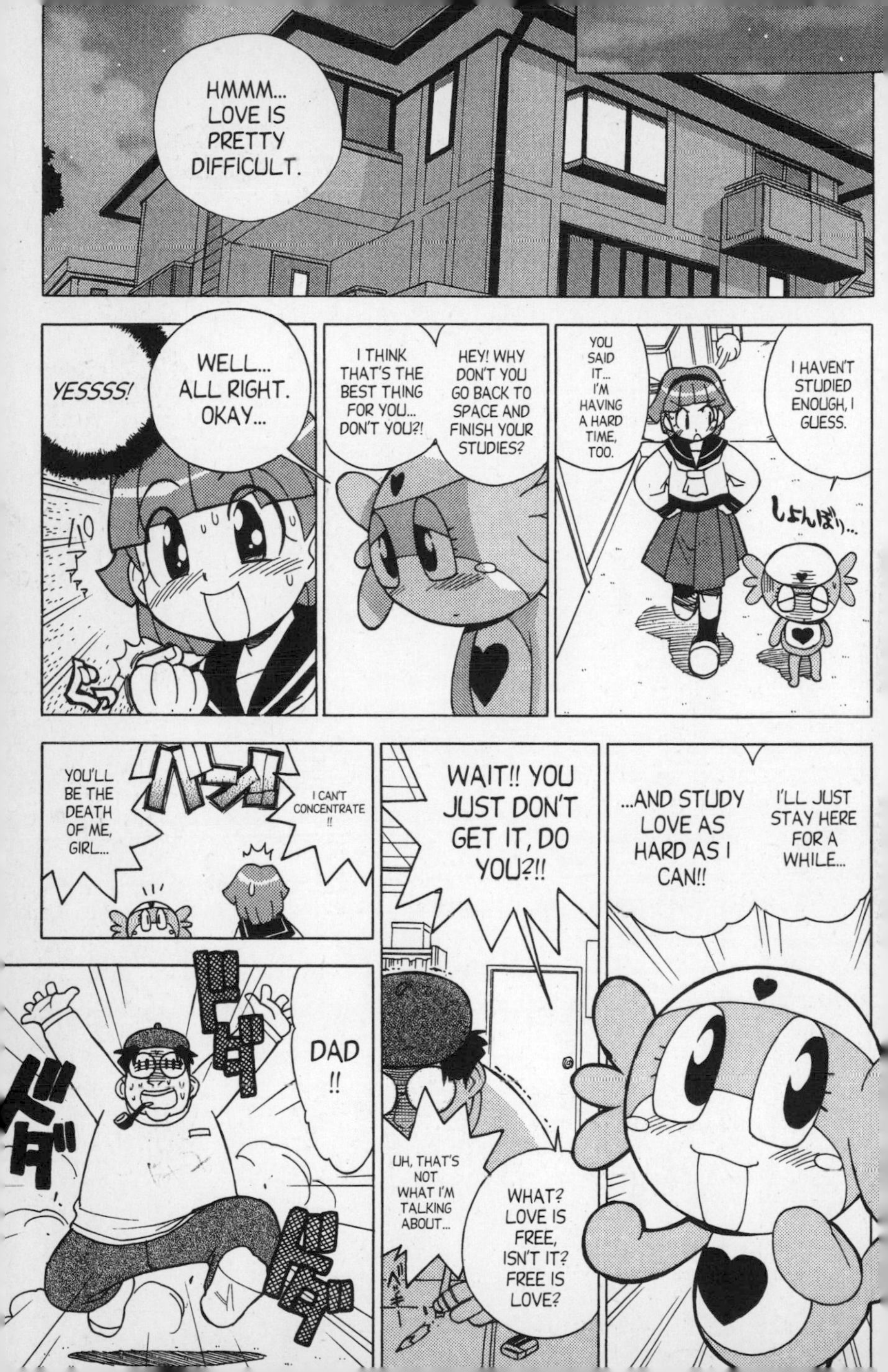
HMMM... LOVE IS PRETTY DIFFICULT.
I HAVEN'T STUDIED ENOUGH, I GUESS.
YOU SAID IT... I'M HAVING A HARD TIME, TOO.
しょんぼり...
HEY! WHY DON'T YOU GO BACK TO SPACE AND FINISH YOUR STUDIES?
I THINK THAT'S THE BEST THING FOR YOU... DON'T YOU?!
WELL... ALL RIGHT. OKAY...
YESSSS!
I'LL JUST STAY HERE FOR A WHILE...
...AND STUDY LOVE AS HARD AS I CAN!!
WAIT!! YOU JUST DON'T GET IT, DO YOU?!!
I CAN'T CONCENTRATE !!
YOU'LL BE THE DEATH OF ME, GIRL...
WHAT? LOVE IS FREE, ISN'T IT? FREE IS LOVE?
UH, THAT'S NOT WHAT I'M TALKING ABOUT...
DAD !!

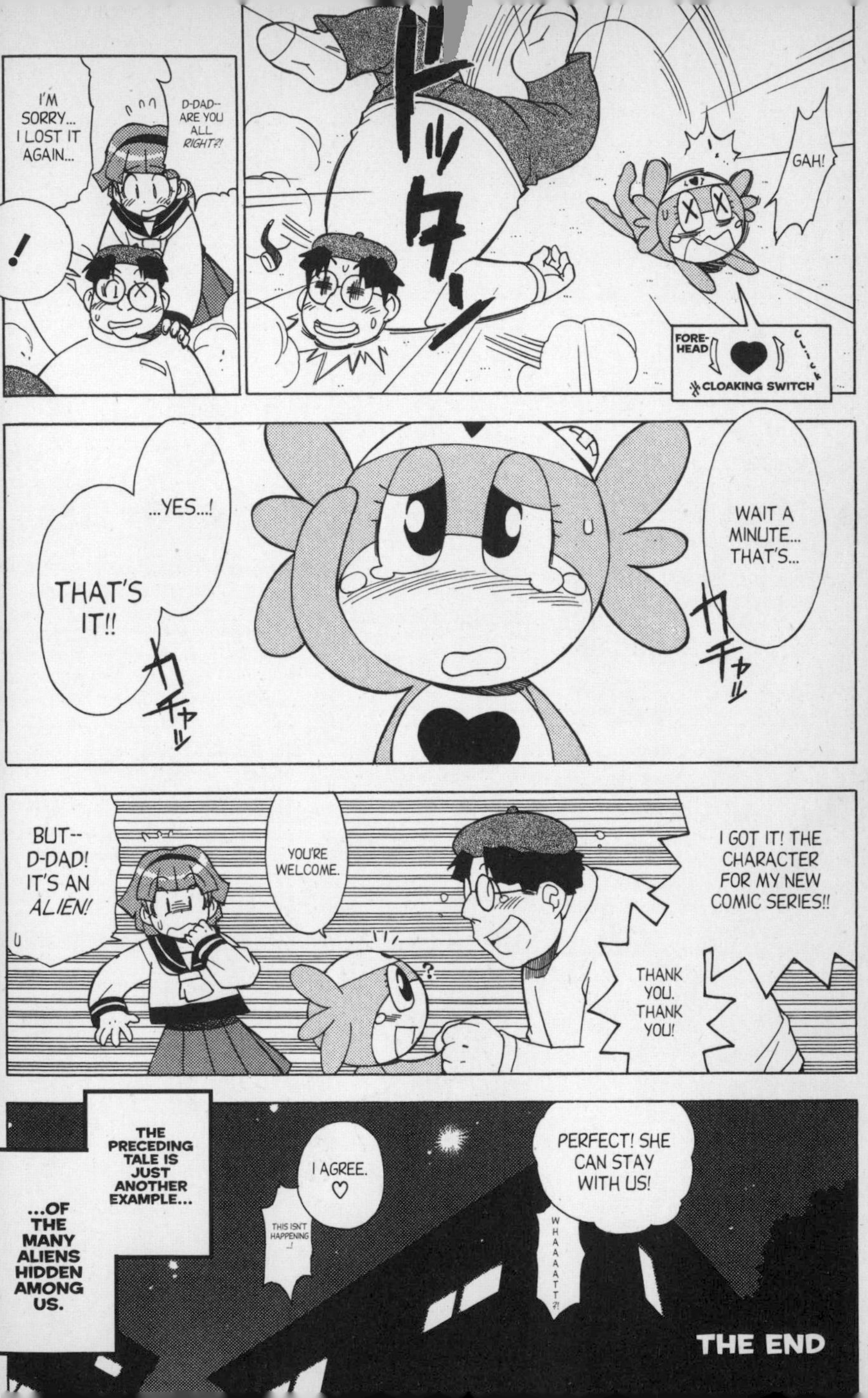
I'M SORRY... I LOST IT AGAIN...
D-DAD-- ARE YOU ALL RIGHT?!
!
ドッターン
GAH!
FOREHEAD
CLICK
CLOAKING SWITCH
...YES...!
THAT'S IT!!
カチャッ
WAIT A MINUTE... THAT'S...
カチャッ
BUT-- D-DAD! IT'S AN ALIEN!
YOU'RE WELCOME.
I GOT IT! THE CHARACTER FOR MY NEW COMIC SERIES!!
THANK YOU. THANK YOU!
THE PRECEDING TALE IS JUST ANOTHER EXAMPLE...
...OF THE MANY ALIENS HIDDEN AMONG US.
I AGREE. ♡
THIS ISN'T HAPPENING ...!
PERFECT! SHE CAN STAY WITH US!
WHAAAATT?!
THE END

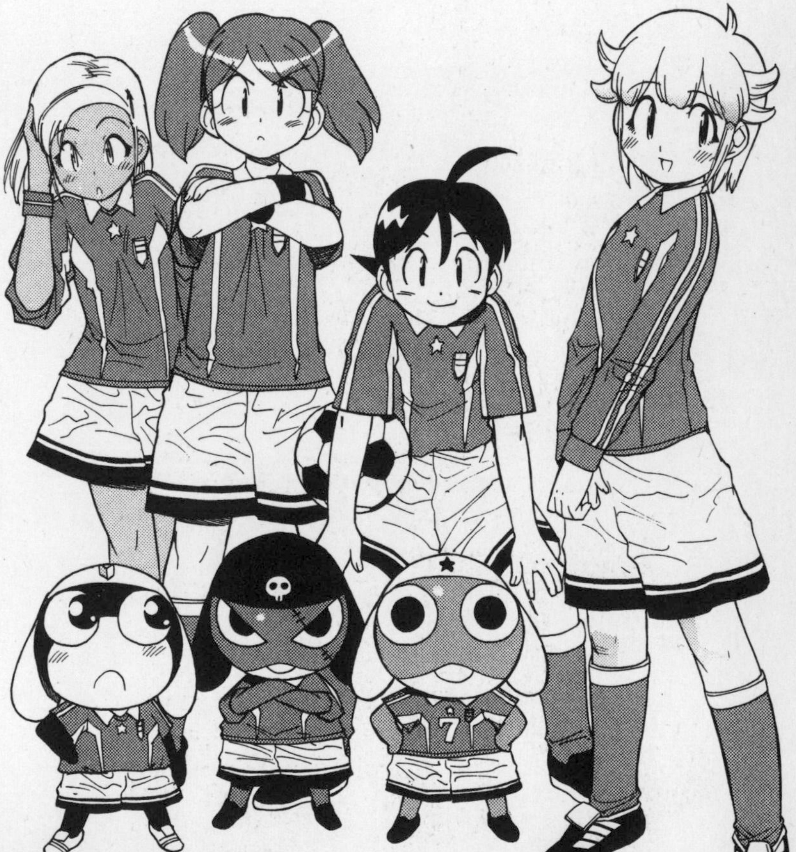

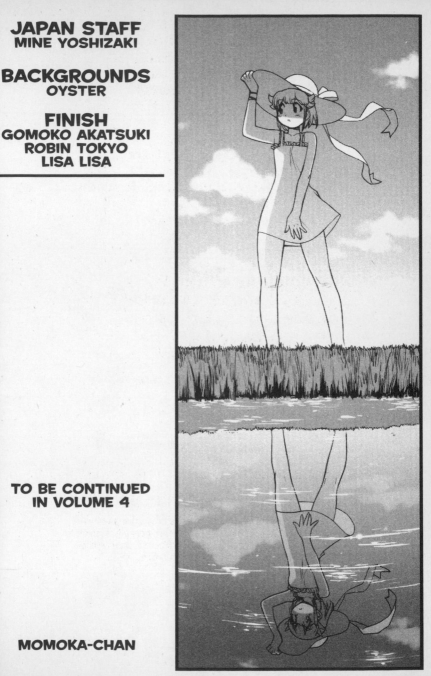

JAPAN STAFF
MINE YOSHIZAKI

BACKGROUNDS
OYSTER

FINISH
GOMOKO AKATSUKI
ROBIN TOKYO
LISA LISA

TO BE CONTINUED
IN VOLUME 4

MOMOKA-CHAN

Translator - Yuko Fukami
English Adaptation - Carol Fox
Copy Editor - Suzanne Waldman
Retouch and Lettering - Jose Macasocol, Jr.
Cover Design - Raymond Makowski
Graphic Designer - Vicente Rivera, Jr.

Editor - Paul Morrissey
Digital Imaging Manager - Chris Buford
Pre-Press Manager - Antonio DePietro
Production Managers - Jennifer Miller and Mutsumi Miyazaki
Art Director - Matt Alford
Managing Editor - Jill Freshney
VP of Production - Ron Klamert
President & C.O.O. - John Parker
Publisher & C.E.O. - Stuart Levy

E-mail: info@TOKYOPOP.com
Come visit us online at www.TOKYOPOP.com

A  Manga

TOKYOPOP Inc.
5900 Wilshire Blvd. Suite 2000
Los Angeles, CA 90036

SGT. Frog Vol. 3

KERORO GUNSO © 2001 MINE YOSHIZAKI
First published in by KADOKAWA SHOTEN PUBLISHING CO., LTD., Tokyo. English translation rights arranged with
KADOKAWA SHOTEN PUBLISHING CO., LTD., Tokyo through TUTTLE-MORI AGENCY, INC., Tokyo.

English text copyright © 2004 TOKYOPOP Inc.

ISBN: 1-59182-705-1

First TOKYOPOP printing: July 2004

10 9 8 7 6 5 4 3 2 1

Printed in the USA

TOKYOPOP PRESS

LOS ANGELES • TOKYO • LONDON • HAMBURG

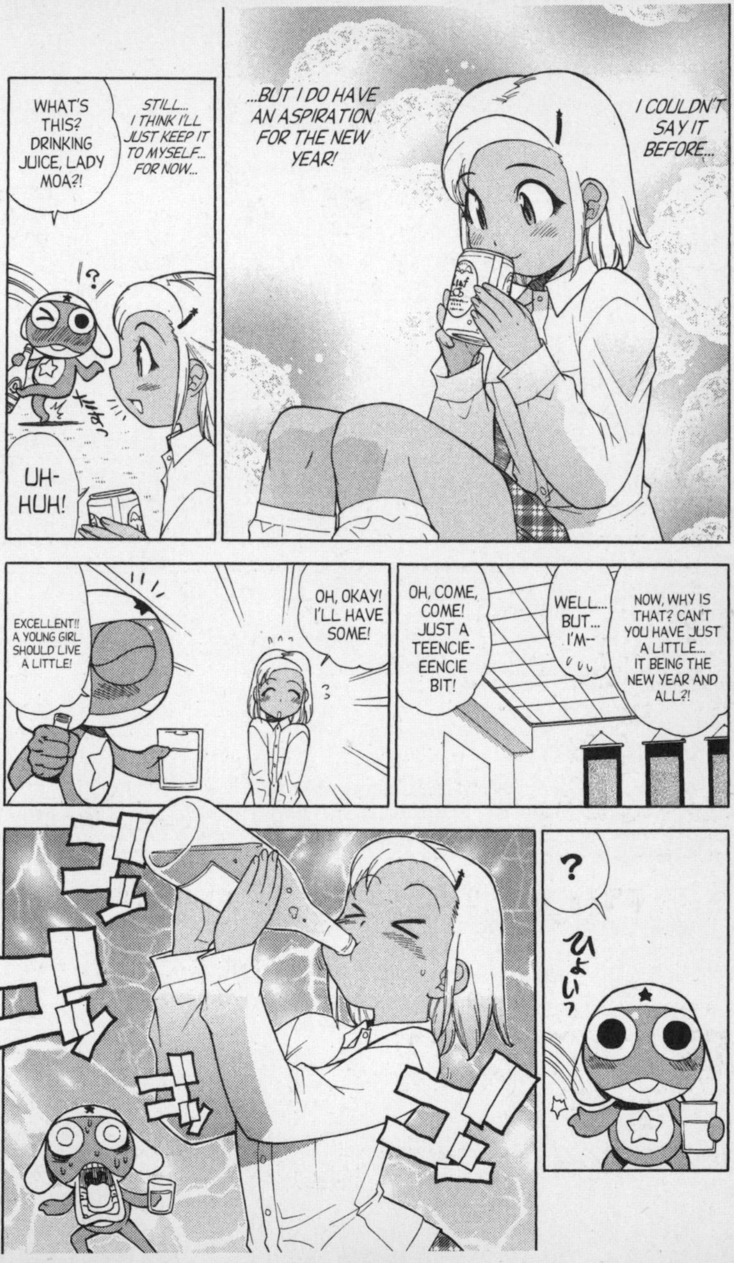

I COULDN'T SAY IT BEFORE...
...BUT I DO HAVE AN ASPIRATION FOR THE NEW YEAR!
STILL... I THINK I'LL JUST KEEP IT TO MYSELF... FOR NOW...
WHAT'S THIS? DRINKING JUICE, LADY MOA?!
UH-HUH!
NOW, WHY IS THAT? CAN'T YOU HAVE JUST A LITTLE... IT BEING THE NEW YEAR AND ALL?!
WELL... BUT... I'M--
OH, COME, COME! JUST A TEENCIE-EENCIE BIT!
OH, OKAY! I'LL HAVE SOME!
EXCELLENT!! A YOUNG GIRL SHOULD LIVE A LITTLE!
?
ひょいっ

TOKYOPOP PRESS

LOS ANGELES • TOKYO • LONDON • HAMBURG

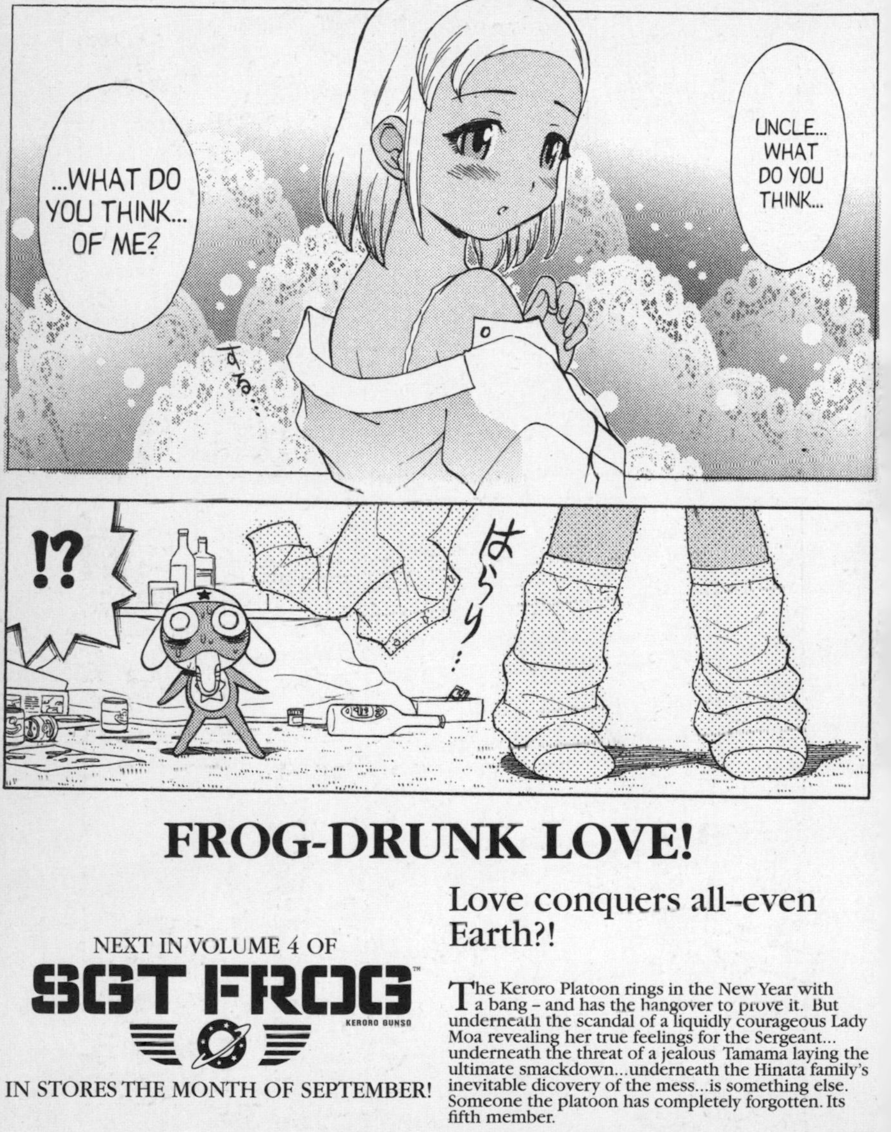
UNCLE... WHAT DO YOU THINK...
...WHAT DO YOU THINK... OF ME?
はらり…
!?

FROG-DRUNK LOVE!

NEXT IN VOLUME 4 OF

SGT FROG™

KERORO GUNSO

IN STORES THE MONTH OF SEPTEMBER!

Love conquers all--even Earth?!

The Keroro Platoon rings in the New Year with a bang - and has the hangover to prove it. But underneath the scandal of a liquidly courageous Lady Moa revealing her true feelings for the Sergeant... underneath the threat of a jealous Tamama laying the ultimate smackdown...underneath the Hinata family's inevitable dicovery of the mess...is something else. Someone the platoon has completely forgotten. Its fifth member.

ALSO AVAILABLE FROM TOKYOPOP®

PLANET LADDER
PLANETES
PRIEST
PRINCESS AI
PSYCHIC ACADEMY
QUEEN'S KNIGHT, THE
RAGNAROK
RAVE MASTER
REALITY CHECK
REBIRTH
REBOUND
REMOTE
RISING STARS OF MANGA
SABER MARIONETTE J
SAILOR MOON
SAINT TAIL
SAIYUKI
SAMURAI DEEPER KYO
SAMURAI GIRL REAL BOUT HIGH SCHOOL
SCRYED
SEIKAI TRILOGY, THE
SGT. FROG
SHAOLIN SISTERS
SHIRAHIME-SYO: SNOW GODDESS TALES
SHUTTERBOX
SKULL MAN, THE
SNOW DROP
SORCERER HUNTERS
STONE
SUIKODEN III
SUKI
THREADS OF TIME
TOKYO BABYLON
TOKYO MEW MEW
TOKYO TRIBES
TRAMPS LIKE US
UNDER THE GLASS MOON
VAMPIRE GAME
VISION OF ESCAFLOWNE, THE
WARRIORS OF TAO
WILD ACT
WISH
WORLD OF HARTZ
X-DAY
ZODIAC P.I.

NOVELS

CLAMP SCHOOL PARANORMAL INVESTIGATORS
KARMA CLUB
SAILOR MOON
SLAYERS

ART BOOKS

ART OF CARDCAPTOR SAKURA
ART OF MAGIC KNIGHT RAYEARTH, THE
PEACH: MIWA UEDA ILLUSTRATIONS

ANIME GUIDES

COWBOY BEBOP
GUNDAM TECHNICAL MANUALS
SAILOR MOON SCOUT GUIDES

TOKYOPOP KIDS

STRAY SHEEP

CINE-MANGA™

ALADDIN
CARDCAPTORS
DUEL MASTERS
FAIRLY ODDPARENTS, THE
FAMILY GUY
FINDING NEMO
G.I. JOE SPY TROOPS
GREATEST STARS OF THE NBA
JACKIE CHAN ADVENTURES
JIMMY NEUTRON: BOY GENIUS, THE ADVENTURES OF
KIM POSSIBLE
LILO & STITCH: THE SERIES
LIZZIE MCGUIRE
LIZZIE MCGUIRE MOVIE, THE
MALCOLM IN THE MIDDLE
POWER RANGERS: DINO THUNDER
POWER RANGERS: NINJA STORM
PRINCESS DIARIES 2
RAVE MASTER
SHREK 2
SIMPLE LIFE, THE
SPONGEBOB SQUAREPANTS
SPY KIDS 2
SPY KIDS 3-D: GAME OVER
THAT'S SO RAVEN
TOTALLY SPIES
TRANSFORMERS: ARMADA
TRANSFORMERS: ENERGON

You want it? We got it!
A full range of TOKYOPOP
products are available now at:
www.TOKYOPOP.com/shop

04.23.04T

MANGA

.HACK//LEGEND OF THE TWILIGHT
@LARGE
ABENOBASHI: MAGICAL SHOPPING ARCADE
A.I. LOVE YOU
AI YORI AOSHI
ANGELIC LAYER
ARM OF KANNON
BABY BIRTH
BATTLE ROYALE
BATTLE VIXENS
BRAIN POWERED
BRIGADOON
B'TX
CANDIDATE FOR GODDESS, THE
CARDCAPTOR SAKURA
CARDCAPTOR SAKURA - MASTER OF THE CLOW
CHOBITS
CHRONICLES OF THE CURSED SWORD
CLAMP SCHOOL DETECTIVES
CLOVER
COMIC PARTY
CONFIDENTIAL CONFESSIONS
CORRECTOR YUI
COWBOY BEBOP
COWBOY BEBOP: SHOOTING STAR
CRAZY LOVE STORY
CRESCENT MOON
CROSS
CULDCEPT
CYBORG 009
D•N•ANGEL
DEMON DIARY
DEMON ORORON, THE
DEUS VITAE
DIABOLO
DIGIMON
DIGIMON TAMERS
DIGIMON ZERO TWO
DOLL
DRAGON HUNTER
DRAGON KNIGHTS
DRAGON VOICE
DREAM SAGA
DUKLYON: CLAMP SCHOOL DEFENDERS
EERIE QUEERIE!
ERICA SAKURAZAWA: COLLECTED WORKS
ET CETERA
ETERNITY
EVIL'S RETURN
FAERIES' LANDING
FAKE
FLCL
FLOWER OF THE DEEP SLEEP
FORBIDDEN DANCE
FRUITS BASKET
G GUNDAM

GATEKEEPERS
GETBACKERS
GIRL GOT GAME
GIRLS' EDUCATIONAL CHARTER
GRAVITATION
GTO
GUNDAM BLUE DESTINY
GUNDAM SEED ASTRAY
GUNDAM WING
GUNDAM WING: BATTLEFIELD OF PACIFISTS
GUNDAM WING: ENDLESS WALTZ
GUNDAM WING: THE LAST OUTPOST (G-UNIT)
GUYS' GUIDE TO GIRLS
HANDS OFF!
HAPPY MANIA
HARLEM BEAT
I.N.V.U.
IMMORTAL RAIN
INITIAL D
INSTANT TEEN: JUST ADD NUTS
ISLAND
JING: KING OF BANDITS
JING: KING OF BANDITS - TWILIGHT TALES
JULINE
KARE KANO
KILL ME, KISS ME
KINDAICHI CASE FILES, THE
KING OF HELL
KODOCHA: SANA'S STAGE
LAMENT OF THE LAMB
LEGAL DRUG
LEGEND OF CHUN HYANG, THE
LES BIJOUX
LOVE HINA
LUPIN III
LUPIN III: WORLD'S MOST WANTED
MAGIC KNIGHT RAYEARTH I
MAGIC KNIGHT RAYEARTH II
MAHOROMATIC: AUTOMATIC MAIDEN
MAN OF MANY FACES
MARMALADE BOY
MARS
MARS: HORSE WITH NO NAME
MINK
MIRACLE GIRLS
MIYUKI-CHAN IN WONDERLAND
MODEL
MY LOVE
NECK AND NECK
ONE
ONE I LOVE, THE
PARADISE KISS
PARASYTE
PASSION FRUIT
PEACH GIRL
PEACH GIRL: CHANGE OF HEART
PET SHOP OF HORRORS
PITA-TEN

04.23.04T

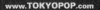

Princess Ai™

A Diva torn from Chaos...
A Savior doomed to Love

Created by
Courtney Love
and D.J. Milky

TOKYOPOP®

T TEEN AGE 13+

www.TOKYOPOP.com

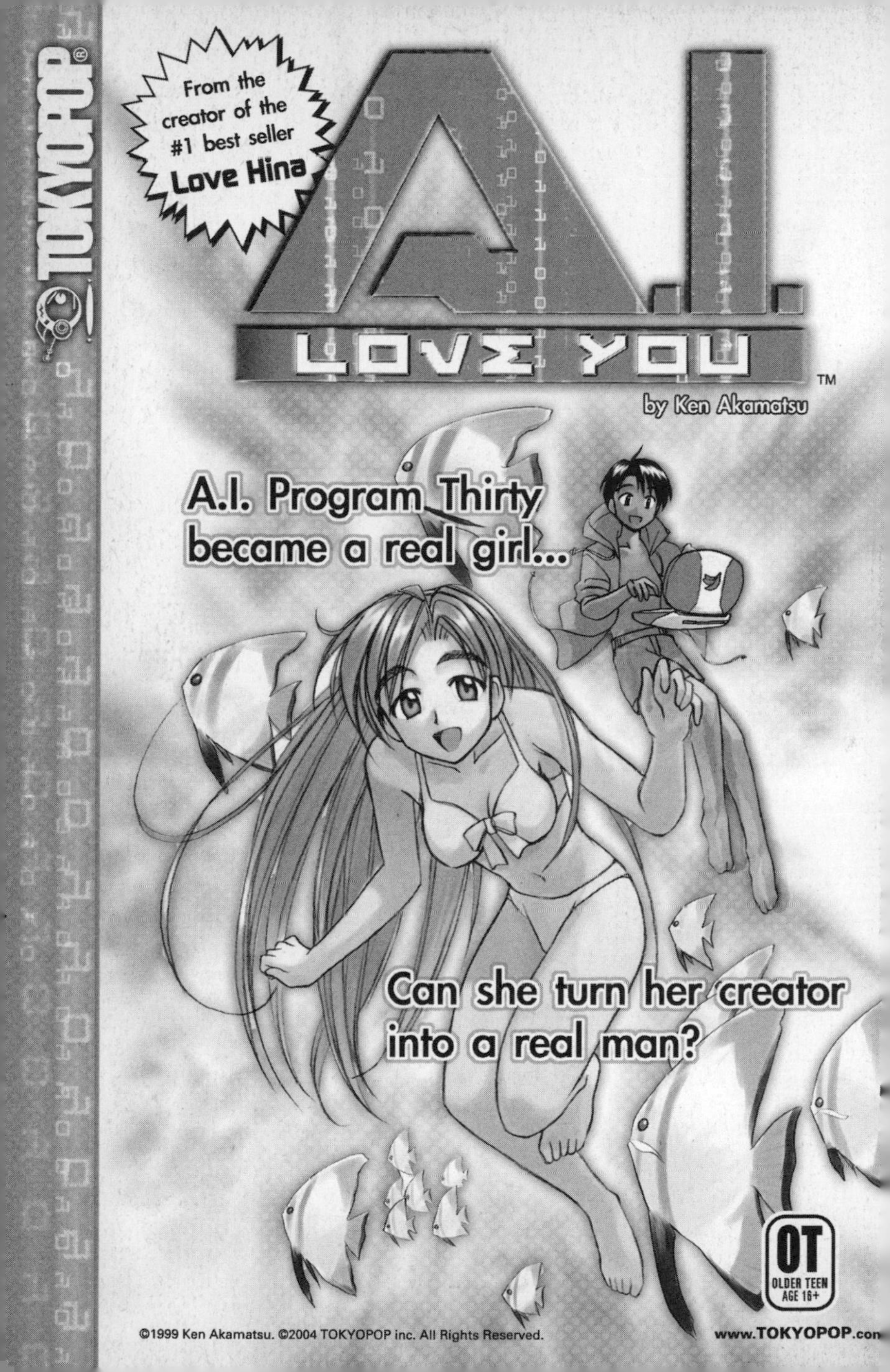
TOKYOPOP®
From the creator of the #1 best seller Love Hina
A.I. LOVE YOU™
by Ken Akamatsu
A.I. Program Thirty became a real girl...
Can she turn her creator into a real man?
OT
OLDER TEEN AGE 16+
©1999 Ken Akamatsu. ©2004 TOKYOPOP inc. All Rights Reserved.
www.TOKYOPOP.com

PITA-TEN™

By Koge-Donbo · Creator of Digicharat

The girl next door is bringing a touch of heaven to the neighborhood.